THE WORLD OF STEAM LOCOMOTIVES

Above: Passenger train of the Saint-Etienne-Lyons Railroad on the line between Saint-Etienne and Givors, that worked without horse or machine traction. *Below:* Coal cars drawn by steam locomotive.

GUSTAV REDER

THE WORLD OF STEAM LOCOMOTIVES

G.P. PUTNAM'S SONS · NEW YORK

Translated from the German by Michael Reynolds

Photo Research: Denise Blum

Illustrations 305 and 347 were taken from the postcard-series
(64 alte und neue Fahrzeugmotive der Bahn) of the Redactor
Verlag, Frankfurt/Main.

G.P. Putnam's Sons
200 Madison Avenue
New York, N.Y. 10016

Published in the United States of America in 1974
© 1974 by Office du Livre, Fribourg (Switzerland)
Library of Congress Catalog Card Number: 74-80030
SBN: 399-11398-3

Printed in Switzerland

CONTENTS

FOREWORD

Although it is common knowledge that the railroad brought about a revolution in the life of the human race, the full significance of that revolution is rarely appreciated. The railroad is in fact one of the more recent links in that chain of epoch-making events that has governed man's material existence — the conquest of fire, the beginnings of agriculture, the discovery of metals, navigation, printing — and of which the most recent has been the harnessing of atomic energy. It was the railroad that made possible the dawn of the industrial age and, with it, that radical transformation of man's life and habitat that has characterized the last hundred and fifty years. For only with the railroad did it become possible to transport large numbers of people and large quantities of goods economically over any distance, thus weaving that network of international trade relationships by which the nations of the world are irrevocably bound together. Recent economic developments have emphasized the fact that, despite great steps forward in other forms of transport, without the railroad the world as we know it today would simply not be viable. Furthermore, taken as a whole, the railroad is the biggest single construction undertaking mankind has ever embarked upon.

The railroad itself was only made possible by the invention of the steam locomotive, and if for no other reason than this it seems to me that there is room for a book describing how this important piece of machinery came into existence and how it gradually evolved to perfection. The steam locomotive stood at the beginning of the machine age. Its requirements gave rise to countless stimuli as regards qualitative improvement of the materials used, more accurate manufacturing methods for components, and theoretical research in the field of heat technology, all of which were then available for exploitation in other technological fields. Without the preliminary work done on behalf of and on the part of the steam locomotive, the machines of our own day and age would be unthinkable.

All of which I have tried to show in the present work.

This is the first book that sets out to describe the evolution of the steam locomotive from the beginning to the end of its existence, and I believe it fills a gap in an otherwise copious literature. There are many works dealing with individual aspects of steam-locomotive development in different countries, but there has been no general survey of the subject since J. Jahn published his magnificent work in 1924. Not even Jahn's book is quite complete, however, for it does not cover the very earliest period, and then of course there is the whole modern period, the final three decades of the steam locomotive's undisputed sovereignty, during which its evolution continued uninterrupted.

I had the great good fortune, first as a railroad fan as a youngster and subsequently as a railroad locomotive specialist, to experience the golden age of steam at first hand almost from the turn of the century, and to do so in a country — Spain — where I have had the unusual opportunity of studying locomotive construction in the form of engines from a wide variety of countries and periods, from the most modern to some that are more than a hundred years old. I have been able to draw on many memories of foot-plate journeys on both large and small engines, speeding across broad plains or toiling up steep gradients through smoke-filled tunnels. It was further my privilege to be personally acquainted with many of the people mentioned in the concluding sections of the book and in some cases even to have enjoyed their friendship. Much of what I know and have tried to set down here I owe to discussions with them.

There is a great deal that I would have liked to say and could not. Although the publishers very kindly allowed me more space than was originally foreseen, I found myself continually having to leave things out. This applies particularly to the modern period, where fortunately there is plenty of literature available already. I opted for dealing at greater length with the considerably less well documented earlier period. Explaining the kinds of problem that the first loco-

7

motive-builders were up against offered me at the same time a good opportunity of initiating the layman in the rudiments of locomotive technology.

Some of my readers will possibly be disappointed not to find their favourites here; indeed I have had to forgo describing many of my own. My principle of selection from among the profusion of locomotive types was and had to be the importance of a particular model in terms of locomotive development or as typifying a particular period or school of construction. Reasons of space have further obliged me to omit all attempts to depart from Stephenson's basic conception — turbine and high-pressure locomotives, water-tube boilers, and so on — since these were of no importance as regards the evolution of the steam locomotive and are in any case already covered in the specialist literature.

Finally I should like to thank my publishers for all the time and work that they have put into presenting this book in so pleasing a form.

Madrid, April 1974

1. THE CREATION AND CHARACTERISTICS OF THE RAILROAD

On February 13, 1804 a steam locomotive ran for the first time. At that time nobody could have guessed that this was the beginning of a new generation in transport, which was to have revolutionary consequences for mankind. However, the intention, on that historic day, was no more than to improve on the horse, which pulled heavily laden coal carts with difficulty over mud-bound roads.

The forests of England were gradually being used up. Domestic heating and industry, which was expanding rapidly around the middle of the 17th century, had to turn more and more to pit coal, which lay beneath the island's soil in great quantities. Once the coal seams at the surface had been exhausted and deeper mining began, water was struck. It was Thomas Newcomen's steam engines that saved the shafts from flooding. James Watt developed the steam engine into a device capable not only of drawing water but of driving machinery. The result was that the need for pit coal increased yet further. A new problem arose at the same time which threatened to stifle coal mining: that of conveying the coal which had been mined from underground to the customers. The route from shaft to ship was a short one so long as shafts ended

Colliery train (see Ill. 6).

9

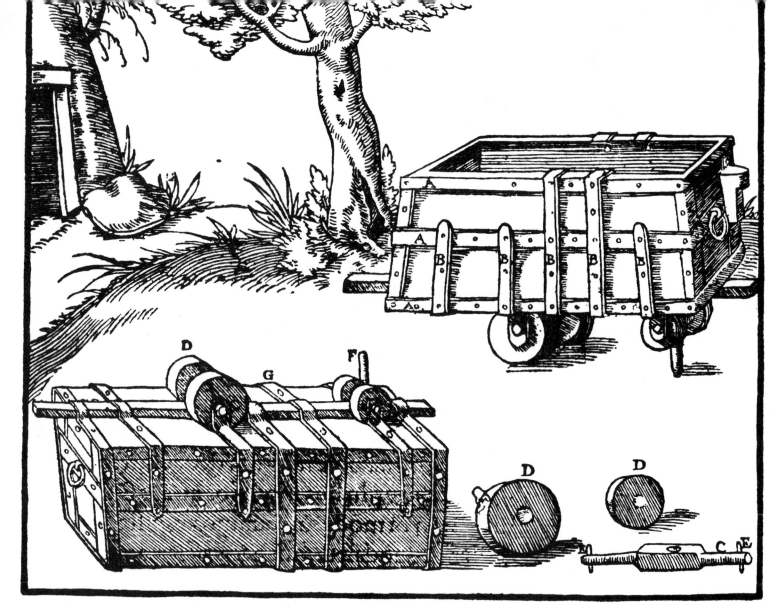

A—RECTANGULAR IRON BANDS ON TRUCK.　　B—ITS IRON STRAPS.　　C—IRON AXLE.
D—WOODEN ROLLERS.　　E—SMALL IRON KEYS.　　F—LARGE BLUNT IRON PIN.
G—SAME TRUCK UPSIDE DOWN.

very close to navigable waterways, such as rivers or canals. It was enough to lay wooden planks so that the heavy coal carts did not sink into the ground.

The first illustrations of such "plank ways" occur in a work published in 1530 in Reichenau (Germany) by Johan Haselberger, *Der Ursprung gemeyner Berkrecht wie die lange Zeit von Alten worde* ("The origin of common mining law as it was from old times"). The *Cosmographia Universalis* by Sebastian Münzer of Basel which appeared in 1550 has pictures of wooden plank-ways such as were used in mining works at Lebertal in Alsace. In 1556 Georgius Agricola gives us a complete description in his comprehensive treaties on mining and metallurgy *De re metallica*. It is worth repeating the first description of a railroad: "If the lumps of rock or earth are carried out in wheelbarrows, planks joined together are laid upon the sleepers; if in open trucks *(Dogs)* then two timbers 9 in. thick and wide are laid on the sleepers, and where they join they are usually hollowed

10

out so that the iron pins of the trucks can move as if in a rut. Indeed these pins prevent the trucks from straying from the groove or rut, whether to the right or to the left." The woodcut (Ill. 1) shows one such truck (or *Dog*) with the iron pin, by which it is guided and follows the rut or groove. The odd name of "dog" was given to them because the noise made by the pin resembled the squealing of a dog when trampled on.

The Thirty Years War prevented the further develop-

already an important centre of coal mining. Until the year 1812 the area between Tyne and Wear saw the growth of a network of short lines, mostly three to eight miles long and crossing one another in places, their use being to convey coal for shipment from more than twenty-four mines. The expression "tramroads" was gradually adopted in a general way for these mining lines. The word "tram" is often, and incorrectly, thought to be derived from the name of Benjamin Outram, who was active

2. Oldest truck with flange wheels. Model.

ment of German mining. Some of the Freiburg miners emigrated, and around 1676 a number of them arrived in England, where coal was already being produced in considerable quantities. It is uncertain whether the use of wooden plank roads in English mining has anything to do with the Freiburg miners or with the influence of Agricola's treatise. A letter of 1610 contains the first mention of "rails" in English mining: the recipient is instructed "to take order with a certain Sir Thomas so that we maie (sic) have libertie (sic) to bring coals down the rails by wagon... for Strekkey cartway is so fowle as few carriadges (sic) can pass". These "rails" were probably wooden planks. There are further mentions in the 17th century of the gradual extension of wooden railroads throughout England, in fact starting at Newcastle which was at that time

around the turn of the 18th century in constructing such lines. In fact the word "tram" is derived from the Latin *trames* which means way or path, and is clearly used in this sense by the 16th century.

The first developments on these "tramroads" laid the foundations and established the principles on which the later railroads were made. The wooden plank roads then in general use deteriorated rapidly, especially after the introduction of cast-iron wheels on the carts, or of wooden wheels with iron tyres fastened round them. There was, initially, an attempt at lessening this deterioration by nailing strips of hard wood onto the planks. Wood from shipwrecks was especially favoured. Early sources make no mention of any means of preventing wheels from slipping off the track. The pins on the mining

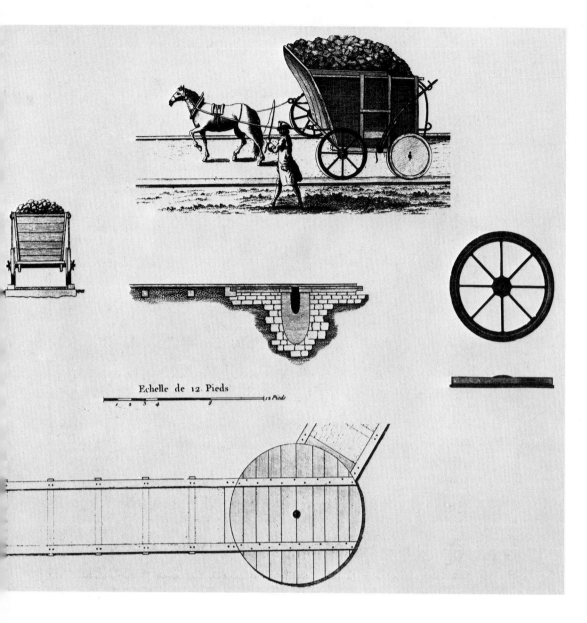

see the next step in the development of flanged wheels in the work *Voyages métallurgiques* by Jars, published in 1765. The flanges are now narrower as are the wheel rims (Ill. 3). This necessitated a much closer adherence to the distance between the rails, still made of wooden planks, and meant a further step had been taken towards the division of transport into road and rail.

The next step in the coupling of wheel and rail was the introduction of the iron rail. It is very probable that this occurred at the Coalbrookdale Iron Works. In 1809, Jabeg Carter Hornblower, the eldest of six brothers who had emulated their father and become engineers, and were serious competitors of Watt, states in a report: "From some adventitious circumstances ... the price of 'pigs' became very low, and their works being of great extent, in order to keep the furnaces on, they thought the best means of stocking their cast iron was to lay it on the wooden rails, as it would help to pay the interest by reducing the repair of the rails, and if iron should take any sudden rise, there was nothing to do but to take them up, and send them away as pigs." There are conflicting accounts as to when these cast-iron sections were first laid, but late 1767 can be regarded as fairly certain. The idea of using them in this way came from Richard Reynolds, who had married into the family and become a partner in the works. The iron railroad proved such a success that Reynolds laid more than 800 tons of these sections between 1768 and 1771. It was clear that the track did not deteriorate so quickly and that, in addition, there was a drastic reduction in the rolling resistance of the trucks. When, for example, this type of cast-iron section replaced the wooden track on the Wylam line in 1808, instead of one wagon, two could now be pulled by one horse.

It was a disadvantage that wagons with normal road wheels could not travel on these smooth narrow sections. This problem was solved when John Curr introduced in 1797 cast angle sections. This sort of track had no significance in the later development of railroad track, but the way in which it was laid did. Because of its angled flange it was "self-supporting" and therefore did not have to be bolted to sleepers running lengthwise as did the shallow, cast sections. It was sufficient to fix them onto sleepers (horizontal supporting beams) running crosswise. Outram, who has been mentioned already, used stone sleepers on damp ground where wooden ones would soon have rotted.

3. Eighteenth-century wagon with narrow flange wheels. From Jars' *Voyages métallurgiques,* 1765.

"dogs" could not be used on carts which were considerably wider and heavier. There were, however, two ways of guiding the wheels. Either the vehicles retained their flat wheels and were prevented from slipping off the tracks by raised rims attached to the planks on each side, or else the rims of the wheels were edged with a projecting strip, the "flange" which guided the wheel along the track. Both methods were used, but only the latter has any significance in the development of tramroad to railroad. In London, in 1734, Jean Théophile Désagulier published *A Course of Experimental Philosophy*. This contains the oldest known picture of a truck with flanged wheels, as well as a description of the trucks built by Ralph Allen for a quarry line opened in 1729/30 (Ill. 4). These trucks were used to transport blocks between the quarry, lying high above the bank, and the loading jetty in the Avon river near Bath. We can

12

4. Prior Park near Bath; in the foreground, Ralph Allen's quarry train.

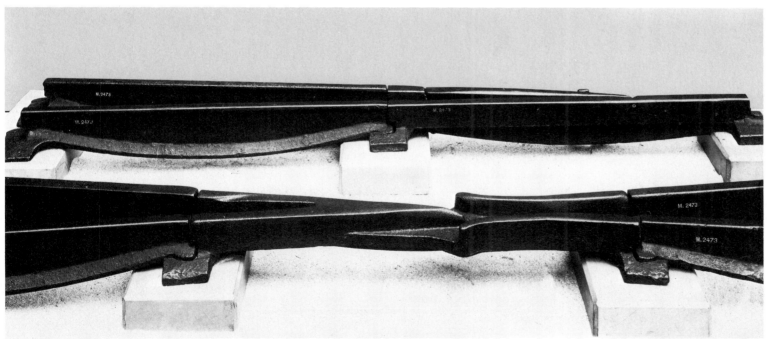

5. William Jessop's new type of rail, 1789. Model.

13

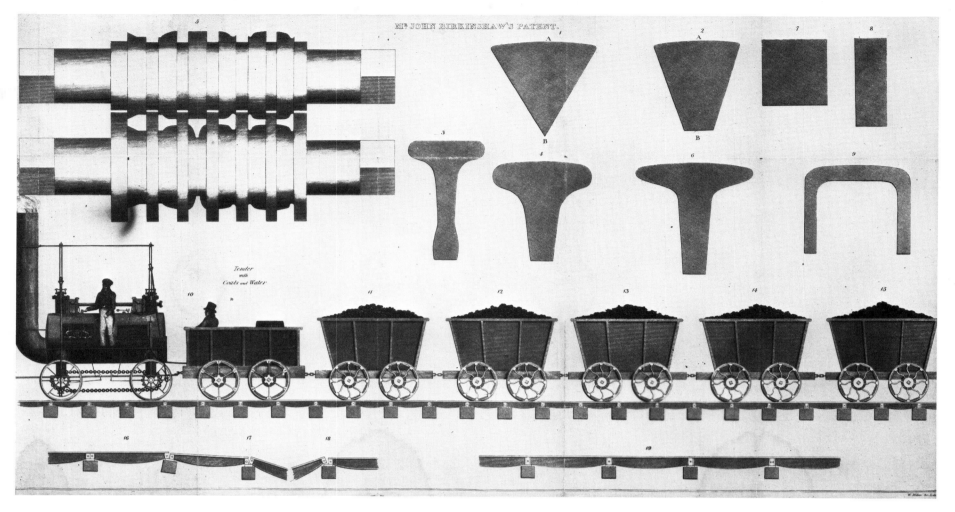

6. Rolled wrought iron rails, John Birkinshaw's patent, 1820. The locomotive is of the type patented by George Stephenson and William Losh, 1816.

The basis for the definitive development of railroad track was the completely new type of rail introduced by William Jessop in 1789. He cast one yard bars with a cross-section similar to a double "T" profile (girder or joist): the head was mushroom shaped, about 2 in. wide, so that there was more material to be worn down by the wheel. The base was also broadened. Running lengthwise the rail had a fish belly shape, drooping downward so that the largest cross-section occurred in the middle which was the point of greatest stress. One end of the bar divided like a fin with a slit in the middle which contained the next section of rail (Ill. 5), and with a hole in the centre for fastening to the stone sleeper. The last step at that time in perfecting the track took the form of rolled wrought iron rails, which were the subject of a rolling patent for John Birkinshaw in 1820 (Ill. 6).

This brought the wheel and the rail together in a way which still holds good today.

14

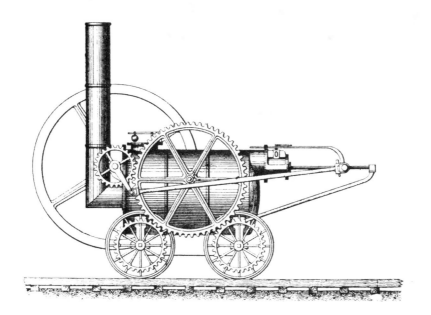

2. THE BIRTH
OF THE STEAM LOCOMOTIVE

2.1 The First Steps

Thus at the end of the 18th century, a smooth track had been created which could carry trucks safely, and along which horses could draw considerably greater loads than by the normal roads. But the horses could not cope with the ever-increasing quantities of goods to be carried, and they were expensive. It was time to think of using the steam engine which had meanwhile been perfected by James Watt. Watt himself had thought of building his steam engine into self-propelled vehicles but it was too heavy and expensive for this. In 1800 his basic patent expired, so ending the practical monopoly he had enjoyed in the construction of steam engines. The path was clear for other constructors.

Of these Richard Trevithick soon came into prominence. James Watt's steam engines worked with a pressure of only 1.56 to 3.13 lb. per sq. in. Thus a considerable amount of the work was performed by atmospheric pressure acting on the vacuum produced in the condenser when a spray of water condensed the steam. For a relatively small output of a few horse-power, very large cylinders were required together

Gateshead locomotive (see Ill. 9).

15

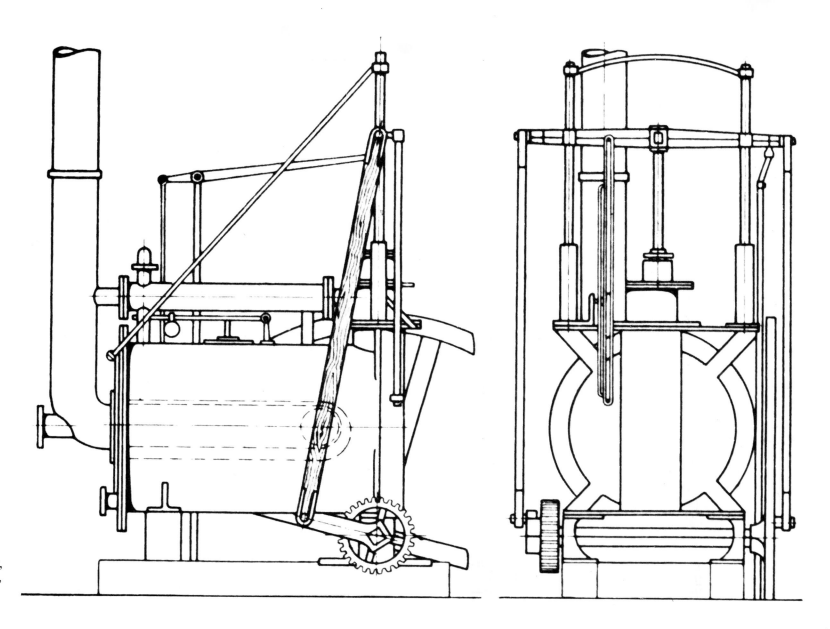

7. Richard Trevithick, portable steam engine, 1803.

with expensive condensers, air and water pumps. By contrast Trevithick created a steam engine which worked by steam pressure alone, without any condenser, and together with his cousin Vivian he was granted a patent for this on March 24, 1800. He envisaged a boiler pressure of 49 to 100 lb. per sq. in. and thus was able to make the cylinder much smaller than Watt's. Weight and space were further saved by the omission of the condenser and its pumps. The so-called "pot boiler" could no longer be used for these higher working pressures. Trevithick built cylindrical boilers which withstood the higher pressures better. He included a return flue for better use of the hot gases inside the assembly. The steam cylinder entered the rear part of the boiler vertically

and was thus well protected against any cooling losses, and the typical heavy swing beam of Watt's low pressure engines also disappeared. In its stead, the piston rod was driven by a cross-head, comprising two vertical driving rods guided by sleeves sliding on two vertical rods. It was of note that the exhaust steam was conducted into the chimney. The exhaust steam pipe was surrounded by a water jacket in which the feed water was preheated. Trevithick thus achieved a compact power assembly, complete in itself, which could be assembled without the need for heavy foundation work and supports, and which took little space wherever it was set up. This was the forerunner of the portable steam engines (Ill. 7). Of course, Trevithick tried to use his steam engine in as

16

many different ways as possible. In 1801 and 1803 he built them into carriages, but this need not concern us here. When Samuel Homfray, owner of the Pen-y-Darren ironworks decided to acquire a steam engine for driving a rolling mill, Trevithick suggested an initial trial using it to drive colliery wagons. This was a daring suggestion, and one of the foremen, Antony Hill, lay on a £500 bet with Homfray that it would not work. The steam engine ordered (Ill. 8) was adapted to its new use by arranging the cylinder horizontally and being able thus to drive both the axles via a toothed wheel. The whole weight of the engine could then be used for the tractive effort. But Trevithick was not at all sure of being able to obtain enough friction between wheel and track in this way. He made provision in his patent specification for enlarging the flange should it prove necessary and attaching bolt heads to the outer edge which would press into the wooden boards laid alongside the iron rails. However, smooth wheels were made, running on angled rails. The engine's cylinder diameter was 8 in., the piston stroke (complete travel of to-and-fro movement) 4 ft. 6 in. and the wheel diameter about 3 ft. 7 in.

On February 15, 1804, Trevithick reported on the first journey of his locomotive to Davis Giddy, President of the Royal Society, who was keenly interested both in this venture and in the work of other engineers at that time. The report runs as follows: "Last Saturday we lighted the fire in the Tram Waggon and work'd it without the wheels to try the engine; on Monday we put it on the Tram Road. It work'd very well, and ran up hill and down with great ease, and was very manageable. We had plenty of steam and power." The letter was dated Wednesday, so that February 13, 1804 was the historic day on which a steam locomotive ran on rails for the very first time.

Other letters from Trevithick to Giddy tell us that the "tram-waggon" easily pulled ten tons, and that with the water in the boiler the engine weighed about five tons, running up a slope of 1 in 50 (2%) empty at forty strokes a minute. Since the engine moved 9 feet at every stroke, the speed was around 4 miles per hour. Trevithick observed that "the fire burned very much better when the steam goes up the chimney than when the engine is idle." He wrote on February 22 that Antony Hill had admitted losing the wager, but was not in the least angry in view of the performance of the locomotive. Trevithick also reports the first official boiler pressure test undertaken on a locomotive, using a water pump. This frequently mentioned journey

8. Richard Trevithick, first locomotive, 1803/04, for the Pen-y-Darren Colliery.

took place on 28 February, his report on it running as follows: "Yesterday we proceeded on our journey with the engine; we carry'd ten tons of Iron, five waggons, and 70 Men riding on them the whole of the journey. Its above 9 miles which we perform'd in 4 hours & 5 mints., but we had to cut down some trees and remove some large rocks out of the road. The engine, while working, went nearly 5 miles pr hour, there was no water put into the boiler from the time we started untill we arriv'd at our journey's end. The coal consumed was 2 Hund[d]*. On our return home abt 4 miles from the shipping place of the iron, one of the small bolts that fastened the axel to the boiler broak, and let all the water out of the boiler, which prevented the engine returning untill this evening..." The engine then entered regular service, and ten days later, it was tried out with 25 tons of iron. Trevithick again reported to Giddy that "we were more than a match for that weight". It seems that the engine was more or less regularly in service for a few months, before it met its final fate, as the drive unit for a rolling mill.

The fact that the locomotive had only one cylinder may well be the principal reason that it did not give complete satisfaction. If the piston was in the position which closes the cylinder steam inlet, the so-called "dead centre", the locomotive could not start by itself. The flywheel had therefore to be turned or the wheels moved with crowbars, to get the vehicle

* Hundredweight.

17

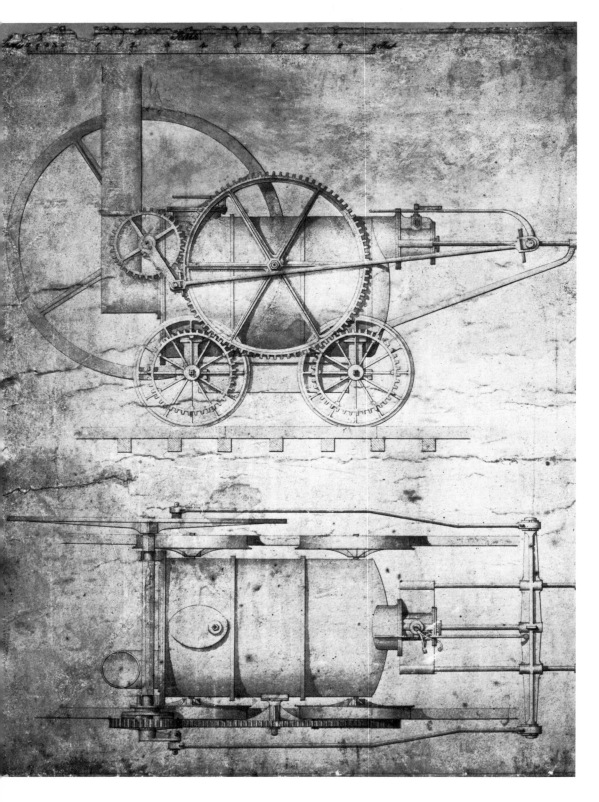

The name of the first locomotive driver in the world, the man who was at the controls of the engine on the trip just mentioned, has been passed down to us: a certain William Richard, who never in fact drove a locomotive again throughout the rest of his eighty years.

In September of the same year, 1804, Trevithick went to Newcastle to negotiate with Christopher Blankett on the construction of a locomotive, Blankett being the owner of the Wylam coal mines. It is not certain whether he himself made the drawing for this locomotive (Ill. 9), which is still preserved in the Science Museum, London. However he undoubtedly gave permission for his patents and the Pen-y-Darren engine to be used as prototype. The new engine was built at the Whinfield Works in Pipewellgate, Gateshead, under the direction of John Steel, who himself had acted previously for Trevithick. In May 1805 it was ready. The position of the cylinder on the boiler was changed, probably because access to the fire door was hampered on the first engine by the guide of the piston rod, which projected far forward. The wheels now had flanges, but since the stretch of track still had plate rails, the locomotive had to be tried out on a short section of track with edge rails. A contemporary report says that it was able to pull three coal trucks each weighing 3 ½ tons when loaded. The intention to adapt the track where the engine was to operate was not carried out, so this second Trevithick locomotive was not used for traction either, but to drive a blower (for ventilating the pits).

Trevithick found other more lucrative activities which stimulated his inventive mind in new ways, but in 1808 he did build one other locomotive which he demonstrated in London on a circular track with a charge for admission. This was known as the "Catch me who can". The engine was more advanced than its two predecessors inasmuch as the rear axle was driven directly from the cross-head. The front wheels ran uncoupled. The demonstration incurred a financial loss but, as we shall see, they did promote a further development of the locomotive. In 1814 Trevithick supplied eight steam pumping engines to the silver mine owners in Peru. Reports on their performance were so promising that Trevithick was persuaded to emigrate to Peru in October 1816, where he met an adventurous fate. Trevithick has often been accused of a lack of persistence, but it must be realized that he did not regard himself as a pioneer inventor of locomotives; he was simply trying to exploit his portable steam engines. Judging that there was no

9. Drawing for the Gateshead locomotive, built by John Steel, 1805.

moving. In addition, the wheels slipped easily as a result of the unequal torque from the single cylinder, especially on rails slippery with damp coal dust. The original sources do not mention that the weight might have been too great for the track or that the rails broke.

18

great future in the building of locomotives, it was only natural that he should have turned elsewhere to study other types of application for his inventions which promised to be more successful commercially. Trevithick's experiments did, however, mean that the question of replacing the horse by other means of traction had become a practical proposition. The Middleton colliery near Leeds had constructed a tramway in 1758 to transport coal to Leeds. The owner of the mine, Charles Brandling, had occasion to go to London frequently as a Member of Parliament. There he had seen Trevithick's "Catch me who can", and he discussed the possibility of trying an engine like this with the foreman or the "viewer" of his mines, John Blenkinsop. It had become vital to solve the problem of replacing horses: as a result of the Napoleonic wars, prices of horse feed and cereal crops had risen out of all proportion. Feeding costs were a major factor for fifty dray horses, and nearly two hundred men were needed to lead and groom them. Brandling probably instructed Blenkinsop by 1810 to get in touch with the ironworks belonging to James Fenton and Matthew Murray at nearby Holbeck. Both Blenkinsop and Murray knew of Trevithick's efforts. They concluded that the failure of his locomotives was mainly due to the fact that the rails were unable to support the load placed on them, since they could not take vehicles of more than 5 tons. This weight was clearly not enough to develop the tractive power required at the Middleton colliery, especially since there was a steep incline to be surmounted at the end of the line. It therefore occurred to Blenkinsop to lay a rack alongside the track. Together with John Straker, he had this idea patented in 1811, although the patent claim does not go into detail on the position of the rack. For the sake of simplicity, Blenkinsop had the cogs cast laterally at the same time as one set of rails. The length of the cast-iron bars chosen after several attempts was 3 ft., the distance between the teeth (i.e., the pitch) was 6 in. and each tooth was 3 in. wide and 2½ in. deep. These rails were attached to stone blocks 20 in. across and 10 in. high. The gauge was 4 ft. ½ in.

The method of construction of Blenkinsop's locomotive (Ill. 10) is clearly visible in the illustration. It is obviously incorrect for a cogged wheel to be shown both sides: this is not possible geometrically: as a result of the different radii of the rails around the curves, the pitch for the inner and outer rail could not be the same. The oval cast-iron boiler of the engine had a 22 in. diameter flue going through it,

and the heating surface amounted to 60 sq. ft. The boiler was mounted on a structure of stout timbers, which also held the cogged wheel and the driving axles, representing a considerable improvement on Trevithick's construction. A second and even more important improvement was the use of two cylinders with cranks set at an angle of 90°, with the result that when one piston was at dead centre, the other was in the middle of its working stroke. Thus the locomotive could always start by itself. The pump visible at the front of the engine for feeding the boiler was not added until later. The diameter of the cylinder was 8 in., the stroke 24 in. The first trial journey took place on January 24, 1812. The locomotive first travelled empty from the canal landing stage uphill to Hunslet Moor. Here, first six and then eight loaded coal-trucks each weighing 3¼ tons were coupled and for the journey some fifty spectators climbed into them. The operation of carrying this "immense load" over the nearly level stretch of one and a half miles was covered in twenty-three minutes without incident.

This first locomotive, christened "Prince Royal", which opened the Middleton railroad on August 12,

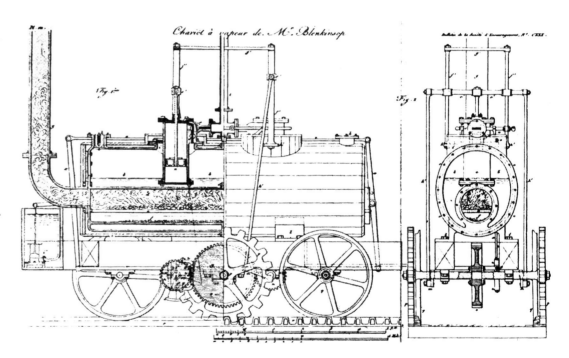

Chariot à vapeur de M^r. Blenkinsop

1812 proved so satisfactory that three more were immediately ordered from Fenton and Murray. The two engines delivered on August 14 were called "Salamanca" and "Lord Wellington", and the third delivered on November 23, 1813 the "Marquis Wellington". The names were chosen to commemor-

10. John Blenkinsop's locomotive with cogged wheels, 1811/12.

19

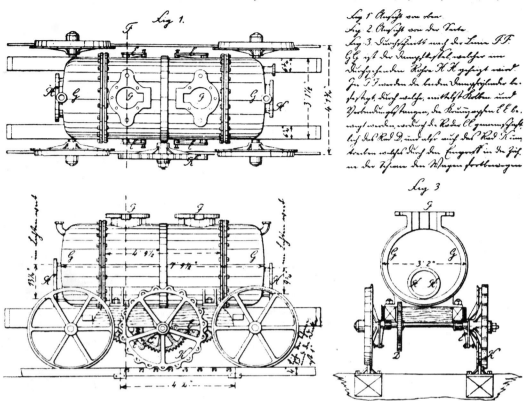

11. Berlin "steam wagon" *(Dampfwagen)*, technical drawing, 1816.

ate the Battle of Salamanca which had just been won in the Iberian Peninsula by a joint English-Hanoverian expeditionary force under Wellington in an alliance with Spanish troops against the French, earning the English commander the Spanish noble title of "Marquis".

These four engines carried twenty-seven loaded wagons in regular service, giving a train weight of around 94 tons. On level ground the speeds were between 2 m.p.h. and 3½ m.p.h. They carried 15 tons on the last 1 in 18 gradient of the journey, which would not have been possible without the rack and pinion. All four locomotives were in regular service until 1839. They can thus be regarded as the first successful steam locomotives, and the Middleton Railway has the honour of being the first steam-operated railroad in the world.

Two German iron and steel experts, Kriegar and Eckard, were among the visitors to come and see Blenkinsop's locomotives in Middleton. On the orders of the Prussian Mines administration, they had travelled to England "to study steam power and its use in transport". On their return Kriegar was appointed Inspector of the Royal Iron Works in Berlin and ordered to construct a locomotive according to the plans brought back from England. At the request of Inspector Schmahel it was to be used for carrying coal in upper Silesia between the Königsgrube and the Königshütte (i.e., the pit and the works).

The *Berlinische Nachrichten* published a notice on June 16, 1816, announcing that the newly built "steam wagon" *(Dampfwagen)* could be visited any day on payment of an entry of 4 groschens. Fortunately a drawing of this locomotive still exists (Ill. 11). The method of construction of the Berlin "steam wagon" was very similar to that of Blenkinsop's Middleton engines. The difference was that the cast-iron boiler consisted of three sections. The flue which ran straight through was made of sheet metal. There are contradictory versions of the bore* of the cylinder, either 6 in. or 5¼ in., the latter probably being correct, since the Berlin "steam wagon" was smaller than the Middleton locomotive. The stroke was 12½ in. The engine pulled a load of 50 *zentner* (hundredweight), and according to a contemporary report, it "carried the same through a distance of 50 paces in 1 minute and only uses 1½ heaped bushels of pit coal per day". On October 23, 1816 this locomotive was packed into

* Diameter.

thirteen crates and arrived via river and canal in upper Silesia. When the assembly work began, it became clear that the wheel gauge was 3 ft. and thus 1 ft. 3 in. narrower than the track. Once the appropriate alterations had been made, the locomotive was tested, but "everyone was afraid to try and handle her". The engine was not able to pull trucks satisfactorily and was therefore converted into a water pump.

Meanwhile, in Berlin, work had proceeded on the construction of a similar locomotive somewhat larger, which was intended for the Bauernwald coal mine in Saarbrücken. This was despatched on September 22, 1818 via the circuitous water route of Spree, Havel, Elbe, the North Sea, Rhine and Saar, arriving finally in Geislautern on February 4 of the following year. But this second engine was also unsuccessful. Its only achievement lay in "going backwards and forwards 20 to 30 feet, with a great deal of assistance from pushing and shoving on the way". The original boiler pressure had also been increased from 17 to almost 43 lb. per sq. in., which resulted in a permanent leak at the boiler joints, which could not be cured although there were plenty of attempts using "enormous quantities of hemp, glue, canvas, oil, a mixture of vinegar and oil, even bull's blood and cheese". The attempt was abandoned and finally in 1835 the engine was put up for sale. Rather against his better instincts, a farmer bought it; he was able to produce many of the bits and pieces as souvenirs, even as late as the 1870s.

This was the inglorious end of the first attempts at building locomotives outside England.

2.2   William Hedley Proves There is Sufficient Adhesion between Wheel and Track

The fact that the Trevithick locomotives were very prone to slip led to the incorrect conclusion that there was insufficient adhesion between the smooth wheel and rail for sufficient tractive effort to be developed. This mistaken belief gave birth to all kinds of suggestions as to how this state of affairs could be remedied. There was a demonstration, and one of the most incredible constructions it produced was Brunton's "mechanical traveller". Instead of wheels, the piston rods worked a sort of assembly of props, which were moved somewhat like horses' legs. One can readily imagine the results of the trial run made in 1814/15 on the Newbottle colliery line. The suggestion by the Chapman brothers of laying a chain alongside

the track was more sensible, the idea being that the engine should haul itself along. But the expensive test made on the Hetton cable track near Newcastle also failed, with the chain continually breaking.

It has already been mentioned that Trevithick's second locomotive had been tested at the Wylam colliery, and that although they had intended to lay a new section of track in order to use it, this work had been postponed. Around 1809, stronger angle plates were laid. Christopher Blackett returned to the question of steam traction, probably as a result of the success of Blenkinsop's locomotives at Middleton. The lively discussions as to whether there was sufficient adhesion between smooth wheels on equally smooth tracks led the foreman at Wylam colliery, William Hedley, to go deeply into the matter: he built a carriage with two hand-cranks attached on each side turned by men standing on running boards. The turns of the cranks were conveyed to four smooth running wheels via toothed gears. The test carriage could be loaded with various weights. In October 1812, attempts were made with this trial arrangement on all parts of the track. By coupling more or fewer trucks and by loading various weights, it was possible to decide on the ratio between traction and load. Unfortunately the values ascertained by Hedley have not been handed down, but the tests did yield decisive proof for the future of the locomotive in that there is sufficient adhesion with smooth wheels on a smooth track to run a train of wagons. A locomotive was then ordered from Thomas Waters of Gateshead, and was little different from that manufactured by his predecessor Whinfield in 1805 on the Trevithick pattern. Delivered in early 1813, the single-cylinder engine soon proved to be rather unpredictable. Several alterations had to made until it was able to pull four or five wagons. However it was unsatisfactory in service because of its unreliability and was therefore abandoned. The boiler explosion which has often been mentioned did not take place.

Blackett was not discouraged by this failure. He now instructed Hedley to build a new locomotive in Wylam itself. The construction took account of their experiences with the previous engines and their observation of Blenkinsop's locomotives. The two cylinders were arranged vertically outside and behind the boiler, probably to avoid sinking them in the boiler which led to steam leakages (Ill. 12). There was an intermediate toothed-wheel gear, like Blenkinsop's, to drive the four smooth wheels. Wrought iron was used for the boiler. There was a return flue, to improve steam production by increasing the heating surface. The exhaust steam was fed into the chimney. This engine soon became known as the "Puffing Billy" because of the puffing noise it made. It was able to pull nine or ten loaded wagons with a total weight of more than 40 tons at a speed of 3½ to

made in the course of time, the main one being the adoption of flanged wheels when the angle plates were replaced by edge rails between 1828 and 1830. It remained in service until 1862 when the mine was closed.

In August 1813 a second and similar locomotive came

12. The "Puffing Billy", William Hedley, 1813.

5 m.p.h. Books mention several dates for its entry into service. Since it is known that Hedley made his adhesion experiments in October 1812, and that the unfortunate Waters locomotive was supplied in early 1813 and that the "Wylam Dilly" following it entered into service in August 1813, we can place the "Puffing Billy" around the middle of 1813, probably May.

There has been much discussion as to whether the original four-wheeled "Puffing Billy" was not subsequently put onto four axles since in view of its weight, the rail plates broke. Fortunately the original is preserved and there are no traces of this kind of alteration, although certain other alterations were

into service, the "Wylam Dilly", already mentioned. It seems certain that this locomotive was on four axles right from the start, for a better distribution of weight on the angled rail plates to be achieved. The engine is illustrated, as shown in a drawing by Nicholas Wood in the *Practical Treatise of Railroads*, 1825 (Ill. 13). The two chassis, each of which contained two axles, were shown for a long time as being pivotable around a vertical pin. For technical reasons, however, this is not possible as L. Troske in 1907 and C.F. Dendy Marshall in 1938 pointed out. What was thought to be a truck pivot on the rear chassis is nothing more than a step by which to mount the

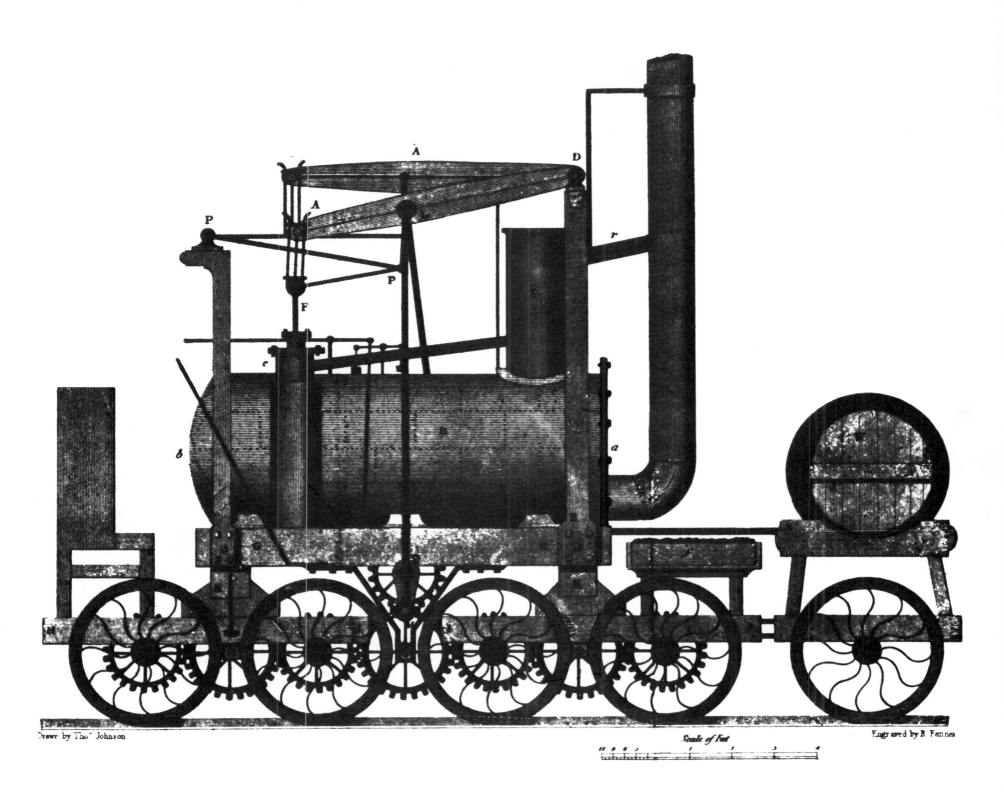

Drawn by Tho.ˢ Johnson   Scale of Feet   Engraved by R. Fenner

locomotive. With angled rails there was always a good deal of clearance between flange and wheel so that even engines with long wheel bases took sharp curves well. This and a third locomotive, "Lady Mary", received four flanged wheels when the track was converted. The "Wylam Dilly" has also been preserved and is exhibited in the Edinburgh Museum in her final condition.

Timothy Hackworth, who was in overall charge of the smith's workshop, got his first spurs as a locomotive builder with the construction of these three Wylam locomotives. He probably played a decisive part in the success of the Wylam engines, for Hedley, the mine foreman, cannot have had any real mechanical qualifications. We will see later that this involvement was why Stephenson later appointed Hackworth resident engineer of the Stockton-and-Darlington Railway.

13. The "Wylam Dilly", William Hedley, 1813.

23

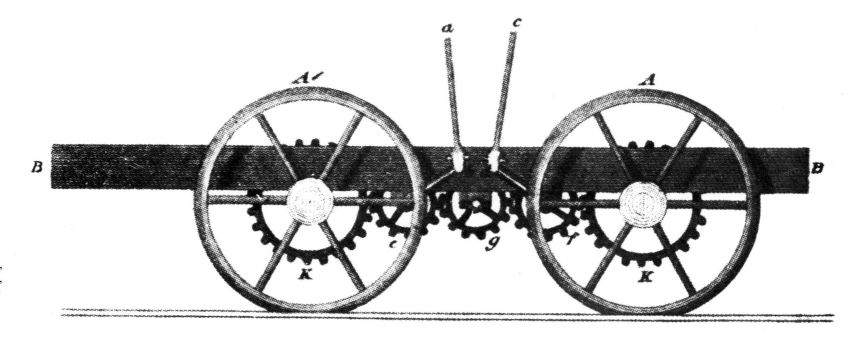

14. The "Blücher", George Stephenson, 1814. Sketch of the mechanism.

2.3 George Stephenson Comes onto the Scene

The creators of the locomotives in Middleton and Wylam were apparently content that their locomotives simply ran; in neither case was there any attempt at further developments. This did not apply to George Stephenson. He had risen to the post of "Superintendent Engineer" — and the technical head therefore — at the Killingworth Colliery. However, since he was also allowed to take part in other projects in the vicinity, for which he built all kinds of engines and tracks, he was able to acquire a wide range of technical experience which helped him later. The mistakes revealed in the locomotives built up until then did not survive his critical scrutiny. He decided "to produce something better"; he failed, however, to achieve this when he built his first locomotive for the Killingworth mine near Newcastle, paid for by Lord Ravensworth. It was christened "Blücher", in honour of the Prussian field-marshal whose timely intervention in the battle of Waterloo led to the decisive defeat of England's arch-enemy Napoleon, and who was therefore highly esteemed. The last existing vestiges of this engine are a sketch of the mechanism from Wood. From this sketch (Ill. 14) and from contemporary reports, it is clear that it was very similar to the Blenkinsop locomotive. It had the same two cylinders of 8 in. by 24 in. mounted lengthwise on the boiler and entering it. The boiler had a single flue. The locomotive was tested on July 27, 1814 on a stretch of track with edge rail, with a slope of 1 in 330. It was able to pull eight coal trucks loaded with a total weight of 30 tons at a speed of about 4 m.p.h. After this trial journey, the engine entered regular service.

Stephenson had carried out experiments along the same lines as Hedley on the adhesion between wheel and rail. According to Warren (1925), he was not sure whether the tractive effort of the "Blücher" was sufficient, and he had therefore prudently increased the

15. Locomotive after George Stephenson's and Ralph Dodd's patent, February 28, 1815.

adhesion weight by putting a cogged wheel on one of the locomotive's axles, carrying an endless chain which drove a second similar one on the one-axle tender. He included this invention in his later patent which was granted to him and to Ralph Dodds on February 28, 1815. But this precautionary measure was soon shown to be unnecessary.

The main point of the trials with the steam locomotive was, of course, to establish whether this method of conveying wagons was cheaper than using horses. Careful notes were thus kept on the costs of both types of operation: at the end of the year, however, steam-traction showed no economic advantage. An additional fact was that the cogged wheels began to rattle badly with increasing wear and the running became extremely jerky. Stephenson had to admit that for the moment he had not produced anything better than his predecessors.

One must admire the fact that despite all this, courage was not lost. Ralph Dodds, inspector at the Killingworth coal mine, was chiefly responsible for encouraging Stephenson to make improvements in the locomotive; and not only that — he also offered to bear a share of the high costs involved in submitting the patent already mentioned. Stephenson's main task was to stop the cogged wheels rattling. Accordingly, he suggested in his patent submission that the four running wheels should be driven directly by the connecting rods from the cylinders which still entered the boiler (Ill. 15). Both axles were to be coupled with a coupling rod. Because of the angle of 90° between the outside crankshafts, this was no simple matter. They had therefore to be attached inside, requiring a double crank axle. A turn-buckle was fitted in order to adjust the exact length of the coupling rods. Stephenson's proposals contained two basic novel ideas which were retained and became normal practice thereafter: coupling rods between the wheels with the possibility of adjusting the exact distance between the crank pins and crank axles.

On March 6, 1815 a new engine incorporating these ideas was tested. Initially it seemed to work. But the forging techniques and the quality of the wrought iron were not sufficiently developed. The double crank axles did not stand up to the stress on them for long and broke, so that Stephenson was forced to go back to the coupling chain.

The engines in those days suffered greatly on contemporary track from hard jolts. In order to overcome this sorry state of affairs, Stephenson suggested two possibilities simultaneously, which he described in a patent submitted jointly with William Losh, owner of an iron foundry in Newcastle, and which was submitted and granted on November 16, 1816. The main reason for the hard jolts was the poor joints in the track, which he set out to improve (Ill. 16). This so-called "overlapping joint" has been "invented" countless times subsequently. The second possibility was an attempt to reduce the jolts which still occurred. Steel leaf-springs* had been met with for a long time on carriages, but it was not yet possible to use them on much heavier locomotives because sufficiently strong springs could not at that time be manufactured. Stephenson arranged steam cylinders open at the top in the base of the boiler, with their downward-projecting piston rods pressing

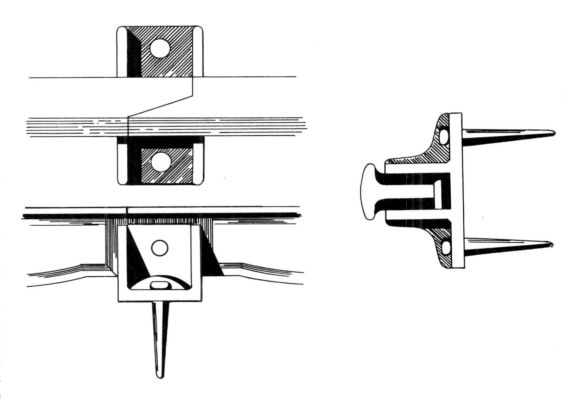

on the axle-boxes (Ill. 17). With this "floating pistons" device, steam in the boiler acted as an elastic fluid and therefore as a shock absorber.

To reduce the stresses on the track, for the first locomotive of this type, which was the third for the Killingworth mine, three axles were provided, coupled by chains. Another innovation for this engine also included in the above-mentioned patent was the fact that the wheels were made from wrought iron instead of cast iron. It entered service in 1815 and must have proved successful initially, since the fourth

16. Rail with overlapping joint after George Stephenson and William Losh's patent of November 16, 1816.

* Springs made up from laminated curved strips of steel.

25

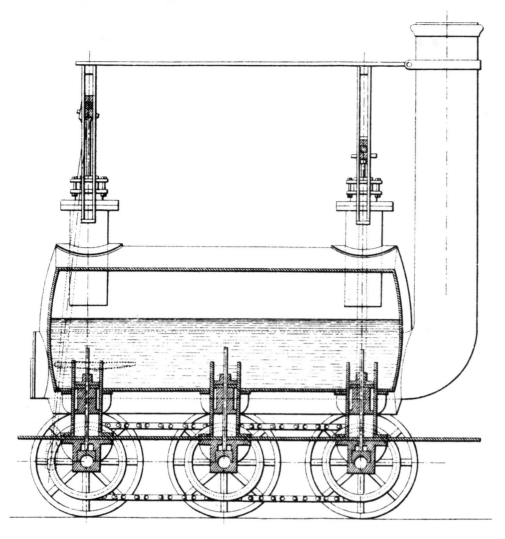

17. Third Killingworth engine, George Stephenson, 1815.

pull eight trucks but only four. To achieve the same transport volume as the two locomotives — 1,788 tons on a total mileage covered of 145 miles — twenty-five horses at 5s each daily would have been necessary, making a total of £6 — proof therefore that steam power was cheaper than dray horses. However these Killingworth engines had been partly converted at that stage: the chain drive had been replaced by coupling rods and the steam suspension cylinders by steel leaf-springs.

The good operational results achieved by the Killingworth locomotives led the Hetton company to turn to Stephenson with a project for a tramway between the coal mine in Hetton-on-Hole and Sunderland. The track was 8 miles long in all. Since it went through very hilly country, Stephenson did not dare plan it for locomotive operation throughout its entire run. Instead, it was divided into sections in a very complicated way: five had stationary steam engines and five had stationary rope ways working by gravity, and two sections of 1½ miles and 2 miles were for steam locomotives. The five locomotives built by Stephenson in his own colliery workshops which were constructed exactly as the last Killingworth engines, pulled sixteen trucks at 4 to 5 m.p.h. On November 18, 1822 the first coal was ceremonially despatched along the complicated route which was to be run by Stephenson's son, Robert. One of these engines was still in service in 1908, but it had been completely transformed in 1857 and then again in 1882. It is today in the York Railway Museum (Ill. 19).

These Hetton locomotives close the first, tentative era in the history of the steam locomotive. Proof had been given that it was possible to build locomotives which would operate satisfactorily and which would stand up to the conditions found on the existing tramways. Operating costs had been less than those incurred where animals had been used.

Stephenson thought the moment had come to build locomotives for his own account. On June 23, 1823 the first locomotive workshop in the world was founded, with financial assistance from Edward Pease, whom he had come to know in connection with the planned Stockton-and-Darlington Railway, and Michael Longridge, owner of the Bedlington ironworks. The workshop was in Forth Street in Newcastle. George Stephenson's son, Robert, was appointed manager. The firm was called Robert Stephenson & Co.: but Robert Stephenson's first work was in South America.

Killingworth engine in the following year followed the same general pattern, with, however, only four wheels (Ill. 18). An innovation was that the boiler steam was fed into the two cylinders via a tube with a slide valve. This enabled better control than the plug valves over the steam flow and therefore improved the performance of the locomotive. It is the origin of the use of slide valves for control purposes, called steam regulator and still in use today.

As can easily be imagined, Killingworth became a place of pilgrimage for all those interested in steam locomotives and their operations, and these included seven people from the founding committee of the projected Liverpool-and-Manchester Railway. With regard to their visit, *The Times* published certain interesting details on February 8, 1825 on the performance of the Killingworth locomotives. An 8 h.p. engine could, it appeared, carry 48½ tons at speeds of just under 4 to 5 m.p.h.

As to a comparison of costs, there exists a report from 1828 showing that the daily costs for two locomotives amounted to £2 9s 2d. Horses could not

26

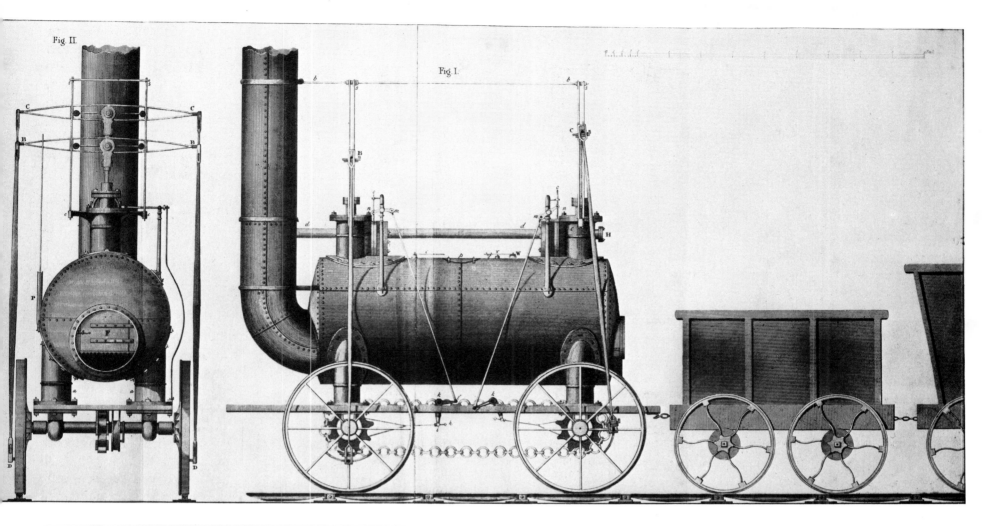

18. Fourth Killing-
worth engine, George
Stephenson, 1816.

19. Hetton engine,
George Stephenson,
1822.

27

3. THE BIRTH OF THE STEAM RAILROAD

20. The "Locomotion" by George Stephenson, 1825, as it is today.

3.1 The Stockton-and-Darlington Railway, the First Public Railroad Using Steam Locomotives

Edward Pease, a Quaker who had grown rich through the wool trade and textile mills as well as through his own bank, exerted all his influence in favour of the construction of a railroad instead of a canal when the rich coal deposits in County Durham began to be exploited. Pease founded a company for the construction of a line between Stockton and Darlington. George Overton had worked out a project. On April 19, 1821 the concession was granted. This spoke both of a "rail-way" and of a "tram-way", on which goods traffic could be conveyed by anybody on payment of a toll. When George Stephenson heard of this concession, accompanied by his former immediate superior, Nicholas Wood, he applied to Edward Pease to offer his services. "Come over to Killingworth and see what my engines can do, seeing is believing, Sir." Pease actually visited the Killingworth track in the summer of 1822. He was even allowed to travel on the locomotives and he returned so enthusiastic that a new bill was prepared to enable

28

locomotives to carry people and goods, and approved by Parliament in 1823.

George Stephenson was instructed to alter Overton's project accordingly. He followed closely the idea of his earlier tracks. The 26-mile-stretch was split into sections for rope haulage, horses, and locomotives. The latter had a 20-mile-section at the end of the track, once an incline had been surmounted. Stephenson succeeded after lengthy negotiations in acquiring Timothy Hackworth as the resident engineer of the railroad and he took up his new position on May 13, 1825.

It had been decided at a meeting of the railroad committee on September 16, 1824 to order two locomotives from the newly formed works, Stephenson & Co. This was the first order executed by the company. The first of the two engines, "Locomotion", arrived just in time, loaded onto three wagons, for the opening of the railroad. It was only a small advance on the last of the Hetton locomotives (Ill. 20; present-day state). The greatest improvement on the old methods was the use of coupling rods mounted outside on the wheels instead of chains inside. Since the cylinder arrangement was retained, the coupling rods meant long counter-cranks on the wheels diagonally opposite to enable the connecting rods to be set at 90°. Originally the wheels were cast in one piece. Later Hackworth used two concentric sections held together by wooden plugs, to avoid having to replace the whole expensive wheel every time the running surface was worn (an arrangement later known as "plug wheels").

The opening of the railroad, which received enormous coverage in the local press, took place on September 27, 1825. The train assembled for this day consisted of the tender, six "chaldron" wagons loaded with

21. Opening of the Stockton-and-Darlington Railway, 1825.

29

coal and sacks of flour, followed by "an elegant covered coach" for the members of the committee, twenty-one wagons fitted with benches specially for the journey and at the far end another six coal "chaldrons" weighing altogether 69 tons. This seems quite a load for a locomotive which later caused complaints about its steaming capacity, and which is reported to have only been able with great difficulty to pull eight wagons on its first test runs. Still, the inaugural train stopped many times on the way and the rider in front with a white flag had trouble dispersing the crowd of people who had gathered on the track. So the train only moved forwards slowly with many stops and there was plenty of time to get up steam pressure in the boiler.

"Locomotion" had a stormy life. Barely a month after entry into service, one wheel broke. On July 1, 1828, the boiler exploded as a result of the driver's carelessness. Once repaired, it was rebuilt twice more in the course of time. It was in service on the track until 1841, was used between 1850 and 1857 as the pumping engine in a mine, and was then mounted on a pedestal near to North Road Station in Darlington as a memento. As part of the 50th Anniversary celebrations for the Stockton-and-Darlington Railway in 1875, it was steamed again. A year later it was exhibited at the World Fair in Philadelphia. In 1881, on the occasion of the 100th Anniversary of George Stephenson's birth, it led the cavalcade of locomotives exhibited. It then appeared at several exhibitions: 1886 in Liverpool, 1887 in Newcastle, 1889 in Paris. In 1892 it was again put on a pedestal as a monument, this time at Bank Top Station in Darlington. But still it had no rest, since it was again displayed at the British Empire Exhibition in Wembley in 1924, and on July 2 in the following year it brought up under its own steam the parade of locomotives on the occasion of the 100th Anniversary of its own track. It then returned to its pedestal in Darlington.

The Stockton-and-Darlington Railway was a severe test for steam locomotives. It became clear that the 20-mile line demanded much more of the engines than had been required on the short freight sections at Killingworth and Hetton. No reliance could be placed on the four locomotives supplied by Stephenson: "Locomotion" and three similar locomotives. The long fly cranks failed and caused damage to the coupling rods. Horses were always having to be brought in and the costs of the frequent repairs ate away the expected savings on horse haulage.

There had been attempts to acquire other locomotives, only no one could be found willing to build them but Robert Wilson. His offer was accepted. Wilson built the first locomotive with four cylinders. The cylinders were outside the rear end of the boiler, next to each other in pairs. The piston rods, also in pairs, worked upwards, and were joined by a common cross-head, which drove the rear of the two axles via connecting rods running down both sides. The crank pins were mounted directly on the wheels without fly cranks, and set at 90°. The two axles were coupled with chains. Because of its noise when travelling, this engine was nicknamed the "Chittaprat". The "Chittaprat" failed, and future for steam operations looked even more gloomy. The "Chittaprat" was nevertheless accepted by the railroad because Hackworth had offered to build a better locomotive than Stephenson's engines, after his own ideas, using the boiler.

Stephenson had not been idle. He supplied a new locomotive at the end of 1827, which in spite of several significant innovations was to prove unsuccessful. Initially its axle loading was too high for the existing track, and so a new frame for three instead of two axles had to be supplied. Stephenson tried to improve the poor steam production of his earlier locomotives by having installed in the forward part of the single 28 in.-diameter flue, and concentric to it, a water drum of 28 in. diameter, connected at the front end with the water space of the boiler. He provided a grate in the rear part of the boiler, which did not consist of the conventional cast fire bars but of eight parallel water tubes of 1½ in. inside diameter. These tubes ran into the water drum at the front and into a cast-iron box at the rear, which was also connected with the water space of the boiler via two elbows. So it was a sort of water tube boiler, the first time that the idea of increasing the effective heating surface by using several narrow tubes had been incorporated in a locomotive. Compared with the single flue the heating surface was nearly doubled. The chimney rose 16 ft. above the track and could be extended a further 8 ft. with a cowl*, to strengthen the draught. What a sight it must have been, a locomotive like this with a chimney reaching upwards 24 ft.! Old prints, which show Stephenson locomotives operating with this sort of excessively long chimney, may well be based on this particular engine. For the first time Stephenson departed from the cylinder arrangement of the classical swing-beam steam engine of Watt. He dispensed with cylinders working upwards, and — in a similar arrangement as that chosen by Blenkinsop for a single

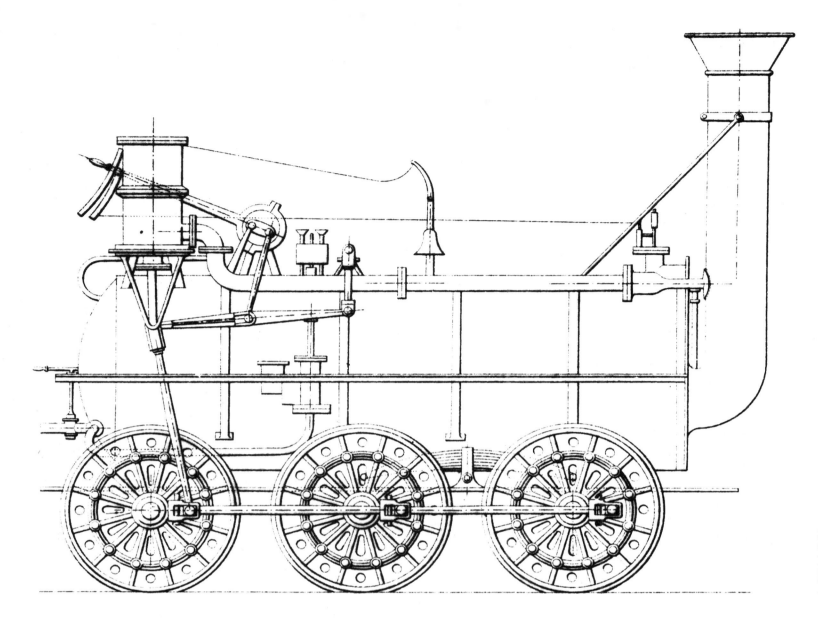

22. The "Royal George", Timothy Hackworth, 1827, Stockton and Darlington Railway.

cylinder — he placed both horizontally next to each other, entering the boiler at the front. The two piston rods each held one of the swing levers, which were mounted on two shafts, matched crosswise behind the boiler, and mounted each independently in three cast-iron bearings. At the outside far end of each of these shafts were further swing levers, which drove the front axle directly via an inclined drive rod. The rear axle was connected with coupling rods. The horizontal arrangement of the cylinders and the long connecting rods allowed the use of leaf springs which had meanwhile become practicable, on all three axles of this locomotive which was called the "Experiment". In his diaries, Hackworth mentions this locomotive as the "quadrant" or the "lever engine". Her crew nicknamed her "Old Elbows". She worked more or less for a few years and did not exceed 5 m.p.h. with twenty wagons. In 1830 Hackworth completely re-built her along the lines of the following engine, and in 1839 she was finally disposed of to a contractor. Hackworth, as mentioned previously, was allowed to use the boiler of the unfortunate "Chittaprat" for a new locomotive he was planning, but he interpreted his permission rather freely. He sent the boiler to the Sumley Forge near Durham where the plates were used for a completely new and much larger boiler with a return flue and many other parts to be cast after patterns sent in. The railroad workshops at Shildon saw the assembly of the components into the finished product. Hackworth could not get away from the traditional vertical cylinders but he arranged them free-standing and working in a downward motion behind the boiler (Ill. 22). Thus the intermediate shafts and beams could be dropped, allowing them to

* Hood.

31

drive the rear axle directly. All three axles were coupled. The rear axle could not take any suspension, and a common leaf spring was attached to the front two, flexible mounted in the middle and acting simultaneously as a load compensating or equalizing device. This arrangement appears here for the first time. An important detail of this locomotive, called the "Royal George", is not visible from the outside: the blast pipe for blowing up the fire. There has been much acrimonious discussion as to who invented this very

into the chimney on principle. Hackworth thought differently. According to the detailed studies made by Ahrons (1924), it was he who for the first time constructed the blast pipe exactly centered and with an aperture shaped like a nozzle, on the "Royal George", and it has survived in that form to this day. The "Royal George" was tested in September 1827. She covered the whole line for the first time on November 29. In normal service she pulled coal trains of twenty-four loaded wagons with an empty

23. The "Wilberforce", Timothy Hackworth, 1833, Stockton-and-Darlington Railway.

important component, which is a very simple method of self-controlled steam production in the boiler according to the performance required. It produces that puffing noise in the steam locomotive which almost makes it appear to be a living creature, breathing more or less heavily according to the work it has to do.

Trevithick had already noticed that the fire burned considerably better when the exhaust steam was fed into the chimney. With the wide chimneys and flues in general use, the natural draught was sufficient to keep the fire bright. On the basis of his experiences with the Killingworth locomotives, Nicholas Wood went so far as to reject feeding the exhaust steam

weight of 24 cwt each and a load of 2.65 to 3.4 tons, thus totalling 93 to 100 tons; she could, however, pull loads of up to 130 tons. Her speed of 5 m.p.h. was the maximum permitted at that time. Her performance far surpassed all locomotives yet built. It was this engine that tilted the balance in favour of steam on the question of whether steam or horse traction were cheaper on the Stockton-and-Darlington Railway.

In 1829, a second, identical locomotive was built, aptly named "Victory".

The year 1829 began on a very hopeful note for the Stockton-and-Darlington Railway. Parliament had approved the extension from Stockton to Middles-

borough which had been applied for. Various new branch lines from mines were started. An order was placed for twelve further locomotives following the well-proven "Royal George" and "Victory", but with improved performances. In the long run the rear axle on the engines, which had no suspension, was not satisfactory. The two cylinders acting in a downward motion were kept but a dummy shaft was interposed which drove the three axles by coupling rods. In this way, all the axles could be sprung. For the first six engines built in this "Majestic" class, the cylinders and dummy shaft were in front of the chimney end of the boiler. Meanwhile Stephenson had shown with his prize-winning locomotive "Rocket" that the steam production of the boiler could be considerably increased by using a multitude of firing tubes. Hackworth did provide such tubes but probably to make building easier he dispensed with the firebox. He preferred a wide flue at the rear end, containing the grate, and then a partition wall. Between the latter and the front boiler plate ran a number of copper fire tubes only 4 ft. in length, which opened into a smoke box set at the front. This sort of construction was often used later for portable steam engines. The six engines which were built

jointly by Robert Stephenson & Co. and by R. & W. Hawthorn, entered into service in 1831/32.

For the second series, constructed in 1833 as the "Wilberforce" class, Hackworth made a number of alterations (Ill. 23). The cylinders and dummy shaft were now at the other end of the boiler, away from the chimney. In the boiler this time the flue and the fire tubes were no longer joined behind one another. The flue opened into an intermediate chamber with a "D"-shaped cross-section. The fire tubes were drawn backwards from here around the flue. For their part, they opened into a saddle-shaped smoke box around the fire door. Robert Napier had patented this type of boiler, and Hackworth came to a friendly agreement with him whereby the Napier patent was to be used exclusively in his locomotives. The success of the "Wilberforce" class ushered in a new era in locomotive construction on the Stockton-and-Darlington Railway, which was to last for decades. Voices have been raised in criticism of the fact that this railroad retained a type of locomotive for so long which was considered outdated when compared with Stephenson's models. But these simple, easily maintained engines were quite sufficient for the slow-running coal trains restricted to 5 to 6 m.p.h.

24. The "Derwent", 1845, Stockton-and-Darlington Railway.

33

From 1838 the "Tory" saw the last series of loco-motives on the Hackworth model, which were built in large numbers until 1845. These later examples were in due course provided with inclined cylinders at the rear end of the boiler and they drove the front axle directly with a long connecting rod without any dummy shaft. Since there was no real overhang and the inclined cylinders did not create as much rocking as the vertical ones, these engines were allow-ed to travel at 15 m.p.h.

One of the last locomotives on this Hackworth pattern, the "Derwent", delivered in 1845 by W.A. Kitching, has been preserved to this day (Ill. 24). It was acquired by the Pease and Partners coal mine in Darlington and was given in 1898 to the North Eastern Railway which had absorbed the Stockton-and-Darlington Railway. This locomotive is displayed in Darlington together with the "Locomotion" at Bank Top station.

3.2 The Saint-Etienne Railroad; the First Public Railroad on the European Mainland with Steam Traction

France had, and still has, one of its richest coal seams at Saint-Etienne. Situated on a plateau between the Loire and the Rhône, it cannot be reached by canal. On October 1, 1828, France's first railroad, 10 miles long, was opened, connecting Saint-Etienne with Andrézieux, which could be reached on the Loire by boat. Following the English pattern, a steep rope-way functioning by gravity was used to overcome the difference in height. The rest of the line was initially horse-drawn. Once the connection had been made to the Loire — and thereby with the north of France — it was time now to connect with the Rhône and thus with the south. Marc Séguin provided the impetus. In the winter of 1827/28 he went on a study trip to England. He himself was scarcely en-thusiastic about rope haulage, which was very com-plicated. In order to avoid this sort of solution he surveyed the planned track with a permanent incline of between 1 in 70 to 84½ in such a way that the loaded trains could roll downhill by themselves to Rive-de-Gier. The next stretch as far as Givors on the bank of the Rhône was less difficult. The steepest incline here was 1 in 154. The last stretch along the bank of the Rhône as far as Lyons was practically level.

Marc Séguin had certainly thought of locomotives right from the start, at least for the more level

stretches, for when he made his trip to England he bought two locomotives from Robert Stephenson & Co. One of these engines was initially given to the engineering firm Halette in Arras to study, and was then transferred to the railroad. There has been no convincing description to this day as to what kind of a locomotive this was. However, fortunately, there is a copy of an old drawing of the second one which was given to the railroad immediately, the drawing copy dating from 1889 and held at the Museon Di Rodo at Uzès (Ill. 25). This was the ninth locomotive built by Robert Stephenson and completely different from those supplied previously. Stephenson had not yet been able to get away from Watt's swing-beam engines, but this time he arranged the vertical cylinders between both axles outside the boiler. It is possible that Robert Stephenson chose this position in order to avoid the long and weak return crank of the "Locomotion" (Ill. 26). There were no springs on the axles. During the winter of 1828/29 many trials were made with the locomotives, both in Arras and in Lyons. These showed that the the boiler did not get up enough steam: no value higher than 600 lb/hour was reached. Both engines were apparently in service for only a short time, if at all, since the annual report of the railroad for 1830 says that "two English locomotives have been put to one side because they were not capable of satisfactory service". This is mentioned again in 1834. One was still in existence in 1859 when the Compagnie du Rhône et Loire which had been formed out of the Saint-Etienne Railroad offered up for sale all the

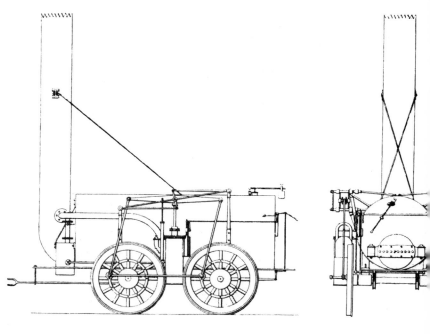

25. Locomotive of the Saint-Etienne-Lyons Railroad, built by Robert Stephenson & Co., 1827.

engines condemned before August 1, 1858, pricing the English one at 2,400 francs.

The same difficulty of getting up enough steam also existed on the tugs on the Rhône, which were run by a steam ship company in which Marc Séguin participated. Séguin reported later that he had begun in 1827 "to realize the idea he had been brooding on for a long time, of increasing the heating area by means of a series of tubes in the water space of the boiler". He dismissed the opposite idea of exposing water tubes to the fire, on the grounds — among other reasons — that it is difficult to achieve in this manner sufficient circulation of water, causing local overheating of the material. It is mainly for this reason that all later attempts to use water tube boilers for locomotives have in fact failed. Séguin constructed a stationary experimental boiler consisting of a water drum with forty-three fire tubes 1½ in. diameter, the drum being 10 ft. long with a stone-built fire chamber with a grate in front of it. Since he did not include a chimney, the fire had to be brought to life. This boiler succeeded in producing up to 2,600 lb/hour of steam. Satisfied with this success, on December 12, 1827, he submitted an application for a French patent for his invention.

Without wasting any time he began to build a locomotive using this new type of boiler at his own rail road workshops at Lyons-Perrache (Ill. 26). He adopted the exact driving arrangement of the Stephenson locomotive which he had bought, but he increased the cylinder diameter. Since the spring beam was able to compensate for small differences in the height of the wheels caused by the track, he took the risk of providing leaf springs on both axles. As on the experimental boiler, forty-three fire tubes were inserted, opening at the front end into an enlarged chimney base. The grate was in a firebox which was placed below the front part of the boiler, consisting of two double-walled water chambers of cast iron, and was closed at the rear by a cast-iron plate with the fire door. The feed water was preheated in the two water chambers at the side. The hot gases passed initially through a double-walled semi-circular chamber around the lower part of the boiler barrel, and were then fed back into the chimney via the fire tubes. This semi-circular chamber was connected with the water space of the boiler barrel and contributed to the effective heating surface. Marc Séguin considered that activating the fire, independently of the variable effect of a blast pipe, was a more convenient way of steadying the steam production and

accordingly provided two large rotary bellows into the tender, the kind of equipment used to clean corn and other cereals. A belt driven by the rear axle of the tender was used to drive their fan blades. The air was blown in under the grate via two leather hoses connected to two holes by the fire door.

The first trial journey took place on November 7, 1829. The locomotive was lit at 11.30 in the morn-

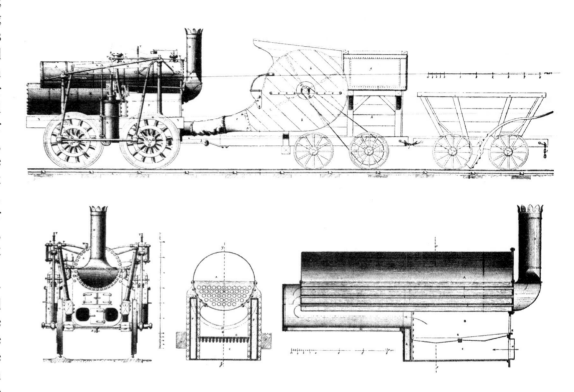

ing and by 12.06 was able to start off along the trial stretch of only 140 yards. This section comprised also the greatest incline on the whole stretch of 1 in 10, and a curve of 460 yards radius. Time after time the locomotive performed to perfection, pulling four wagons loaded with 15 tons of cast-iron pieces representing a total weight of 19 tons. But it was not possible to reach a speed higher than 2 m.p.h. on the short trial stretch. When the second trial was made on the following day the axle boxes had been greased so liberally that on heating the fat dripped onto the rails and the wheels kept slipping on the greasy rails. Thus it was only possible to pull 17 tons; but it was considered as proven that the locomotive would be able to pull at least eight wagons each with an 11-ton load along the section Rive-de-Gier–Saint-Etienne and Marc Séguin received an order for two more locomotives.

26. Marc Séguin's locomotive with multi-tubular boiler for the Saint-Etienne-Lyons Railroad, 1829.

In view of the dispute as to who was the first to use a multitubular boiler, it should be stressed that Marc Séguin began work on constructing his locomotive before Stephenson began the "Rocket", but he completed it later. The tests on the Saint-Etienne Railroad took place just one month after the Rainhill Trials.

The two newly ordered locomotives entered service in July 1830 on the stretch which had meanwhile been completed, running from Rive-de-Gier to Givors. Initially they were very prone to mishap and Séguin altered them several times. The firebox was converted from coal to coke burning. Séguin replaced the bellows in the tender by a blast pipe in the chimney. As a result the engines were able to take thirty to thirty-five trucks in less than three hours along the 17½-mile-stretch between Givors and Consort near Rive-de-Gier without any problems. With the bellows in the tender they had broken down

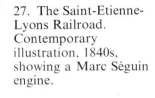

27. The Saint-Etienne-Lyons Railroad. Contemporary illustration, 1840s, showing a Marc Séguin engine.

for lack of steam so often that a wagon containing four horses had always to accompany the locomotive, so that these could be harnessed whenever it ran out of steam. When the various faults had been corrected, a total of twelve engines of this type were built before 1835 at the Lyons-Perrache workshop. Because of their loose levers they were known as "Scieurs de Long" or "Alternating Saws". In 1834 Marc Séguin left the company after differences of opinion with the board of directors. His successor Tourasse set out on a completely different track and we will return to him later.

3.3 The Liverpool-and-Manchester Railroad Leads Steam to a Decisive Victory

The Stockton-and-Darlington Railway had proved conclusively that steam locomotives could be used to

transport coal economically, but, until the end of its life, it remained a mineral railroad; passenger traffic was small and was initially satisfied by using horses. Much more challenging was the project for a railroad linking the neighbouring cities of Liverpool, with its international port, and Manchester with its flourishing industry. This was a chance to carry goods of all possible descriptions and a large number of people at higher speeds than were possible on the canals. George Stephenson was appointed chief engineer for the construction of the railroad. As he had to take up residence in Liverpool to supervise the construction work, it was fortunate that his son

Robert returned from South America in 1827 and was able to devote his attention to the locomotive works in Forth Street, where all was not well.
Both Stephensons agreed that the locomotives built hitherto were not suitable for the new railroad. Two basic problems had still to be solved before faster and more efficient engines than those on the colliery lines could be built: a good suspension system, to save wear both on the track and the locomotive, and a free-steaming boiler which maintained a good head of steam for a sufficient length of time. We see the first step in this direction with the "Liverpool Travelling Engine", intended for the construction

28. The Liverpool-and-Manchester Railway, 1831. In descending order: freight train; train for cattle transport; passenger train with first-class cars; second and third-class cars.

trains in 1828 working on the Liverpool-and-Manchester Railway, but was handed to the Bolton-and-Leigh Railway which was shortly to be opened. This engine was able to be tested more thoroughly in this way, and, as the "Lancashire Witch", it became very well known. This new design (Ill. 29) had the cylinders mounted at an angle for the first time, and they drove the axle at the chimney end directly, the axle being joined to the second axle with coupling rods. There were thus no other intermediate components between cylinders and wheels. Both axles could be sprung because the play had less effect on the pistons than when the cylinders were vertical. Since an engine, built with a water-tube boiler — the "Experiment" of the Stockton-and-Darlington Railway — had not proved a success, the general secretary of the company, Henry Booth, to whom we owe the building of the Liverpool-and-Manchester Railway, suggested another way to increase the heating surface. In addition to the central flue (marked "X" in Ill. 29) two smaller return flues (Y) were provided on each side. Additionally two water tubes (W) were drawn through the central flue. The construction of these tubes caused great difficulties. As a result, the final version simply had two flues running from the front to the rear in parallel (shown hatched in the figure). Thus the heating surface only amounted to 66 sq. ft. which was not much more than that of the "Locomotion". Each of these flues had its own built-in grate. The "Lancashire Witch" (Ill. 30) entered service on the Bolton-and-Leigh Railway in this form. So far there had not been any progress in boiler performance but there had been a major simplification of the mechanical arrangement. The "Lancashire Witch" represents the transition from the slow-moving colliery railroad locomotives to the "Rocket" which came later. Another remarkable feature of the "Lancashire Witch" was the possibility of either admitting steam throughout the whole course of the piston stroke or of shutting it off earlier. Thus, for the first time on a locomotive, we find a valve gear with variable cut-off.

On one of the axles a toothed bevel wheel is fixed, which turns another bevel wheel placed horizontally and attached to a vertical shaft. This, passing through the boiler, operates a rotating valve. There are two toothed quadrants which the driver can turn by handle through a quarter of a revolution about their centres; in their first position they allow the rotary valve to produce its effect by causing the steam to work by expansion; in the second, they stop this and steam acts only by the effect of its elasticity on its entry into the cylinders. The early cut-off of steam into the cylinder was used when starting, when the bellows originally provided were not yet effective: steam, therefore, had to be used sparingly until the locomotive began to move. When going properly, the steam supply was then turned on full. Obviously the value of expansion had not yet been recognized, for the variable cut-off was used in exactly the opposite way to that adopted later on.

In the meantime Rastrick and Walker took stock of all the stationary and locomotive engines working on railroads and delivered the report on them commissioned by the committee of the Liverpool-and-Manchester Railway. Their report was far from emphatic in its support of the locomotive. The curious situation is that here was an expensive railroad being built without any idea of how it was going to be operated, a circumstance which was to be repeated later when the mountain line was built over the Semmering Pass. This report was a bitter disappointment for the Stephensons. George Stephenson submitted a contrary report in favour of the

29. The "Lancashire Witch", George Stephenson, 1828. Sketch showing cross-section of boiler.

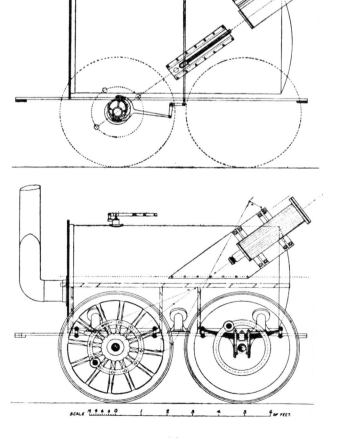

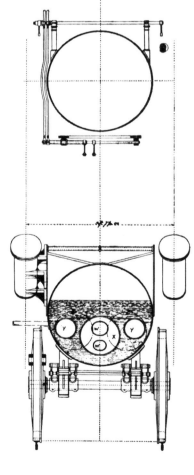

38

steam locomotive in vain. After many debates conducted even in the press, the company committee decided at its meeting on April 20, 1829 to accept Rastrick's suggestion and to organize a competition with a prize of £500 for a locomotive which was better than those already constructed. This decision was amplified at the following meeting on May 4, when it was added that it did not have to be a steam locomotive but could be "an improved Motive Power". Whereupon the members of the committee

should be able to pull a train weighing 20 tons, on a well laid stretch of horizontal track, including the tender at a rate of 10 m.p.h. with the boiler pressure not exceeding 50 lbs. per sq. in. "The engine and boiler must be supported on springs and rest on six wheels. The weight of the machine, with its complement of water in the boiler, must, at most not exceed six tons."

c) "An engine of less weight would be preferred if it drew after it a proportionate weight." If the locomo-

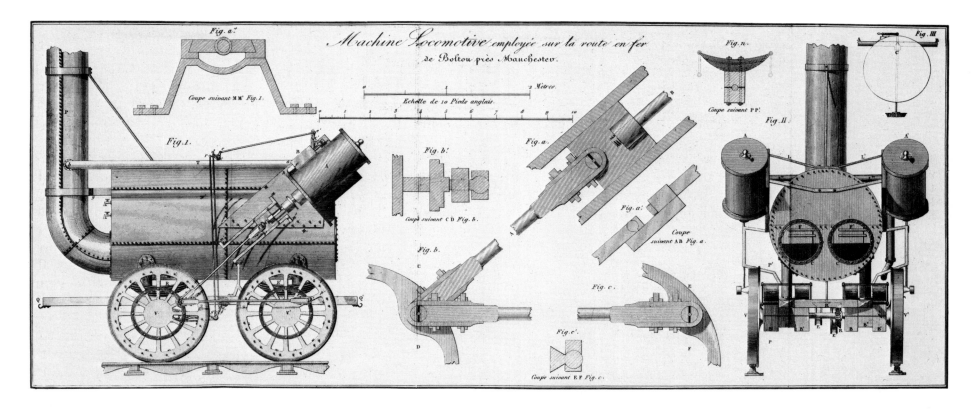

were overwhelmed with a flood of the most bizarre ideas. Henry Booth writes: «Every scheme which the restless ingenuity or prolific imagination of man could devise was liberally offered to the Company." By April 25 the conditions for the locomotives participating in the competition had been decided. These regulations, which were decisive for the history of the steam locomotive, are a summary of the practical experiences acquired up to that time. The basic points contained in the conditions for the competition were:

a) in accordance with the regulations for the Railway Act the locomotives should consume their own smoke. (This regulation was observed while coke was burned, because it is almost smokeless. For this reason it was used in almost all cases until well into the 1850s.)

b) A locomotive weighing 6 tons maximum by itself

tive did not exceed 4½ tons it could run on four wheels only.

d) Two safety valves should be provided, one of which had to be "completely out of the control of the engine man" (a regulation which remained in force right to the end of steam operation). "A mercury gauge should be affixed to the engine shewing the steam pressure above 45 lbs. per sq. in. The railway company shall be at liberty to put the boiler, fire-tube, cylinders etc to a test of a pressure of water not exceeding 150 lbs. per sq. in."

e) "The price of the engine which may be accepted should not exceed £550 delivered on the railway."

f) The locomotive had to be delivered "complete for trial at the Liverpool end of the Rail-way no later than the 1st October 1829." The railway company would provide the water and fuel necessary for the

30. The "Lancashire Witch", George Stephenson, 1828.

test runs free of charge. Only in the appendix is it mentioned that the "distance between the rails" is 4' 8½".

George Stephenson was instructed to prepare a stretch of 1¾ miles for the trials at Rainhill near Liverpool, with 200 yards of track attached at either end to allow the train to get up speed for the complete journey and to brake at the end.

Both Stephensons, of course, had decided to take part in the competition. With the "Lancashire Witch" they had discovered a workable answer for a drive gear which enabled all the wheels to accommodate the sprung suspension required. On the other hand there were still problems with the boiler. But the cross-section of the boiler (Ill. 29), originally intended for the "Lancashire Witch", shows that they were on the right track. Once again it was the non-technical Henry Booth who made a valid and feasible suggestion for a boiler and who proposed to George Stephenson that they should share the costs of construction. Booth's new idea was to include a large number of smaller fire tubes in the boiler, each of 2 to 3 in. diameter and with a wall thickness of ⅛ in. The idea was not new in itself. Boulton in 1816 was among others to have thought of it; he had received a patent in 1816 but had not carried it through to execution. It is possible that Booth knew something of this; what, on the other hand, cannot be proved is whether or not he had heard of Marc Séguin's attempts. Robert Stephenson was responsible for the actual design of the locomotive to be built for the competition in close contact with his experienced father. As is customary in ship-yards, the plans for the engine were drawn on the floor with chalk with the result that we do not have any authentic drawings. The new method of building the boiler using a lot of narrow fire tubes did not allow the grate to be constructed inside the boiler barrel as was customary. Marc Séguin had therefore arranged the firebox underneath the boiler barrel (Ill. 26). In contrast Robert Stephenson placed it in front (Ill. 32). It was not until Rastrick's notebook was found in 1929 that the question of the original shape of the firebox of the "Rocket", as this engine was called, was cleared up. Rastrick acted as judge in the Rainhill competition. According to his notes, the firebox consisted of double-walled side sheets, connected with the water space of the boiler barrel by curved pipes above and below. Both sheets of the double walls were held against each other by means of a number of screws, the predecessors of the stay bolts which

were to come later. The lower part of the front wall and the lower part of the rear wall consisted of single sheets.

Since the conditions for the competition favoured a lighter locomotive, Robert Stephenson decided on a twin-axled engine under 4½ tons in weight. In these circumstances a single-drive axle was sufficient to achieve a tractive power of 3 to 3½ times the weight of the locomotive. He thus circumvented the difficulties which then existed with two coupled axles — the unequal wear on the wheel tyres which were made of soft steel and the consequent extra forces exerted on the coupling rods. The frame consisted of two bayonet-shaped bent flat iron sections which were braced at the front by two round bars at an angle and which were joined front and rear by other flat bars. At the rear a covering plate served both as a reinforcement and as a platform for the driver. The cylinders which were set at an angle of 35° rested on an iron plate attached to the boiler shell. The whole assembly was mounted on four leaf springs above the axle boxes. It is quite clear that the resistance against the hot gases through a large number of narrow tubes is much greater than when one wide flue is used. On the "Lancashire Witch" Stephenson had produced an artificial draught, just as Marc Séguin had done, but using ordinary bellows. This time

31. The "Sanspareil", Timothy Hackworth, 1829.

making stationary tests, the Stephensons established the extent to which the effect of the steam being led into the chimney could blow up the fire, a principle which was already known to them. However they led away the exhaust steam from each cylinder through separate pipes. It was not until the trial runs were being made, that they altered the exhaust pipe nozzle in line with Hackworth's design, having observed the exhaust from the competing locomotive "Sanspareil". While the locomotive was being built, all the parts were carefully weighed so as not to exceed the permitted weight. The final empty weight amounted to 3 tons 10 cwt. 1 qr., and to 4 tons 5 cwt. 1 qr., with 15 cwt. of water in the boiler, thus remaining below the permitted limit of 4 ½ tons for a two-axle engine. The tender, supplied by a carriage-builder in Liverpool, had a new method of axle suspension (Ill. 6). It was normal for coal trucks to mount the axle bearings inside the wheels, but, on this tender, they were out-side (Ill. 32) and since they were sprung, they ran inside two-axle guards. George Stephenson had intro-duced this kind of construction as early as 1827 in order to be able to build a wider carriage, but it seems that the first time this was manufactured with suspension springs was on the tender of the "Rocket". It was then introduced on all the cars on the Liverpool-and-Manchester Railway and has since become normal practice on railroad rolling stock.

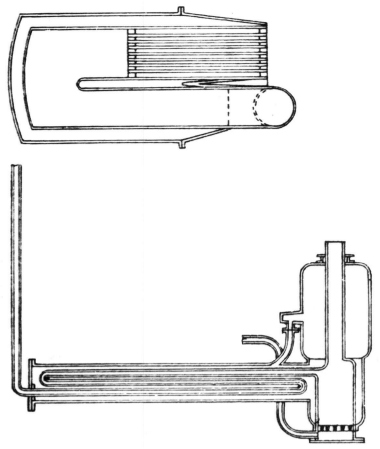

33. Boiler system of the "Sanspareil" and the "Novelty", 1829.

34. The "Novelty", John Ericsson and John Braithwaite, 1829.

Hackworth was also quite naturally determined to participate in the competition. He was allowed to build a locomotive for it at his own expense in the Shildon workshops of the Stockton-and-Darlington Railway. Working a normal day at his regular job he was only able to get his design onto paper at night.

He had to have many of the parts made outside: the Bedlington ironworks made the boiler, for example, and Robert Stephenson the cylinders. The tight time schedule often compelled Hackworth to work right through the day and all night. He had no time to make a thorough test, but had to be content with a short trip made at midnight. His locomotive, proudly christened the "Sanspareil" was very similar in construction to the proven "Royal George" but was mounted on two axles (Ill. 31). He increased the heating surface by using a return flue which he brought back out of the boiler and surrounded it with a conical water jacket (Ill. 33). The wheels had cast-iron bosses which took the crank pins. The wooden spokes were set into cup-shaped sleeves mounted radially around the hub. The wheel rim was probably also of wood with wrought iron tyres around it. The rear axle could not be sprung because of the vertically mounted cylinders, and the front axle was not suspended either. In this respect the "Sanspareil" did not comply with the rules of the competition and its operational weight of 4 tons 16 cwt. exceeded the admissible 4½ tons, the limit for four-wheeled engines.

A certain Mr Burstal from Leith had also put forward a candidate. Robert Stephenson reported to Booth that he had entered the Newcastle works by stealth and had had a good look at the "Rocket" which was under construction, before he was discovered. The construction of his "Perseverance" as it was called resembled mechanically one of his steam-driven carriages (Ill. 35). The evening before the trial runs began it was damaged while being unloaded. Subjected to a short preliminary test it was not able to comply with the conditions. Burstal withdrew his locomotive, but was given £25, very probably as compensation for the accident.

The "Novelty" designed by John Ericsson and built by John Braithwaite in London aroused most interest and admiration (Ill. 34). It was fully worthy of its name, and was completely different from the engines which people were accustomed to. Its boiler was unique (Ill. 33). The hot gases were to flow through a triple coil installed within a horizontal barrel, with the result that the fire needed a strong draught produced with bellows. The fuel was fed in via a wide flue running down through a vertical boiler, and the mouth of the tube had then to be tightly closed. As the cylinders were vertical they were not able to drive the axle beneath them directly, the axle being sprung. Thus the movement of the pistons was very compli-

cated, using bevel cranks and rods similar to those used on Stephenson's quadrant engine, connected obviously with a double crank to the likewise sprung axle near the overhanging boiler. The "Novelty" was the only one of the competing engines to carry its own fuel and water. For the water, a tank was hung on the frame, while the fuel container was above the frame and also acted as a counter-weight to the overhanging boiler. The "Novelty" qualifies thus as the first tank locomotive.

Since the rules of the competition allowed other forms of motive power than steam, Brandreth from Liverpool announced his "Cyclopede", worked by two horses trotting on an endless belt, an idea which cropped up several times later on. Increased speed was achieved by a transmission gear; the horses were thus not driven too hard. This Brandreth "locomotive" ran at approximately 12 m.p.h., with the horses trotting at a maximum of 4 m.p.h. It was not allowed to take part in the tests because its power output was too low, but was allowed to be shown to the public aside from the competition.

October 6, 1829 was fixed as the date for the competition. The event attracted thousands of curious residents of the area as well as many interested scientists and experts. After various preliminary trial runs, the three judges announced further stipulations for the test. They decreed that the participating engines should first be weighed with full boilers at 8 o'clock in the morning to determine the load to be coupled up on the basis of the engine's weight, the rules being that the load assigned should be three times that of the weight of the locomotive itself. Once the necessary fuel had been loaded, the boiler could be steamed and the locomotive could take the wagons it had been allotted to the starting board. As soon as the boiler pressure had reached the prescribed 50 lbs. per sq. in., the test runs could begin. Each locomotive had to haul its load ten times there and back along the 1¾ mile length of track, approximating the distance between Liverpool and Manchester of 35 miles. 30 miles had to be covered at a speed of not less than 10 m.p.h. Once these ten trips had been successfully completed, a fresh supply of fuel and water was delivered and the programme repeated.

The "Rocket" was the first to be put to the test. Hauling its assigned load of 12 tons, 9 cwt. on the

36. The "Rocket", George Stephenson, 1829, as it is today.

first ten trips, not counting stops at the marker boards, it reached a mean speed of 13½ m.p.h. and, on the next ten trips, a speed of 14 m.p.h. These results would have been better if the train had not had to be pushed on each return journey. The highest average speed at the second trial measured over one round trip was 24 m.p.h. and the lowest, upwards, 11 m.p.h. On the final trip the engine must have been run at full speed because it reached a top speed of 29½ m.p.h. The "Rocket" gave a subsequent extra demonstration: pulling a carriage with twenty people, it ran up and down a steep incline of 1 in 96 without any difficulty, an achievement that was considered impossible over a stretch of track designed for rope haulage.

The "Sanspareil" came next. When weighed it was officially determined that it was about 5½ cwt. too heavy. It was therefore officially excluded but still allowed to run, to see whether it might not be chosen to operate on the railroad in spite of this. When it set off, it seemed to be outdoing the "Rocket" with its glowing coke cinders gushing out behind. It was pulling a load of 19 tons 8 cwt., proportionate to its own weight. Initially all went well. But on the eighth trip, the feed pump failed and the water level in the boiler fell so low that the fusible plug in the firebox melted. Nevertheless it had shown that it was able to make a round trip at a mean speed of 16½ m.p.h. at a maximum speed of 18 m.p.h. Travelling on the locomotive, which had no sprung suspension, cannot have been very comfortable, for an eye witness reported: "It thundered and roared and reeled like an empty beer barrel on a bad road."

In the meantime, Braithwaite and Ericsson had got on so well with their engine the "Novelty" — which they had not been able to try out before their arrival at Rainhill, and which still required a number of modifications — that they thought they were able to enter. It was a great favourite and everyone was pleased at the sharp contrast with the "Sanspareil" when it set off, gently pulling its two carriages with 6 tons 17 cwt weight. But before it had covered 6 miles, the joints in the boiler leaked and, to the great disappointment of the spectators, it had to be completely withdrawn from the contest.

Thus the "Rocket" was the only engine to comply in all respects with the conditions of the competition and was awarded the prize of £500.

Hackworth never got over the defeat of his "Sanspareil". It affected his hitherto good relationship with both Stephensons and developed into real hatred on his part; we shall hear more of this later, however. The "Sanspareil" was bought by the Liverpool-and-Manchester Railway for the £500 established in the conditions for the competition, but this did not defray all his expenses. Three years later it was passed on to the Bolton-and-Leigh Railway. Since operating conditions on this railroad were easier, it performed very well. It was in regular service there until 1844; it then served as a stationary steam engine at a coal mine and was presented to the South Kensington Science Museum in London by the owner of the coal mine, John Hick, in 1863, where it is exhibited today, next to the remains of its victorious competitor, the "Rocket".

In regular service many faults soon became apparent

LOCOMOTIVE ENGINE, "THE ROCKET," 1830.
BUILT BY GEORGE STEPHENSON.

on the "Rocket" involving several structural alterations. Initially a blast pipe nozzle was built in, as used by Hackworth. The performance improved considerably as a result of a better steam production capacity which was now achieved. On new test runs, the "Rocket" was now able to pull 40 tons at 13½ m.p.h., i.e. around ten times its own weight. But at higher speeds it ran very unsteadily. It was thought that this was because of the inclination of the cylinders, and between 1831 and 1833 these were lowered to such an extent as to be practically horizontal. At the same time a separate smoke box was added with a door to allow easy access to the fire tubes for cleaning. The firebox which was only loosely connected to the round boiler gave trouble and was twice replaced by different shaped boxes. Since the "Rocket" did not live up to the extra operational demands which came to be required of it in the course of several years, it was sold for £300 in 1836 to the Midgeholme colliery near Brampton, and was used there to pull coal trucks. Around 1839/40, it was no longer performing satisfactorily, was pensioned off and partly dismantled. For the Great Exhibition in London of 1851, Thompson, owner of this colliery, exhibited it after Robert Stephenson & Co. had restored it, unfortunately not to a very high standard. After the exhibition, it was handed over to the technical collection of the British Patent Office, many of

45

THE NORTHUMBRIAN ENGINE.

Published by I. Shaw, Liverpool, & Grundy & Fox, Manchester.

whose exhibits passed to what is now the South Kensington Science Museum. The later and inexpert additions were removed here so that the "Rocket" as exhibited today displays only the original parts still existing (Ill. 36). Using old plans and reports, Ford had an operational copy of the original built for his traffic museum in Detroit (Ill. 32).

The encouraging performance of the "Rocket" decided the Liverpool-and-Manchester Railway to place an immediate order with Robert Stephenson & Co. for four locomotives on the same principle as it but with larger boilers, eighty-eight fire tubes and horizontal cylinders. The two engines ordered in 1830 were the first to have a smoke box. The "Northumbrian" whose firebox and boiler barrel finally formed one unit, was the last of this family of engine (Ill. 38). This was the achievement of the final form of the Stephenson locomotive boiler, which has never been replaced by any other form, despite many attempts.

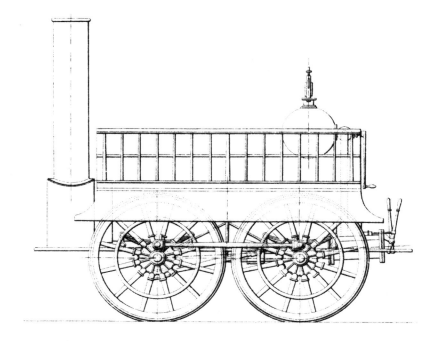

4. THE TECHNICAL PROBLEMS OF STEAM TRACTION

4.1 Hackworth's "Globe", a Trial Balloon

As just mentioned, the locomotive boiler reached its final form on the "Northumbrian", but many other aspects nevertheless remained unsatisfactory. The important fact had been realized that horizontal cylinders provided a smoother ride than inclined ones. The piston action was thus no longer influenced by the suspension movement. The question was how and where the cylinders could best be located. As had happened in the case of the multitubular boiler, suggested solutions fused almost simultaneously from various sides. But priority in this case belongs to Hackworth.

The planned extension of the Stockton-and-Darlington Railway as far as Middlesborough made the conversion of passenger traffic from horse to steam haulage seem a desirable and a practical proposition. As soon as he had returned from Rainhill, Hackworth began to design a locomotive suitable for this purpose. It was not possible to build this locomotive in the fully occupied railroad workshops at Shildon. He was therefore forced to give the contract to Robert Stephenson & Co. After laborious negotiations from

39. The "Globe", Timothy Hackworth, 1830, Stockton-and-Darlington Railway.

March 4-6, 1830, Hackworth handed over his plans for the new locomotive. His design (Ill. 39) shows that he had brought many new ideas away with him from the Rainhill trials. He was convinced that the main problem was that the single flue was not sufficient to provide the required heating surface, and he designed a number of radial water tubes on the inside, set at an angle to one another. The heating gases were thus forced to pass through in a spiral flow. This construction was adopted by Galloway later for stationary boilers and became well known under his

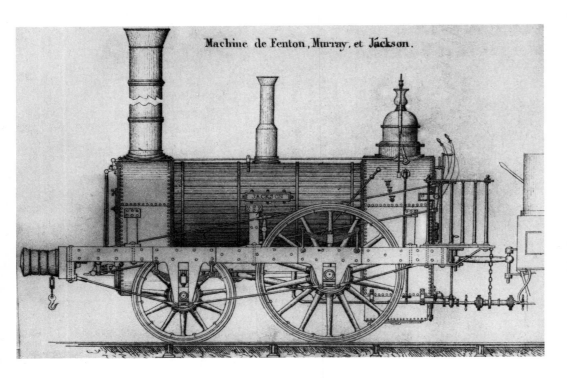

40. The "Jackson", "Planet" type, Paris-Saint-Germain Railroad, 1835.

name. It was clear that in the short boiler of the unsprung "Sanspareil", the water was shaken about so much that it flooded into the cylinders. Hackworth therefore now designed a spherical-shaped container above the boiler to catch the water thrown up. This innovation seemed so momentous, and in fact was so important, that he accordingly christened the engine "Globe". This spherical container was the predecessor of the dome. In order to provide springs for the locomotive, he designed the cylinders horizontally at the rear end, inside the wheels, to drive the front axle directly. This necessitated a crank axle which he designed with a special shape, taken as a model for later versions. Another detail borrowed from the "Novelty", like the crank axle, was a platform with hand-rails which ran round the whole locomotive. The crew were thus able to check the driving gear easily while the engine was in motion.

The construction of the "Globe" underwent considerable delay. Quite deliberately, remarked Hackworth mistrustfully, because Stephenson had also started work on a completely new type of locomotive and intended to outdo Hackworth with it. It was not until December 27, 1830 that the "Globe" went into service on the occasion of the opening of the new Middlesborough line. It worked satisfactorily for nine years until the boiler burst owing to negligence on the part of the driver who let the water level fall too low.

4.2 The Stephensons Attain the Final Form of the Steam Locomotive

On the "Rocket" as well as on its successors, it was noticed that a lot of water spewed forth from the chimney. This was attributed to the severe cooling of the unprotected cylinder walls which were completely exposed to the oncoming wind, resulting in partial condensation of the steam. In his new design, Robert Stephenson also placed horizontal cylinders inside the wheels. It has not been determined to this day whether he was prompted to do so by Hackworth's drawings. The total arrangement of the new design, which became known as the "Planet" after its first performance in 1830 on the Liverpool-and-Manchester Railway, was similar in terms of basic construction to a later machine built with certain improvements in 1835 for the Paris-Saint-Germain Railroad at Jackson's works (Ill. 40). The two horizontal cylinders were now at the front end for the first time, resulting in a shorter and more direct route for the exhaust steam to the blastpipe. They were attached to the lower part of the smokebox and were thus well protected against cooling. To give good support to the crank axle, a strong external bearing frame of heavy timber beams was provided, with the four bearings for both axles mounted in iron double guides called hornplates, one inside and one outside, allowing room for suspension movement. In addition, between the cylinders and the front wall of the firebox were two stiffeners, initially in wood and later in wrought iron, supporting each crank in two places. In all, therefore, the crank-axle was supported in six places. These inner frames also served to relieve the crank-axle of the horizontal stresses from the pistons and to support it should any break occur. The four inner bearings were therefore not sprung. As can be seen, the whole design was well thought out. But what had not been realized was that the tractive effort was

48

transferred to the tender coupling pin attached at the rear of the frame via the boiler and its reinforcements.

Although the dimensions of the boiler of the "Planet" were hardly greater than those of the "Northumbrian", the locomotive was considerably superior in terms of tractive power. This was because the driving axle bore 25 per cent more load, and also because of the position of the cylinders which were well protected against cooling, resulting in the saving of steam by reducing condensation. Since the "Planet" was principally intended for freight traffic, on December 4, 1830 it was attached to a freight train of eighteen wagons, weighing 80 tons including the locomotive. Apart from the two inclines of 1 in 96 at Whiston and at Hutton, where another engine pushed from behind, it achieved a mean speed of 12½ m.p.h. In places it travelled at more than 16 m.p.h.

The way the "Planet" was built gives a first glimpse of the final basic shape of the steam locomotive: a boiler with multiple fire tubes, horizontal cylinders with direct drive, a strong frame as the basis for the whole construction. What followed were continual improvements in the individual components and gradual improvements in performance. The first step towards improved performance was soon made. As already briefly mentioned, the original intention for the two inclines on the Liverpool-and-Manchester Railway had been rope haulage, but this was abandoned once the "Rocket" had proved that locomotives could overcome these obstacles. Nevertheless a second locomotive had to push as well. In order to avoid this as far as possible, the board decided at its meeting on September 20, 1830 to order two more powerful locomotives from Robert Stephenson & Co. They were aptly called "Samson" and "Goliath". Their construction was exactly like that of the "Planet" but their dimensions were increased. In order to achieve greater power, the adhesive weight was increased by coupling the front axle.

In 1832, a locomotive of this same type (Ill. 41) was supplied to the Loire Railroad which had been formed in the meantime by amalgamating the Saint-Etienne-Lyons Railroad and the Andrézieux-Roanne Railroad. The frame was now constructed in the so-called "sandwich form", with the timber beams reinforced by iron sheets from front to rear. More details can be seen from the drawing on which the wheels have been omitted from one side (Ill. 42). The slide valves were operated from the front end, and the reversing gear was also at the front.

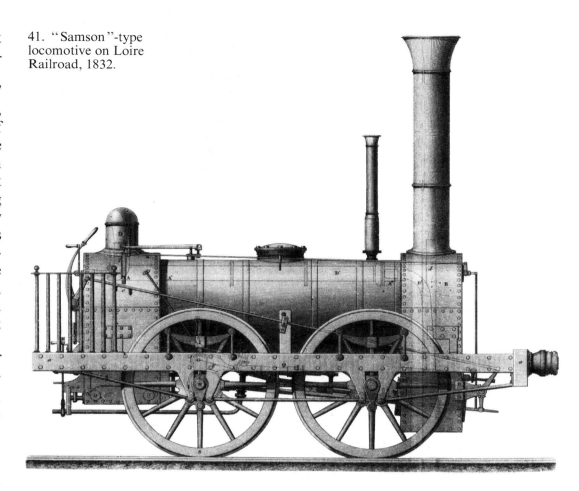

41. "Samson"-type locomotive on Loire Railroad, 1832.

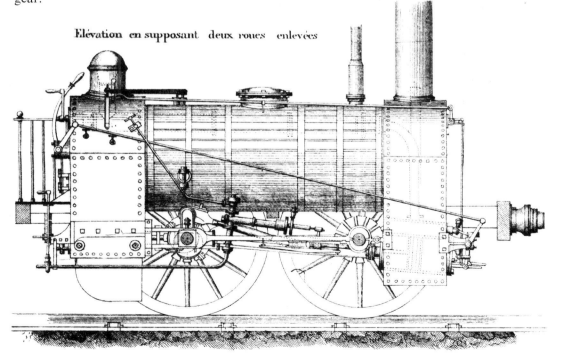

42. "Samson"-type locomotive on Loire Railroad, 1832, showing the driving gear.

Elévation en supposant deux roues enlevées

49

On the test run on February 25, 1831, the performance of the "Samson" caused such astonishment that the *Manchester Guardian* considered it worthwhile issuing a report. The engine reached a speed of 20 m.p.h. before coming to the 1 in 96 gradient, pulling thirty fully laden wagons amounting to a total weight of 151 tons. It was helped by three locomotives up the

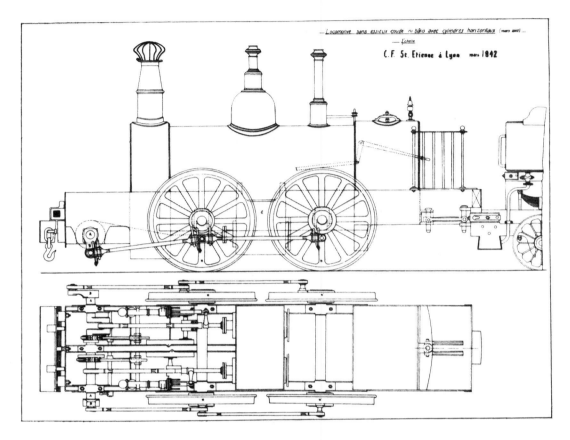

successful in France. On May 8, 1842, no fewer than forty-four such engines existed, some built by Schneider of Le Creusot. In Germany the first to receive the "Samson" type was the Leipzig-to-Dresden Railroad which had nine — undoubtedly the only ones of this type on German tracks. In Austria there were only the "Austria" and "Moravia", both "Planet"-type engines, on the Kaiser Ferdinand's North Railroad, opened in 1838.

The "Samson" type received a strange modification from Tourasse in 1842 when locomotives came to replace horses on the stretch between Givors and Saint-Etienne. Tourasse thought that a locomotive with a short wheel base was suitable in view of the many sharp curves on the line, but that the overhanging cylinders which caused unstable running should be avoided. He therefore transferred the cylinders to the plane of the centre of gravity between both coupled axles (Ill. 43). They worked in a forward movement attached to a cranked countershaft, thus excluding the danger of a derailment if the shaft broke. The engine was too heavy for the existing track and was given a rear carrying axle.

4.3 Edward Bury, the First Serious Rival to the Stephensons

The third locomotive builder to use horizontal inside cylinders driving the axles directly was Edward Bury, who achieved this simultaneously with Hackworth and Robert Stephenson. His first locomotive was not ready in time for the Rainhill trials, but was subsequently offered to the Liverpool-and-Manchester Co. There is uncertainty as to how this locomotive was constructed. It is known from the reports of the meetings that George Stephenson found a number of faults with it, as, for example, the excessive wheel diameter of 6 ft. instead of the normal 5 ft., the crank axle which was only supported at two points, and so on. There was a lively discussion on the merits of the outside frame as compared with the inside frame. This was not to be the last such discussion.

Bury was requested to build the two engines he had offered using an outside frame similar to that of Stephenson and also to undertake certain modifications on the firebox the better to guard against explosions. One of these locomotives was passed on to the Bolton-and-Leigh Railway before it was even accepted, the other one was called the "Liver" after the legendary winged beast contained in the coat-of-arms

43. "Samson"-type locomotive, Tourasse, 1842, Saint-Etienne-and-Lyons Railroad.

incline. As the truck coupling links slackened with the pushing from behind, it was observed that the "Samson" pulled sixteen wagons up the slope, amounting to about 80 tons.

Both types, the "Planet" (2–2–0)* and the "Samson" (0–4–0) were in such demand on the rapidly spreading railroads of England, that Robert Stephenson & Co. could not meet the demand which suddenly arose. The company realized that it had to put its plans at the disposal of other workshops for a fee. Initially they employed the firm of Fenton, Murray & Jackson (Ills. 40 to 42), founded in 1830 by Matthew Murray who had built the Blenkinsop engines. Stephensons gave financial support for the founding in 1831 of R. & W. Hawthorn company in Newcastle which was not finally taken over by Robert Stephenson & Co. until 1937.

On the Continent, the "Planet"-type engine was most

* Whyte notation of wheel arrangement of steam locomotives.

Machine d'Edward Bury, de Liverpool.

BURY

of the city of Liverpool. There are drawings showing an inside for this engine which were made on various occasions at later dates. They are false, as is shown by the above. Although the "Liver" used relatively little fuel compared with the total consumption of the "Planet" over a six-day comparison in the spring of 1832, and although De Pambour (1840, 2nd edition) considered that this was one of the ten best engines of this railroad, no further locomotives were ordered from Bury. But Bury was reimbursed when he entered a contract for the conveyance of passengers and freight at a fixed rate of remuneration on the London-and-Birmingham Railway on August 5, 1836. Part of the contract was that the locomotives to be acquired by the company should be built according to Bury's ideas. Thus he was now able to put his ideas into practice completely. Although the period of four-wheeled locomotives was in fact already past, he remained a devoted adherent of these, and initially equipped the railroad exclusively with 2–2–0 and 0–4–0 locomotives of his type of construction.

Bury's engines had various plainly visible structural peculiarities (Ill. 44). Unlike that of Stephenson, the firebox was cylindrical. Since it was directly connected to the round boiler the lower part of the assembly seen in cross-section was D-shaped; it was capped by a hemispherical top. The frame was a further development of that of the "Rocket", consisting of flat and round iron sections, laid completely inside the wheels with four sprung axle bearings attached to it. The rear part of the frame surrounded the firebox in the form of a semicircle and carried the draw hook. Bury thought that a middle support for the driving axle was superfluous. He proved this with a daring test: a crank axle which had not been used because it had been supplied with a smaller diameter than required was sawn next to the journal collar all around so that the only part holding was a 1 in. thick core.

This was built into an engine and Bury set off. The axle broke as intended, but it did not cause a derailment because the axle was held firm in its bearings. All in all, Bury's locomotive was a considerable simplification of the "Planet" and the "Samson". On the other hand it was a disadvantage that there was room for only a small grate. Bury's 2–2–0 locomotives normally pulled trains on the London-and-Birmingham Railway at a mean speed of 23 m.p.h. for trains weighing 57.5 tons, with occasional peaks of up to 38 m.p.h. He remained an adherent of four-wheel locomotives. Because of their unsatisfactory performance, conditions on the London-and-Birmingham Railway became critical; it was quite common for freight trains to set off with four engines coupled at the front. He finally had to come to terms with the facts and construct more powerful six-wheel engines

Museum in London and will be redisplayed at the National Railway Museum in York to be opened in 1975. Bury's type of construction influenced Stephenson as will be shown later. It introduced a completely new development to the United States... but that is a chapter in itself. And the first successfully built locomotive in Germany, the "Saxonia" of the Leipzig-and-Dresden Railroad, followed Bury's construction.

4.4 Stephenson's "Patentee" and its Further Development

It has often been stated that Robert Stephenson added a rear-carrying axle to his "Planets" in order to take up the heavy rolling motion during running owing to the long overhang of the firebox. But this was only

45. The "Comet", Edward Bury, London-and-Birmingham Railroad.

from 1843 onwards (Ill. 45). Bury lost his field of activity when the London-and-Birmingham and the Grand Junction Railways were amalgamated in July 1846.

His method of construction was adopted by other railroads in England and France. One locomotive built in 1846 for the Furness Railway, a 0-4-2 type which stayed in service there until 1898, has survived to this day. Known as "Old Copperknob", it was until recently exhibited at the Clapham Transport

a happy coincidence. The main reason for the switch to six-wheel locomotives can be clearly discerned in the patent granted to Robert Stephenson on October 7, 1833, following the designation of the engine as the "Patentee": the additional axle "will sustain the extra weight of a larger boiler than herebefore used". In fact the weight of the locomotive had risen between 1829 and 1831 from 4.5 tons in the case of the "Rocket" to 10 tons in that of the "Samson". And people were wary of permitting greater axle load on

52

existing tracks. In order to take curves smoothly despite the extended wheel base, Stephenson omitted the flange on the middle wheels. This also avoided the severe strain caused on the crank axle from the lateral flange pressures, the wheel acting as a lever on the shaft. The frame, boiler, and drive arrangement of the new "Patentee" type were the same as the later engines of the "Planet" type but the slide valves of the cylinders were no longer operated from the front but directly. No drawings of the first "Patentee" are known but there are illustrations (Ill. 48) of a later model of about 1837, when it had already been introduced on a large scale.

On April 28, 1834 Robert Stephenson offered a locomotive manufactured according to these patented ideas for £1,000. This shows that, since the "Rocket", not only the weight but also the price had been doubled.

The "Patentee" type proved to be very promising for the future. With a basic 2-2-2 wheel arrangement, the driving-wheel diameter between 5 ft. and 6 ft., it was initially the "Jack of All Trades". As the driving-wheel diameter became larger, it developed into a typical express locomotive. Various faults, which were still present initially, were eliminated in the course of time. Since the axle-box horns attached to the frame easily became loose, Sharp, Roberts & Co. made the frames for the locomotives with a shallow arch in the middle (Ill. 47). Thus the axle-box horns became shorter and were also welded to the framing to form one unit. The inside arrangement of the frame was also different from that of Stephenson.

46. Entrance of the locomotive house at Camden Town.

53

The two inner plates on the inside simply had cut-away sections for the driving axle but no bearings. This dispensed with the difficult adjusting of all the crank-axle bearings. The middle driving wheel had flanges, probably so as not to infringe Stephenson's patent.

The Sharp locomotives, often nicknamed "Sharpies" in England, were a great success everywhere because of their careful and well conceived design and because of the obvious attempts which had been made for the first time to design the locomotive and the tender to look like one harmonious whole — which was the responsibility of their chief draftsman at that time, Charles (Karl Friedrich) Beyer, a German. Sharp became Stephenson's most significant competitor, outside England especially. In 1839 Sharp supplied the Baden State Railroad with six engines which were assembled in Heidelberg. At that time Kiefer, an artillery officer, and drawing instructor at the military school in Karlsruhe, made exact plans which would enable a replica to be built today with the greatest of ease. One may hope that this will one day happen. On the Continent it was mainly in France that engineering workshops built countless engines on the Sharp model. In Germany the first nine locomotives built in Karlsruhe by Emil Kessler were an exact replica of the Sharp engines supplied to the Baden State Railroad. A Sharp 2–4–0 engine delivered in 1854 to the Spanish Barcelona-and-Martorell Railroad is being preserved by the RENFE for its future railroad museum.

Time passed and various English railroads were amalgamated, with freight traffic rising to such an extent that in many cases it was impossible to get by with uncoupled locomotives because of their low adhesion weight, or because of insufficient boiler performance as in the "Samson". When the Leicester-and-Swannington Railway, built by George Stephenson, was opened in 1832, it had already been necessary after two years to use more powerful engines for coal trains than the "Samson" which had been used until then. Thus Robert Stephenson supplied a more powerful "Samson" which had a carrying axle at the rear for the first time so that a more powerful boiler could be provided. This engine, called "Hercules", was delivered in December 1833, followed immediately by a second such locomotive for the Stanhope-Tyne Railway (Ill. 49).

47. Sharp locomotive, "Patentee"-type of the French Nord Railroad.

48. "Patentee"-type
locomotive, 1838,
built by Stephenson.

Until about 1846 this type multiplied rapidly in England as a freight locomotive. Such an engine, which was supplied to the Liverpool-and-Manchester Railway in 1838 by Todd, Kitson and Laird has survived to this day as the "Lion" and with several alterations has often been used for filming purposes. This type of engine was not frequent on the Continent. But a similar type is the "Ajax" which still exists, built for the Kaiser Ferdinand's North Railroad in 1841 and preserved today in the Railroad Museum in Vienna.

Even greater adhesion than with two coupled axles could be achieved if three were coupled together. On the "Patentee" type this first occurred with the "Atlas" (Ill. 50) delivered in February 1834 by Robert Stephenson to the Leicester-and-Swannington Railway. In contrast with the 2-4-0 engines described above, this time the flanges on the middle wheels were omitted. The "Atlas" became the mother of the classic English outside frame freight engine, being built in large quantities until the end of the 1890s. In its time, the "Atlas" was considered to be the most powerful locomotive. It proved itself so well that it was used for twenty-five years. It was then rented to coal mines and ended its career forty years later.

49. Freight train engine, "Hercules", 1833, Stanhope-Tyne Railroad.

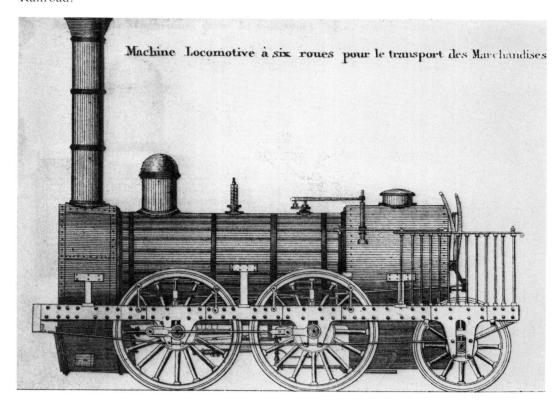

50. The "Atlas",
Leicester-and-
Swannington Railway,
1834.

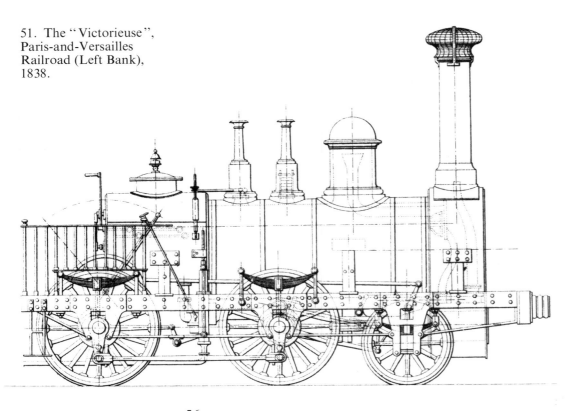

51. The "Victorieuse",
Paris-and-Versailles
Railroad (Left Bank),
1838.

With the low-mounted boiler which was customary at that time, the cylinders had to be arranged very low and inclined upwards to leave room for the piston rods to pass under the leading axle. If smaller leading wheels were added, the cylinders were able to lie horizontally without the front coupled axle being in the way. Robert Stephenson tried this method of construction in 1837 as well, employing it on four locomotives of which two were delivered to North America for the Baltimore and Susquehanna Railroad and one to the Paris-and-Versailles Railroad (Left Bank). This was the frequently pictured "Victorieuse" (Ill. 51) which was intended to haul both passenger and freight trains. It was able to pull 110 tons at about 15 m.p.h. on an almost constant gradient of 1 in 250 (0.4%).

According to the law outlined by John Jahn (1924) on the "progressive development of types", it was from the "Victorieuse" type that there developed in England the typical express locomotive of the Victorian era, which continued to be built until the 1890s.

4.5　Improvements in Cylinder Performance

After Stephenson's multitubular boiler had solved the problem of the best way of producing steam, people began to think about the best way of utilizing the steam produced. On the earliest locomotives, steam was admitted for roughly the full piston stroke. However, engineers had already realized the importance of allowing the valve to act ahead of the piston, the so-called "lead". The boiler steam was cut off at a point shortly before the piston reached the end of its stroke, and allowed to enter the opposite side and act as a cushion as the piston movement was suddenly reversed. Wood had already observed during trials on the Liverpool-and-Manchester Railway that admitting steam throughout the piston stroke was in fact an unnecessary waste of steam. But it was not until the Frenchman, Benoît Paul Emile Clapeyron came onto the scene that any use was made of the property of steam expansion. Clapeyron was led to do this as a result of preliminary trials by Flachat and Petiet using locomotives on the Paris-and-Versailles line (Right

57

Bank). In 1840 Clapeyron altered the valve gear on the engine "Le Creusot" which was identical to "La Gironde" (Ill. 53), so that the valve cut off the steam after the piston had run through about 70 per cent of its stroke. The steam then acted on the piston only through expansion. The result was, of course, a decreasing steam pressure and therefore a lower mean working pressure than full cut-off. If, however, the performance of the cylinder was to remain unaltered, its diameter had to be increased accordingly. In the present case, the cylinder was bored out from 13 to 15 in.

Clapeyron's expectations were exceeded, with the result that other locomotives were immediately modified in the same way. Because of the improved use of the steam through its expansion, the coke consumption of the modified engines fell from their previous 70-90 lbs. per train mile to 40-45 lbs. Additionally the locomotives with expansive working could pull 40 to 50 per cent heavier trains while producing the same amount of steam in the boiler.

The next goal was to alter the degree of expansion in accordance with whatever performance was required. At that time the original valve gears had already been actuated by loose eccentrics engaged by means of axle straps, replaced by the so-called "gab motion" (Ill. 55).

Two eccentric rods were provided for each cylinder, one for forward motion and one for reverse, with gabs at their free ends.

Using the lifting links, these gabs could be raised and lowered together and the bolt heads located on a vertical rocking lever embraced by them. The rocking levers thus actuated the valves. This gab gear enabled the direction of travel to be changed easily but did not allow the cut-off to be varied. The Belgian Thomas Cabrey therefore altered the shape of the gab for the forward motion in such a way that the bolt of the rocking lever could now be gripped in two different places, either right at the bottom or further out, by the extended, now parallel gab jaws. This allowed two possible points of cut-off, one at 70 per cent, and one at 50 per cent.

Countless inventors tried to devise controls enabling operation using variable expansion. The only one of all these devices — which were theoretical rather than practical — to have a wider significance was the variable expansion valve gear of Jean-Jacques Meyer of Alsace. He delivered the first locomotive using his valve motion (Ill. 54) on July 6, 1842, called "L'Espérance", to the Alsace Railroad. His engine was similar to those of the Sharp type. Gab rods, as before mentioned, drive a main slide valve with fixed

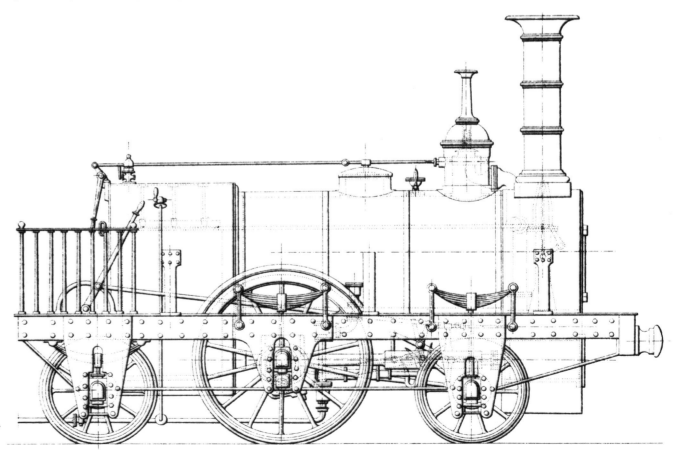

53. "La Gironde", Paris-and-Versailles Railroad (Right Bank), 1840.

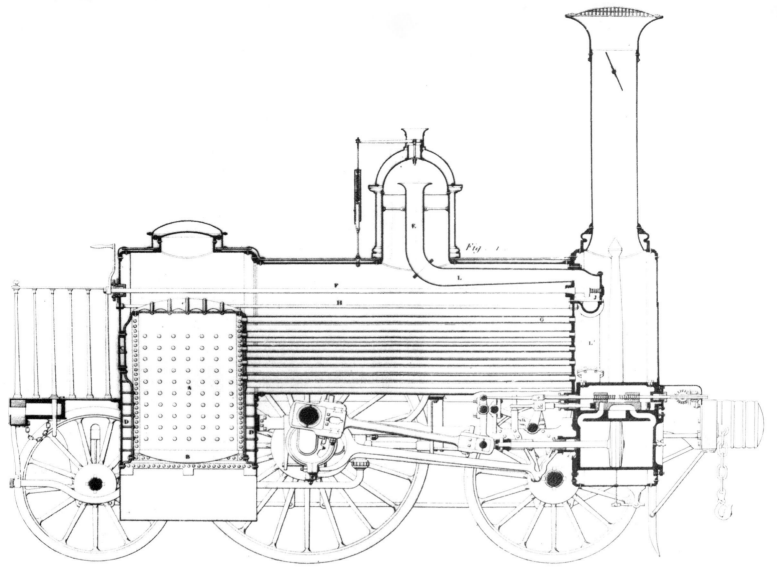

54. "L'Espérance", 1842. Cross-section showing Meyer's variable expansion gear.

55. "La Gironde", 1840. Cross-section showing gab valve motion.

cut-off. On its back rides a second auxiliary slide valve composed of two blocks which controls the variable steam admission — thus the American term "riding cut-off". The auxiliary valve is worked through a vertical lever from one of the two gab rods. The variations in cut-off are made from the driver's platform via a bevel gear visible at the front on the valve chest: the valve rod and the two valve blocks have a left-hand and a right-hand thread. According to the direction in which the valve spindle is turned, the two blocks either move apart or come closer together. As a result the amount of steam let in is either greater or less (the cut-off is increased or decreased). On trial runs, "L'Espérance" used 13.3 lbs. of coke per train mile in place of the 18.3 lbs. to 27.8 lbs. used by the other locomotives.

The Alsace Railroad immediately ordered an identical engine, which was appropriately named "Le Succès". Meyer built a third locomotive at his own expense, the "Mulhouse" which was subjected to thorough

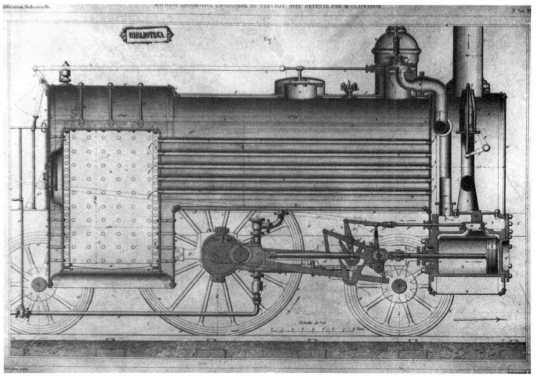

tests on the Paris-and-Versailles Railroad in November 1843, and resulting in an average drop in coke consumption of up to 31 per cent. Having been demonstrated on various other lines, this engine finally ended up on the Paris-Orléans Railroad, running as No. 39 (later No. 6). The Meyer riding cut-off valve gear was especially popular in Germany and Austria, and in places was even preferred to the Stephenson link motion which is described below. A similar principle was the basis of the equally often used riding cut-off valve gears by Gonzenbach, Borsig and Baldwin and others, which avoided the use of threads that had a tendency to stick.

At the same time as Meyer was making his first trials, Robert Stephenson developed the link motion, named after him. Its discovery can be attributed to William Williams, a skilful draftsman at R. Stephenson's factory, and to the works foreman, William Howe. The engines with gab gear (Ill. 55) were often arranged with both forks pointing at one another. It was but a short step from there to join the two forks and form a connecting link. We can see the general arrangement of this new gear on a Sharp locomotive (Ill. 57), and a description is superfluous. The original intention was supposed to have been to achieve smooth engagement between the forks on the bolt

56. Scene at a railroad station, first half of 19th century. "Patentee"-type locomotive, with open cars for the summer.

60

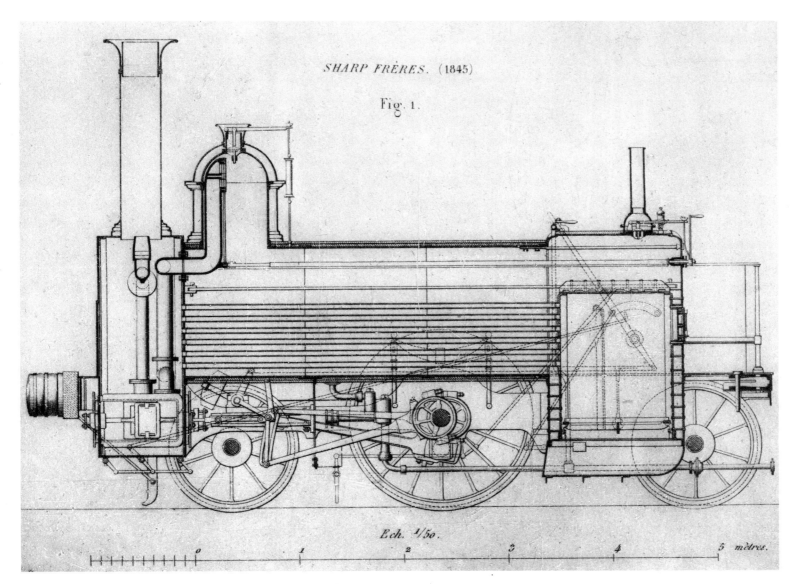

SHARP FRÈRES. (1845)

Fig. 1.

Ech. 1/50.

heads. For that reason only three notches had been provided on the reversing lever brakes on the driver's platform, for forward, reverse, and middle position. The drivers simply discovered as a matter of instinct that they could save steam by pulling the reversing lever back, and accordingly they filled further notches for intermediate positions. The Stephenson link motion was incorporated in a locomotive for the first time in 1842 and, thanks to its advantages and simple construction, soon displaced all other systems. It was retained in England up to very recent times for inside cylinders.

Both the Meyer system and the Stephenson basic idea underwent several variations. Gooch turned the connecting link the other way round so that instead of the two eccentric rods it was only the valve operating rod which had to be lowered and raised. Allan and Trick simultaneously made the link straight. That simplified its construction but also necessitated simultaneous raising and lowering of the eccentric rods and the valve operating rod. All these variations had certain advantages but corresponding disadvantages as well. We will come later to various applications for these modifications.

5. AMERICA BEGINS TO TAKE AN INTEREST IN RAILROADS

5.1 The First Steam Locomotives in North America

Colonel John Stevens, a wealthy farmer from Hoboken, New Jersey, can be called "Father of the American Railroad". As early as 1811, he handed an application to the government of New Jersey for the construction of a railroad, and the following year he published a pamphlet advocating the use of railroads in place of shipping canals. Initially Stevens's ideas were rejected everywhere. When the State of Pennsylvania was about to build a canal between Philadelphia and Pittsburgh, Stevens laid a circular length of track about 200 yards long on one of his properties and built a small demonstration locomotive in order to prove that a railroad was a viable alternative.

This first locomotive in America had a vertical boiler containing a group of twenty iron water tubes (Ill. 58). A cylinder 3¼ × 14½ in. mounted horizontally at the bottom of the boiler served as the drive, driving a large cogged wheel via a pinion; the cogged wheel engaging into a rack laid along the centre of the track. The running wheels had no flanges. They probably ran on simple wooden boards, because horizontal rollers controlled the steering of the train along the track, these rollers being mounted on four posts in each corner of the frame and running along the inside of the rails. This demonstration locomotive weighing only 9 cwt. was first run on October 23, 1824 and was shown often thereafter. A speed of 12 m.p.h. is said to have been reached.

The next attempt to use steam locomotives was made by John Bloomfield Jervis, chief engineer of the "Delaware and Hudson Co.", founded in 1823. Stevens's small demonstration locomotive led him to use steam locomotives for the railroad planned to ascend the valley of the Lackawanna River, where no canal was possible. When his assistant Horatio Allen made a study trip to England, John Jervis instructed him to buy four locomotives there as well as the rails. One of these was ordered from Robert Stephenson. Initially named "Pride of Newcastle", later renamed "America", it was a sister engine of the "Lancashire Witch" (Ills. 29 and 30). It arrived in New York on January 15, 1829 and was assembled at the West Point Foundry there. It is not known what happened to it. Forster and Rastrick supplied the three other engines. The first of these which arrived in New York on May 17, 1829 was also assembled at the West Point Foundry and was then handed over to the railroad. It was called the "Stourbridge Lion". Its construction was similar to that of the old Hetton locomotives (Ill. 19). Although the engine was too heavy, it was tested on August 8, 1829. Driven by Horatio Allen himself, the "Lion" clattered along the precariously shaking wooden bridge of the test track and scraped round the subsequent curve which had a radius of only 100 yards with a terrible screech. They decided not to use it. The "Lion" was put aside for fourteen or fifteen years, and later its boiler was used from time to time at Carbondale as a stationary steam engine. Other parts were sold as scrap iron, some being recovered between 1889 and 1913 and used for the construction of the replica which is now at the National Museum in Washington. The other two Foster and Rastrick engines never actually reached the railroad and have disappeared. Operations continued until 1860, using horses and stationary steam engines with rope haulage.

Even the Baltimore-and-Ohio Railroad, for which the concession was granted on February 28, 1827 and which opened on January 1, 1830, used horses to pull wagons along the first 36-mile stretch as far as Ellicott's Mills. A New York businessman, Peter Cooper, who had bought parcels of land along the track, tried in vain to interest the board of directors in steam locomotives which would have been able to convey the traffic better. As John Stevens had done before him, he had a small demonstration locomotive built at his own expense, which was called, after the fairy tale character, "Tom Thumb" (Ill. 59). It weighed just over a ton and produced about 1.4 h.p.

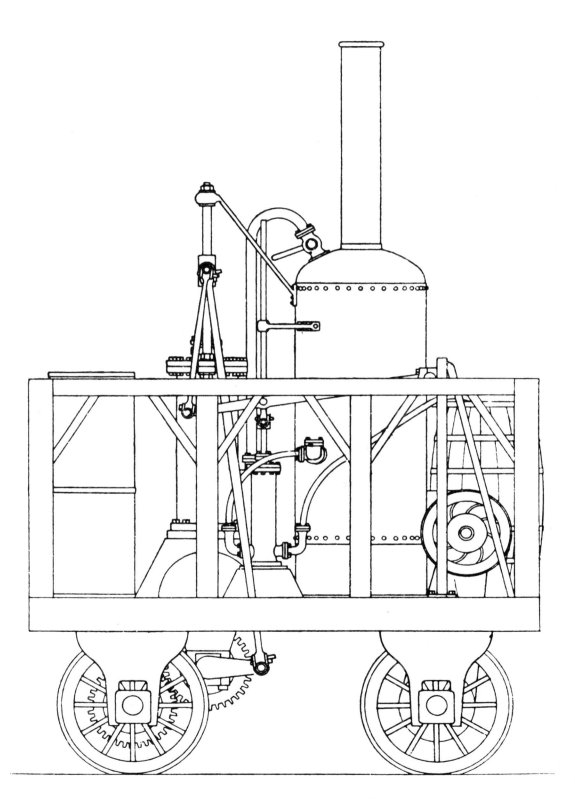

59. The "Tom Thumb", Peter Cooper, 1830.

was held the frequently pictured race between "Tom Thumb" and a coach pulled by horses along the other track. Initially "Tom Thumb" pulled away victoriously, but when the belt driving the bellows that kept the fire going slipped off, it lost steam and fell behind the horse-drawn coach. It made various journeys for a week and then disappeared. These trials had some result, however, as we shall see later on.

5.2 America's First Regular Steam Railroad Service

The honour of being the first American railroad with a regular steam-operated service goes to the South Carolina Railroad. Horatio Allen, who has already been mentioned, succeeded in persuading the Board of Directors of the railroad to try out steam locomotives. He got in touch with the West Point Foundry already mentioned. The track was to run inland from Charleston to Hamburg, and the population of Charleston became very excited, hoping that the railroad would help to restore their cotton trade, which Savanna was threatening to take over by the construction of a canal. Thus the locomotive ordered was given the hopeful-sounding name "The Best Friend of Charleston" (Ills. 60 and 61). This engine arrived at the railroad on October 23, 1830. It had a vertical boiler, overhanging one end of the frame. The lower part containing the firebox was double-walled and filled with water. The inner wall had multiple "tits" so as to increase the heating surface exposed to the fire. The inclined cylinders, which were mounted at the opposite end to the boiler, drove a double-crank axle. This engine was tried out for the first time on December 14, 1830. Forty none-too-willing recruits from among the railroad's labourers took their places in a high-sided covered wooden wagon, which was coupled up. A speed of 20 m.p.h. was reached. The first official trip took place on December 24 with two wagons, and on the next day the first regular steam-locomotive-operated service in America began.

On June 17, 1831 the fireman shut the safety valve, annoyed by the constant hissing of escaping steam, with the result that the boiler burst, killing him and badly burning the driver, Mr Darrell. The locomotive was subsequently completely rebuilt and renamed the "Phoenix". The boiler was now in the middle and the cylinders set horizontally outside. A working replica of the original model was built in 1928 by the Southern Railroad, which had taken over the

60. "The Best Friend of Charleston", 1830. South Carolina Railroad.

The vertical boiler had heating tubes made out of gun barrels, and the two cylinders were taken from a small stationary steam engine.

The first trial run took place on August 28, 1830. Six men travelled on the engine, with Peter Cooper himself acting as driver and fireman. A car with sixteen people on board was coupled up. This little train took 1 hour, 12 minutes for the gentle slope of 1 in 23 as far as Ellicott's Mills. On the return journey

South Carolina. As usual, this engine was shown at exhibitions and anniversaries.

Even before the "Best Friend" had exploded, a second and more powerful locomotive, also built at West Point, had arrived. Designed according to Horatio Allen's plans and named "West Point", it had a horizontal boiler, the first such in the United States (Ill. 62). It was different from Stephenson's boiler, for there were only six to eight fire tubes (the number is not certain) each of 3 in. in diameter. For the first time the firebox top was not round but flat, and later a dome and a square smoke box were added. This engine made its first test run on March 5, 1831, and for reasons of safety a "safety car" loaded with cotton bales was coupled between the engine and the four trucks carrying 117 people. The first 2½ miles were covered in 11 minutes, and the other 2¼ miles in 8 minutes, corresponding to 13½ and 18 m.p.h. Following the accident to the "Best Friend", and until it was back in service as the "Phoenix", the "West Point" pulled all the line's traffic by itself.

the first articulated locomotives and we shall see how this method of construction was adopted later on.

5.3 *The Baltimore-and-Ohio Railroad Contest*

Even if the "Tom Thumb" was too small for service in practice, it had nonetheless convinced the Board of the Baltimore-and-Ohio Railroad that steam operation was feasible. Following the example set by the Liverpool-and-Manchester Railroad, a contest was announced for locomotives. In January 1831 the conditions were set out in several daily papers at Baltimore, New York and Philadelphia. Prizes of $4,000 for the best engine and $3,000 for the next best were offered. The locomotives were not to be more than 3½ tons in weight and had to be able to pull a train of 15 tons at a minimum speed of 16 m.p.h. in regular service. They had to be able to burn both coal and coke and had to have two safety valves, one of which had to be inaccessible to the driver or fireman while

Finally Horatio Allen ordered yet a third locomotive, the "South Carolina", which was completed by the West Point Foundry in January 1832 (Ill. 62). It was a duplex locomotive with two boiler barrels opposite one another and a common firebox. Both boiler barrels rested each on a wooden frame pivoting around a vertical pin, and each had a carrying axle on the outside and a driving axle on the inside. Each of these driving axles was driven by only one inside cylinder. This locomotive, and a few others built subsequently, were in service until 1838. They were

the train was in motion. The boiler pressure had to be below 100 lbs. The engine would only be accepted once it had run without trouble for thirty days. The railroad would supply a tender, water and fuel. As at Rainhill, four locomotives were entered, as follows: "Childs", built by Ezekiel Childs, a watchmaker from Philadelphia. This was driven by a rotating steam engine located at the bottom of the vertical boiler, but it did not work.

The second engine was from Stacey Costell of Baltimore. This had two oscillating cylinders located

61. "The Best Friend of Charleston" with a passenger train at the opening of the South Carolina Railroad, 1830.

65

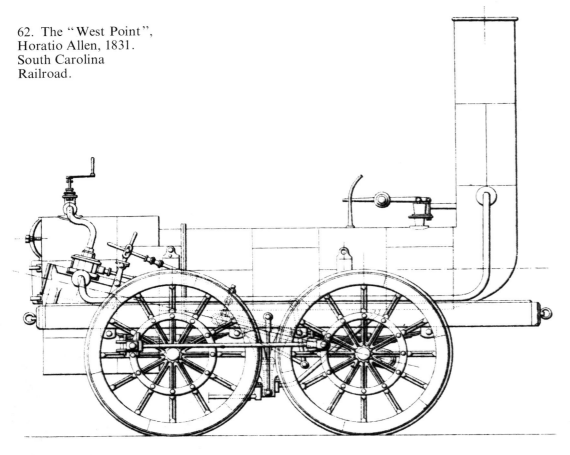

62. The "West Point", Horatio Allen, 1831. South Carolina Railroad.

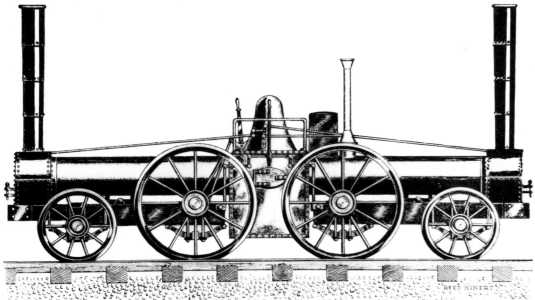

63. The "South Carolina", Horatio Allen, 1831. South Carolina Railroad.

drove the two coupled axles simultaneously. Reversing was effected via sliding cog wheels, forerunner of the gearshift on a modern automobile. Very little has been passed down about this locomotive but it seems to have run quite well, in the initial stages at least.

Later on, apparently after the boiler had exploded, the cylinders were moved to the front and inclined at 30°, now only driving one axle via spur wheels (Ill. 64). The link-gear valve motion (seen in the illustration) must have been added when the alterations were made, for the original provision with gearshift would have made it superfluous.

The fourth locomotive was the "York". This, too, was designed by a watchmaker, Phineas Davis from Pennsylvania. He had built it together with a mechanic called Gartner or Gardner. It had a vertical water tube boiler of the John Stevens locomotive type, with two cylinders operating vertically downwards each one mounted at the top on both sides. The connecting rods were linked with coupling rods in a sort of truss frame (Ill. 65). Phineas Davis was the winner with his engine, the only one to comply with the conditions of the contest, and he not only received first prize but the appointment as "master mechanic" (chief mechanical engineer). From July 1831, the "York" entered regular service with daily return journeys between Baltimore and Ellicott's Mills. It pulled a "brigade", as the trains were then called, of five light passenger cars. The cost of steam operation turned out to be half that of horse-haulage. The "York" was soon modified in the same way as the "James", i.e., the cylinders were mounted at an angle behind the boiler. They now drove only one axle via spur wheels. This engine remained in service until 1834, but disappeared thereafter. A full-size replica of the original was made by the Baltimore-and-Ohio Railroad in 1927 on the occasion of the "Fair of the Iron Horse" and was then presented to the Museum of Science and Industry.

5.4 The "Grasshoppers" and "Crabs"

The "York" introduced a peculiar development for steam locomotives on the Baltimore-and-Ohio Railroad which we can regard as the first true American school.

By the autumn of 1834 the track had reached as far as Harper's Ferry. The small "York", which was operating in conjunction with horses, was no longer

alongside a horizontal flue boiler, the cylinders driving one of the two coupled axles via a counter-shaft and spur wheels. It is uncertain whether this locomotive actually took part in the competition.

The third engine was the "James" from William James of New York. The two cylinders were arranged vertically behind the vertical boiler and acted upwards on a counter-shaft which was mounted in a wooden frame. From there connecting rods forming a triangle sufficient for the traffic. In the meantime, Phineas Davis had set up a workshop for locomotive building in Mount Clare together with Gartner and his assistant Ross Winans, and began to build a more powerful engine there. The first of this type, the "Atlantic", entered service in the summer of 1832. Initially it was uncoupled, but in contrast, all the succeeding engines had two coupled axles (Ill. 66), being identical in other respects.

The vertical boiler was retained because the water did not swirl about as much as in the long horizontal round boilers. Because of the large diameter, four hundred fire tubes, 1 in. internal diameter, could be inserted, but they were only 3 ft. 2 in. long. The large boiler was also suitable for the grate which was designed to burn anthracite, for anthracite needs a large surface area and only burns in thin layers. This fuel does not produce a high flame and therefore the firebox above the grate can be low. Originally the fire was fanned by means of a pair of bellows mounted next to the boiler, and interestingly, they were operated by the exhaust from the cylinders. Later these bellows were dismantled and the exhaust was led into the chimney as usual. The type of axle drive is visible from the illustration. Initially the "Atlantic" entered passenger service between Baltimore and Parr's Bridge (40 miles). It made a daily round trip with a "brigade" of five passenger cars there and back. These cars, built by Ross Winans, were the first in America with bogies (or trucks) but the bodywork still had stage-coach compartments with side doors. The weight of this train inclusive of passengers was 51 tons. It travelled at a speed of 12 to 15 m.p.h. along the average incline of the track in question which amounted to 1 in 143. After only four years service, the "Atlantic" was withdrawn from service for reasons unknown. Probably various parts were used in the construction of the succeeding engines of the same type.

Until 1837, sixteen engines of this "Grasshopper" type were built in all, they being so called because the movement of the swing beams and connecting rods reminded people of grasshoppers' movements. In 1836, the Leipzig-and-Dresden Railroad acquired one of these locomotives. Its boiler, which was designed to burn anthracite, was not suitable for the coal used in Saxony. The engine could barely operate even on the so-called Lobejün coal but since this was unsatisfactory, it was soon sold.

A fault of the "Grasshopper" was that it was top-heavy, which meant effectively that it was easily overturned in any derailment. Phineas Davis lost his

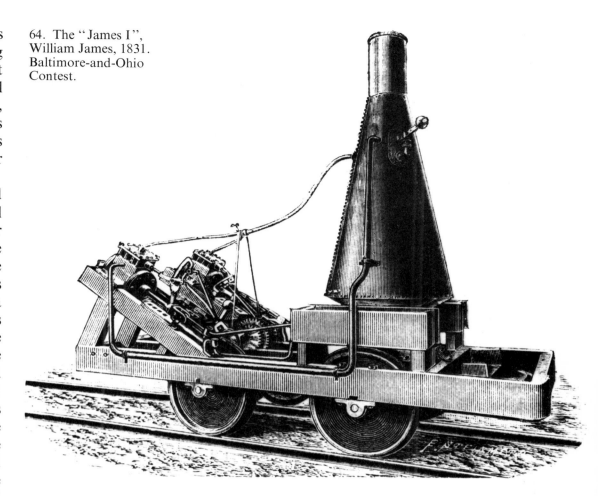

64. The "James I", William James, 1831. Baltimore-and-Ohio Contest.

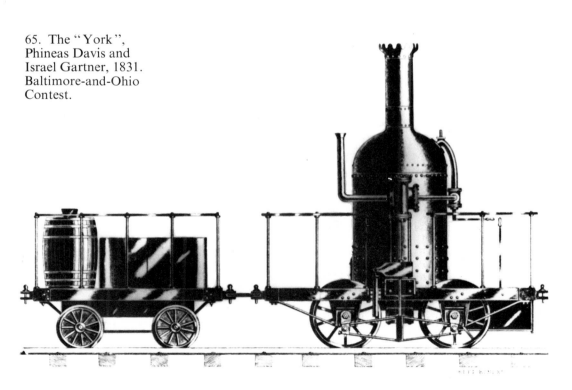

65. The "York", Phineas Davis and Israel Gartner, 1831. Baltimore-and-Ohio Contest.

life in such an accident. In addition, it was very uncomfortable to ride in when travelling fast because of the up and down movement of the rods. In order to counter these objections, Ross Winans arranged the cylinders on the last two engines, "McKin" and "Mazeppa" (Ill. 67), horizontally outside the frame. The locomotives were called "Crabs" because they appeared to be running backwards. Ross Winans supplied more than thirty such engines by 1842, all of them four-wheeled, for the Philadelphia-and-Columbia, the Reading Railroad and the Patterson-and-Hudson River Railroad. In 1892 four "Grasshoppers" from the Baltimore-and-Ohio Railroad arrived at the Mount Clare workshops as shunting engines. These were rebuilt for the Columbia World Exhibition in Chicago and represented the four types of basic construction. Renamed and renumbered, they were often shown at exhibitions. Today's no. 1 is now in Carillon Park in Dayton, Ohio, and nos. 2

and 3 in the Baltimore-and-Ohio Railroad Museum. The fourth was scrapped.

In time, these "Grasshoppers" were relegated to hauling freight trains because as already stated they were unsuitable for high speeds. They proved so successful in this rôle that Ross Winans ordered two more powerful locomotives from Baldwin in 1842 for the Western Railroad of Massachusetts, which were manufactured according to the patent he was granted on July 23, 1842. The basic arrangement was similar to the "Crabs" but four coupled axles were arranged in two sets well separated to leave room for the boiler which was pitched low (Ill. 68). They closed the first period of locomotive construction in America. The vertical boiler had reached the limit of its performance. But we find this type of vertical boiler once again for rack and pinion locomotives later on and frequently on cheap, easily maintained industrial locomotives both with and without cranes.

As the Delaware and Hudson Canal Co. had done, so the Camden-and-Amboy Railroad now sent its chief engineer to England in 1830 to buy a locomotive and rails. Robert Stevens, son of the Colonel Stevens we have already met, at last saw the fruit of his father's efforts. This trip was to be important in two ways. On the way Stevens conceived a new type of rail, the flat bottom rail which was subsequently to be introduced to Europe in a slightly altered form by the Englishman Charles Vignolles, becoming well known in association with his name. This is the type of rail still in general use today; even England has abandoned the bull-headed rail.

The other product of this trip was the "John Bull", built by Stephenson but altered in many respects according to specifications supplied by Stevens (Ill. 69). The frame, drive and the boiler barrel were exactly the same as those used for the "Samson" class. The firebox followed Bury, but with a flatter hemispherical top. The original cylinder diameter is uncertain, and the cylinders were probably altered over the years. Isaac Dripps, the railroad's master mechanic, assembled the "John Bull" without any assistance or a single drawing from the factory, and it entered regular service on the 20½-mile stretch of track between Camden and Bordentown on November 12, 1831. It was not well suited to taking the sharp curves on the track, and Dripps had therefore to remove the coupling rods. It is said furthermore that he attached the wooden frame running at the front to achieve a better guide at the curves in the track. But there is something of a contradiction here, in the fact that the engine got stuck on the curves despite its short wheelbase and then negotiated them better once the distance between axles was increased to 24 ft. 9 in. by adding the leading truck. The uncoupled front axle had 1 in. lateral play. It is possible that the pins by which the wooden frame was hinged to the front axle allowed a certain amount of radial play. But whatever the details, this was the first time that the idea was put into practice of using a free carrying axle at the front to achieve better guidance round curves. To remove cattle from the track, which was not fenced in, without causing any damage or danger of derailment, Dripps added after several attempts a plough-shaped track clearer at the front on the frame, called a "cow-catcher", which was soon to become a conspicuous feature of the American locomotive. The "John Bull" lasted in regular service

67. The "Mazeppa", Ross Winans, 1837. Baltimore-and-Ohio Railroad.

68. The "Buffalo", Ross Winans, 1844. Baltimore-and-Ohio Railroad.

69. The "John Bull",
1831. Camden-and-
Amboy Railroad.

until 1865/66, with various alterations being made in the course of that time, principally in the replacement of the wooden wheels by iron ones, after which it was then reverently put aside. The Pennsylvania Railroad, successor of the Camden-and-Amboy Railroad, presented it to the National Museum in Washington in 1885. As usual, it was shown at various exhibitions, and as late as 1893, it passed the severe test of running under its own steam along the 920-mile stretch between New York and Chicago, pulling an original coach which had been rediscovered.

All of the locomotives imported from England at that time, like the "John Bull", had two axles with no lateral play. The general complaint was not only the difficulty of taking curves but the frequent derailments on the uneven track. When a study group from the Baltimore-Ohio Railroad visited Robert Stephenson in 1828, he had already suggested the idea patented by William Chapman on April 12, 1812 of a vertical pin around which a truck turned, in order to take curves more easily. This system was not initially adopted. Instead John Jervis, who has been mentioned already, was the first to realize the idea of the truck. As he himself wrote in 1871, he discussed this matter with Horatio Allen in 1830 and 1831. Allen

preferred the solution he used on the articulated locomotive "South Carolina" which has been mentioned. By contrast Jervis decided to attach a truck in place of the front carrying axle.

On the basis of his drawings, the first locomotive in the world with a front truck was constructed at the West Point Foundry and supplied to the Mohawk-Hudson Railroad in August 1832. This engine, aptly called the "Experiment" by Jervis but soon nicknamed "Brother Jonathan" (Ill. 70), had a boiler and main frame corresponding to Stephenson's "Planet". The difference was that the driving axle was placed behind the firebox. As a result the cylinders underneath the smoke box had to be tight against the outer frame so that the connecting rod could operate between the frame and the firebox. The second innovation worthy of note was the truck. This had a wooden frame reinforced by iron plates outside the wheels. The weight was taken by a roller rim as in Chapman's patent, but instead, there was simply one roller provided on each side so that the truck could also swing vertically and could thus follow the rise and fall in the track. This engine was a complete mechanical success but the firebox had to be replaced because it was not suitable for burning anthracite. It is reported that this locomotive was the first to reach the speed of one mile per minute (60 m.p.h.) which was a constant goal in later years, and that it achieved this speed along the 4 miles between the two steep inclines on this line.

The "Brother Jonathan" had realized a locomotive type which fully met the operational requirements of the American railroads at that time, and it was quickly taken up and developed by others. The English 2–2–0 and 0–4–0 engines were modified on the same pattern. In April 1833 Robert Stephenson supplied his first truck locomotive for the Saratoga-and-Shenectady Railroad, working on specifications supplied by Jervis who was also in charge of this railroad, and other models were supplied by other factories up until 1841. Mathias Baldwin, who had built his first locomotive "Old Ironsides" in 1832 exactly on the pattern of Stephenson's "Planet", inspected Jervis's engine. He was so impressed that he immediately built his second engine, the "E. L. Miller", as an identical locomotive. It entered service on the South Carolina Railroad in February 1834. Baldwin remained faithful to this type of construction and until 1841 supplied this type of 4–2–0 engine almost exclusively. The "Martin van Buren" (Ill. 71) was of this type of Baldwin engine, and was ordered by the Philadelphia-and-Columbia Railroad in 1839. These Baldwin 4–2–0 locomotives had fireboxes on the Edward Bury pattern, who had delivered his first two locomotives in 1832 to the little Shuikill Navigation and Railroad Co. and who subsequently became the second most successful seller of

70. The "Experiment", also known as "Brother Jonathan", John B. Jervis, 1832. Mohawk-Hudson Railroad. First locomotive with a leading truck.

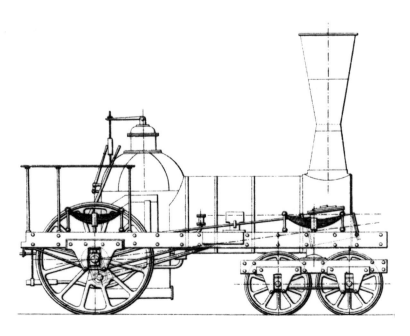

locomotives to American railroads after Stephenson. The Bury firebox was a great success because it was easily maintained and effectively prevented water from passing into the cylinders, especially when poor track meant that the boiler water swilled about. It became almost a characteristic feature of the first era of American locomotive construction. An individual feature of Baldwin's 4–2–0 locomotives was that the crank pins were pressed into the wheel hubs on the inside. As a result each side only required one crank web on the driving axle. This shape was called the half-crank axle. This type of drive required less space between the wheels, thereby allowing a wider firebox to be installed.

William Norris became a decisive influence on early American locomotive building and in certain countries of Europe, as we shall see later. He had a dry-goods business and from 1833 onwards he had built a few unsatisfactory locomotives without any initial success in partnership with Colonel S.H. Long of the US Army (Engineers), who had received certain patents. Fortunately when this partnership ceased, he found a skilful constructor in the Austrian Fred David Sanno, and his fortunes changed. His first decisive success was the "George Washington" and he knew

71. The "Martin van Buren", 1839. Philadelphia-and-Columbia Railroad.

how to exploit this in terms of publicity. Very few details are known about this engine except that the driving axle was located in front of the firebox and thus supported a higher load than was the case for the Baldwin 4–2–0 locomotives; on the other hand, details are known about the incredible performances achieved. The engine was built for the Philadelphia-and-Columbia Railroad in 1836 and was thoroughly tested in July of that year on the stretch of line which had

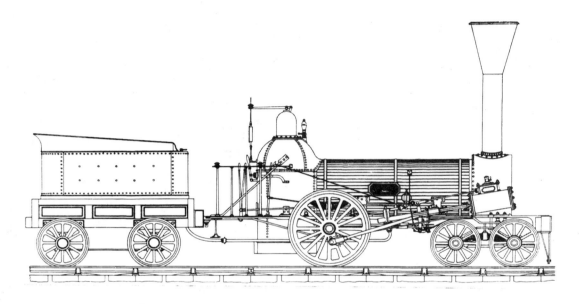

72. The "Washington Country Farmer", William Norris, 1836. Philadelphia-and-Columbia Railroad.

been built for rope haulage up a 1 in 14 gradient. On July 10 it pulled a train weighing 8.7 tons including the tender in 2 minutes, 2 seconds, and on July 19 one weighing 14 tons in 2 minutes, 24 seconds, on both occasions against the gradient. To achieve this on an incline which was considered impossible for locomotives seems unlikely at first glance, but Dewhurst proved (1950) that it was possible: the boiler pressure must have been considerably greater than that shown by the inaccurate spring-loaded pressure gauge. The draw bar between the engine and the tender was of a bent form and this increased the friction when the tractive effort was transmitted. In addition there was the weight of the people travelling on the locomotive. In October 1836 there followed the "Washington Country Farmer" (Ill. 72) which achieved equally good results on similar trial runs. This engine, authentic diagrams of which still exist, was the first to combine all the features which were to distinguish Norris locomotives: inside bar frame, outside inclined cylinders mounted outside the smoke box working directly

onto the driving axle on the outside, Bury-type firebox and a driving axle located in front of the firebox, and thus carrying a great load.

These Norris locomotives proved their worth in operation elsewhere. They were not susceptible to damage and were easily maintained thanks to their simple construction with no crank axle and with all parts easily accessible. They quickly became popular on American railroads and we shall see the influence they had on European locomotive construction. Norris seems to have been the first to make the truck in flat iron plates and what is more the first to offer a range of standard types. This embraced four classes and all his locomotives were built in accordance with them.

5.6 The Origin of the "American" Type

As the American railroad network extended, the demands made by the traffic it carried also increased. The tractive effort achieved by a single driving axle was no longer sufficient for the ever-heavier trains. Henry R. Campbell, an engineer on the Philadelphia, Germanstown-and-Norriston Railroad, made the logical step of attaching a second coupled axle to the 4–2–0 engines and received a patent for this on February 5, 1836. It is clear from the patent description that Campbell understood quite correctly the effect of the truck running in front acting as a lever guiding the machine gently round curves. He referred to this appropriately as the "guiding truck". Later builders were not always aware of this effect.

As shown by a comparison with the "Brother Jonathan" (Ill. 70), Campbell's locomotive (Ill. 73) was basically a development of this engine. In one respect however a step backwards was made: the two truck axles were not suspended independently. Campbell regarded the truck as a substitute for a single axle at the front and considered it sufficient for the whole assembly to be suspended by means of a leaf spring inserted on each side of the main frame. In order to allow easier passage round curves he omitted the flange on the front-coupled wheels. In this way he avoided the lateral play of the truck pivot which for geometrical reasons is necessary for four-coupled locomotives.

Campbell's first 4–4–0 locomotive was built by James Brooks in Philadelphia and delivered to the Philadelphia, Germanstown-and-Norriston Railroad on May 8, 1837. Because of its high adhesive weight, it was intended for freight trains. Campbell stated that it was capable of pulling 140 tons up inclines of 1 in 100 and 104 tons up inclines of 1 in 67. Unfortunately he does not mention the speeds attained. When this type of 4–4–0 locomotive was used for passenger trains, they tended to derail on the uneven track with the coupled wheels coming off. This was attributed to the unequal distribution of weight on the coupled axles which were suspended separately, and which could not easily follow the irregularities in the uneven track sufficiently well.

The first to consider how the weight could be properly equalized was Joseph Harrison Jr., works foreman of the locomotive factory of Garret & Eastwick, founded in Philadelphia in 1836. In 1838 he had patented various ideas in this connection. One was used for the first time on the "Hercules" (Ill. 74) delivered in early 1837 to the Beaver Meadow Railroad. There is a common leaf spring between the two coupled axles, attached to the lower edge of the main frame with an extended buckle and fixed to a heavy cast-iron compensating lever. This lever in turn acted on the axle boxes via two vertical rods. Harrison also thought about the truck. He positioned the truck pivot a little farther back in order to make space for a transverse leaf spring transferring the load to the middle. Thus the main frame of the locomotive rests on three points, the middle of the spring already mentioned and the two articulated bolts of the equalizer. The significance of this construction will be clear if one remembers that a three-legged table never rocks whereas a four-legged table always has to have a wedge under one leg where the floor is uneven to prevent any rocking. The idea of three point suspension has always been con-

sidered the ideal solution for an effective weight distribution.

We find a further development in the 4–4–0 engines with the locomotive named after an English bank "Gowan & Marx" (Ill. 75). It came from the same factory as the "Hercules" but Garrett had left in the meantime and had been replaced by Harrison. When the Philadelphia-and-Reading Railroad needed new motive power for freight trains, they decided to have them fired with anthracite. Eastwick & Harrison achieved the large grate area required for this by mounting for the first time the firebox above the frames instead of between them. In this way, the total width between the wheels could be used. This was possible, despite fears at that time of mounting the boiler too high, because the grate did not have to be low and the driving wheels were only 3 ft. 6 in. in diameter. Additionally the Bury-type firebox was made slightly oval in length. The weight was distributed on the rear coupled axles just as on the "Hercules", but a new construction was used for the truck. It was built in line with a patent of Ross Winan's in 1834 and has no frame at all. A long leaf spring moving around a bolt is mounted directly onto both truck axles. The whole is held together by a strong cross-stretcher which

73. The "Campbell", Henry R. Campbell, 1837. Philadelphia, Germanstown and Norriston Railroad.

74. The "Hercules", Joseph Harrison Jr., 1837. Beaver Meadow Railroad.

73

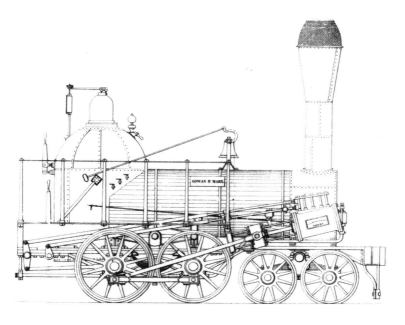

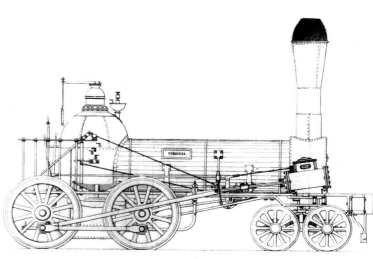

75. The "Gowan & Marx", 1839. Philadelphia-and-Reading Railroad.

76. The "Virginia", 1842. Winchester-and-Potomac Railroad.

77. Passenger train engine on the Camden-and-Amboy Railroad, Mathias W. Baldwin, 1846.

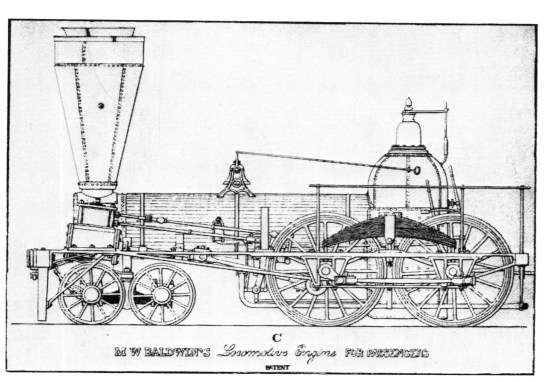

bears the truck pivot and ends in bolt heads at the side, around which the springs move. There are no lateral support surfaces for the cross-stretcher and it thus forms a transverse compensating lever. Together with the compensating levers of the coupled axles there is therefore three-point suspension. For its time the "Gowan & Marx" performed very well. On February 20, 1840 it pulled a train weighing 280 tons at an average speed of 10-12 m.p.h. The stretch of track had curves of as small a radius as 250 yards, and the steepest incline was 1 in 67. Rebuilt several times, this engine was in service for about twenty years and was then handed to Baldwin in part-payment for a newly ordered locomotive.

Norris himself obviously began very quickly to build 4–4–0 locomotives. Almost nothing is known about his first engines of this type which were supplied from 1839 onwards. In 1842 he delivered a locomotive called "Virginia" to the Winchester-and-Potomac Railroad (later taken over by the Baltimore-and-Ohio Railroad). A drawing of this has been preserved (Ill. 76) from a French source. Norris also developed a way of compensating the weight for both coupled axles, and together with Knight he was granted a patent for this on February 10, 1843. Both coupled axles were mounted in a separate independent frame whose sides were attached by a leaf spring at its centre and supported at both ends to the main frame. This independent frame had some lateral play and was guided by draw bars running at an angle upwards from the front axle boxes, and that were attached to the main frame above the truck wheels. In this way, the truck pivot did not have to have any lateral play.

Baldwin meanwhile had gone on his own way, as will be described in the next section, but in 1845 he realized that he had to take up 4–4–0 locomotives. For this he had to pay license fees for Campbell's patent and also to Eastwick & Harrison for their weight-compensation device. One of Baldwin's first 4–4–0 engines was delivered to the Camden-and-Amboy Railroad in 1846 (Ill. 77). This still had connecting rods on the inside of the coupled wheels using half-cranks and thus an outside frame was required. The latter, however, was now completely of iron bars and had heavy cast-iron pedestals (or horn blocks) for the axle boxes. The weight was distributed by one of the other solutions suggested by Harrison in his patent of 1838. This consisted of a large inverted leaf spring arranged with its buckle attached to the frame and with its ends resting directly on both axle boxes. As the wheel base had increased greatly, the cylinders drove the first coupled axle.

We can see the end of the old American 4–4–0 Baldwin locomotive in an engine built in 1849 for the Pennsylvania Railroad (Ill. 78). Although the cylinders were still inclined, they were no longer simply attached to the smoke box but also mounted on an auxiliary frame running from front to rear. They now acted externally on the driving wheels thus omitting the inside cranks and allowing more room for the Bury-type firebox which was still retained. It is especially interesting that the load compensation for the coupled axles was already in the final form of a short and light lever between the two main springs.

We can also see the shape of the first American driver's cabs on this engine, which were made completely of wood until about the turn of the century. This type of cab appears to have been used first of all at the end of the 1830s on locomotives of the railroads to the north of the country, where the engine crew had to be protected against the severe winter climate. But it did not become general until the 1850s.

A few words should be said on the striking chimneys of the older American locomotives. Initially wood was burned almost exclusively, resulting in a heavy shower of sparks. The oldest device known so far to arrest the sparks was adopted by the Camden-and-Amboy Railroad for its locomotives in 1833. An inverted cone of cast iron with rounded-off sides was located inside a bonnet-shaped hood above the chimney. This caused the sparks to fall into a funnel-shaped outer casing located around the chimney, where they were extinguished. Since then countless of spark arresters have been tried out with varying

degrees of success. Ludwig von Klein was probably the first to use a stationary baffle in the form of turbine blades to withdraw the sparks, which thus fall harmlessly into the hopper of the outer casing. This device was introduced in 1845 on the Württemberg State Railroads. Since fine anthracite also produces many sparks, until very recently a funnel-shaped chimney was used in America for this fuel. The same was true for turf and brown coal when used in Europe.

As a kind of express service gradually developed, some railroads began to prefer locomotives with cylinders inside for this purpose. We give as an example of this type of early American inside connected locomotive, an engine built in 1851 by the short-lived Amoskeag

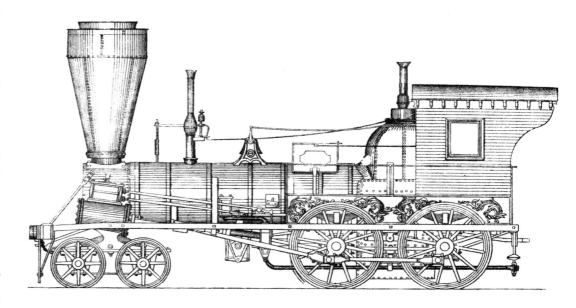

Manufacturing Co. in Manchester (N.H.) (Ill. 79), but unfortunately it is not known for which railroad this engine was intended. This locomotive is remarkable for its boiler pitched very high for those times, necessitating a high saddle to take the smoke box, but also for its good accessibility to the inside valve gear resulting from the bar frame. All in all it represents a modification of English tradition to American conditions.

The 4–4–0 locomotive originally intended for freight trains had developed by the 1850s into an all-purpose locomotive, following Jahn's Law on improved development of types, and it was so typical of America that it was simply called "American".

78. Freight train locomotive, Mathias W. Baldwin, 1849. Pennsylvania Railroad.

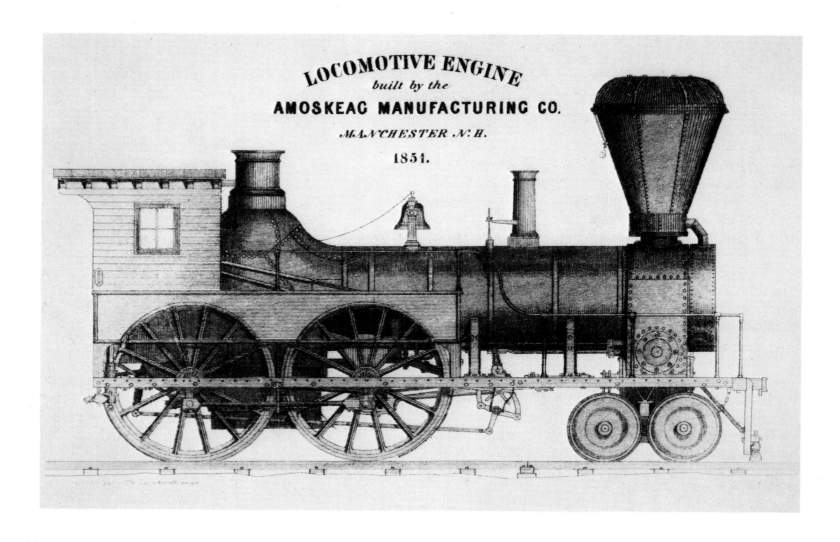

5.7 *Origins of the American Heavy Freight Locomotive*

It has previously been mentioned that Baldwin initially went his own way to develop a locomotive with more tractive power than was obtainable on one with a single driving axle, but that had the capacity to negotiate without difficulty the sharp curves on American tracks at that time. His first attempt, in August 1841, to drive the wheels of the truck by means of gearing was a failure. His second attempt to solve the problem — successful this time and which got around Campbell's patent rights — was his flexible beam truck. On each side there was an independent beam which could swivel on a centre pin while maintaining parallel axles. Thus, when the engine was on straight track, the truck was a rectangle, while on a curve it was an oblique parallelogram, both axles being pushed in opposite directions following the curve radius.
The first locomotive of this type, with Baldwin's flexible beam truck, patented on September 10, 1834, was

80. Six coupled engine
on the Central of
Georgia, 1842, with
Baldwin's "flexible
beam truck".

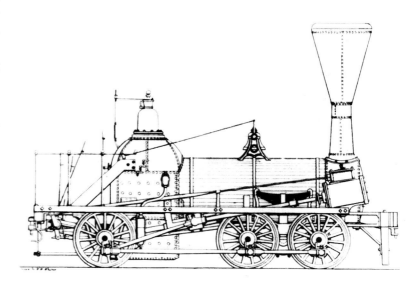

76

for the Georgia Railroad in 1842 (Ill. 80). This figure shows clearly how this six-coupled engine had been developed from the 4–2–0 engines. The two front axles mounted in the flexible beam truck are still located very close to one another, just as in the first truck, whereas the third axle remains behind the firebox and was driven by inclined cylinders using long connecting rods. The loads pulled by these Baldwin triple locomotives were far greater than anything achieved hitherto. One locomotive of this type supplied to the Philadelphia-and-Reading Railroad, with a weight in working order of 18 tons, travelled at an average speed of 7 m.p.h. and pulled one hundred and fifty wagons, which loaded weighed 1,130 tons. This was the first time that a train weighing more than 1,000 tons has been mentioned. However in normal service, trains weighing only 575 tons were working along the 94-mile line, at an average speed of 12 m.p.h. This type of construction was a success. All in all about one hundred and twelve engines of this type were built, most of them before 1855. A few of these were different, with all three axles located in front of the firebox, so as to negotiate curves even better.

Baldwin also used his flexible beam truck to offer a competitive 2–4–0 engine as opposed to the 4–4–0 engines. On this one, the carrying axle at the front was linked to the nearest coupled axle with this truck. Very few of this type were built, but three of them were supplied by Baldwin in 1845 to the Württemberg State Railroad.

Baldwin had just as much success using his flexible beam truck for eight-coupled locomotives, and he was granted a patent for his construction in 1842. The "Atlas" was probably the first engine of this type (Ill. 81), and was supplied in 1846 to the Philadelphia-and-Reading Railroad. The four axles were still located very near to one another. Although each pair of axles had common main springs, the weight must have been unevenly distributed and as a result of the rear overhang of the firebox, the running of this engine was not satisfactory. Thus later versions had all four axles spread out with the firebox between the rear four wheels (Ill. 82). This was how the eight-coupled counterpart to the long wheelbase 4–4–0 engines arose. When the last engines of this type were supplied in the early Fifties, the firebox, which was now of the Stephenson type, was over the rear axle and the boiler barrel was by now of the normal "wagon top" type of the time. All in all, there must have been one hundred and fifty of these eight-coupled Baldwin engines built, the last being for the Sabanilla and

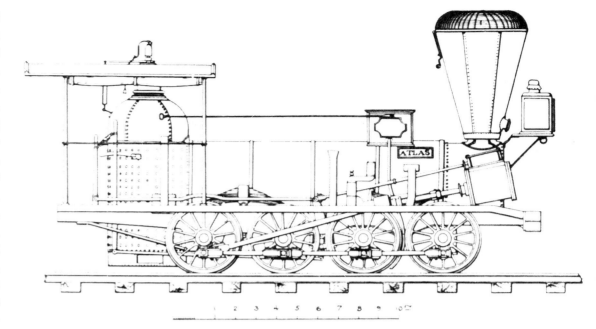

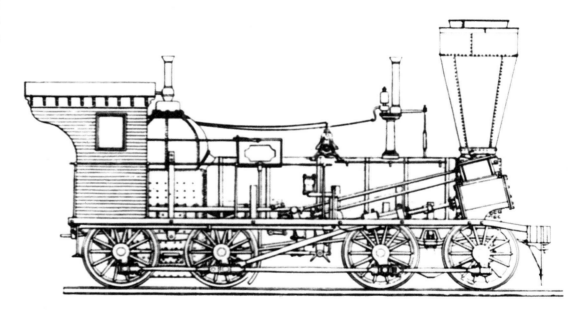

81. The "Atlas", Mathias W. Baldwin, 1846.

82. Eight-coupled engine with long wheel-base, Mathias W. Baldwin, c. 1850.

Moroto Railroad in Cuba, one of which was still in existence in 1911.

Baldwin's flexible beam truck had nearly the same guiding effect as that of the centre pivot truck, but the whole assembly was unstable because the two side beams could not be properly stiffened while retaining their mobility. There were also a great number of

77

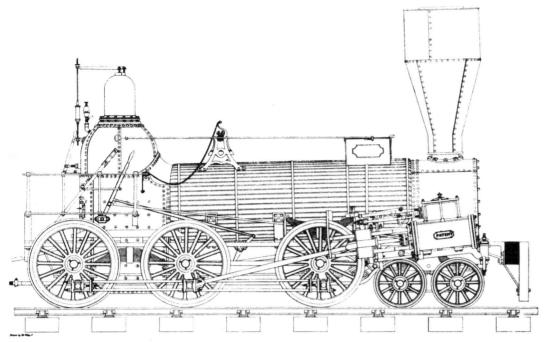

NORRIS BROTHERS *10 Wheel Freight Engine. Manufactured at their Works in* PHILADELPHIA. PA.

83. The "Chesapeake",
William Norris, 1847.

84. The "Monster",
Robert Stevens and
Isaac Dripps, 1834.
Camden-and-Amboy
Railroad.

formance and quality. Norris restricted himself initially to locating all three coupled axles as closely as possible in front of the Bury-type firebox. To lessen the overhang at the front he retained the inclined cylinders mounted on the smoke box. With the wheelbase reduced so drastically it was no longer possible to provide a boiler with sufficient steaming capacity. Thus in March 1874 William Norris's brother Septimus built a locomotive for the Philadelphia-and-Reading Railroad which can be regarded as a lengthened version of the 4–4–0 engine, with another coupled axle inserted between the two coupled axles at the rear and the truck at the front. This engine, called the "Chesapeake", is considered the world's first 4–6–0 engine (Ill. 83). There were, in fact, worries as to how this engine would behave round curves, but these fears proved groundless, since the flanges on the two front coupled axles were omitted. The contract conditions specified an ability to pull one hundred loaded coal cars weighing 720 tons in all, and when the engine entered service on March 19, 1847, it fulfilled these with ease.

Another engine of the 4–6–0 type entered service a day before the "Chesapeake", for the Boston-and-Maine Railroad. This was supplied by Hinkley. Other factories soon began to supply their locomotives with the same wheel arrangement. Thus the "Chesapeake" was the forerunner of an extensive family of American freight locomotives, which were only supplanted by the lighter 2–6–0 locomotives once the Bissel "pony truck" had been introduced. Following John Jahn's Law, the 2–6–0 engine was developed initially into a heavy passenger engine for mountainous sections of line and finally into a real express engine.

When Robert Stevens and Isaac Dripps created their extraordinary locomotive for the Camden-and-Amboy Railroad, which has with perfect reason become known under the name of the "Monster" (Ill. 84), they probably intended to make use of very fine anthracite as their fuel, obtainable cheaply because it remained behind as a waste product after the normal grades had been sieved. To build the very large grate required for this type of fuel he omitted the frame completely, so that the cylinders had to be attached to the boiler itself. The wheels were subject to a complicated drive arrangement, with the front pair of wheels being coupled to the rear by gear wheels. This intermediate gear arrangement allowed a certain amount of play in the front wheels to negotiate curves. Valve control was effected by catching and releasing the long eccentric rods. No details of the boiler are

articulated joints subjected to heavy wear and tear. This explains why Baldwin's articulated frame disappeared in the mid-fifties once other, simpler solutions had been found for six- and eight-coupled locomotives. However a slight variant was adopted later in Europe, and we shall come to this later.

Baldwin was unwilling to grant licences on his patent. His competitors were thus forced to seek other solutions to be able to offer locomotives of the same per-

78

given by the sources consulted. These merely state that for the first time a combustion chamber was provided, in other words that the inner firebox extended partially into the boiler barrel.

It is not certain exactly in which year the "Monster" entered service, but it must have been between 1834 and 1838. Steam production by the boiler turned out to be unsatisfactory. Before long the steam dome blew off. Dripps added another, improved boiler, after which, despite occasional failures, in the spur gear system, the engine matched up to its operational requirements and a further three were ordered as late as 1853 from the Trenton Locomotive Works, in which Dripps was a partner. At least one of these engines was completely rebuilt in 1869 (Ill. 85), and this lasted until 1875, with the running number 635, on the Pennsylvania Railroad. These "Monsters" may be regarded as predecessors of the "Camels" and as the first eight-coupled engines, apart from Hedley's "Wylam Dilly".

85. The "Monster", after its rebuilding, 1869.

6. THE BATTLE OF THE GAUGES AND ITS CONSEQUENCES

6.1 Brunel's Broad-Gauge Locomotives

As is well known, the gauge most commonly used throughout the world is 4′ 8½″, but this "standard" gauge was not created for technical reasons, and was the product of pure chance. When vehicles were divided into those with smooth running treads and those with flanged wheels, George Stephenson established the exact distance between the edges of rails as the distance quoted. Right from the outset he recommended: "Make them of the same width, though they may be a long way apart now. Depend upon it, they will be joined together one day."

Not all railroad builders agreed with this gauge, especially Isambard Kingdom Brunel. When he was appointed chief engineer by the founders of the railroad planned to run between London and Bristol, the fact that he suggested the name "Great Western Railway", which was the first time that the prefix "Great" had been used, showed that he was planning something out of the ordinary. He cunningly omitted all references to gauge specifications in the application for a concession which was granted on August 31, 1835. He thus had a free hand to put into practice the gauge that he believed in: the 7 ft. gauge.
He chose this broad gauge for several reasons. From

80

a technical point of view, he was thinking in terms of speeds greater than those considered possible at that time, and with this in view, he wanted to build very stable vehicles with a low centre of gravity suitable for this purpose. The body of the coaches was not to lie above the wheels — as in George Stephenson's vehicles — but rather remain within them. Taking the normal width of coach at that time as about 6 ft. 6 in., the gauge therefore had to be 7 ft., in width or to be more precise, 7 ft. ¼ in. The trial coach built on

met his ideas on fast travelling. His enquiries of various locomotive works, which specified little more than the gauge and the desire for high speeds at low piston rates, brought engines which, "with one or possibly two exceptions, formed the most extra-ordinary collection of 'freaks'", Ernest Ahrons wrote in 1925: locomotives with driving wheels 10 ft. in diameter, poorly related to their cylinder dimensions and their boiler heating surfaces, and some of which hardly managed to move themselves, like the "Vulcan" and

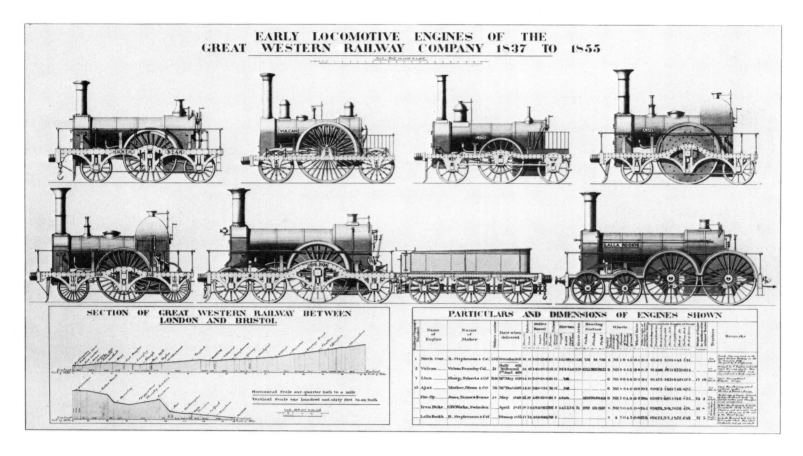

86. Locomotives on the Great Western Railway between 1837 and 1855: "North Star", "Vulcan", "Lion", "Ajax", "Fire fly", "Iron Duke", "Lalla Rookh".

this plan was not approved by the railroad board, that took the quite understandable line that if the gauge was to be so wide, then the coaches should be made equally wide to accommodate as many passengers as possible. This disposed of one of Brunel's arguments.

On the other hand, Brunel's view that the difference between the gauges would make it more difficult for other railroads to start operations in the Great Western area carried more weight, for this would ensure a monopoly situation.

If he did not have his way with the coaches, Brunel did at least have a completely free hand with the locomotives and was able to produce engines which

the "Ajax" (Ill. 86). In addition they were so prone to mishap that, for this reason alone, they were unusable in regular service.

This was the situation which Daniel Gooch found when, at the age of twenty-one, he was appointed by Brunel to take charge of the locomotive department and took up office on August 28, 1837. Working day and night shifts and training his workshop employees at the same time, he succeeded in improving some of these "freaks" to such an extent that they were capable of limited service. That being the situation, he acted immediately when he learned that Robert Stephenson had two locomotives ready which had been intended for the New Orleans Railroad,

87. The "North Star", 1837.

88. The "Lord of the Isles", Daniel Gooch, 1851.

pletely ready for service. On a test run in preparation for the railroad's opening, the "North Star" achieved a speed of 30 m.p.h. pulling a train of 110 tons including locomotive and tender, and with a load of 45 tons it reached a mean speed of 39 m.p.h. and a peak of 45 m.p.h. With certain subsequent alterations, the "North Star" was in service until 1870. It was then preserved in the railroad's Swindon works but broken up in 1906 because the Science Museum was unable to take it in for reasons of space. Using a few of the parts preserved, a full-size non-workable replica was built in 1925 as part of the centenary celebrations of the British Railways, and this replica is preserved in the Great Western Museum at Swindon today.

The "North Star" was only the beginning. Gooch subsequently built ten locomotives of the same type and sixty-two more powerful examples then followed, with fireboxes for the first time in the new Stephenson "Gothic" form (Ill. 86 "Firefly"). The exact drawings for the engines were made under Gooch's direction and patterns were then made for those parts which were to be interchangeable with one another. Both items were sent to the locomotive works concerned, who were instructed to adhere to these rigidly. This was the first time that a railroad had stressed the value of standardization and interchangeability. Gooch had a superb assistant, Thomas Russel Crampton, soon to become one of his fiercest competitors. When the Great Western began to put out its feelers northwards towards Wolverhampton, the "battle of the gauges" broke out. Those railroads using Stephenson's gauge prepared to defend themselves against this attack on their territory. The mobilized Parliament, which appointed a Royal Commission on June 9, 1845 to settle the question of the gauges. Robert Stephenson was heard first, naturally speaking in favour of his standard gauge. Other railroad experts were then heard, who mostly agreed with his ideas. Only a few said that a somewhat broader gauge of 5 to 6 ft. would be better to allow more space for the inside motion. Nonetheless they recommended keeping Stephenson's gauge. Only one, William Cubitt, spoke in favour of rebuilding all existing railroads using Brunel's gauge before it was too late. Daniel Gooch gave the commission a factual account of the advantages of the broad gauge. He compared the performances achieved by Great Western locomotives with those operating on the standard gauge; this comparison gives a good picture of traffic conditions at that time, deserving to be reproduced in brief:

but had been kept at the factory because payment had not been forthcoming. These were the "North Star" (Ill. 87) the "Morning Star", and since they were both built for a 5 ft. 6 in. gauge, it was easy to modify them to the new gauge. They were delivered in December 1837 but again Gooch had to make several modifications before they were com-

| Railroad | Average weight | | Average speed of Passenger trains m.p.h. |
	Passenger t	Freight t	
London-Birmingham	42.2	162	20
Grand Junction	43.5	152	20.8
South Western	36	121	24
Birmingham-Gloucester	38.5	152	21
Great Western	67.0	265	27.5

89. Bristol Station on the Great Western Railway.

As can be seen, the Great Western was far and away the best performer.

Meanwhile the adherents of the standard gauge had not been idle. As we shall see, in terms of performance their locomotives were threatening to compete with Gooch's and even to exceed them. This would have further reinforced the main technical argument in favour of the broad gauge, namely its superior performance. Something had to be done quickly in order to keep ahead. In a matter of thirteen weeks, ending on April 1, 1846 a new and considerably more powerful locomotive was built at Swindon, baptised the "Great Western". As before, it was a 2–2–2 engine of the "Patentee" type. In June 1846, it pulled a train of 100 tons from London to Swindon — a distance of 77¼ miles — at about 60 m.p.h. and shortly afterwards to Exeter, 194 miles non-stop, making the journey there at 55½ m.p.h.

83

90. The last broad-gauge through-train. May 20, 1892.

The overloaded front axle broke shortly afterwards and Gooch simply replaced it with two carrying axles. A wheelbase of this length was no problem on the very gentle curves which Brunel had laid out on a grand scale. With this 4–2–2 wheel arrangement, the "Great Western" became the forerunner of the express locomotives which were now built to a total of thirty and which hauled all expresses on the Great Western until the broad gauge ended on May 20, 1892. At that time, twenty-three examples were still in existence. The "Lord of the Isles" (Ill. 88) was one of the batch delivered in 1851. It was in service until 1881 and was subsequently preserved at Swindon, but unfortunately in 1906 it was scrapped together with the "North Star".

When the Great Western extended its lines to the hilly country of South Wales, the tractive power of these 4–2–2 engines was no longer sufficient. For this reason, in 1855 Gooch asked Stephenson to build ten 4–4–0 engines, designated as the "Waverley"

84

class. On these the sandwich frame which the railroad preferred for so long was inside. And in this case, too, there was no need of a truck for the front pair of axles.

6.2 Stephenson's Long-Boiler Locomotives in the Battle of the Gauges

In service it had been noticed that plates in the smoke box and the chimney of the "Planet" and the "Patentee" had gradually burnt away. This was a clear indication that much of the heat of the combustion was not being used. In order to obtain an idea of temperature conditions in the smoke box, Robert Stephenson placed small conical cups with metal samples of various melting points inside it. As a result of this test, he decided to increase the previous length of the fire tubes from about 9 ft. to between 13 and 14 ft., so as to make better use of

the hot gases. If the firebox slung between the two rear axles had been retained, the distance between these axles would also have had to be increased to accommodate the longer boiler barrel. However this

would have been beyond the capacity of all the turntables which had been laid at every large station and which were used to transfer locomotives and cars from one track to another. Thus there was nothing for it but to return to the overhanging firebox of the "Planet". As he revealed later, Robert Stephenson was encouraged to do this once he realized that there had been no complaints of poor riding of the many four-wheeled Bury locomotives. Bury's influence is also unmistakable in the replacement of the sandwich double frame by the far simpler and cheaper inside frame, which was made out of single plate sections instead of flat bars. Bury had also proved that it was perfectly feasible to omit any inside bearings for the crank axle. This was therefore omitted by Stephenson when he used inside frames. Robert Stephenson also exploited the advantages of Bury's raised hemispherical firebox which was better for the supply of dry steam. However he made it into a four-sided "Gothic" dome, as he

91. Hastings Station, 1852, South Eastern Railway.

92. 2–2–2 Longboiler locomotive No. 43 of the PO (Paris-and-Orléans Railroad), 1843.

85

York and Midland and the other to the Northern and Eastern Railway. Points in their favour were their simple construction, which made maintenance easy, the considerable savings in fuel resulting from better utilization of the hot gases, and the Stephenson link motion which was soon standard equipment on these locomotives. With all this, their unsteady running was overlooked at first. They were immediately built under licence, not only in England but on the Continent as well. They were already to be found by 1843 on the Paris–and–Orleans Railroad, supplied simultaneously by Robert Stephenson and by Meyer of Mulhouse (Ill. 92). The No. 30 "Montgolfier", supplied by Stephenson, was the first locomotive either in France or on the Continent fitted with Stephenson link motion. The dimensions of these French engines were typical of the "Longboiler" except for the driving wheel diameter, which was normally 5 ft. 6 in. On test runs in May 1844 on the Paris–Orleans line, one of these engines hauled passenger trains of 65 to 86 tons at 31 and 34 m.p.h. In Germany the first to receive this type of locomotive, in 1842, was the Baden State Railroad which was still on the broad gauge at that time.

93. The "Tarasque", 1846. Avignon-and-Marseilles Railroad.

94. Hallette's "Sézanne", 1847, Montereau-and-Troyes Railroad.

had done with some of the "Patentee" models for the Great Western. (Ill. 86).

The patent which Robert Stephenson claimed for his new construction was granted him on June 23, 1841. The first two engines of the new class with the lengthened boiler were delivered in 1841, one to the

In early 1843, negotiations with French engineers who wanted to build "Longboilers" under licence revealed that there were worries as to whether they would be able to manufacture the crank axles to the same standard as those made in England. Robert Stephenson therefore agreed to provide outside cylinders. These "Longboilers" with outside cylinders were introduced by the Paris-Orleans Railroad for the first time in 1845, and soon spread to all French railroads, and as they were so simple they spread quickly over the whole Continent, as we shall see. Two engines of this type have fortunately survived to this day: the "Pierrot", supplied by Robert Stephenson in 1846 to the Avignon-and-Marseilles Railroad and the "Sézanne" (Ill. 94), built in 1847 by Hallette in Arras for the Montereau-and-Troyes Railroad, which was initially the No. 5 but later the No. 291 of the Est Railroad. This has a special place in the locomotive history: it was the first to undergo tests for oil firing, made in September 1868. Withdrawn from service on May 1, 1871, it was then used as a stationary boiler for the Epernay railroad works. Private initiative had it restored to its original condition and it has today been given to the Mulhouse Railroad Museum in Alsace.

But let us return to England, where the battle of the gauges had become even more intense. When other

95. Station scene in Gloucester. For the change between broad-gauge and narrow gauge, passengers had to descend, and baggage and freight be unloaded. Contemporary caricature.

railroads tried to rival the example of the Great Western by attaining the same speeds, the defects of the "Longboiler" were soon clearly revealed. As a result of its poor riding, there were several accidents. The government considered imposing a speed limit. It appointed its inspector, Major-General C.W. Pasley, to write a report on this aspect. For this purpose, he travelled on every type of locomotive in express passenger service and decided "that the 'White Horse of Kent' (a 2–2–2 'Longboiler' with outside cylinders) was unsteady and unsafe if pushed to a speed exceeding 45 miles per hour".

This was a severe blow to the supporters of the standard gauge. The increased steam production of the "Longboiler" was one of the arguments that they had used in favour of their case, but it lost its value when the poor riding of this engine was considered. In order to end the long debates before the Gauge Commission which were leading nowhere, Brunel suggested at the meeting of November 22, 1845 that

comparison runs should be made, and he suggested the broad gauge track from London to Exeter and a standard gauge stretch of track which ran through similar country. This suggestion was accepted.

The weapon which Robert Stephenson forged to meet Brunel's challenge was a modification to his 2–2–2 "Longboiler". He could not do without the advantages of its boiler performance. He tried to alleviate its poor riding that stemmed from the large overhangs at both ends by locating the driving axle farther back. Thus when the springs of the driving axle were overloaded, the engine did not tend to rock around this axle as before so that the leading axle was dangerously relieved. He also arranged the cylinders near the centre of gravity so that they no longer overhung, and moreover the piston forces now did not affect the smooth running of the engine as badly as before.

In 1846 Le Benet of La Ciotat, near Marseilles, delivered a rear drive locomotive built on these lines to the Avignon-and-Marseilles Railroad: it was called the "Tarasque" (Ill. 93), and the railroad received at the same time three more engines built in the same way by Robert Stephenson. The three English engines had larger driving wheels than the "Tarasque" (diameter 6 ft.).

Breaking with the existing practice for locomotives of this class, the engine built by Robert Stephenson in 1845 for the comparative runs was simply designated the "A", instead of being given a name, for it was not intended for any railroad. It was later acquired by the York and North Midland Railway. To accommodate an even greater number of fire tubes, the boiler had a slightly oval cross-section. Gooch's rival weapon was the "Ixion", a sandwich frame locomotive of his standard 2–2–2 type and belonging to the "Firefly" class of 1840/42.

Comparative data for "Ixion", "Great A" and "Namur"

	Cylinder		Diameter of driving wheel	Heating surface (sq.ft.)		Tractive weight in tons
	diam. in.	stroke in.		firebox	boiler tubes	
"Ixion"	15	18	7 ft.	13.4	699	21
"Great A"	15	24	6 ft. 7 in.	9.5	836.8	23.5
"Namur"	18	20	7 ft.	14.5	989	22

The "Ixion" was the first to make the comparison runs. Pulling a train weighing 81.5 tons it reached an average speed of 47.8 m.p.h. between London and Didcot and 52.4 m.p.h. when pulling a train of 61 tons. The corresponding average speeds for the return journey, which was slightly downhill, were 50 and 54.6 m.p.h. The "Great A" was subjected to similar tests on the stretch of track between Darlington

96. The "Namur", the first Crampton locomotive, 1846.

and York of the Great North of England Railway, which was comparable with the stretch chosen by the Great Western. Pulling 80 tons, it reached an average speed of 43.5 m.p.h. and pulling 50 tons, 47.2 m.p.h. Three weeks later it achieved 60 m.p.h., but this was pulling only 40 tons. There was no doubt that, load for load, the "Ixion" was the better performer. But there was no decisive outcome as to which converted more water into steam per pound of coke, for the standard gauge supporters had pre-heated the feed-water. The first comparative runs showed that the running of the "Great A" left a great deal to be desired. Gooch, who made one of the trips on the driver's platform, dissuaded Brunel from accompanying him because he considered it too dangerous. Thus Stephenson's 4–2–0 locomotive offered no advantages over his other "Longboilers", and hence few examples were actually built.

Robert Stephenson then tried out two ways of improving the riding qualities of his 4–2–0 Long-boilers". The first was to copy the example of the "Planet" and to add another carrying axle below the rear overhang. Only two examples of this 4–2–2 arrangement were constructed for the London and North Western Railway in 1848/49. The second way was partially to balance the piston forces from the two outside cylinders by locating a third cylinder inside. All three cylinders were placed in the same transverse plan and, taken together, had the same volume as the two of the "Great A". However, the volume of the inside cylinder was twice as great as that of each of the outside ones. The cranks actuated by the two outside cylinders worked parallel with the same dead points, while that of the inside cylinder was set at 90°. Again only two such engines were built and again they were for the London and North Western Railway, being supplied in 1847. These first three cylinder locomotives did not have any special advantages. They were therefore consigned to the York, Newcastle and Berwick Railway later on, and were completely rebuilt in 1853.

6.3 A New Weapon in the Battle of the Gauges: the "Crampton" Engine

A new weapon in the battle of the gauges was forged by Thomas Russel Crampton, who has already been mentioned as being Gooch's assistant before the battle commenced. He left the Great Western, probably because in the final analysis he would not have been able to execute his ideas on improvements to the

97. Railroad bridge over the Manzanares Canal on the Madrid-Aranjuez Railroad. Illustration by Mendiolagoitia.

steam locomotive under Gooch, who was basically conservative. These ideas were first set out in the patent which was granted him on February 15, 1842. Closely following the concept at that time, he summarized his ideas in his patent application as follows: "A method or methods to lower the centre of gravity of the steam locomotive by a better arrangement and combination of the various components."

Of the various possibilities listed, some emerged which led to the concept of the "Crampton locomotive", which was to become well known. The driving axle was located behind the firebox, so that the boiler could be located as low as the front carrying wheels permitted, unhindered by large wheels. Not only was this low centre of gravity considered important in achieving smooth running, but Crampton also placed the cylinders in the middle, as in the Stephenson rear driver engines already mentioned. Thus there were no dangerous overhangs on the Crampton locomotive. The drawings for the new type of construction were made in February 1834. Crampton did the rounds of various English railroads to show them, but no one was interested. Not until July 1845 did he succeed in receiving an order for two locomotives from the English company founding the Namur and Liège Railroad, which had not even been laid yet. One of the two, Crampton's first engine, was called "Namur" (Ill. 96) and the other "Liège". The order was executed at the Lowka Works of Tulk and Ley in Whitehaven. This firm, decidedly, although new to locomotive construction, wished to get off to a good start.

Crampton had indeed created enough space for large driving wheels, but it was a wrong move to assume that there were no obstacles in the way of the boiler, since the firebox was now in a very restricted position. To accommodate a large enough grate without shortening the fire tubes, the lower part of the firebox was extended in front below the level of the boiler barrel and went under the driving axle at the rear. In addition Crampton built the boiler barrel with an oval cross-section. The normal valve

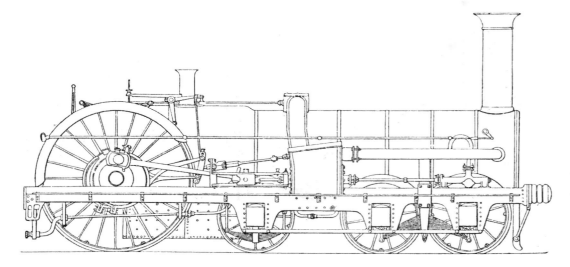

98. The "Liverpool", 1848, London and North Western Railway.

locomotive, which was also built by Tulk and Ley. It was called the "London". A comparison with the dimensions of Gooch's "Great Western" shows the extent to which Crampton tried to match the latter:

	Cylinder		Dia. of driving wheel (ft.)	Heating surface (sq. ft.)		Boiler pressure (lbs./sq.in.)	Tractive weight (tons)
	dia. (in.)	stroke (in.)		firebox	boiler tubes		
"Great Western"	18	24	8	22.6	1733	100	21
"London"	18	20	8	21.5	1529	100	24.4

The "London" was delivered in June 1848. In the meantime, on July 16, 1846, there had been a merger between the London-and-Birmingham Railway, the Grand Junction Railway and the Manchester-and-Birmingham Railway to form the powerful London and North Western Railway (LNWR). Between Wolverton and London, the "London" achieved an average speed of 58½ m.p.h. and a peak of 65½ m.p.h. pulling twelve coaches, but it was not entirely satisfactory, nor was the somewhat smaller "Courier" which had been built by the Northern Lines in its own works at Crewe in early 1847.

But when Gooch made the new 4–2–2 engine of the "Iron Duke" class (Ill. 86), Crampton replied to this ultimatum from the broad gauge with an ultimatum from the standard gauge, the "Liverpool" (Ill. 98). A comparison between the two is again revealing:

	Cylinder		Dia. of driving wheel (ft.)	Heating surface (sq. ft.)		Boiler pressure (lbs./sq.in.)	Tractive weight (tons cwt.)	
	dia. (in.)	stroke (in.)		firebox	boiler tubes			
"Iron Duke"	18	24	8	21.6	1790	100	12	6
							25	10
"Liverpool"	18	24	8	21.5	2290	120	12	0
							35	0

The "Liverpool" was built by Bury and Kennedy in Liverpool. To achieve a very large heating surface, Crampton had to extend the boiler forwards and to place a third axle under it. This axle was located very close to the next one, so that the wheelbase should not exceed that of the "Iron Duke". In addition, as he had done with the "London", Crampton made the boiler out of two half-cylinders, with the upper one having a larger diameter than the lower. The halves were joined with sideplates bent slightly inwards. Thanks to this device it was possible to insert three hundred fire tubes. For the first time with a Crampton engine, a continuous double frame was constructed, which allowed the cylinders to be mounted much better than with an inside frame. There was enough space between the two frame plates to accommodate the valve gear and the connecting rods between them. The driving axle had only bearings in the inside frame plate. The "Liverpool" was also

gear inside the frame was obstructed by the firebox at the rear. For this reason the two eccentrics were attached on each side to a return-crank. The mechanism was thus easily accessible, with even the slide valve chest located outside. The driving axle suspension was unique, using a large transverse spring located very high up behind the firebox. This was how Crampton created a great deal of lateral room for the firebox. These elements were copied later, both the transverse spring, and especially the outside valve gear.

Because the construction of the Namur and Liège Railway was very much behind schedule, the "Namur" made its test runs on the Grand Junction Railway track. It covered 2,287 miles there in all, pulling all kinds of trains. It reached 62½ m.p.h. with 50 tons behind the tender, and running light even reached 74½ m.p.h. — performances which almost matched those by the broad gauge locomotives. And it ran smoothly and steadily.

Neither the "Namur", nor the "Liège", nor a third locomotive ordered subsequently, went to Belgium. They were accepted by the South Eastern Railway as Nos. 81, 83 and 85. Three more identical locomotives, which Crampton had built optimistically at his own expense, were eventually sold to small railroads after a lot of efforts.

The reaction of the Great Western to the advent of the Crampton locomotive has already been described. The London and Birmingham Railway was in strong competition with the Great Western on their lines running north. Of course the small Bury engines used up to now could not match the Gooch creation. The good results achieved by the "Namur" led the London-and-Birmingham Railway to place an order with Crampton for a similar, but more powerful

90

the first engine to have the regulator valve mounted in a cast-iron box set on the top of the boiler, thus allowing easy access. It was delivered to the LNWR in July 1848, but not put into service until June of the following year. Curiously, there are very few surviving details about its performance. It is said to have reached 78½ m.p.h. on one occasion. It is also said that it once achieved an average speed of 50 m.p.h. with 150 tons behind the tender. The "Liverpool" was exhibited as one of the marvels of the Great Exhibition in London in 1851. Painted brick red, which was normal for the LNWR at that time, it appeared somewhat puny beside the towering, broad-gauge "Lord of the Isles" of the Great Western. It had only a short career. The track where it was to have been used in express service was not laid out as well as that constructed by Brunel, and it soon became clear that it was causing severe damage to the track. It was withdrawn and broken up in 1858. Despite the limited success of his type of construction, Crampton did not admit defeat. During the battle of the gauges, the type built with inside cylinders had

shown that they ran more smoothly. Crampton therefore switched to the inside cylinder which his fellow countrymen preferred and abandoned the feature which he prized so much, namely the accessible valve gear. In 1849 he had a variation of his type of construction patented. Inside cylinders were not able to drive directly the driving axle located behind the firebox, so that he inserted a cranked counter-shaft between them. Crampton thought that this counter-shaft would offer certain other advantages, including a good, if not perfect, balance of masses. He also assumed that the play in the springs would not affect the working of the valve gear. However he was not able to keep faith with his basic idea of a very low centre of gravity, for the boiler had to be pitched considerably higher because of the counter-shaft cranks. The South Eastern, the only English railroad to have been satisfied with Crampton's earlier models, ordered from Stephenson ten engines of this new type, which were delivered in 1851. One of these, the "Folkestone" (Ill. 99), was also shown at the Great Exhibition. The first trial run by the "Folke-

99. The "Folkestone", 1851, South Eastern Railway.

stone", pulling nine carriages along the level 26½ mile line between Tonbridge and Ashford non-stop, saw the achievement of the amazing speed of 78 m.p.h. This class of engines was in service until 1869, when they were converted to 2–4–0s, because their adhesion weight was no longer sufficient.

The final result of the battle of the gauges was that standard gauge was imposed by law, in order to preserve a uniform railroad network. From a technical point of view, however, it soon became clear that the standard-gauge supporters were not able to offer loco-

On the other hand, the Cramptons were greeted enthusiastically in France. In 1848 a direct link between Paris and the Channel coast had been forged when the smaller companies involved had merged to form the Nord company. But they had no suitable express locomotive. It is probably thanks to the efforts of the Derosne et Cail Locomotive Works that the Crampton model was chosen. This firm had been granted a licence by Crampton to use the French patent he had been granted on October 24, 1846 against payment of a fee of £100 (then 2,500 French

100. Crampton locomotive No. 137 on the Nord Railroad in France, 1855.

motives with performances comparable to those of the broad-gauge locomotives. Nonetheless valuable experience for the future had been gained. There was final confirmation that overhangs were dangerous on fast-running engines and that smoother running was afforded by inside cylinders. And to a certain extent, the correct ratio between the heating surface of the firebox and that of the fire tubes had been found by trial and error.

In England, the Crampton locomotives did not supplant the 2–2–2 locomotives, now radically improved. All in all, only twenty-four outside cylinder "Cramptons" entered service, that were bought individually here and there. As already mentioned, the South Eastern Railway was the only one to be so satisfied that it even converted a few rear driver "Longboilers" into Cramptons.

francs) per engine. Cail's Crampton models, designed by their engineer Hauel, are derived from the "Liverpool". Nothing about them was in itself new, but all aspects of their construction had been carefully considered, simplicity and accessibility had been rightly valued and all components had been built accordingly. In this way, an express engine of such excellence was created, that without any real modifications the Nord, the Est and the PLM (Paris-Lyon-Méditerranée) Railroads all ordered the engine.

Cail supplied their first two Cramptons to the Nord in March 1849. They were part of a batch of twelve, Nos. 122–133. A second delivery was made in 1853, Nos. 134–145 (Ill. 100) differing from the first series and all subsequent ones in that the driving wheel diameter was increased to 7 ft. 6½ in. in place of the normal 6 ft. 10½ in. All French Cramptons were

double framed and had the same motion arrangement, visible in the illustration. None of Crampton's devices in connection with the boiler was adopted. An innovation was the firebox crownplate, made flush against the round boiler, which was probably Cail's idea but which was soon used extensively and known as a Crampton firebox. All models were fitted with Stephenson gear, with the exception of the 165–170 series for the Nord Railroad in 1859 — the first in France to have Heusinger-Walschaerts valve gear. The location of the regulator valve in a cast-iron box on top of the boiler became almost synonymous with French locomotives and was used a great deal elsewhere as well. The only engines with domes were the thirty Cramptons Nos. 31–40 of the PLM, built by Koechlin, who was always a supporter of large domes. These, and the Nos. 174–188 supplied by Le Creusot to the

Est Railroad, were the only Cramptons among the 127 on French railroads not made by the Cail works. Already the trial runs by the two first Cramptons on the Nord saw speeds of up to 60 m.p.h. with smooth running, but before long there were four unexplained derailments. It was finally realized that the cause lay in the balanceweights on the driving wheels. Louis Le Chatelier had advised that the reciprocating masses should be completely equalized; this had been done without it being realized that the balanceweights mounted on the wheels opposite the cranks also acted up and down, and that no vertical compensating force had been provided. As a result, the driving wheel was lifted from the rail when the engine was travelling fast. After that, each balanceweight was reduced by 25 per cent, and no further derailments occurred.

There had been very early recognition of the fact that

101. Passengers in a train. Conditions in third-class carriages were anything but comfortable.

balanceweights on the wheels aided smooth running, but there was confusion over where to locate them and how large they should be. The first to make systematic tests on the balancing of masses was Heinrich Nollau, chief engineer of the Holstein Railroad. In 1848 he published his results in the German review *Eisenbahnzeitung*, which was translated by Louis Le Chatelier into French. The procedure was further developed by Clark in England and Henri François Couche in France. In 1861, Professor Gustav Zeuner of Zurich Technical High School

102. Coupled Crampton-type locomotive No. 2.522 of the French Est Railroad.

included the play of the springs in the calculations. The question of balancing the masses became acute at the turn of the century, when locomotives with more than two cylinders were introduced, and more sophisticated calculation methods were introduced.

When the balanceweights were altered, the French Cramptons showed their worth. They pulled regular express trains of between eight and twelve cars (up to 96 tons in weight) along the main Nord Railroad line, which had gradients of up to 1 in 250 or 1 in 200, and realized average speeds of 38 to 46½ m.p.h. The journey from Paris to London was shortened to twelve hours, and Paris to Cologne (via Brussels and Aix-la-Chapelle) to sixteen hours. Using its Crampton engines, the Nord Railroad became top express train operator on the Continent, and was able to retain this position until it lost its independent status. The Cramptons also succeeded on the Est Railroad. They lasted here until 1881, a few of them remaining until

even 1902, when twenty-six were still in service. The last of them, "Le Continent", was not withdrawn from service until August 21, 1914. From time to time it was exhibited on the linking platform of the Gare de l'Est in Paris. In December 1946 it was fully restored and made several runs with other historic trains. Today it stands in the Mulhouse Railroad Museum.

The Est was so delighted with its Cramptons that it bought twelve from the PLM, where they no longer met the prevailing conditions, and the chief engineer Salomon even tried to give them a new lease of life in 1889. He mounted a Flaman-type boiler, which will be discussed later, onto one of the engines. It outdistanced all its competitors in a trial run, but did not have sufficient tractive power. Further proof of the Est's high regard for the Crampton was shown by the fact that it was the only railroad to build a locomotive on identical lines, which became known in France as the "coupled Crampton". This type of locomotive, entering service in 1878 as Series 501–510 (Ill. 102), had a coupled axle in place of the second set of carrying wheels. The firebox, with a flat Belpaire top (which we shall come on to later) was another variation on the original Crampton. Also there was a dome, but the typical Crampton regulator valve box on the boiler was maintained. This coupled Crampton was further improved until 1884/85. Later, the grate was located over the rear axle. The last series of this engine was one of the most powerful 2–4–0 locomotive types ever built.

Brief mention should also be made of the fact that Jules Petiet, chief engineer on the Nord, also tried to improve the Crampton. In view of his partiality for tank locomotives, he adopted this system for the two engines built in 1856, the No. 162 "Alma" and the No. 163 "Inkerman". A third carrying axle was inserted just in front of the firebox to carry the extra supplies taken. Thus these were 6–2–0 engines. There was not sufficient water for very long non-stop runs, so in 1860 they were converted into tender engines and were given steam driers of a type which will be described later. Both engines were scrapped at the end of the Seventies.

After France, the German railroads were the most enthusiastic about the Crampton locomotive. The number constructed — 135 — exceeded even that of France. By contrast with the standard type of construction in France, in Germany there was a varied spectrum of four different main types and many differences in detail.

The first Cramptons in Germany were introduced

by the Prussian Eastern Railroad*. They were used on express trains between Berlin and Königsberg. The "Folkestone" (Ill. 99) served as a model, and an engine called "England" of this type was ordered from Robert Stephenson in 1852. At the same time Johann Friedrich Wöhlert of Berlin was given an order for eight similar locomotives with many variations.

The "England" and Wöhlert's "Baude" were subjected to thorough comparative tests with Borsig's 2–2–2 locomotives by an official commission which

road suffered from this fault. As a result, no further engines were ordered.

The Hanover State Railroad introduced its first Cramptons a year after the Eastern Railroad, choosing fortunately the French model, and it acquired easily the highest number of Cramptons of any German railroad with nineteen supplied by Wöhlert between 1853 and 1857 and nineteen coming from Egestorff in Hanover.

The third main type of Crampton was developed in

103. The "Pölnitz" with the Bavarian Royal train at the old Ludwigshafen Station, Germany.

was appointed in 1853 by the Prussian government to "examine locomotives and to ascertain the best method for its construction." The smooth running of the Cramptons was praised, but it was considered a disadvantage that "initially the piston force is transmitted to the comparatively small mass of the counter-shaft which, even on small clearances, due to its wear and tear, cause severe and dangerous impacts being unavoidable despite careful maintenance." The disadvantages of the counter-shaft which were noticed at that time were to plague the designers of the first electric locomotives later on. Indeed breaks in the counter-shaft were frequent, and it must be because of this that the Eastern Railroad Cramptons were scrapped by the middle of the 1860's. The two counter-shaft Cramptons of the Aix-la-Chapelle-Düsseldorf-Ruhort Railroad, another construction of Wöhlert, and the two of the Magdeburg and Halberstadt Rail-

South Germany. Its frame construction was similar to the outside frame developed by Joseph Hall which will be considered in more detail in the next section. The Bavarian Palatinate Railroad was the first with four engines supplied by Maffei in 1853, and these were followed by fourteen from Emil Kessler by 1864. This batch included the "Pölnitz". It is shown on a photograph at the head of the Bavarian Royal train in the old station of Ludwigshafen on the Rhine (Ill. 103). The traffic museum in Nuremberg has a full-size replica of the Maffei engine, "Die Pfalz", and also has a reassembled original "Phoenix" engine. The Baden State Railroad possessed the largest number — twenty-nine — of this main type of Crampton. Following an idea of Kessler, the first two engines built at the Karlsruhe Locomotive Works in 1854 had a boiler with a pear-shaped cross-section in order to get the centre of gravity as

* Köningliche Preussische Ostbahn.

104. The "Carlsruhe",
Crampton-type
engine with truck,
Baden State Railroad.

105. American
modified Crampton-
type locomotive, 1849.

low as possible. The lower, wider part of the boiler was completely filled with fire tubes, and the upper section served as the steam chamber. Where the two boiler sections met there was a perforated partition wall which acted simultaneously to reinforce the join and as a splash plate to prevent priming. The chimney was set back to the middle of the boiler for some reason. This affected the efficiency of the blast-pipe nozzle and was immediately altered. This peculiar construction was not followed in later batches.

Another characteristic of European Cramptons was to be found only in the Series 69–76 which was also supplied by the Karlsruhe works. Although the wheelbase of only 12 ft. 4 in. on the foregoing batch was very short for a Crampton, it was considered advisable to fit a truck rather than fixed carrying axles (Ill. 104), for these engines were to be used on the southern main line section from Freiburg onwards by the Baden State Railroad, where there are curves of only 260 to 360 yards radius. The truck was an old American type, modified for Europe as has already been described. It had longitudinal frames on both sides made of two parallel plates with a large enough distance between them to accommodate the common spring for both axles. In service, the slide plates stuck when taking curves, with the result that the truck was omitted from later batches, and instead, the overall wheel base was decreased to 11 ft. 10 in. The No. 76, "Basel", of this series could be seen at the International Exhibition in Paris in 1855. These truck Cramptons pulled eighteen cars with a total weight of 51 tons 2 cwt. between Freiburg and Waldshut. Their maximum speed was restricted to 44 m.p.h., and they could pull 45 tons at this speed. The fourth main type of German Crampton represented a return to the old "Namur". It was Emil Kessler who returned to this when he supplied to the Hessian North Railroad six engines in 1858, and again in 1863, when the Crampton type had already been superseded by a further eight. Meanwhile, in 1861/62 he built identical locomotives for the Nassau Railroad. These simply constructed machines were very popular for the light trains running in this level countryside, with the result that the last of them did not disappear until the end of the 1890s.

There were a few other Cramptons in Europe outside France and Germany, and most of these were in Denmark, with twelve going to the Zeeland Railroad and four to the Warsaw and Petersburg Railroad. One engine even found its way to Egypt.

The number of Cramptons in the United States — thirteen — was also very small. But they were even more individual.

In 1849 Baldwin supplied the Pennsylvania Railroad with three derivatives of this locomotive (Ill. 105). The Bury-type firebox was retained, as was the drive to the driving wheels via inside half-cranks. The frame was built up of iron slabs. A third carrying axle was inserted just in front of the firebox to support the enormous boiler. Of course a front truck was retained. The predecessor of these three locomotives was the "Governor Paine", supplied in 1848 to the Vermont Central Railroad. The "Lightning", another 4–2–2–0 engine, was more like the English "Liverpool" and was supplied to the Uticah-and-Shenectady Railroad with a very high Stephenson firebox made by Edward S. Norris.

The eight locomotives of the Camden-and-Amboy Railroad were "a fearsome truck type" (Hamilton Ellis, 1949) (Ill. 106). John Stevens, President of the Railroad Company, was the moving force behind these engines, following his acquaintance with Cramptons shortly after they were first built, in the course of a European trip. He instructed his chief engineer, Dripps, to design an engine to outdo everything which had gone before. The plans were ready in 1847 and were given to Richard Norris in Philadelphia for execution. The driving wheels had the huge diameter of 8 ft. The piston stroke was correspondingly long: 38 in., with a cylinder diameter of only 13 in. The driving axle was not behind but under the sloping firebox. Thus the firedoor lay under the axle, with the result that a very low platform had to be provided for the fireman. In contrast, the driver stood on a sort of conning-tower, high above the boiler, as if on a ship. This high driving position occasioned a tall chimney, which seemed even higher because of the spark-arresting funnel. The long thin cylinders, the complicated system of rods, the wheels covered in wood between the spokes to prevent air turbulence, and the six-wheeled truck, all resulted in a bizarre creation, and a worthy bedfellow of the "Monster" (Ill. 84) designed by the same engineer. The first of these engines, No. 28, "John Stevens" was tried for the first time on April 17, 1849. It was immediately apparent that, as a result of the lack of weight on the driving axle, it was very prone to slip and that owing to the unsuitable ratio between the dimensions of the cylinders and the boiler, it was hardly capable of keeping up steam. With something of an effort, it pulled six four-wheeled cars. It would appear that

by trial and error, the ratio between boiler and cylinders was improved on subsequent locomotives. They were fitted with smaller driving wheels of 7 ft., and various cylinder dimensions were tried. Finally all these engines were rebuilt into 4–4–0 locomotives, with driving wheels of 6 ft. They remained in service in this form until 1869.

The Crampton was one of the very few types which was born into the world as an express locomotive. They are a perfect example of fixed prejudices leading to errors, even when they are so unfounded as was the axiom of the low-pitched boiler. Nonetheless — or maybe precisely because of this — the Crampton brought invaluable knowledge on smooth running and the limits of the rigid wheelbase. Many components used in their construction, such as the flush firebox crown, the cast-iron regulator box, the easily accessible external valve gear with counter-cranks, were used on a large scale later on. Crampton's concept of good accessibility for all components had a lasting influence on locomotive construction on the Continent.

106. American Crampton-type engine, Camden-and-Amboy Railroad, 1848.

6.4 The "Longboiler" Conquers the European Continent

While the Longboiler method of construction was not popular in England because of its unsteady running, it was taken up on the Continent with real enthusiasm. We have already mentioned its advantages. Its short wheelbase meant that it took the more frequent and much shorter curves on the lines, which were rarely laid out as well as in England, and it did not have to be driven as fast. Nevertheless the 2–2–2 type of Longboiler was quickly abandoned or modified. On January 21, 1851, a train driven by a 2–2–2 Longboiler was derailed at Gutersloh Station on the Cologne-and-Minden Railroad, and one of the passengers in it was the future Kaiser Friedrich. When it was discovered that unsteady running was the cause, in 1853 Prussia introduced a ban on the use of this type of locomotive for express trains.

The 2–4–0 Longboilers were very versatile, being used both for freight and for normal passenger trains. As a result, they acquired a lasting popularity. The outside cylinder type was normally preferred. On the early examples of this type, the Stephenson raised Gothic firebox was still provided (Ill. 108). The engine illustrated belongs to a series of fifteen which were built in 1846/47 at Le Creusot for the Centre Railroad which was later merged with the Paris and Orléans. These engines were classed Series 345–359. They could travel on the level at about 30 m.p.h. pulling 180 tons; the last were not scrapped until just before 1880.

The 2–4–0 Longboilers with outside cylinders were also used extensively in Germany. It was used in particular on the gently graded lines of Prussia, and here it lasted well into the Sixties for freight trains. In 1866/67, another twenty-four engines were built for the Cologne-and-Minden Railroad (Ill. 109), and these were typical in every aspect of the North German method of construction then being practised, although they came in fact from Haswell in Vienna. The ample steam space offered by Stephenson's old Gothic firebox was not abandoned; indeed, this explains why Borsig introduced the very high, vaulted firebox crown in 1862. An experiment with these engines was to build them with steel plate for the boiler. The idea

107. 2–4–0 locomotive No. 212 on the French Est Railroad with a passenger train.

was to avoid the frequent cracks caused by rust on the material commonly used, and to reduce weight by using lighter sheets. The main idea was not successful. Rust pockets and cracks formed to such an extent that it was not long before new boilers of iron plates had to be installed. It was not until the middle of the Nineties, when better quality steel was obtainable, that steel began to be used for boilers. Another innovation on these engines was an arrangement to prevent the formation of boiler scale. Small pockets open at the top were riveted to the side walls of the boiler, with the feed tubes opening into them. The idea was that the particles forming the boiler scale should be deposited here. It was not a complete success and was thus not repeated. It is not until very recently that a successful way of preventing the formation of boiler scale was found. It was with these engines that at last the Borsig separate cut-off gear so popular in Prussia was omitted, once comparative tests held by the railroad had shown that the system did not offer any improvement in steam consumption.

There was only one other attempt to develop the 2–4–0 "Longboiler" into an express engine. This ambitious attempt was made by Victor Forquenot, chief engineer of the Paris-and-Orléans Railroad, in 1864. The 2–2–2 engine's adhesion was not adequate for the inclines on the lines between Limoges and Agen and Brives and Toulouse, which were between 1 in 100 and 1 in 60. Forquenot designed an express engine for this purpose (Ill. 110). His suspension system, involving one very large leaf spring on each side for the coupled axles was unique, and resulted in hard riding. The front carrying axle had lateral play controlled by inclined planes on the axlebox. The firebox was short and very deep, with a Ten Brinck water chamber inserted to increase its heating surface. This consisted of a flat water chamber set at

an angle over the grate, which was connected to the lower jacket of the firebox below the heating tubes, and to the upper jacket at the rear via double elbow pipes. This Ten Brinck device, introduced in 1860, was very popular in France right into the Nineties. The Paris-and-Orléans Railroad alone fitted more than 1,200 engines with the system. They were not, however, much used in other countries. Taken as a whole, its construction was not very suitable for an express engine. When the No. 203 was exhibited in Paris in 1867, reactions to it in England were very negative. But the Paris and Orléans was so satisfied that it ordered in all ninety-four engines by 1873, Series 171–264. This type of engine was also adopted by the PLM and the Etat Railroads. When the axle box-guides eventually became worn, the engines began to run so badly that Forquenot decided from 1873 onwards to add a rear carrying axle to all locomotives coming in for overhaul. There thus arose a typical French express engine, called the Orléans type, which we shall return to later.

The 2–4–0 Longboiler was also built with inside cylinders. This is probably the older version, for it appeared in England in 1842, supplied to several railroads either by Stephenson or on his instructions. The No. 71, a member of the same family, supplied in October 1842 to the North Midland Railway, was

108. "La Hyène", of the Centre Railroad, later the PO (Paris-and-Orléans Railroad) No. 353 (Series 345-359), 1846/47.

109. The "Herford", Cologne-and-Minden Railroad, 1866.

99

110. Engine No. 203 of the PO (Paris-and-Orléans Railroad), Victor Forquenot, 1864.

111. "Mammouth" ("Mammoth") type engine, No. 246 of the Spanish Madrid-Zaragoza-Alicante Railroad, 1857/58.

the first locomotive to be fitted with the Stephenson link motion. But this series did not become popular in England either. It was found, above all, in France, appearing on the Paris-and-Orléans Railroad in 1842, and in the countries where the influence of French engineers was felt, such as Italy and Spain. There are only isolated instances of its use in Germany, Austria and Switzerland.

It was the six-coupled Longboiler engines which were easily the most popular, again another Stephenson creation. The first two engines of this type entered service on the York-and-Midland Railway in 1843. This was the only type of Longboiler engine which was to become reasonably popular in England, where from the outset there was a need for powerful freight engines. Their short wheelbase made them more suitable than the long 0–6–0 "Atlas" (Ill. 50) engines to take the sharp curves on the colliery and dock branch lines. As a result, they lasted longest on tracks in Scotland and north-east England, heavily engaged in hauling coal, and they were ordered for example up to 1875 by the North-Eastern Railway.

They were tried on the Continent for the first time in 1845, the Paris-and-Orléans having ordered some as an experiment as heavy freight engines. The first was called the "Mammouth", and gave its name to the whole class. This engine still had the original Longboiler form, with a high Gothic firebox. The Paris-and-Orléans only acquired seven, as Polonceau soon designed his own, which we shall consider later. But on the other hand, all other French railroads placed large orders. When the orders ceased, in 1886, more than six hundred had been supplied. Because the inner and outer cranks of these locomotives were set at 180°, and the reciprocating masses were equalized with balance weights, speeds of up to 40 m.p.h. were allowed with driving-wheel diameters between 4 ft. 7 in. and 4 ft. 11 in. This meant that these engines were highly valued for their versatility. Series 1214–1217, supplied by Koechlin in 1848 to the PLM (Paris-Lyon-Méditerranée), replaced the Gothic firebox with a vaulted, slightly raised crown, and the flush firebox of Crampton later became practically a standard feature. From 1857 onwards, the dome was often omitted, with the result that the most austere locomotive of all in appearance was created. These "Mammoth" types, like the 2–4–0 engines already mentioned, were adopted particularly by those railroads where French influence was strong. They appeared in Italy in 1849; statistics for the year 1878 reveal ninety-one "Mammoths" of this type already. In Spain, where this type was introduced in 1857 as one of the three standard engines on the Madrid-Zaragoza-Alicante Railroad, a classic "Mammoth" has been retained to this day (Ill. 111). It was produced at E. B. Wilson's and entered service on February 2, 1858. It had run 1.6 million miles by its 100th anniversary and had only suffered two slight accidents. All subsequent additions were removed from the engine on the occasion of this anniversary, under the direction of the present author, and it is now being preserved by the Red Nacional de los Ferrocarriles Españoles (RENFE), the Spanish National Railroads, for the planned Railroad Museum.

The six-coupled Longboiler with outside cylinders was easily the most successful. It was the only type not

born in England, and was never popular there. It was born in France, on the Nord Railroad, whose lines included the important coal-mining area of north-east France which soon generated considerable freight traffic. For this purpose no fewer than sixty-four engines were built, Series 201–264 (later 3.210–264) at three factories: Meyer, Cail and Gouin. They had all the features of the original Stephenson Long-boiler, including the high Gothic firebox. Too much attention was paid to tractive effort in the design and the boiler turned out to be too small. Thus by 1852 they were fitted with new Crampton style boilers, larger, domeless and with the regular valve box behind the chimney. They lasted in this form until 1880–88. They pulled twenty-one cars weighing 294 tons at

16 m.p.h. A few engines assigned to the subsidiary company Nord-Belge ran until 1904.

There was then a pause in requirements. When the so-called Bourbonnais Railroad was built, fifty loco-motives were ordered from Cail and Koechlin, and these were supplied in 1854/55. Their boilers and other components were the same as those of the 2–4–0 engines ordered at the same time. They were designed, as were the Cramptons, by Hauel. They began the long series of 1,054 French engines known as the "Bourbonnais", once the Bourbonnais line had been merged with the PLM. In various versions they quickly spread throughout the Continent. They were popular because of their simple, robust construction, their good negotiating of curves resulting from their

112. 0–6–0 passenger locomotive of the Spanish Lérida-Reus-Tarragona Railroad, 1885.

101

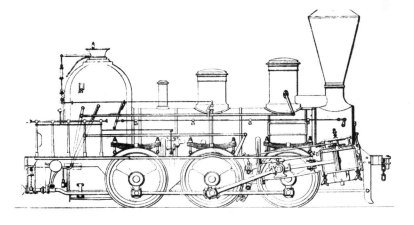

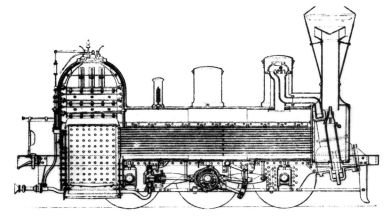

113. Locomotive on the "Geislinger Steige" in the Swabian Mountains, 1848.

In 1845 Kessler of Karlsruhe first supplied the Baden State Railroad with 0–6–0 Longboilers with outside cylinders. These were eight engines built for broad gauge, still then in existence. After these, which still belonged to the old Stephenson school, it was not until 1856 that the first six-coupled engines entered service, this time "Bourbonnais"-class engines. The six-coupled examples built by Maffei between 1847 and 1850, series C1 on the Bavarian State Railroads, belonged to the pre-"Bourbonnais" period. These were banking engines with small wheels, and acted as banking engines along the stretch between Neuenmarkt and Markschorgast, which had inclines of up to 1 in 45. To increase their adhesion weight, a large box was mounted on top of the boiler, which could be filled with sand.

The unique mountain engines designed by Josef Trick of the Esslingen Machinery works were also banking engines (Ill. 113). They were intended for the Geislingen incline, which climbs the Swabian mountains (Schwäbische Alb) with gradients of up to 1 in 45. They had the oval boilers which had become so popular by then. As many parts as possible, including the wheels, were made of cast iron, so as to increase adhesion. The suspension was too much of a good thing: all the main springs were linked via balance beams, with the result that there were only two support points and the suspension gear was thereafter unstable. Thus immediately after the first trial run, on November 1, 1848, the balance beams were removed. A load of 120 tons was then pulled up the Geislingen incline at 11 m.p.h. These mountain engines played havoc with the existing track. The front coupled axle was therefore soon uncoupled, and eventually they were converted into 2–4–0 engines. On this showing, the Württemberg State Railroad did not introduce any further six-coupled engines until 1864, and thereafter it introduced classic "Bourbonnais" engines of this type.

There was no need of six-coupled engines in the flat country of North Germany until the early Sixties, but this type of engine was then bought in quantity. They were typical "Bourbonnais". One peculiar feature on the Prussian six-coupled engines was sometimes a dummy frame which ran outside from front to rear. The cylinder and piston cross-head guides could be fixed firmly between this dummy and the main frame. This construction, designed by Borsig, was incorporated in the "Simplon" which came to the Cologne-and-Minden Railroad in 1865 (Ill. 115).

The development of the "Bourbonnais" in Germany

short wheelbase, and their economical consumption of coal measured by the standards of that time. According to its performance chart, the PLM "Bourbonnais" could pull 1,228 tons on the level, 508 tons up an incline of 1 in 200 and 306 tons up 1 in 100. On a 1 in 33 gradient it was rated to pull 118 tons at 10 m.p.h. It is impossible to describe even just the main types of "Bourbonnais", as there was not a single railroad company in Europe which did not operate them. One of them became known as the "Ardennes" type (Ill. 114), because it was included in the stocks of the Ardennes Railroad which was taken over by the Est on March 15, 1863, and further models were then ordered by the Est. It had a slightly longer wheelbase than the PLM "Bourbonnais" and its cylinders were located more towards the front, the idea being better to equalize the weight of the overhanging firebox. Between 1856 and 1884, the Est bought a total of 346 engines of this "Ardennes" type. Forquenot introduced a new type on the Paris-and-Orléans (PO) which had outside Gooch valve motion as fitted on the 2–4–0 express engine described earlier. The Ouest ordered identical engines in 1867. In 1892, for Series 2245–2269, an external Heusinger-Walschaert valve gear was incorporated for the first time in the Bourbonnais.

ended with the standard locomotives of the Prussian State Railroad in 1877. Altered slightly in 1896, and redesignated type G4, these were the last "Bourbonnais", which were also ordered for the longest period, namely until 1903.

The "Bourbonnais" class was introduced in Austria by the eight locomotives supplied by Haswell of Vienna in 1846/47, half going to the Vienna-and-Raab Railroad (later the Gloggnitz Railroad) and half to the Hungarian Central Railroad. These were the "Fahrafeld" type. With driving wheel diameter of 4 ft. 8 in., they represented the first move towards the hauling of passenger trains. But other trends intervened, that will be discussed later. Not until the 1870s was a return made to the "Bourbonnais" locomotive.

It was not long before the further improvement of the 0–6–0 Longboiler engine into the multi-purpose and even the local passenger engine occurred. Again it took place in France. In 1860 the Series 1529–1565,

with a driving wheel diameter of 5 ft. 1 in. was introduced as a *machine mixte** on the secondary lines of the PO which had by now been constructed. They were easier to maintain than the "Mammouths" which had also been used on these lines, and they gradually replaced them. They continued to be built in large numbers until 1883. The Midi hit upon the idea of building the locomotive in such a way that they could be set on wheels either 4 ft. 4 in. diameter for freight trains or 5 ft. 6 in. for local passenger trains. These engines proved so suitable for local trains that it was not until 1927 that eleven of them were given the smaller wheels. Between 1876 and 1886, Forquenot introduced this type of engine with Gooch valve motion on the PO. Owing also to his influence, as consulting engineer for the Spanish Norte, this railroad, too, received such engines, Series 1461–1480, from Hartmann. They were a problem at first because at higher speeds there were derailments, until finally the suspension system was altered. The Vulkan

* General purpose.

114. The "Childeric II", "Ardennes"-type, No. 0.414 of the French Est Railroad.

115. The "Simplon",
Cologne-and-Minden
Railroad.

Works in Stettin built two similar locomotives in 1885 for their one and only delivery to Spain. These engines were later assigned to the Norte as Nos. 1481–1482, once the latter had been acquired by the Lérida-Reus-Tarragona Railroad (Ill. 112).

In Germany, where these engines had not been greeted with great enthusiasm, they soon acquired a bad reputation. One of the thirty engines supplied to the Baden State Railroad by the Karlsruhe Machinery Factory in 1864–69, trying to catch up on time on a downhill run, was the cause of a serious accident in which sixty-three people were killed.

115. The "Simplon", Cologne-and-Minden Railroad.

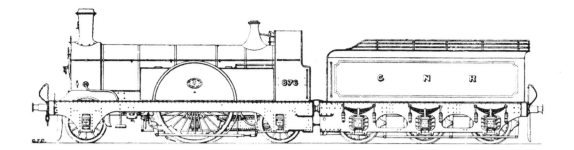

7. NEW SCHOOLS OF LOCOMOTIVE BUILDERS

In the development of the steam locomotive, the 1840s stand as a period of consolidation, when the locomotive firmly took root. The trunk — Stephenson's foundations — began to bear fruit of all sorts, the seeds of which sprang up and produced new plants. But the old trunk — at the start of everything — withered. In 1848 George Stephenson died. His son Robert turned permanently to bridge-building, where he won new laurels. Others now were at the source of the new developments, so that new "schools" of locomotive construction arose, leading in turn to further progress.

7.1 The "Jenny Lind" and "Bloomer"

John Gray, the newly appointed chief engineer of the Hull-and-Selby Railway, used his experience on the Liverpool-and-Manchester Railway and simplified the frame construction of the "Patentee". He did, in fact, retain the double frame but restricted himself to mounting only the running axles in the outer frame. By contrast, the driving axle was supported by the inner frame only, which ran from the inside cylinders to the outside front of the firebox. Gray had two locomotives on this pattern, the "Star" and the "Vesta",

116. 2–2–2 engine of the Great Northern Railway "Jenny Lind" type, Patrick Stirling, 1885.

105

built by Shepherd Todd. He subsequently introduced this type of construction to the London-and-Brighton Railway, when he was appointed chief engineer there in 1846. He ordered twelve locomotives of this type from Timothy Hackworth, who, after withdrawing from the Stockton-and-Darlington Railway, was managing a locomotive works in New Shildon together with his son John, the so-called "Soho Works". Gray's construction proved so good that the railroad placed a further order for ten more identical engines, this time from E. B. Wilson, Nos. 61-70. Gray had

117. 2–2–2 express of the Brunswick Railroad, built by Egestorff (Hanover), 1853-67.

left, so the firm sent its chief draftsman, David Joy, to make a thorough study of the locomotives on the spot. From this arose the "Jenny Lind" class, called after the first such engine to be built, christened in its turn after a Swedish singer of that name who was proving a sensation at the time (Ill. 119).

Between Derby and Masborough on the Midland Railway, on May 4-6, 1848, several comparative test runs were made between two "Jenny Lind" locomotives and two "Jenny Sharp" models, the latter being the competing version which Sharp had immediately brought out. The first 20 miles of the line ran upwards at a gradient of 1 in 330, followed by a downhill run at the same gradient for the second 20 miles. The "Jenny Lind" engines took the gradients at speeds between 44½ and 52½ m.p.h., whereas the "Jenny Sharp" engines, using more fuel, could only manage nearly 43 and 48 m.p.h. These results contributed to the "Jenny Lind's" reputation. But although various English railroads ordered locomotives of the classic "Jenny Lind" system of separate bearings for the driving and carrying axles over a period of more than forty years, and although they even reappeared as 4–2–2 engines on the Midland Railway, they were never able to replace other types completely. The longest the "Jenny Lind" lasted was as a 2–2–2 engine on the Great Northern, where they were taken up by Patrick Stirling in 1868 and were successively enlarged until 1894, when thirty-five in all had been supplied as express engines (Ill. 116). The very long wheelbase is a remarkable feature, and this explains why the front axle was given a certain amount of lateral play with no control. These engines kept the same schedules as the Stirling 4–2–2 engines which will be considered later. They pulled 220 tons on the level at 60-62 m.p.h. Once, when running late, one such engine allegedly reached 87 m.p.h. We shall see how these Stirling 2–2–2 locomotives heralded a new era on the Nord Railroad in France.

It has already been stated that Hackworth never got over the defeat of his "Sanspareil" in the Rainhill

118. 2–2–2 engine, "Bloomer" class, London-and-North Western Railway No. 249, 1851/52.

JENNY LIND.

contest. Having built the Gray engine described above, he started a very similar engine with certain modifications, and the small number of spokes on the wheels is a noticeable external feature. Another remarkable feature was the extensive use of welding, not as used today, however, but the difficult forge welding: the parts to be joined were heated in the forge fire and welded to one another by hammering. Once this "Sanspareil 2" had made successful test runs in late 1849, Hackworth thought the moment had come to get his own back for the defeat he had suffered long ago. On October 29, 1849 his son addressed a letter to Robert Stephenson, referring to the Rainhill competition and suggesting that comparative trials should be held between the new "Sanspareil 2" and the 2–2–2 longboiler just delivered by Stephenson to the York-Newcastle-Berwick Railway. There was no reply.

There were only isolated examples of the "Jenny Lind" type which ran outside England. Georg Egestorff of Hanover took up this model in Germany and supplied thirteen engines of this type to the Brunswick Railroad between 1853 and 1867 (Ill. 117),

and six somewhat smaller to the Altona-and-Kiel Railroad. Germany was still some way from appreciating the mature smooth lines of English locomotives, but the Egestorff versions were particularly ungainly, covered as they were with unnecessary decorations. They were the first express engines on the Brunswick Railroad, running the direct express service between Berlin and Cologne.

It was possible to improve the dangerously unsteady running of even the inside-cylinder Longboilers when the short boiler of the "Patentee" was readopted, thus avoiding the overhang of the firebox. J.E. McConnell had used these ideas to build a few 2–2–2 engines for the Birmingham-and-Gloucester Railway. When he succeeded Bury in July 1866 on the southern section of the LNWR*, annoyed at the behaviour of the ninety four-coupled small Bury engines and a few other types ordered as experiments — among them the Crampton engines already mentioned — he returned to his 2–2–2 locomotive of the Birmingham Railway. He was now convinced that far too much importance had been attached to the axiom of a low centre of gravity. Thus he did not hesitate

119. The "Jenny Lind" was named after a fashionable Swedish singer.

*London and North Western Railway.

107

120. 0–6–0 locomotive, DX class, for mixed traffic, London-and-North Western Railway.

NEWCASTLE AND CARLISLE RAILWAY.

Newcastle RACES.

A SPECIAL TRAIN

WILL LEAVE THE COMPANY'S STATION, CARLISLE,

On WEDNESDAY, June the 23rd,

AT SEVEN O'CLOCK IN THE MORNING,

FOR NEWCASTLE;

And will return on the Evening of the following day (THURSDAY); Leaving Newcastle at Half-past Seven o'Clock.

FARES:---Carlisle to Newcastle & Back,

First Class,	Second Class,	Third Class,
11s. **0**d.	**8**s. **6**d.	**5**s. **0**d.

And in Proportion from all the Stations West of Haydon Bridge.

Railway Office, Forth, Newcastle,
June 8th, 1847.

By Order, JOHN ADAMSON, Clerk to the Company.

☞ The Maryport and Carlisle Railway Company have signified their intention of running a Train in connexion with the above.

SCOTT AND BENSON, PRINTERS, 11, ENGLISH STREET, CARLISLE.

121. Announcement of a special train from Carlisle to Newcastle for the Horse Races, June 23, 1847.

to pitch the boiler as high as was required by the crank stroke of driving wheels of 7 ft. in diameter. As these engines had no outer frame to cover up the wheels—even the wheel splashes were widely cut out—they were nicknamed "Bloomer", after the American lady Amalie Bloomer who was much in the news at that time because of her efforts to replace the cumbersome long dresses worn by women by more masculine apparel. Remembering the Crampton, McConnell was no longer so anxious about the wheelbase. He made it as long as was required by the firebox design which was provided with transverse mid-feathers inside to compensate for the reduced heating of the shortened boiler tubes.

The first ten "Bloomers" (Ill. 118), Nos. 247–256, were supplied by Sharp in 1851/52. They caught on so well that they became the standard model used by the LNWR as express engines on its southern section. They were bought in various dimensions up until 1862 in large quantities. They included three "large Bloomers" with driving wheel diameter of 7 ft. 6 in. so that the height of the centreline of the boiler was 7 ft. 5 in. — and much criticized by the supporters of the low centre of gravity. At the beginning of this century, these "Bloomers" often had to be used as pilot engines for the three-cylinder compound locomotives of Francis William Webb, which we will consider in due course. The design created with the "Bloomer", with inside cylinders, inside frame and firebox placed between the two rear axles was constructed frequently not only on the 2–2–2 but also 2–4–0 locomotive. McConnell developed this type into a 0–6–0 engine with a long wheelbase when he ordered eleven engines with a wheel diameter of 5 ft. 6 in. of this type from James Kitson in 1854 for fast freight trains. They were followed by similar freight engines built at the Wolverton Railway Works, which became standard on the LNWR between 1854 and 1863. John Ramsbottom, who was still chief engineer of the northern section, took up the McConnell type, and when he was appointed locomotive superintendent for the whole network he ordered no less than 857 as standard type class DX between 1855 and 1872. This was the first time that a locomotive type had been built in large numbers for years on end with hardly any variation. His successor, Francis William Webb, then converted five hundred of these DX models and added a driver's cab which became a typical feature of the LNWR for decades (Ill. 120). Webb himself then continued with another five hundred engines with wheel diameters of 4 ft. 3 in. They were intended as coal

engines and entered service between 1873 and 1892. A further 310 engines with a larger wheel diameter of 5 ft. 1 ½ in. then came between 1880 and 1902, and, because of the coat-of-arms painted on one of the wheel splashes, were nicknamed "Cauliflowers". The Webb engines were the first to be fitted with the Joy valve gear as a standard feature.

These six-coupled engines with extended wheelbase were soon seen on all English railroads and were to England what the "Bourbonnais" were to the Continent. One can hardly imagine a greater contrast than between these two types.

7.2 The "Allan-Crewe" School

If the crank axle on the "Planet" and "Samson" types, always prone to damage and difficult to maintain, had to be avoided, it was necessary to provide outside cylinders. It meant a new overhang and it resulted in poor running qualities, for these engines had a short wheelbase. George Forrester, who ran

the Vauxhall foundry in Liverpool from 1827 on, restricted the overhang of the cylinders by mounting an external frame along the engine. The cylinders could therefore be moved closer to the front carrying axle. To make them more secure he added a second, dummy frame outside. The "Vauxhall" (Ill. 123), which was supplied to the Liverpool-and-Manchester Railway in 1834, was an engine of this type. The piston rods were guided through a parallelogram instead of by the usual system of a crosshead running on guide bars, and in the illustration, part of the linkage and the crescent shaped opening can be seen in which one of the articulated lever joints is in place. Forrester reverted to the usual crosshead for the locomotive built later for the London-and-Greenwich Railway. Since it was not yet known how to provide balanceweights to balance the revolving and reciprocating masses, these engines ran even worse than the "Planet" and were therefore nicknamed "Boxer". They were not developed any further.

The Grand Junction Railway was joined to the Liverpool-and-Manchester via two sharp curves. The

122. English station about 1840 with, in the foreground, a 2–4–0 locomotive of Allan-Crewe type.

109

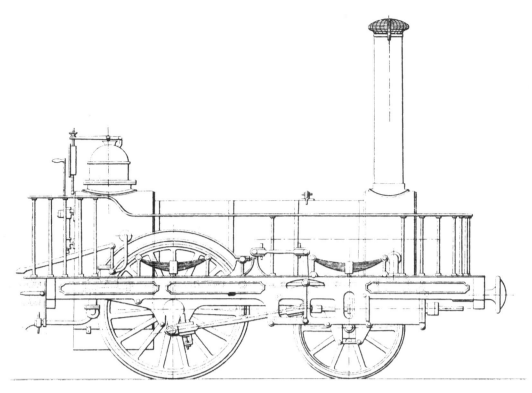

123. The "Vauxhall", Liverpool-and-Manchester Railway, 1834.

of the works in Edge Hill the permission he requested to convert three locomotives which needed new frames and crank-axles into Forrester-type engines. Alexander Allan knew these engines well as a result of his previous position with Forrester. He fitted an outside frame, but this time with both carrying axles running in it. He had to arrange the cylinders at a slight angle so that the piston rods could clear the front. He mounted the driving axle in the inside frame which had been retained. The characteristic of these engines is a section cut away at the front end of the outside frame to gain access to the crosshead.

Once the LNWR was founded, it was built as a standard type in large numbers at the railroad works set up in Crewe in 1843, and has thus become part of railroad history under the name "Allan-Crewe" type. By 1844 it had also been built as a 2–4–0 freight engine (Ill. 124). In all, over four hundred "Allan-Crewe" locomotives ran on the LNWR. One of these is still in the York Railway Museum, the "Columbia", a 2–2–2 engine, No. 49, built on February 20, 1845, the first to follow Allan's designs.

Joseph Locke, who has been mentioned already, is one of the greatest railroad contractors of all time. As was usual he not only undertook the earth works, but also supplied all the fixed and rolling stock.

2–2–2 engines of the "Patentee" type, with driving axles which probably had flanges — the omission of the flange was a patent held by Stephenson — got stuck so badly that crank-axles often broke. Joseph Locke, chief engineer of the railroad, gave the foreman

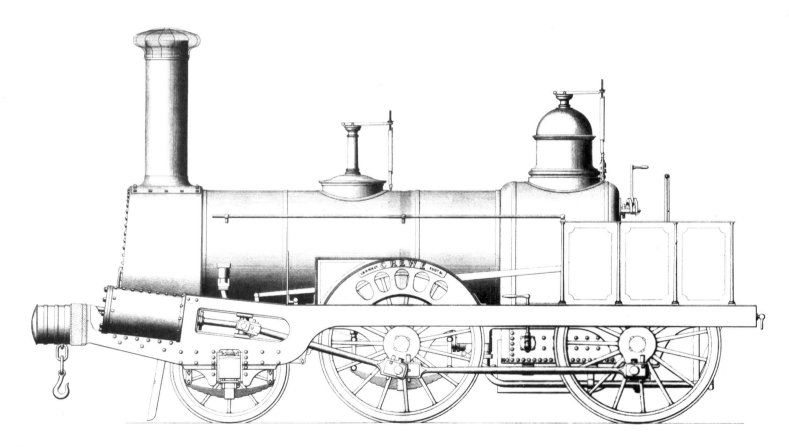

124. 2–4–0 freight engine, "Allan-Crewe" type, 1844, London and North Western Railway.

Wherever he made railroads or acted as consulting engineer, it was only natural that he preferred the "Allan-Crewe" type which he had sponsored. It thus came to several Scottish railroads and was continually being developed further here. It was under Benjamin Connor of the Caledonian Railway that these engines reached their peak as express engines. He firstly introduced 2–2–2 express locomotives with 8-feet driving wheels in 1859, and in 1868 there followed 2–4–0s with equally unusually large coupled wheel diameters of 7 ft. 2 in. The final stage of development was reached with the Highland Railway: the "Allan-Crewe" was introduced on it from 1884 on as a 4–4–0 engine by D. Jones and was built until 1901 with successive modifications (Ill. 125).

Locke's activity was not restricted to England, so that "Allan-Crewe" locomotives reached many countries, in Europe and beyond, without, however, inspiring many followers.

Only in France did this type of engine have a lasting influence. When Locke was appointed resident engineer for building for the Paris-and-Rouen and Rouen-Le Havre Railroad, two of his former engineers, Buddicom and Allcard, transferred the locomotive works they had just founded from Warrington to Sotteville and Chartreux. On payment of a licence fee they were given permission to construct the locomotives required for these two railroads using the Allan-Crewe design, which Locke had suggested to the railroad company. Buddicom and Allcard were given an order for thirty-eight 2–2–2 engines, but they made certain alterations to the frame construction and in the cylinder fastening. The cylinders were not mounted between the two main frames, but above the front wheel where a third parallel plate was inserted which took, together with the inner plate, the cylinder flange abutting onto them. The valve chests were mounted outside and the slide-valves were thus operated by a rocking shaft actuated by the inside valve gear. The locomotives supplied to the Paris-and-Rouen in 1843/44 (Ill. 126), small as they were for those times, nevertheless pulled trains weighing 80 tons from Paris to Le Havre at the remarkably high average speed of 36 m.p.h. If one disregards twenty minutes for the five stops en route, this figure represents 38½ m.p.h. As time passed and they could no longer meet traffic demands, twenty-five of them were converted to tank engines between 1860 and 1865. They were so useful on branch lines that ten of them were still in service in 1914. The No. 0.135 was restored

125. The "Nairnshire", 2–4–0 engine of the Highland Railway.

111

to its original condition at the railroad workshop in Sotteville and has been given to the Mulhouse Railroad Museum.

The thirty identical 2–2–2 locomotives supplied by Buddicom to the Amiens-and-Boulogne Railroad in 1838, which had a somewhat larger driving wheel diameter of 6 ft. 1 in., were also converted to tank engines around the same time. An additional axle was added behind to carry the fuel supply.

Benoît Clapeyron tried to combine the "Buddicom" and the "Longboiler" in a remarkable way (Ill. 127).

He had been entrusted with acquiring the rolling stock for those stretches of track built by the French State*, which were then transferred to the Nord. His intention was clearly to retain the advantages of the Longboiler but to improve the very poor cylinder arrangement used on them. Unlike Buddicom, he ran a plate frame from front to rear with the coupling hook fitted to its rear cross-piece. In this way, he avoided having to attach the coupling hook to the firebox, as had been customary, and which was not at all suitable to take the strain. This series of engines,

* Etat Railroad.

126. 2–2–2 locomotive of the Paris-and-Rouen Railroad, Buddicom system, 1843. Legend has it that the engine driver with the top hat is the company's founder, Edward Blount.

127. 2–2–2 locomotive, with outside cylinder. Series 17-50 of the French Nord Railroad, Clapeyron type, 1846.

128. No. 157 of the Paris-and-Orléans Railroad, first engine built by Camille Polonceau, 1850.

129. "L'Auroch", Paris-and-Orléans Railroad, Series 658-719, 1854–56.

delivered by various engine works, and later designated Nord Series 17–50, had the defect of all "Longboilers". To try and achieve a better running, the rear axle was moved behind the firebox, thus increasing the wheelbase to 15 ft. 1 in.

As had happened in England with the "Allan-Crewe", the "Buddicom" was also made in France as a 2–4–0 engine, but in small numbers. There were even a few examples in France of 0–4–2 engines and — what is more — of a large-wheeled 0–6–0.

7.3   The "Polonceau" School

A contract signed on August 1, 1848 leased the operation of the Paris-and-Orléans Railroad to Camille Polonceau. It was only natural that he should then immediately begin to build engines of his own design, intended to replace the mixed bag of existing types. The first to appear were five 2–4–0s for mixed traffic (Ill. 128), and these had many striking characteristics. The boiler followed the Crampton style, with a flush firebox crown and a small dome. The cylinders were located inside, but the slide valve chest was outside, to ensure easy access. This prevented the cylinder casting from being mounted on the outside frame, which was of a sandwich construction. Polonceau therefore inserted two shorter inside frames only 1 ft. 8½ in. apart which took the cylinder casting. These inside frames ran from the rear wall of the smoke box to a cross-member located in front of the firebox. Since the cylinders had been mounted closer together, there was enough space between the outside frame and the driving wheel to mount the eccentrics outside the wheels, thus actuating the valves directly. The valve gear was of the Gooch type. Polonceau had already used this gear for previous 2–2–2 engines and it remained thereafter the prevailing system on the PO until 1900. This series, 153-157 (later 381-385), built at the Ivry railroad works, was used for local passenger services, mixed and freight trains.

Polonceau then tried several wheel arrangements for his type of construction. There were, firstly, fourteen 0–4–2s with fireboxes between the two rear axles, Series 367-380. The boiler was probably too small, for the next batch one year later, Nos 386-393, was practically the reverse of the 2–4–0 engine described above, with an overhung firebox.

THE GREAT SEMAPHORE SONG.

THERE'S DANGER ON THE LINE.

WRITTEN & COMPOSED BY
G . P . NORMAN.
SUNG WITH THE GREATEST SUCCESS
BY
G . H . MACDERMOTT.
LONDON; HOPWOOD & CREW, 42, NEW BOND ST.

130. English station
guard signalling danger.
Illustration accompa-
nying the song "There's
danger on the line".

The most successful Polonceau type, built in larger quantities than any other, was a six-coupled freight engine, 134 of which entered service on the PO between 1854 and 1856. The frame construction was drastically simplified. The outside frame was made of a simple continuous plate. Inside there was also just a single plate in the middle, which took the crankshaft and to which both cylinder castings were bolted. The first series, 658-719, had the firebox placed between the two rear axles (Ill. 129). But the next series, 720-791 of 1856, saw it overhung. The engines in the first series were modified to those of the second series between 1861 and 1864, to ensure that their boiler performance became comparable. With replacement boilers from time to time, these engines have lasted a very long time: indeed none had been scrapped by 1914. They were only discarded in any quantity once the PO began to electrify its main lines, and even so, thirty such engines were still running in 1930. It was not until 1939 that the last were scrapped.

In 1859 Polonceau left the Paris-and-Orléans Rail-road. As so often happened, there were radical changes as a result of the departure of the company's chief engineer. The engines of his successor, Victor Forquenot, have already been considered in sec-tion 6.4.

In 1857, the Ouest Railroad adopted Polonceau's type of construction, and ordered thirty-five six-coupled engines, Series 541-575. They were intended for mixed traffic and had a somewhat larger driving wheel diam-eter of 5 ft. 1½ in. and slightly larger overall dimen-sions. They were not succeeded by any others, prefer-ence being given to the simpler "Mammouth" type. The 2-4-0 engines, Series 369-380, which were ordered the same year from Ernest-Alexandre Gouin following Polonceau's principles and plans supplied by the railroad, were subject to an interesting development. They were the first express engines in France with large coupled wheels. The series quoted had the front carrying axle located very close to the front coupled axle. The crank-axle, supported in the middle as in Polonceau's design, had only two bevelled crank webs, located inside. As in Mathias Baldwin's half-cranks, the wheel boss itself formed the others. All the axles were mounted in the outside frame. The inner and outer cranks were not at 180° as usual, in order to balance the moving masses, but they ran together to reduce the stresses on the axle bearings. The firebox was overhung. With the second series, 381-400, which entered service between 1860 and 1874, the cylinder castings were located well before the smokebox, so

that the front axle had to be placed further forward. The larger examples of Series 707-743 appeared in 1877. To accommodate the enlarged grate without increasing the overhang at the rear, the grate was located above the second coupled axle. From 1880 onwards, the engines of Series 636-706 appeared (Ill. 131), with driving wheel diameter increased from 6 ft. 1 in. to 6 ft. 8 in. and several variations. Finally a new series, 621-623, emerged in 1886, and these were the final development of the Polonceau type. The firebox was now hung between the two rear axles.

The valve gear was still outside, but the slide-valve chests were now moved inside, with the result that a transmission shaft had to be included. These engines pulled the 120-ton expresses between Paris and Le Havre at an average speed of 36 m.p.h., three stops included. In all, 327 2–4–0 Polonceau-type express locomotives entered service on the Ouest. Between 1901 and 1911 the front axle on all engines built after the year 1880 was replaced by a truck, with the result that the maximum permitted speed was increased to 68 m.p.h.

131. 2–4–0 express locomotive of the French Ouest Railroad, No. 637, 1880.

132. Paris-Bordeaux mail train on the bridge over the Loire at Saint-Côme, 1871. Victor Forquenot locomotive of the PO (Paris-Orléans Railroad), No. 247.

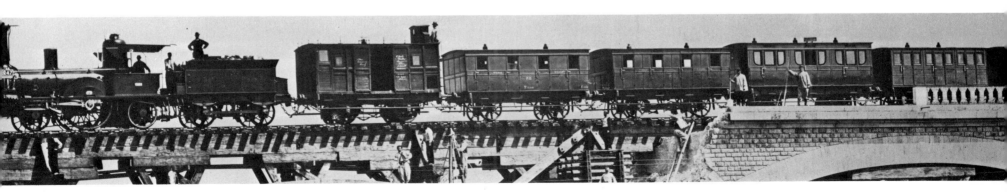

7.4 From the George Forrester to the Joseph Hall School

Forrester's 2–2–0 locomotive, described in section 7.2, followed a new and different method of construction, in which he attempted to steady the running by the addition of another carrying axle at the rear. This variant, first introduced on four engines supplied to the Birmingham-and-Gloucester Railway in 1838, caused as little enthusiasm in England as his "Boxer" had earlier. The cylinders were this time secured only to the outside frame, which was consequently extended underneath and used also to take the running axle. Two locomotives built in 1840 for the Grand Junction Railway had a remarkable valve gear. A single eccentric keyed into the driving axle on the inside engaged both eccentric rods which were directed upwards. Their upper gab-ends engaged and disengaged with a three-armed lever mounted on the boiler, for forward or reverse motion. The middle arm of the suspended lever, which pointed downwards, controlled via a rocking shaft the valve mounted above the cylinders (Ill. 133).

It is amazing that the Brunswick State Railroad should have come across one of these very few Forrester locomotives. It is possible that Philipp-August von Amsberg met them on a trip he made to England. He had been instructed to purchase stronger rails than those originally envisaged for the railroad planned between Brunswick and Wolfenbüttel. But whatever the reason, this first railroad in Bruns-wick was opened on December 1, 1838 with two Forrester engines. No further locomotives of this type were purchased.

When there were plans in Bavaria to build railroads, Friedrich Pauli, a member of the Building Commission, got to know of these Brunswick engines. Possibly because the simplicity of its construction and the easy access to all components seemed impressive, he took these as his models for the first locomotive order from the Bavarian State Railroad. Initially there were no further orders for Forrester Class A I engines, but other types were tested. When the Bavarian network was connected to the railroads farther north, however, Forrester locomotives were again chosen as the first express engines. Batch A IV, which comprised eight engines, was very similar to the A I in terms of general construction, although the firebox was supported on the rear axle.

The next batch, A V, opened the era of the Hall type (Ill. 134). In 1839 an Englishman, Joseph Hall, had come to Bavaria as the chief traffic superintendent of the Munich-and-Augsburg Railroad. The opening was delayed, so while waiting, he helped with the construction of the first locomotive for the railroad. When the railroad was nationalized, he entered service

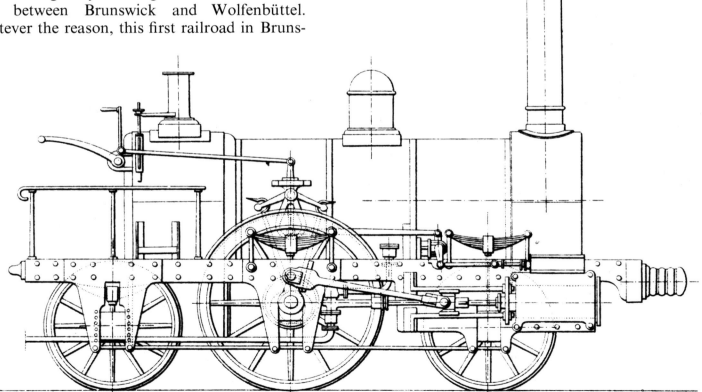

133. 2–2–2 locomotive of the Grand Junction Railway, George Forrester, 1838.

with the firm of Maffei and became their technical director.

A disadvantage of the Forrester model was the great distance between the cylinders. As a result, the engines swayed badly when running. To reduce this distance, Hall first designed the so-called eccentric crank, and was granted a patent for this in 1853. This had the crank web forged together with the eccentrics in one piece, then turned right round and keyed into the axle emerging at the wheel boss. The crank and eccentrics by this method became much narrower.

Hall's second patent was in connection with the so-called bearing collar crank: a turned pin was welded to the crank web to act as a bearing collar, and was mounted on the axle stub. This bearing collar replaced the normal axle journal which ran into the axle box. Because of its greater circumference, the bearing collar could be kept narrower than a normal axle journal without any increase in stress on the bearing surfaces. The former method was used on locomotives with outside motion, the latter where the motion was inside.

The first series to be fitted with Hall's eccentric cranks was the A V, with outside motion. But the supplementary Meyer double-valve expansion gear remained inside, with the drive being transmitted via a bayonet-shaped intermediate assembly. The sandwich frame was replaced by an iron frame consisting of two parallel plates of sheet metal with filling plates between, a type of construction called the "filled frame". In all, twenty-three A V engines, with slight variations, entered service in 1853/54, all built by Maffei. Since their firebox was hung between the two rear axles, despite the relatively small driving wheels, a maximum permitted speed of 50 m.p.h. was allowed. In Bavaria, turf was sometimes used as locomotive fuel because coal had to be transported over a long distance and freight costs were therefore high. An effective spark arrester was needed since burning turf sent out a welter of sparks; this was initially pear-shaped, but later cone-shaped following Ressig's design. The tender had to be covered to keep the turf dry. Turf does not have a high calorific value, so that a great deal had to be shovelled into the firebox. The normal tender did not hold a sufficient amount for long journeys, and a second "ammunition" turf tender was coupled up, meaning that a second fireman was obviously needed.

The A V was the start of a very large family of engines. The Bavarian offspring commenced as early as 1852, with 2–4–0 engines. Up to 1887, in all 329 2–4–0s ran

on the Bavarian State Railroad. The first six-coupled engines appeared in 1857-59, five locomotives with support tenders styled after the Engerth model, which will be considered later. The next ones reverted to the normal tender. In this form, the Hall models were bought until 1879, that were also used on other railroads in South Germany.

The Hall type of construction spread so extensively through the Austro-Hungarian Empire that it may be cited as typical of the second half of the last century.

134. The "Innsbruck", Group A V, Bavarian State Railroad, 1853.

135. Engraving of Munich Main Station, 1848.

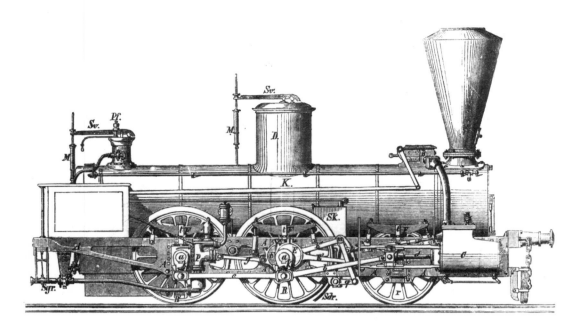

136. 2–4–0 locomotive, Austrian Southern Railroad, 1859–73.

or outside motion. The overhang of the firebox and the horizontal cylinders were common to all. A filled frame was normally used. The Austrian Südbahn acquired its first Hall six-coupled engines in 1860. Because of the large number of sharp curves, the rear axle was driven and thus the wheelbase was kept as short as possible. By 1872, a total of 202 of this type, designated Series 29, entered service; and besides these, there were another three belonging to the Graz-and-Köflach Railroad, which were operated occasionally by the Southern Railroad. For its part, the Graz and Köflach (GK) acquired a further fourteen engines. In 1965, four of these locomotives were still in service as switchers, including No. 680 (Ill. 137). They have hardly been altered since entering service, with the exception of the later additions of the cab, the air brake pump and the spark arrester, known as "Kobel". No. 671 still exists today. In first-rate order, affectionately maintained, its finest moments come when it pulls special trains for enthusiasts and emits clouds of smoke for the benefit of photographers.

Hall locomotives were also acquired by several railroads in Russia and the Balkans, supplied by Austrian and German works. By now there were twenty-six such engines on the line on the Rechte Oderufer Railroad (Oder Right Bank Railroad) and, as an unusual feature, these had the firebox supported mid-way over the rear axle. There was a different version in Prussia, created by August Wöhler, who was the chief engineer of the Lower Silesia and Brandenburg Railroad**. Prussia had always valued simplicity: for this reason, the outside frame was simply built of plates and was not a filled frame. As was normal, the slide valves and the Allan gear normally fitted were inside. Hall's bearing collar cranks were used on the driving axle, but normally mounted cranks were used on the coupled axle. The Lower Silesia and Brandenburg Railroad began to purchase Wöhler engines in 1864 (Ill. 138). Until 1875, a total of fifty-one local passenger engines with a coupling wheel diameter of 5 ft. 1½ in. were ordered. From 1869 onwards a lovely express engine followed, thirty-five examples of which were built by 1871. Wöhler was one of the few locomotive builders on the Continent who took pains to design good-looking engines. As they had to be built according to his plans, the factory accretions which were normally added in those days were omitted. The Berlin-Potsdam-Magdeburg Railroad also introduced this Wöhler type between 1870 and 1874, acquiring twenty-nine engines. They had the reputation of being among the most powerful engines of their

In 1858, Hall took over as manager at Günther's Locomotive Works at Neustadt in Vienna. In fact he left by 1860, to take over the rail-rolling mill he had begun at the Austrian Southern Railroad*, but his short stay there was enough to introduce on a broad scale his design in the twin Empire, where most further development was carried out, and it even reached the stage of 4–4–2 engines. The versatile 2–4–0 locomotive spread quickest; one such example was also made with Hall's eccentric cranks, as is visible in the illustration (Ill. 136). Between 1859 and 1873, seventy-three such locomotives were built, Nos. 467-539, by every domestic constructor and by Ludwig Kessler of Esslingen, all for the Austrian Southern Railroad. A strictly Austrian touch was the regulator box of the Crampton type. As elsewhere, the last series built in Austria saw the overhung firebox replaced by the supported one. With a driving wheel diameter of 6 ft. 6 in., these engines entered the express locomotive class. The final stage in the improvement of Hall's 2–4–0 locomotives was reached by the engines built in 1880 as series IIb3, supplied by STEG to Kaiser Ferdinand's North Railroad, with the cylinders located close to the first coupled axle and not overhung at the front.

But most common in the dual monarchy were undoubtedly the Hall six-coupled engines. As in South Germany, these can be divided into two categories: with middle axle drive or rear coupled axle drive. In both cases there were two types, with inside

* Südbahn.

** Niederschlesisch-Märkische Bahn.

day, but at the high speeds which were customary with this particular railroad they did not run satisfactorily. A very large number, fifty-five of them, ran on the Breslau-and-Freiburg Railroad. Apart from that, only a small number of these locomotives were ordered. All in all, only 199 were built for North German railroads, a very small number compared with the figures for the more conventional 2–4–0 engines.

7.5 The European Norris School

It is a surprising fact that the "Norris" locomotive, discussed in section 5.5, had such an influence on German locomotive construction, especially in South Germany and Austria.

The initiative came from Austria. The same problems existed here for railroad building as in America: the terrain was difficult to cross and meant severe curvature and steep inclines. It was thus only natural to look to America to see how problems were being tackled. Matthias von Schönnerer, who made the Austrian Monarchy's first railroad — the horse-drawn Budweis-and-Linz Railroad — went on several study tours of the United States in the late 1830s before participating in the building of the Vienna-and-Raab Railroad between 1839 and 1842, after which he became its manager.

Schönnerer arrived in America at just the time when the two Norris locomotives "George Washington" and "Washington Country Farmer" were making their remarkable runs. He was very impressed and arranged for the Vienna-and-Raab Railroad to order a similar Norris 4–2–0 locomotive. It arrived in Trieste in April 1835 and was called the "Philadelphia". It was this engine which introduced the American-type truck to Europe.

The expectations of this engine can be seen in the report of the Vienna-and-Raab Railroad General Meeting of October 1, 1835, which runs: "Since the construction is simpler than the English one, it will be an easy matter for Austrian factories to build further examples on the same lines. Furthermore it requires fewer repairs, and those that are needed will be easier to carry out. It is able to take sharp curves and steep inclines, and finally the chimney retains the glowing coal fragments better than English designs, so that there can be no doubt that its introduction will be especially useful." It would appear that the "Philadelphia" did not prove disappointing, for the Vienna-and-Gloggnitz Railroad, which succeeded the

137. 0–6–0 locomotive of the Graz-and-Köflach Railroad, No. 680, Series 29, 1860–72.

138. 2–4–0 locomotive, No. 451 of the Lower Silesia and Brandenburg Railroad, 1874.

119

Vienna-and-Raab Railroad, ordered another two identical Norris engines, which arrived in 1838/39. Nothing is known about what happened to these three engines. Kaiser Ferdinand's North Railroad followed the example of the Vienna-and-Raab Railroad and ordered four engines, as did the K.u.K. (Kaiserliche und Königliche). Northern State Railroad, which obtained four of this type in 1845. Norris thus supplied eleven 4–2–0 engines from Philadelphia to Austria. William Norris was encouraged by this success to set up a locomotive works in Vienna. But between 1846/47, it only built six locomotives, because what the Vienna-and-Raab report (quoted above) had contended proved true: these engines were, indeed, easy for local works to copy, and Norris could not compete against them.

The name John Haswell is closely linked with the further development of the Norris type of construction. The Vienna and Gloggnitz Railroad had decided to erect its own works both to maintain its existing engines and to build new ones. Haswell came to assemble the machinery for this purpose ordered by Schönnerer from W. Fairbairn and Co. He then remained as manager of the works. It is strange that two Englishmen, Hall and Haswell, should have created as un-English a type of locomotive as could possibly be imagined, designed for the special railroad conditions in Austria.

The first locomotive built by Haswell, the "*Wien*" ("*Vienna*"), entered service on June 6, 1841. As planned from the outset, it was very similar to the Norris engines. Haswell soon made various changes in the design: on engines built after 1844 the frame was no longer made of iron bars but of plates. The truck was also constructed in the same way. The Norris firebox was shaped differently: it was slightly raised, with a semi-cylindrical cross-section, and at the rear the cover was shaped like a quarter-sphere, a type of construction which was thereafter much used in Austria.

Wenzel Günther, who had originally worked under Haswell and then in 1842 had taken over as manager of the locomotive works just established in Neustadt/ Vienna, also turned to the Norris type when he bought

139. Train of the Swiss Ouest-Suisse Railroad near Renens (Lausanne), c. 1860.

140. Arrival of the trains at Kaiser Ferdinand Nord Station, Brno (present-day Czechoslovakia) on July 7, 1839.

the factory. He supplied his first engines to the K.u.K. Northern State Railroad. They were built with the Haswell-type plate frame, but retained the Bury firebox.

Once again it was Haswell who took the next step in the further development of the Norris locomotive. In 1844 he supplied the Vienna and Gloggnitz Railroad with the first pair of 4–4–0 locomotives. Apart from this they retained the structural characteristics of the 4–2–0 engines. The front coupled axle was driven by the cylinders, still inclined. The front and second axle had a common spring balanced together on the American pattern. These two engines were the predecessors of the engines which Haswell later supplied to the K.u.K. Southern State Railway

and the Vienna-and-Gloggnitz Railroad, which became very famous as the "Kleine Gloggnitzer" and the "Grosse Gloggnitzer" ("Small Gloggnitz" and "Large Gloggnitz").

Between Mürzzuschlag and Laibach, depending on the incline, which was as much as 1 in 300, the "Grosse Gloggnitzer" pulled between 145- and 160-ton passenger trains and 190- to 380-ton freight trains, while the corresponding figures for the "Kleine Gloggnitzer" were 122-135 tons and 155-290 tons. This was more than had been expected, and the builders of the Semmering Railroad were even more confident that locomotive operations would be successful. One of the "Small Gloggnitz" engines, the "Steinbrück", came to the Graz-and-Köflach Railroad in 1860

121

141. Lithograph show-
ing a railroad signal-
man's cottage, c. 1850,
in Bavaria.

where, renamed "Söding", it was in service until 1878. It is today in the Vienna Railroad Museum, restored to its original condition and re-christened with its original name (Ill. 143).

As was the case with the 4–2–0s, the 4–4–0 Norris types soon had several variations, with the Austrian quarter-sphere firebox, with the tall cylindrical Meyer-type and finally with the Stephenson Gothic variety. The cylinders were sometimes located horizontally in front of the truck.

The twelve engines supplied by Cockerill to the K.u.K. Northern State Railroad in 1825/53 were of a very unusual construction (Ill. 142). They attempted to provide a radical solution to the cause of the poor running by all Norris engines, firstly by placing the firebox between the two coupled axles instead of over-hanging at the rear and secondly by locating the cyl-inders inside. The slide-valve chests were located outside, to make them more readily accessible. As a result the cylinders had to be overhung at the front, for no one yet dared to pitch the boiler high enough to make room for the cylinders above the truck. This

engine was in fact an attempt to use the very popular Norris type of construction for faster trains. But it did not achieve the success hoped for it. The 4–4–0 arrangement became established in Austria with these Norris engines. Together with the Hall type, they took Austrian locomotive construction along a new path which will be the subject of a later section.

The second centre from which the Norris influence spread was Württemberg. Ludwig Klein, who had been to America as early as 1838 and who had worked with the Kaiser Ferdinand's North Railroad on his return, was appointed to the Württemberg Railroads Commission in 1843. His knowledge of the railroads of America, which had exerted such an influence in Austria, led him to suggest these as the most suitable for Württemberg, in a report submitted on April 3, 1844. He also suggested that "the locomotive of the preferred type should be obtained from its original makers" and that these, as in Austria, should then be used as the basis for further examples to be built in works planned for Esslingen. At Klein's sugges-tion in 1844, the Railroads Commission ordered from

Baldwin, in August, the 2–4–0 locomotives with flexible beam truck, as seen in section 5.7. In September, three 4–4–0 locomotives similar to the "Virginia" (Ill. 76) were ordered from Norris in Philadelphia. The Baldwin engines were not as satisfactory as the Norris and were resold to the Swiss Central Railroads. The Norris engines, which survived until 1867, became the basis on which locomotive building in Württemberg was launched.

Emil Kessler, who had been building locomotives to the English pattern at his Karlsruhe factory since 1841

142. 2–4–0 engine of
the Northern State
Railroad of Austria
(K.u.K. Nördliche
Staatsbahn), 1852.

143. The "Steinbrück",
"Small Gloggnitz"
type, 1848.

for the Baden State Railroad, was given an order from Klein in 1846 to construct fifteen Norris-type engines. The first six were built at the Karlsruhe factory, and the remainder at the Esslingen works which was acquired by the former. But Kessler did not produce a true copy of his American model. He replaced the Bury firebox with the Stephenson four-sided Gothic firebox. The main frame and the truck were made from plates, as in the Norris-type engines built by Haswell in Austria. In contrast, the cylinders were located horizontally in front of the carrying axles.

To begin with, of these initial Norris-type engines built by Kessler at the Karlsruhe works, the "Rhein" (Ill. 144) and the "Reuss" were delivered to the Swiss North-Eastern Railroad in 1847. They succeeded Switzerland's famous first locomotives and were used on the "Spanisch Brötli-Bahn"* (Ill. 146) between Zurich and Baden, the only Norris-type engines which Kessler built as single driving wheelers. They were too light for the traffic and as a result the 4–4–0s already mentioned were the next to be ordered. Whereas these four Norris engines were the only ones

to come to Switzerland, in Württemberg this was the only type of locomotive to be pursued. In 1854 an express engine appeared, Class A, with driving wheels 6 ft. ½ in. diameter and a flush fitting firebox. Strangely, from 1856 onwards this was built as a strictly freight engine, with a driving wheel diameter of 4 ft. 6½ in. On these Class E slow-running engines, the last one, the cylinders were located behind the truck and the coupled wheels were even smaller (Ill. 145). In contrast, the front overhung cylinders were retained on the express engines for as long as they were built, until 1868. Thus in Class E the only Norris feature which remained was the short truck. The Norris types were not used after Heinrich Brockmann, who came from Hanover, was appointed chief engineer on the Württemberg State Railroads in 1865. The existing engines were for the most part modified into engines without trucks.

Locomotives of the Norris variety were supplied to Hessen by the Esslingen works in Württemberg. The famous first engine built by Henschel, the "Drache"**, was a copy of the Kessler type.

* "Little Spanish Bread Train."

** "Dragon".

123

144. The "Rhein",
North-East Railroad,
Switzerland, 1847.

145. The "Einkorn",
2–4–0 passenger train,
class E of the Württem-
berg State Railroad.

7.6 The "Spinning Wheels"

The Norris engines which came to North Germany gave the decisive impetus to a development that took quite another form from that followed in Austria and Württemberg. The Berlin-and-Potsdam Railroad, which had opened its whole line on October 30, 1898 with English locomotives of the "Patentee" type, acquired two 4–2–0s from Norris in Philadelphia the following year. But by 1845 these were being used merely as stationary steam engines for track building purposes. The Norris types which were tried out by other North German railroads did not fare much better. The only satisfied customer was the Lower Silesia-and-March Railroad which, with fifteen, had most Norris engines. In a book appearing in 1844, *Die Eisenbahnen Deutschlands ("The Railroads of Germany")*, von Reden writes thus: "... Not suitable for fast running, like the English types, because of the way they are constructed, but they prove to be more powerful."

August Borsig began building locomotives in Berlin-Moabit during the initial euphoria over the Norris. His first completed locomotive, ready in July 1841 and ordered on a trial basis by the Berlin-and-Anhalt Railroad, was a fairly straight copy of the Norris engines working on the Berlin-and-Potsdam Railroad at the time (Ill. 147). It had an extended boiler, and the consequent increase in load on the driving axle was taken up by an extra carrying axle added at the rear. On July 21, 1844 the first trial run, against an English engine, was made on the track towards Jüterborg. To the amazement of the spectators, the "Borsig" took ten minutes less than its competitor. Like all first efforts, the "Borsig" had its share of teething troubles. Its performance was no longer satisfactory by 1850, and it was withdrawn from service.

It was the short truck which made the Norris engines "not suitable for fast running", and this will be considered further in section 8.1. The North German railroads ran over flat country with no severe curvature, so the truck was superfluous. Thus only six 4–2–2 Borsig engines were built. By 1844, Borsig had replaced the truck with a simple front carrying axle on the locomotive which he had called "Beuth" (Ill. 148) in honour of his former teacher at the Berlin Technical School. Compared with the "Borsig" the frame construction was also considerably improved. The engine was shown at the 1844 Industrial Exhibition in Berlin. On the occasion of the 75th anniversary of the Borsig firm in 1912, a non-working full-size model of the "Beuth" was made and presented to the German Museum in Munich.

The introduction of the uncoupled express engine to North Germany began with the "Beuth" which was built for the Berlin-and-Anhalt Railroad. They were generally called "Spinning Wheels", on account of their resemblance to such instruments. In brief, the further stages in the development of the "Spinning Wheels" were in 1847 the mounting of the cylinders in a horizontal position, and the moving of the valve chest inside so that the valves could be operated directly by the motion, which was also inside. In addition to the Stephenson link motion, the Borsig expansion gear was often used. This system had an expansion valve mounted on the back of the main valve. A second link transmitted the movement of the reverse eccentric, and the guide-block of the valve-rod could be adjusted to different settings in this link. The result was to shorten or to increase the trajectory of the expansion valve. The Borsig double valve gear was incorporated in over a thousand locomotives. From 1847 onwards, the Bury round firebox was replaced by the Stephenson four-sided Gothic dome, which was nicknamed the "haystack firebox" by the

124

drivers and was a characteristic of most Borsig locomotives until around 1868.

At about this time higher boiler pressures began to be used, and these did not suit this type of construction. Instead Borsig introduced a very high firebox, semi-cylindrical at the top, which has already been described in section 6.1. This type of firebox no longer had to be made square, like the four-sided type, so that it was possible to extend the grate at the rear, thus enlarging the grate area. The "Spinning Wheels", which were easy to maintain and undemanding, spread so far and so quickly, that they may certainly be called typical of North Germany. In various forms they were also taken up by other locomotive works. In 1869, Richard Hartmann supplied the Cologne-and-Minden Railroad with four engines exactly on the Borsig pattern, among them the "Oker" (Ill. 150).

It was Hartmann who also introduced these engines

146. 4–2–0 engine of the "Spanisch Brötli-Bahn" Line from Zurich to Baden. First railroad in Switzerland.

125

to Saxony. They soon represented a real challenge to the spread of the Crampton, as is shown by the order figures: 228 engines (2–2–2) between 1851 and 1875 as against 115 Cramptons between 1852 and 1864. They performed as well as the Cramptons on the test runs arranged by the Prussian Railroad Commission which have been mentioned already. With 6 ft. 6 in. driving wheels they became known as "Racers".

In France and in England, different paths led to very similar engines. As had happened in many other places, several French railroads had moved the rear axle of the 2–2–2 Longboiler back, so as to obviate the troublesome rear overhang. On new-built engines, this was first used in 1847 on the Paris-and-Lyons Railroad. The chief engineer on this railroad, Alexis Barrault, drew up the plans and Jean François Cail undertook the construction of this Series 1–45 (later PLM 101–145) (Ill. 152). These engines, which have become well-known as the "Perraches", together with a subsequent, slightly different series (PLM 146–160) ran to the same timetable as the Cramptons bought at the same time. They hauled express trains with eight or nine cars weighing 50-60 tons, at a speed of about 36-37 m.p.h. When their performance was no longer adequate, in the 1860s, they were easily converted into 2–4–0s with an extended boiler and an overhanging firebox. On the other hand the Cramptons were either given to the Est Railroad or scrapped.

Of the French engines to have derived from the "Perraches", those of the Midi have a special place. They were undoubtedly the first single-wheelers with outside motion. Originally built in 1855 as tank engines, they could not accommodate sufficient fuel and water, so the second batch had normal tenders. They were in service on expresses on the line from Bordeaux to Toulouse and Bayonne, and pulled 100 tons at 31 to 37 m.p.h. In 1918 at least twelve of them were still in service on secondary lines, undoubtedly the 2–2–2 variety, the most long-lived.

In England two paths led to the 2–2–2 locomotive, both similar to the Borsig design, but almost entirely restricted to two of the big railroad companies.

When McConnell left the LNWR, in late 1861, John

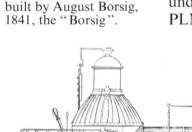
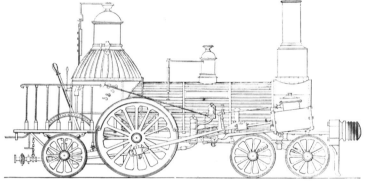

147. 4–2–2 locomotive of the Berlin-and-Anhalt Railroad, first engine built by August Borsig, 1841, the "Borsig".

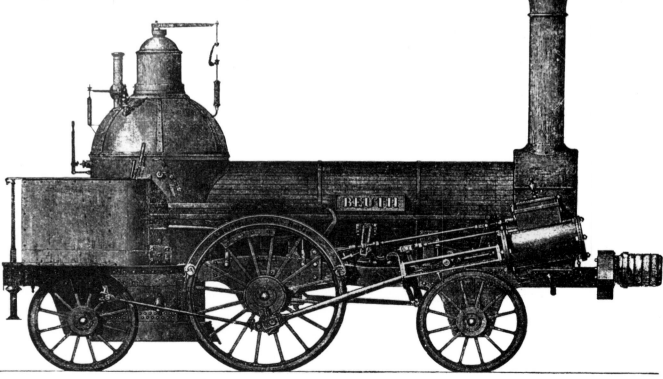

148. The "Beuth", 2–2–2 locomotive of the Berlin-and-Anhalt Railroad, August Borsig, 1844.

Ramsbottom was appointed sole locomotive super-intendent. The board was pursuing a policy of very strict economy, and he was instructed to build an engine which was as cheap to construct and maintain as possible. The desire for simplicity shows itself in his first express engine of the "Problem" class, often called the "Lady of the Lake" class after the name of the engine exhibited in London in 1862 (Ill. 151). It is a simplified version of the Allan-Crewe type, with the omission of the external blind frame. Between late 1859 and mid-1865, sixty engines in the "Problem" class were acquired. The "Watt" became especially famous. Pulling a special train, conveying the United States Government's answer to an English protest, it covered the 130-mile stretch between Holyhead and Stafford at an average speed of 54½ m.p.h. despite a strong headwind. This distance could be run non-stop because of the water troughs, invented by Ramsbottom, which had recently been laid between the rails; as a result the tender was refilled en route while travelling at full speed. In Webb's time even the "Problem" had to serve as a pilot engine. The last was not scrapped until 1907.

The other variation, quite remarkable in many ways, is due to Joseph Beattie. Since Joseph Locke had been involved in the building of the London-and-South Western Railway, Allan-Crewe-type engines had been used on it since 1843. This was the time when rising price of coke forced a change to coal. The latter produces more smoke than coke in burning and so there were attempts to counter this disadvantage with every possible design of the combustion chamber. Beattie joined in and produced a firebox, which was sub-divided into several parts to obtain mixing of the heating gases with the air for burning, and after-burning of the gases. This necessitated a firebox, unrestricted by any axle boxes, so that Beattie used outside bearings for the rear axle as on the Allan-Crewe engines. In contrast, the front axle was mounted normally in the inside frame and fixed to a plate spring. Outside a small steadying bearing was pro-vided. This was held only by a much weaker spring which was underhung, taking its load from the lower slide bars of the crosshead. This peculiar method used on Beattie's "Canute" class lasted until 1875 as a characteristic feature on all LSWR locomotives with outside cylinders (Ill. 153). The load on the driving axle could be varied by the driver according to the requirement, by means of the worm gear visible below the connecting rod.

The large number of water tubes which divided the

149. Timetable of the Berlin-and-Anhalt Railroad for Summer 1842.

Berlin-Anhaltische Eisenbahn.

Fahr-Plan für die Sommer-Monate 1842.

150. The "Oker",
Cologne-Minden Rail-
road, 1869.

151. The "Lady of the
Lake" London-and-
North Western Rail-
way, 1862.

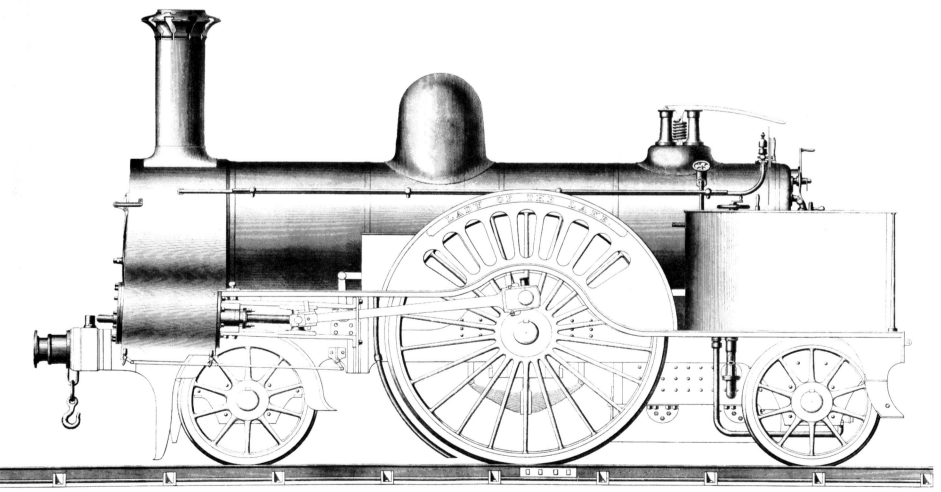

firebox were very susceptible to temperature variations, which often occurred with the piston pumps then used to force feed water into the boiler. After several initial tests, Beattie developed a feed water heating unit to avoid this problem. It was more effective than the method of introducing part of the exhaust gas into the tender, as Heinrich Kirchweger of the Hanover Railroad had done. The heating occurred in two stages. First, the feed water was pumped cold into a long cylindrical vessel called the condenser, and mounted vertically in front of the chimney, receiving part of the exhaust steam. This mixed with the water sprayed in and imparted to it its condensation heat. If the boiler was not being fed, the warm water was passed into the tender. If feeding was required, the return flow was sealed off to some extent by a tap operated by the driver. A second pump, this time a hot-water pump, conveyed the water flowing past the tap via another pipe into a drum. This was mounted inside the smokebox above the blast pipe and several fire tubes ran through it. Exhaust steam was routed through here to give the second pre-heat, running on its way to the condenser. Beattie succeeded with this unit in raising temperatures above boiling point. Fuel savings of up to 20 per cent were achieved on test runs. The Beattie

152. 2–2–2 locomotive of the Paris-and-Lyons Railroad, No. 124, Alexis Barrault, 1847.

153. The "Canute", London-and-South Western Railway, Joseph Beattie.

154. 2–4–0 locomotive No. 910, Class 910 of the North Eastern Railway, Edward Fletcher, 1875.

* On the LNWR (London-and-North Western Railway).

feed water heating apparatus, subsequently simplified, was used by the LSWR for more than twenty years. It may be regarded as the predecessor of modern units of this type.

7.7 Front or Rear Carrying Axles

It can be said that the main European railroad networks had grown together to form a comprehensive network by the middle of the 1850s. The lines served by through-trains, mostly designated "express" or "courier" trains became longer and longer, and the result was that people spent more hours in railroad cars. This meant that greater comfort had to be

offered, in turn entailing heavier cars. Single coupled locomotives, like the English "Single" and the North German "Spinning Wheels" were not able to pull these heavier trains owing to their lack of adhesion. The previous sections have already described in several instances how various types of 2–4–0 express engines were developed. In general the overhanging firebox, which caused poor running at higher speeds, was abandoned. The firebox was now hung between the rear axles. A front carrying axle was normally retained, giving a 2–4–0 wheel arrangement.

Initially the double frame method of construction remained popular in England, as a further development of the old "Victorieuse" (Ill. 51). This was pursued above all by Kirtley on the Midland Railway and also lasted a long time on the Great Western. In addition the "Jenny Lind" also spread, as the outer bearing on the carrying axle gave a wider spring distance, which made for less side rolling. As an example, we are illustrating one of the heaviest and most powerful 2–4–0s of its time (Ill. 154). It belonged to Class 901, which was introduced in 1872 on the North Eastern by Edward Fletcher, and by 1882 fifty-five engines of this class had been built. Details and dimensions changed with the various batches. The introduction of the 901s meant a decrease in the journey time of the "Flying Scotsman" between London (King's Cross Station) and Edinburgh to nine hours, whereas the West Coast route required ten hours, twenty-five minutes and the newly opened Midland route ten hours, forty-five minutes. The North Eastern engines ran right through between York and the Scottish capital, although the section from Berwick onwards belonged to the North British Railway. The average speeds of the "Flying Scotsman" in 1876 between York and Newcastle (a distance of 80¼ miles) were 47.8 m.p.h., between Newcastle and Berwick (66½ miles) 47 m.p.h. and from there to Edinburgh (57½ miles) 45 m.p.h. When the famous race to Scotland took place in 1888, an engine of this type reached an average speed of 50½ m.p.h. pulling eight cars between York and Newcastle. The No. 910, fitted with a new boiler, as were all her sister engines, is preserved at the York Railway Museum.

Despite earlier English versions, the last big English family of 2–4–0 locomotives can be regarded as a further development of the "Bloomer". The first of this type to emerge* was the "Samson" class, comprising ninety engines from Ramsbottom in 1863 with 6 ft. coupled wheels, followed from 1866 by ninety-

155. The "Charles Dickens", "Precedent" class, on the London-and-North Western Railroad, 1874-1882.

six "Newton" class engines with a coupled wheel diameter of 6 ft. 8 in. The engines then built by his successor Webb with some modifications were typical examples of the latter's policy of building as simple and small a type as possible. These were the "Precedent" (seventy engines, 1874–82 [Ill. 155]), the "Precursor" (forty engines, 1874–79) and the "Improved Precedent" (ninety-six engines, 1887–94). In the black colour with white stripes introduced by Francis Webb, these comparatively small, often overloaded engines which spurted fire and flame managed the complete express service on the LNWR without any serious competition from the Webb type of compound locomotive which will be discussed later. The "Precursor" was intended for the Crewe to Carlisle run, where there were steeper inclines. It therefore had smaller coupled wheels of 5 ft. 6 in. The "Charles Dickens" (Ill. 155) became famous because it ran more than two million miles during its working life.

The further development of Borsig's "Spinning Wheels" made up a large family. These engines were also to be found outside North Germany. The stages of development already described apply to its boiler: we can regard the locomotive of the Cologne-and-Minden Railroad, known as the "Flieger"*, remarkable in several respects, as the final stage of this type (Ill. 156). A deep grate was provided for the Ruhr coal used by the railroad, which was as good as English coal, and, after tests, the best grate area was found to be 16.9 sq. ft. The unusually long wheelbase, which seemed admissible as there were no sharp curves on the main line, despite the front axle

without sideplay, resulted from the considerable length of 14 ft. 5½ in. of the boiler tubes. In fact there were no troubles in service. These thirty engines, twelve supplied by Borsig in 1871/72 and eighteen by Hartmann in 1873/74, replaced the earlier 2–2–2 "Racers". They pulled the Berlin to Cologne expresses which consisted of seven to ten four- or six-wheeled carriages, making the occasional non-stop run along 30 miles between Dortmund and Oberhausen in forty minutes, which was the equivalent of 45½ m.p.h.

This long wheelbase could not be used everywhere. As a result, the grate was sloped over the rear coupled axle. The first 2–4–0 locomotives of this type appeared, thirty-four in number delivered by Borsig, in 1863–68 on the Bergisch-and-Brandenburg Railroad**. From the outset they were destined for express trains. Almost all North German railroads, including Saxony, took on these 2–4–0s with outside cylinders and supported firebox, and they were built in considerable numbers until the 1870s. They were often to be found abroad. They were also the basis of the Prussian so-called "Standard" locomotive. Attempts to standardize the various types, which were very similar to one another, were begun in 1871. But they had no success until the engineers of each individual railroad company met in 1874/75 at the invitation of the Prussian Minister for Public Works. After eight days of talks, the type of engine to be acquired in future was agreed in essence to such an extent that the directorate of the Berlin Region was able to finalize plans for two basic types, a 2–4–0 locomotive for local passenger service and 0–6–0 freight locomotive with either inside or outside Allan gear. Such standardization

* "Flier".

** Bergisch-Märkische Bahn.

156. The "Metz", 2–4–0 locomotive of the Cologne-Minden Railroad, 1871–74.

157. 2–4–0 standard locomotive of the Prussian State Railroads, Type S1.

of 6 ft. 6 in. diameter. This type of construction, called the S1 (Ill. 157), saw a total of 261 engines built by 1895, seventy-five of which were for the Magdeburg Region company alone. For 2–4–0 locomotives they proved very powerful. On the 159-mile stretch of line between Berlin and Hanover via Stendal, they worked the expresses at a running speed of 53 m.p.h. in three hours, fifty minutes, the average with stops being 42 m.p.h. The weight of the train was about 172 tons, easily twice that pulled by the locomotives on the Berlin-and-Potsdam Railroad described in section 7.4. The Prussian S1 saw the final development of the simple 2–4–0 engine in Europe.

The 2–4–0 wheel arrangement seems perfectly logical to us today since the concept of small front carrying wheels ensured a safe passage along the track. Nevertheless at various times, a serious rival emerged with the reverse arrangement. In section 4.4, we considered this as it affected the freight train engine. For a rear carrying axle had many advantages: a lower rear axle gave designers a free hand in arranging the firebox. As long as the firebox between the frames was retained on the 2–4–0s, it was not a simple matter of distributing the load with the main weight of the locomotive resting on the two coupled axles, where the adhesion was most needed. Various efforts were made to overcome this difficulty. The dome was placed at the rear boiler end and the high fireboxes with four-sided or semi-circular crown, which were retained for such a long time in Germany, also served the purpose of concentrating more weight at the rear. In England and elsewhere heavy ballast weights were often built in to the rear draw-bar casing. In contrast, in the 0–4–2 arrangement, the main weight naturally rested as required on both rear axles, with the additional advantage that the front axle was not overloaded, as often happened.

For these reasons Sharp devoted special attention to 0–4–2 engines. They were used very widely, especially in Scotland and the North of England, but initially as freight locomotives only. It was not long, however, before their use in mixed traffic was appreciated, especially where simple operating conditions applied. This was the case in France where twenty engines of the Sharp type were built by Ernest-Alexandre Gouin in 1851 for the Paris-and-Lyons Railroad on the basis of Sharp's original plans (later PLM Series 301–303 and 351–367). They became known as the "Rhône" type. Although their coupled wheel diameter was 5 ft. 11 in., they were intended for mixed traffic. This type, but with smaller wheels, spread quickly to other

was nothing new in itself but was normally restricted to a single railroad; on this occasion it was a much further-reaching standardization, involving several railroad companies.

The first "Standard" locomotives entered service at the start of September 1877. Their construction was altered in the so-called extended Standard types. The famous Series P3 of the Prussian State Railroads, which eventually comprised 695 engines built between 1884 and 1897, was one of these. There was no real improvement on the 2–4–0 engines used by the private and public railroads which had amalgamated into this company. The P3 was not very suitable for express trains on the level track with its driving wheels of a mere 5 ft. 9 in. diameter. Thus the Magdeburg Region company worked out a new design based on the P3 for a more powerful 2–4–0 with larger coupled wheels

railroads in France and elsewhere where French influence was felt. Only the Nord line was cool at first; initially it preferred, as we will see, four-coupled Engerth locomotives, then abandoned these and replaced them with the "Rhône" type. Between 1867 and 1881 it acquired the largest number of any French railroad, 180 engines (Ill. 159). Apart from the very fastest trains, which were reserved for Cramptons, they were used on passenger and express freight trains, including the fish trains which ran to Paris virtually at express train speeds bringing daily the freshly caught fish and shellfish.

The final improvement towards the express engine came about with the "Gladstone" class (Ill 161), created by William Stroudley, entering service on the London, Brighton and South Coast Railway in 1882. Seldom has as much been written about an engine as about the "Gladstone", and it was indeed a quite extraordinary express engine. In 1878-80, six similar locomotives had preceded it, with 6 ft. 6 in. coupled

wheels, but these were still designated as mixed traffic locomotives. It was not until the "Gladstone" that William Stroudley exploited all the possibilities of the 0–4–2 arrangement to offer an engine rivalling the 4–4–0 types which were then growing popular. By 1891, thirty-six in all of these engines were built, and ten did not enter service until after Stroudley's death. Refitted with new boilers of the same dimensions, most of them survived until the end of the 1920s and early 1930s. No. 214 was acquired by the Stephenson Locomotive Society in 1927 and given to the York Railway Museum. Despite their large wheels at the front, they never came off the rails. But when the Nord Railroad in France built a similar express locomotive as an experiment in 1886, its running was so dangerous that it was modified to a 4–2–2 engine (see section 11.1.3).

Of course, the 0–4–2 arrangement was also fitted with outside cylinders which had to overhang at the front. This type, which became known as the "Shearing

158. Scene of the arrival of a train at the North Station in Vienna, painting by Karl Karger, 1875.

133

159. No. 468 of the French Nord Railroad (Series 2.451-2.486), "Rhône" type.

160. Train of the French Nord Railroad with engine No. 2.619.

Machine" because of the reciprocating action of the motion, became quite important in North Germany where the flat terrain meant that only two-coupled axles remained adequate for a long time. The Prussian Eastern Railroad made a start in 1856 with engines with driving wheels of only 4 ft. 4½ in. The engine of the Berlin-and-Hamburg Railroad of 1865, built by Borsig (Ill. 162), was known as an "Intermediate

161. The "Gladstone", London, Brighton and South Coast Railway, 1882.

162. 0–4–2 locomotive of the Berlin-Hamburg Railroad, 1865.

Train Locomotive". Whereas maximum speed for the earlier 2–4–0s with overhanging firebox had been restricted to 28–31 m.p.h., this one was allowed to travel at 47 m.p.h.

There were only two unsuccessful attempts to develop further the 0–4–2 with outside cylinders into a fast express engine. At the Vienna International Exhibition in 1873, the Esslingen works put on show one of the twelve locomotives with 6 ft. 3 in. driving wheels, intended for the Galician Ludwig Railroad*, but these tended to come off the rails in icy conditions. Very similar, but with smaller driving wheels of 5 ft. 7½ in.

were the four engines supplied by Richard Hartmann in 1885 to the Spanish Almansa-Valencia-Tarragona Railroad, which were in service with the Norte as Nos. 300–303. At some time they were rebuilt by the latter as 2–4–2 engines, an indication that their running qualities were not considered satisfactory.

We should like to mention here briefly the "Coutances" which are also part of this family, with a driving wheel of 5 ft. 6 in., acquired by the Ouest Railroad between 1855 and 1859. In Zola's novel *La Bête humaine*, the engine-driver who goes mad is driving an engine of this type.

*Galizische Ludwigs-Bahn.

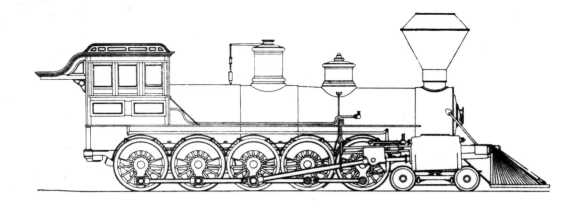

8. "WESTWARD HO!"

"El Gobernador"
(see Ill. 174).

8.1. The Four-Wheel Truck is Perfected

Once railroads in North America had penetrated inland, higher speeds were necessary to cover the distances in reasonable times. As in Europe, it was observed that on the straight, the short trucks oscillated and caused the engine to run unsteadily. This was attributed initially to the use of inclined cylinders. In order to locate these horizontally with the normal inside frame, with no overhang at the front, the distances between the two truck axles had to be increased. This raised the problem of how to spread the weight evenly over four wheels widely separated from one another. It was clear that the same procedure had to be adopted as for the coupled axles. Thomas Rogers was probably the first to find a solution in 1850, with his "swan-neck balance lever", so-called because of its shape. It was made initially with a very curved shape as can be seen on this locomotive built by Danforth, Cooke & Co for the Delaware, Lackawanna and Western Railroad in 1857 (Ill. 164). These swan-necks were paired and carried between them a long leaf-spring. Thus in principle the American truck was born.

136

Another improvement, equally typical of North America, was the replacement of the old Bury firebox by the "wagon top" boiler. This is characterized by a firebox greatly increased in height and diameter, connected to the round boiler with a tapered ring. The intention was to increase the steam space where the steam was generated most strongly, as in the case of Stephenson's Gothic dome and the Borsig tall, round-top firebox in Europe. The illustration reveals other typical American features. Firstly there is the cast-iron smokebox saddle, with the cylinders attached to its sides, although normally the two cylinder castings themselves formed the saddle. This variation was occasioned in this engine by the unusually large gauge of 5 ft. The side sheets of the driver's cab do not come down to the upper edge of the frame, as in Europe, but remain above the wheels, with benches for the crew attached at the side. The comparison with the Austrian "Rittinger" coming some twenty years later (Ill. 212) shows how limited and uncom-

fortable drivers' cabs in Europe were. In the smokebox, the blastpipe can be seen, with several jets mounted on it called "petticoats". These jets spread the effect of the blastpipe evenly over the boiler tubes. We shall see later how they occurred more recently in Europe.

Rogers also introduced the inside Stephenson link motion, with the outside valves actuated by rocking levers ("rockers"). These are all structural features of the American locomotive until the turn of the century. The elaborate, rich ornamentation, in fashion for a time, which gave such a bizarre appearance to these "Prairie Steamships" as people liked to call them, disappeared during the Civil War which broke out in 1861, and American locomotives took on their purely functional appearance typified by the example supplied by Rogers in the mid-1880s to the New York, West Shore and Buffalo Railroad (Ill. 166). Details of a trial run made by this engine have survived, the test train consisting of three truck cars weighing

163. The "Sagua La Grande", typical American 4-4-0 engine with rich decoration, 1856.

137

164. 4–4–0 broad-gauge engine of the Delaware, Lackawanna and Western Railroad, 1857.

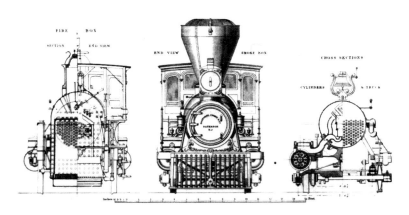

anthracite in locomotives, and these had not been abandoned. From 1848 Ross Winans continued such attempts, and made a peculiar eight-coupled locomotive for the Baltimore-and-Ohio Railroad, which became known as the "Camel Back". The firebox was long and narrow and its semi-circular crown was steeply inclined at the rear. As the front part of the grate could not be reached with a shovel, there was another fire door at the top with a hopper. The driver's cab was set at the back of the boiler. James Milholland introduced a similar arrangement on the Philadelphia-and-Reading Railroad in 1859, and this found its final form in the version named after his successor, John E. Wootten, from 1866 on. He dared to mount the boiler so high that the firebox could be spread out above the wheels.

The railroad in question built a locomotive with the Wootten firebox in its own works in 1880 (Ill. 165). There remained, nevertheless, a prejudice against a high boiler, and thus the grate was mounted at almost the same height as the lowest boiler tubes. To prevent the tubes being obstructed there was a bank of refractory bricks at the front of the grate, followed by a combustion chamber. The fireman stood on the tender and fed the grate through two fire doors.

Apart from these special types, the "American" type continued to develop steadily. As track laying gradually improved, higher axle loadings were allowed. The boiler could be enlarged, but as its diameter increased, it could no longer be fitted between the cou-

69¾ tons running between Buffalo and Frankfurt on July 9, 1885. Between Buffalo and Genesee Junction an average of 65½ m.p.h. was achieved. Travelling on to Newark (94 miles from Buffalo) the train arrived in ninety-seven minutes, which gives an average speed for the whole run from Buffalo of 58 m.p.h., or, not counting two stops en route totalling nine minutes, a running average of 64½ m.p.h. Of course these speeds were not as a normal rule achieved. The table shows 30 m.p.h., for example, for a load of 710 tons up an incline of 1 in 264, one of 485 tons up 1 in 132 and one of 360 tons up 1 in 88.

In section 5.7 on the "Monster", an account was given of the attempts to burn cheap, small size

165. 4–4–0 locomotive of the Philadelphia-and-Reading Railroad, 1880.

166. 4–4–0 locomotive of the New York, West Shore and Buffalo Railroad, c. 1855.

167. Record-holding locomotive No. 999 with the "Empire Express", New York Central Railroad, 1893.

168. 4-4-0 locomotive, Class P, of the Pennsylvania Railroad, 1880.

169. 4-4-0 locomotive, class L (later D 16 a) of the Pennsylvania Railroad, 1895-1902.

pled wheels, and had to be pitched higher. As a result fears over a high centre of gravity were gradually appeased.

The locomotives of the Pennsylvania Railroad illustrate this change (Ills. 168 and 169). The first shows the typical old method of construction in Class P of 1880, with the centre line of the boiler 7 ft. 2½ in. high. In an unusual fashion for American engines, the firebox crown was flat, as in the Belpaire, the type which became normally used on the Pennsylvania railroad. These engines ran for the most part around Philadelphia and Pittsburgh, where the gradients were steep, so the driving wheel diameter was 5 ft. 8 in.

The second illustration shows the final stage in the development of the "American" type. This is Class L (later D 16 a) which was ordered between 1895 and 1902. This engine was partly intended to pull the luxury train "Pennsylvania Limited" which normally consisted of seven Pullman cars weighing 300 tons in all. The centre line of the boiler was now 8 ft. 10½ in. high. The earlier short tapered boiler shell ring was superseded by a more extended taper along the whole boiler barrel. The axle loading was 21.5 tons.

In discussing the "American" type, mention must be made of the famous record-breaking engine No. 999. There was intense competition between the New York Central and the Pennsylvania Railroads. When the

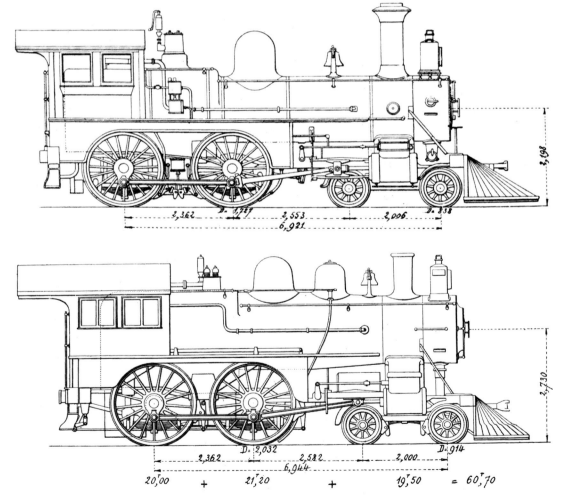

139

170. 2–6–0 locomotive, "Mogul"-type, Louisville-and-Nashville Railroad.

11,218 simple expansion locomotives and a further sixty-five compound engines in service. According to Bruce (1952), about 25,600 were built between 1831 and 1950, only about nine hundred of them between 1901 and 1950.

8.2 The Bissel "Safety" or "Pony" Truck

As speeds gradually increased, one fault became apparent: trucks with rigidly fixed central pivots stuck when certain curves were being negotiated, and derailments were thus caused. If lateral play was simply given to the central pivot, the truck ceased to guide the train into the curve. Levi Bissel discovered a solution which was to have a far-reaching influence on construction methods for axles built to adjust radially to curvature in the track. He built the truck frame like a radius bar which could swing on a centre pin behind the truck axles. The central pivot was replaced by a cast-iron plate loaded centrally through a pair of "V"-shaped inclined planes on each side. They in turn were mounted on a cross-member on which rested the balance beams of the leaf springs. Every time the radius bar moved sideways, the lower plans fastened to the truck frame were pushed up onto the upper plans attached to the locomotive frame, and thus effected the counter-force needed to centre the truck frame back into position again. With the aid of a small demonstration model, Bissel succeeded in convincing the Central Railroad of New Jersey to fit a 4–4–0 locomotive, the "Lebanon", with his arrangement. The test runs showed that, even at high

World Exhibition was held in Chicago in 1893, the Pennsylvania Railroad decided to operate a special express service, to be called the "Empire Express". William Buchanan, chief mechanical superintendent since 1881, designed an engine suitable for this purpose, which was deliberately given the eye-catching designation of No. 999. It was similar to the Class L of the Pennsylvania already described, with the exception of the shape of the firebox. At a demonstration run in Syracuse on May 10, 1893, it is alleged to have pulled a train along a level straight track west of Batavia at a speed held over a brief moment of 112½ m.p.h. It is not known who recorded this speed, nor how it was recorded. Anyone who has ever tried to measure the speed of a fast-moving train by using the track joints or even the mile posts, must know how inaccurate such measurements are. Other sources give the speed as 100 m.p.h. It is evident how the 4–4–0 engines spread throughout America from the fact that when they were all in the process of being replaced, on December 31, 1904, there were still

171. 2–8–0 locomotive, Class R (later H3) of the Pennsylvania Railroad, 1885.

speeds, the previous oscillatory movement along the straight had been cured and that the engine was guided smoothly and safely into the curves. Bissel was then granted a patent on August 4, 1857, his previous application having been refused. After much use, the "V"-shaped planes tended to stick, so that the truck shifting was jerky. In 1862, Alba F. Smith replaced them by a swing bolster, whose swing links lifted the front of the locomotive when the radius bar swung out, thereby putting an increased load on the wheels running along the outside rail and achieving the force necessary to return the truck to its normal position. This swing bolster also allowed normal trucks with central pivots to be given a controlled degree of lateral play. It was used very extensively.

At the suggestion of the Englishman Colburn, who had been publisher of the well-known technical journal *The Engineer* since 1858, Bissel modified his design, originally intended as a replacement for the normal four-wheel truck, into a design with only one carrying axle. This was granted a North American patent on November 2, 1858 and an English patent on December 1, 1858. Initially there was no demand in the United States for the four-wheeled Bissel truck, the engines in use being mainly 4–4–0s. It was only in hilly regions that small-wheeled 4–6–0s were used,

and eight-coupled ones were frequent on coal lines. But in the course of the 1860s, the weight of freight trains increased to such an extent that the adhesion from two-coupled axles was no longer sufficient. To use one more coupled axle rather than a second truck axle, the Bissel arrangement came into its own, following a further improvement discovered by William S. Hudson of the Rogers Locomotive Works, which enabled a good distribution of the load between the front running axle and the first coupled axle. His system was to place a heavy balance-beam lengthwise along the centre of the locomotive, resting on the cradle of the radius link at the front and attached to a transverse equalizer between the main springs of the front coupled axle at the rear. This equalizer was pivoted on a main frame cross-member, so that the weight of the front section of the locomotive was spread over the whole suspension system. This was such a good arrangement even with the two-wheel truck that from then on this "pony truck" became a special feature of the American freight locomotive.

The 2–6–0 wheel arrangement, known as the "Mogul", spread so rapidly and extensively throughout the Sixties that it became, with the 4–4–0 arrangement, the second standard American type. In the 1880s, Rogers supplied typical "Moguls" as standard factory items, and they

172. The "McKay", 4–4–0 engine, Little Rock-and-Fort Smith Railroad.

141

173. The "Champion", 4–8–0 locomotive of the Lehigh Valley Railroad, 1882.

174. "El Gobernador", 4–10–0 locomotive of the Central Pacific Railroad, 1884.

fangled Bissel truck onto an eight-coupled wheel arrangement, but close cooperation between Alexander Mitchell, chief engineer on the railroad, and the Baldwin Works resulted in such a successful type that the "Consolidation" became the third standard type in North America. It dominated practically all freight traffic until the First World War; numerically, it beat all the others, with 22,900 examples built. Of course, the first "Consolidations" had the standard structural features of their time. It is known that the engines acquired by the Lehigh Valley Railroad in 1873 were capable of pulling a train of thirty-five laden coal trucks weighing 330 tons at a speed of 9 m.p.h. up a 12-mile incline of 1 in 55.5 (just under 2%). These "Consolidations" were later built with growing dimensions. Class R (later H 3) (Ill. 171), built at the Pennsylvania Railroad's own works at Altoona in 1885, had a much higher pitched boiler as a sign of things to come. As an experiment, some of these engines were fitted with the Belpaire firebox, and this was then adopted as standard. Between 1885 and 1890 alone, 111 engines of this type entered service. The last "Consolidation" on the Pennsylvania, Class H 10 of 1915, had a weight in working order of 112¼ tons, as we shall see later.

went to the Louisville-and-Nashville Railroad (Ill. 170) among others. He offered them in various sizes, with cylinder and coupled wheels dimensions from 16 × 24 in./4ft. to 20 × 24 in./4 ft. 6 in., and with total weights from 31¾ tons to 44½ tons. They had the standard structural features of their time. The "Mogul" was often used in mixed traffic, and was exported all over the world with Bissel trucks, coming to Europe as well (England, Finland, Spain). Between 1860 and 1910, about eleven thousand engines of this type were built in the United States.

Slowly at first, but from 1880 on, when train weights were steadily increasing, the 2–8–0 locomotive began to replace the 2–6–0 in North America. It first appeared on the Lehigh and Mahoning Railroad in 1866, at a time when the company was in financial difficulties and had been recently consolidated with the name the Lehigh Valley Railroad — which explains why this 2–8–0 engine was called "Consolidation". It was a move of some daring to mount the new

8.3 The First "Heavyweights"

There were two reasons why, in the early 1880s, particularly large locomotives began to be built. One was that coal traffic on the lines in the Alleghenies increased to such an extent that ever larger locomotives had to be used. The other was that the Pacific Railroads, which had meanwhile started oper-

ating, needed very powerful locomotives to act as bankers up the steep inclines of the Rocky Mountains. As already stated, 2–8–0 locomotives had been introduced on the Lehigh Valley Railroad, but they had been preceded here by a 4–8–0. Philip Hofecker, responsible for the engines of the Southern Beaver Meadow section of this line, had been in charge of this. The "Champion" (Ill. 173), as it was called, was built in the railroad's own works in 1882 and stands as the first 4–8–0 engine — despite the fact that Ross Winans had supplied the Baltimore-and-Ohio Railroad with a tank engine with the same wheel arrangement in 1854, for, in fact, this one hardly ran at all. The dimensions of the "Champion" were only slightly greater than those with the 2–8–0 arrangement.

That year the rivalry for the biggest engine in the world began, when the Central Pacific Railroad had an engine built at its Sacramento works to the design of its chief engineer Andrew J. Stevens, which was a 4–8–0 nearly 10 tons heavier than the "Champion". Two years later, in 1886, the Central Pacific outdid this, achieving a new record with the famous 4–10–0 engine given the Spanish name of "El Gobernador".

This was also built at the Sacramento works and, like its predecessor, was intended for banking service on the mountainous stretches in the Sierra Nevada, where there were long gradients of 1 in 44. A second fireman was needed to keep it going. It proved too cumbersome around the curves, and as a result was rebuilt.

The record set by "El Gobernador" (Ill. 174) did not last long. That same year, two engines of the North Pacific Railroad, 2–10–0s Nos. 500-501, beat it. In 1898 it was the turn of the Great Northern Railroad to set a new world record with its 4–8–0 engine, No. 100. This locomotive was designed to pull 500 tons up an incline of 1 in 44. Because of its size, it was aptly called "Mastodont", and this became the common name for the 4–8–0 wheel arrangement. In the United States, the 4–8–0 remained simply a freight engine. It offered hardly more advantages than the 2–8–0, and as a result only six hundred were built.

Two other "Heavyweights" of these times should be mentioned. Firstly, the world's first 0–12–0 (Ill. 177), built by James Milholland in the Reading works of the Philadelphia-and-Reading Railroad, to act as a

143

banker for the coal trains over the watershed between Schuylkill and Delaware. The firebox was in the shape of the "Camel Backs" already mentioned. To save weight, no coal was accommodated. The grate was refuelled at either end of the short incline. Since this engine was very hard on the track, and had such an enormous draw-bar pull that the car couplings broke, it was modified in 1870.

The second remarkable locomotive was the first 4–6–2 engine in the world. The reason for this wheel arrangement was the use of a double corrugated flue firebox like a ship's boiler, the weight of which was taken by the axle inserted underneath (Ill. 139). The diameter of the corrugated tubes was only 3 ft. 2½ in. As a result, only a very small grate could be mounted inside them and two corrugated flues had to be located next to each other. A peculiar, very intricate valve gear was devised to keep the exhaust always fully open. Neither the corrugated flue firebox nor this gear proved satisfactory, so this engine did not have a very long life. But this "Duplex" has a place worth mentioning in the history of the locomotive as a predecessor of the later "Pacific" with its wide projecting firebox.

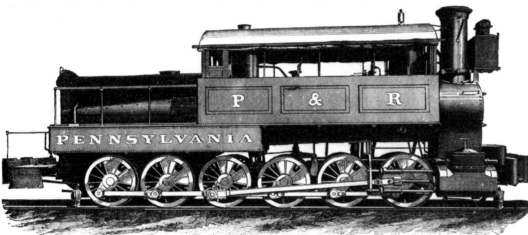

176. A train of the Union Pacific Railroad runs into a herd of buffalos.

177. First twelve-coupled locomotive in the world on the Philadelphia-and-Reading Railroad, 1863.

178. The "Duplex", first 4–6–2 locomotive in the world No. 444 of the Pennsylvania Railroad.

144

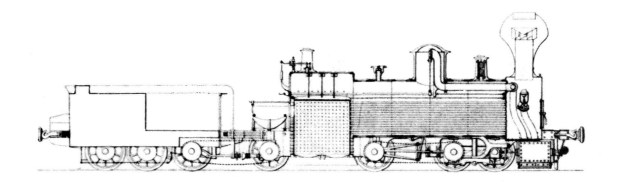

9. VICTORY OVER THE MOUNTAINS

9.1   The Semmering Contest

The connection between Vienna, the capital, and Trieste, then the only Austrian port, and with the upper Italian provinces which were then still part of the Empire, was of vital importance. But the Alps lay between them, and it seemed impossible to cross them by rail. Nevertheless, under the leadership of Karl, Count of Ghega, who had made a thorough study of railroads in America, a start was made on the construction of a railroad, despite the fact that, as in the case of the Liverpool-and-Manchester, it was not yet known how it was to be operated. Acting on a suggestion by Karl von Etzel in the Stuttgart *Eisenbahnzeitung (Railroad Magazine)*, the Austrian Administration decided to organize a contest for suitable locomotives to operate on the Semmering line. The conditions which the locomotives, "preferably for freight traffic", had to fulfill were set out in the rules of the competition, and were essentially as follows:

Under normal weather conditions they had to be able to pull 2,500 *zentners* (125 tons) minimum exclusive of tender as a normal load around the sharpest curves existing on a gradient of 1 in 40 (2.5%). A minimum speed of 7 m.p.h. had to be achieved for a minimum distance of 4.7 miles. The boiler pressure had to be less than 97 lb. sq. in. The wheel loading

The "Bavaria" (see Ill. 179).

145

179. The "Bavaria",
built by Josef Anton
Maffei for the
Semmering Contest,
1851.

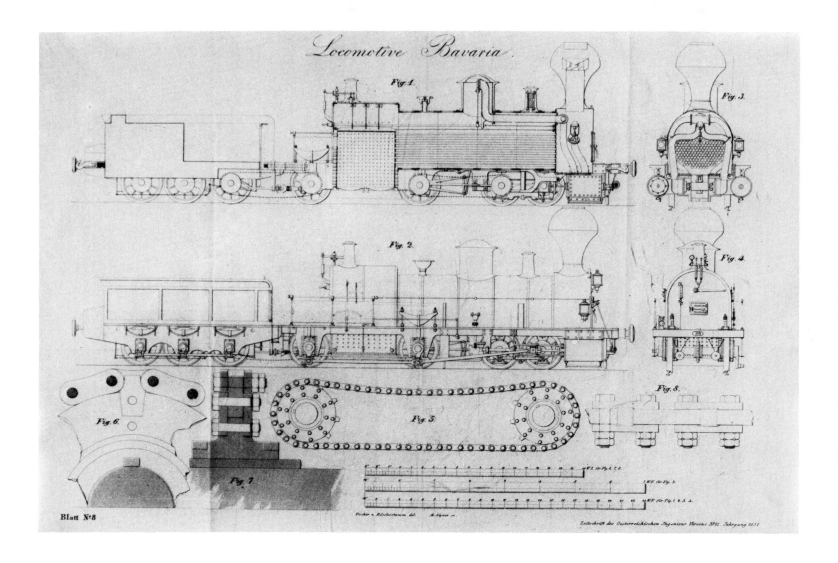

was not to exceed 6¼ tons. The wheel arrangement had to take the curvature of the track into consideration (the sharpest curve had a radius of 200 yards.) The engines had to run satisfactorily downhill at a speed of up to 19 m.p.h. and to be able to stop within 160 yd. on the steepest gradient.

The test runs were to be made by every engine at least twelve times and at most twenty times: twelve of these runs had to count and had to comply with all the conditions. The engine to perform best would receive a prize of 20,000 ducats, the next best would be bought for 10,000 ducats, and the following two would receive 9,000 and 8,000 ducats respectively.

On July 31, 1851, the date set for the arrival of the competing locomotives, the following confronted the adjudicating commission:

the "Bavaria" built by Josef A. Maffei in Munich, works No. 72;

the "Wiener Neustadt" built by W. Günther in Neustadt/Vienna, works No. 73;

the "Seraing" built by John Cockerill in Seraing, works No. 200;

the "Vindobona", built under Haswell's direction at the Vienna and Gloggnitz Railroad's engine works, works No. 186.

The "Bavaria" (Ill. 179) consisted of two axle groups, each with two axles coupled by rods. The cylinders worked on the two rear axles, which themselves ran on the main frame. The front group formed a sort of swivelling truck with inside frame, whose two coupled axles were driven by the driving axle by means of chains. To use the weight of the tender for increasing the adhesion weight, its three axles, also coupled, were driven by a second chain. The boiler was slightly oval. Besides the Stephenson gear there was another expansion valve, and in the illustration the bevelled wheels of this can be clearly seen under the front buffer beam — they were used to adjust the cut-off.

The "Wiener Neustadt" (Ill. 180) ran on two four-

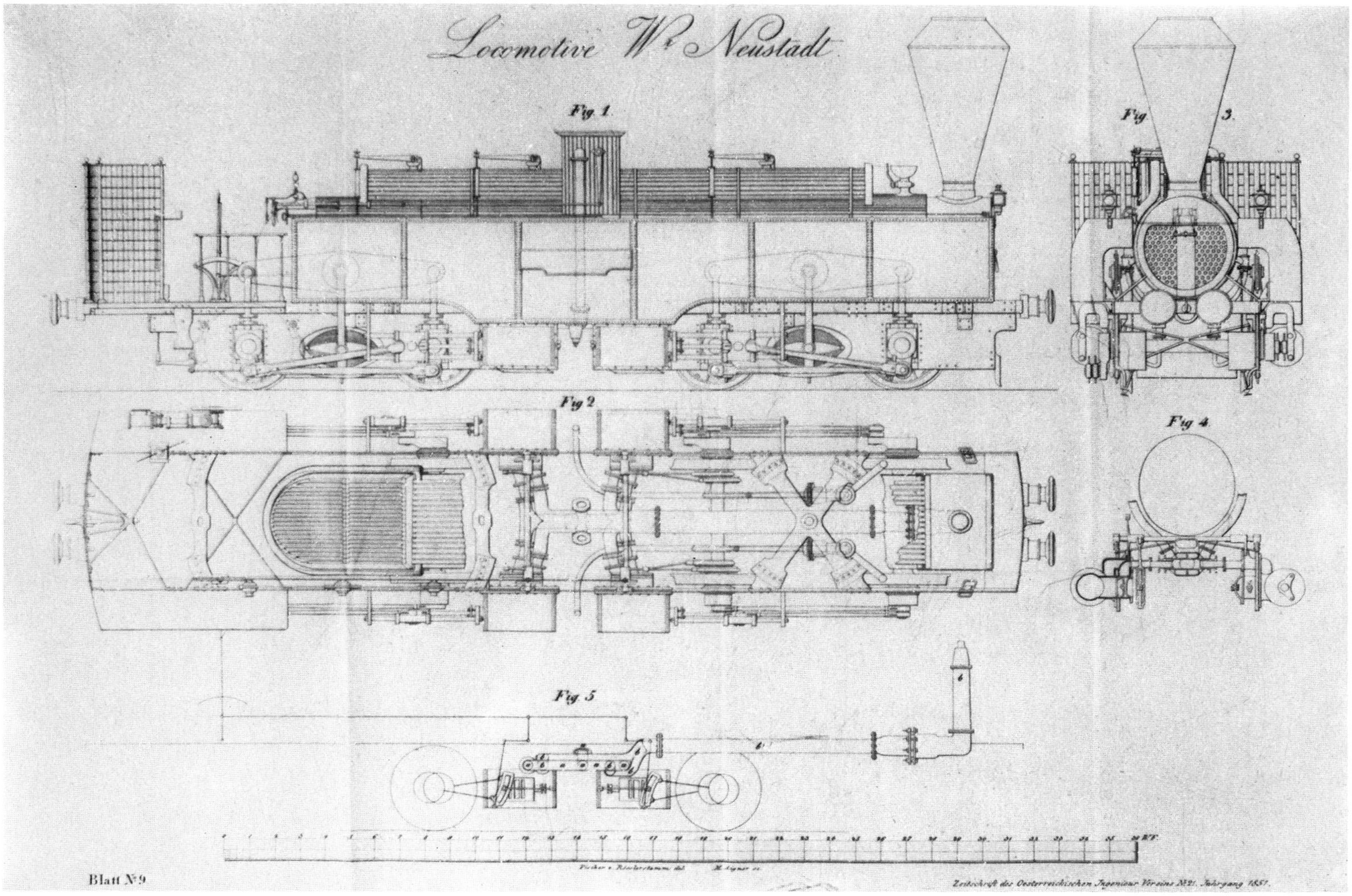

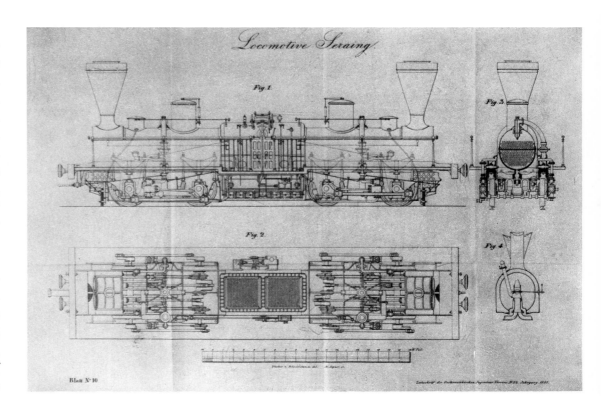

Locomotive W. Neustadt.

Fig 1.

Fig 2

Fig 5

Blatt N.º 9

Fig. 3.

Fig 4

180. The "Wiener Neustadt", built by Wenzel Günther for the Semmering Contest, 1851.

181. The "Seraing", built by John Cockerill for the Semmering Contest, 1851.

wheeled frames, each of which had two inside cylinders. Because of the firebox, it was not possible to mount a fixed pivot on the rear truck as it was on the front one. Instead there were curved guides, which are clearly visible in the illustration. The boiler had a pronounced oval cross-section. There was a long, semi-cylindrical container mounted on it, connected to the steam chamber via two rows of holes. The dome which surmounted this container was, unusually, of a rectangular cross-section. Unlike all the other locomotives, which required tenders, the "Wiener Neustadt" carried its own supplies.

The "Seraing" (Ill. 181) also had two four-wheeled frames, with inside cylinders mounted near the end. To avoid very long boiler tubes, there was a common firebox in the middle and horizontal boiler barrels connected front and rear. It was thus a symmetrical layout. This overall arrangement had been patented in Prussia by Johann Friedrich Laussmann, chief engineer on the Bergisch-and-March Railroad, who

Locomotive Seraing.

Fig 1.

Fig 2.

Fig 3.

Fig 4

Blatt N.º 10

147

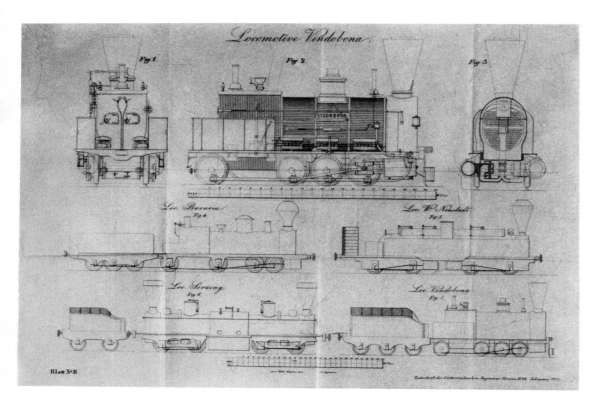

182. The "Vindo-
bona", by the
Locomotive Works of
the Vienna-Gloggnitz
Railroad under
John Haswell built for
the Semmering Contest,
1851.

had sent the plans to John Cockerill to engage his
firm's interest. They were used without Laussmann's
knowledge, and he subsequently protested, but unsuccessfully. The two grates were fed from the side,
and two fire doors were provided for this purpose.
The "Seraing" was the first time that a steam cylinder
was fitted to assist the driver in reversing the valve
gear. Originally the "Seraing" was conceived as a
tank engine, but when fully laden, it turned out to
be heavier than the permitted weight, so the supplies
had to be reduced. However they were then not
enough for the test stretch of track, so a four-wheel
tender was coupled to the engine.

John Haswell had no luck with his "Vindobona"
(Ill. 182). Originally it was six-wheeled, but when
weighed at Payerbach it transpired that the front axle
loading went considerably over the maximum weight
allowed. The engine was then fitted with an additional
pair of coupled wheels. As on the "Seraing", the
boiler consisted of two semi-cylindrical drums, joined
by flat walls with a perforated plate acting as cross-
stiffening. This device, often used at that time,
enabled Haswell to insert no less than 286 boiler
tubes, as against the "Bavaria's" 229, the "Wiener
Neustadt's" 180 and the "Seraing's" twice 170. To
increase the heating surface directly exposed to the
fire, there was a double-walled water-filled chamber

the length of the firebox. This necessitated two grates
and two fire doors. Besides the long, fixed wheelbase,
the "Vindobona" was also remarkable in that, unlike
the other engines, it did not have brake blocks, but
was braked by back pressure in the cylinders. For
this purpose the driver first shut the regulator valve
and put the gear back, so that the cylinders worked
as an air pump. He then closed a shut-off valve
fitted in the exhaust pipe which prevented the exhaust
gas from being sucked out of the smokebox, and
simultaneously he opened a valve which sucked in
fresh air from outside. A valve mounted on the top
of the boiler could control the amount of air sucked
in by the cylinders, and thus regulate the amount of
braking power required. This principle was adopted
later by Nikolaus Riggenbach and it became known
under his name.

The 8-mile stretch of track between Payerbach and
Abfaltersbach was prepared for the trial runs, for it
was here that the basic conditions for the competition
existed. The Commission and the participants agreed
on comparative figures to be worked out to evaluate
the trial run results; these figures were reckoned as
follows: the average speed of all successive runs made
with the same load was taken. This value was then
multiplied by the load hauled and divided by the
average amount of wood burned on each group of
trips. The figures thus reached for each series of runs
with the same load were then classed into the twelve
best runs made, and totalled. The average value thus
reached was the deciding factor.

In this way, the "Bavaria" achieved the highest value
of 485.5, for it pulled the heaviest load at the fastest
average speed and also consumed the least fuel. It
was thus awarded the prize. The "Wiener Neustadt"
was the next best performer with a value of 374.7.
It was recommended that this engine should be purchased provided the owners increased the size of the
fuel store, which had proved too small. The "Seraing"
was actually the only engine to have made all twenty
trips in accordance with the conditions, but its fuel
consumption was higher than the others, due to the
low position of the two regulator valves which meant
that water was drawn in on downhill runs. It was
recommended for purchase with a value achieved of
322.4. The "Vindobona" came out worst from the
contest. It had been noticed at the preliminary test
— when it was being decided whether it could take
part — that the long wheelbase placed great stress on
the track at curves. The "Vindobona" was admitted
to the competition but, for safety's sake, it was

decided that the other engines should make all their test runs first. Since it was impossible to predict whether the stress on the track would prove dangerous, all test runs made by the "Vindobona" were made with the front axle uncoupled. As a result of the loss of adhesion, a great deal of slipping occurred. In addition, it was difficult to keep up steam with the prescribed test loads. Thus it only achieved a value of 272.2 and it was decided not to place an order for it.

In time the three locomotives which the State Railroad did acquire proved unusable in normal service. Nonetheless the Semmering Contest achieved its purpose of gaining valuable experience in the development of locomotive construction for a variety of new engines. We shall see in due course how the "Wiener Neustadt" reappears as a Meyer system at the Vienna World Fair in 1873, and the "Seraing" in 1865 as a Fairlie locomotive.

9.2 Wilhelm Engerth's Tender Supported Locomotive and its Derivatives

When the Semmering Contest locomotives failed, the Trade Ministry President at that time deduced that neither chains nor complicated articulated locomotives should be used. Chains had not succeeded in using the weight of the tender to increase the adhesive weight, but a cogwheel transmission might succeed, meaning that the front tender axle had to be located as close as possible to the rear coupled axle on the locomotive. For this purpose the frame of the tender had to embrace the lower part of the firebox and be converted into a sort of truck. This resulted in another advantage: the coupled axles could be located very close together, thus improving the ability to negotiate curves. The frame of the tender took the rear overhang of the firebox, and better running ensued. Since there was also one more load-bearing axle it was possible to mount a larger boiler than one used with the normal six-coupled engine, without exceeding the permitted axle loading.

The end-result of this reasoning was the tender supported locomotive which became known under the name of Wilhelm Engerth (Ill. 183), who received a patent for it on December 11, 1852. Three spur-wheels mounted in a common frame transmitted the drive to the tender. This frame was fixed firmly to the rear axle of the locomotive at the front, and to the front axle of the tender at the rear. The middle cog-wheel could be moved aside to disengage the drive.

183. The "Kapellen", Engerth tender supported locomotive on the Semmering Line, 1853, model.

149

The bearings of the third spur wheel were on vertical guide cheeks in the frame, to allow the tender to twist independent of the locomotive when negotiating the cant of the curved track. The tender pivot was located exactly above the point where the first pair of gears engaged.

The Esslingen Engine Works and John Cockerill undertook the construction of the first twenty-six Engerth locomotives simultaneously. The first test run took place on November 30, 1853 along the whole 25½ miles of the Semmering track. Compared with a locomotive deriving from a Norris engine, it hauled 68 tons more with a total train weight of 136.4 tons at 8.5 m.p.h. — a speed increase of 1.8 m.p.h. — and the fuel consumption was reduced by a third. This engine proved satisfactory in service on the Semmering track but in time it again became apparent that the cogs were not good enough to stand

the wear and had to be dismantled. From 1857 onwards, a further fifty Engerth locomotives entered service without cog transmission. There were two types, one with 4 ft. 2 in. driving wheels for freight trains, and the other with 4 ft. 6 in. wheels for passenger trains.

The advantages of the Engerth locomotive seemed so evident that they were soon used far and wide: initially as freight locomotives, even on inclines easier than that of the Semmering — not only in Austria but also in Switzerland and, above all, in France, where it was immediately further developed into a passenger engine for level lines. As such it had only two coupled axles, but with six-wheeled tender as against four-wheeled (Ill. 184). For express train service, it was built with inside motion. Kessler supplied the Nord Railroad in France with the first engines of this type in 1856, and these were followed until 1857 by others supplied by Cavé and the La Chapelle works, Series 401–436. They were designed to pull trains of 21-24 cars weighing between 177 and 204 tons up a gradient of 1 in 200 (0.5%) at 28 m.p.h. They were used mainly for the express fish trains between Boulogne and Paris. Initially they were satisfactory in every respect, but a later order gave preference to the simpler 0–4–2 engines described in a later section. How the railroad world was impressed by the Engerth locomotive is shown by the fact that two Swiss railroads, the Sankt-Gallen-and-Appenzell Railroad (forerunner of the United Swiss Railroad) and the Central Railroad cancelled

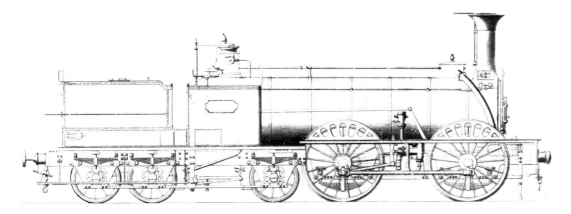

184. Engerth tender supported locomotive of the French Nord Railroad, No. 427, 1856.

185. The "Basel", Engerth tender supported locomotive of the Swiss Central Railroad.

150

orders with Kessler for Norris-type engines, probably
with a 4–4–0 arrangement, and ordered Engerth
engines instead. In Switzerland they were mainly
four-coupled engines with six-wheeled supporting
tenders, like the "Basel" (Ill. 185), for example. This
belongs to a series of twenty-six supplied by Kessler
between 1854 and 1858 to the Central Railroad.
Despite its small driving wheel diameter it was designated a passenger engine and used as such. On the
level it pulled 260 to 360 tons, on an incline of
1 in 100 (1%), 160 to 220 tons, but only 75 tons
on the difficult Hauenstein stretch. In contrast to the
Nord Railroad's French engines, they had outside
cylinders and motion and large water tanks on the
side. The "Basel" was in service until 1905, once a
substitute boiler had been fitted. In all, 110
Engerth locomotives were in service in Switzerland,
mainly on the two railroads mentioned, with just

eight running on the Jura-and-Industrial Railroad.
But in time various disadvantages of the Engerth
locomotive became apparent. They were difficult to
get back on to the rails after a derailment, because
the tender could not be disconnected without a great
deal of difficulty. Their maintenance costs were
greater than those of normal engines, since for all
repair work on the firebox, the tender and engine
had to be separated, involving a major operation. In
addition there was the wear on the pivot and guide
plates on the tender. Once the original idea of using
the weight of the tender to increase adhesion had been
dropped, the Engerth locomotive had lost its *raison
d'être*. The tender was often separated, and sometimes replaced in Switzerland by a two-wheel tender.
Desgranges converted them to eight-coupled engines
on the Semmering line, by replacing the front pair of
tender wheels with a fourth coupled axle.

151

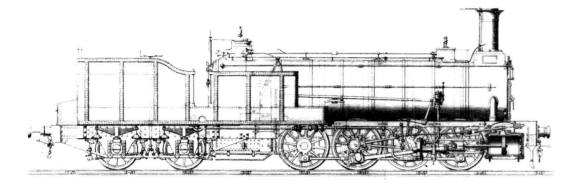

187. Eight-coupled freight locomotive of the French Nord Railroad, Creusot-Engerth system, 1856.

188. Eight-coupled locomotive of the PLM (Paris-Lyon-Mediterranée) Railroad, No. 4086, 1878.

which were hung on the upper edges of the tender frame-plates by double articulated links. The use of fine coal was soon abandoned and only a few engines of this type were used.

By 1854, the old six-coupled engines were no longer adequate to deal with the increasing coal traffic on the Nord Railroad in France. An attempt was made to use the Engerth six-coupled engines of the Semmering variety. But as the cogs had to be dismantled very early on, there remained insufficient adhesion. Thereupon the Schneider Works in Le Creusot designed an eight-coupled engine with overhanging firebox, but provided with a tender which would help to bear the weight of it. The tender frame was extended in the form of two prongs embracing the firebox and resting by means of a cross-frame built from flat irons on the springs of the fourth coupled axle. The cross-shaped braces took the spherical centre pivot, around which the tender swung (Ill. 187). The performance of these locomotives fulfilled all expectations. They pulled forty wagons each holding 10 tons, the equivalent of a gross weight of 450 tons, on the main Nord tracks, which had curves no smaller than 1,000 yards in radius and gradients no steeper than 1 in 200 (0.5%). These engines gave complete satisfaction and, apart from the twenty engines supplied by Le Creusot in 1855, another ten came from Grafenstaden in 1857. In contrast, the Est Railroad, which had placed a simultaneous order for twenty-five engines, often suffered derailments. This resulted in a lively discussion in the technical

Of course, there was no lack of attempts to utilize the advantages of the supporting tender with other methods, which would enable the two components to be separated more easily. The Bavarian State Railroad extended the frame of the tender forward far enough to locate the front axle of the tender just behind the firebox, and supported the locomotive frame on this pair of wheels. But the running qualities did not prove satisfactory so that only the six trial engines were built. The Brunswick Railroad tried to use cheap, fine coal as fuel. For this purpose they included a horizontal combustion grate and a sloping after-burner grate. The result was a long overhanging firebox at the rear. The locomotives built on the Behne-Kool system by Egestorff between 1861 and 1875 had the tender frame extended as far as the firebox, so that the first tender axle was located under it. The weight was spread via a cross-member mounted under the grate, the projecting side ends of

press by the experts, which showed that the track of the Est Railroad, with sharper curvature and less careful maintenance, resulted in constant shifts in the weight borne by the axles. From 1860 on it was decided to separate the locomotive and the tender. Since the firebox had been made as wide as possible within the prongs of the tender frame, the locomotive main frame ended in front of the firebox front wall. Thus a wider endpiece had to be added behind. This bayonet-shaped main frame was retained on the eight-coupled engines built later on, because the rear overhang was thereby lessened. In this way, a special version of the French eight-coupled engine was developed, which was also adopted by the PLM (Paris-Lyon-Marseille) Railroad. The heaviest of its type, the number of these engines officially recorded as ordered between 1868 and 1887 was 164 (Ill. 188). The performance records included a load of 1,175 tons at 19 m.p.h. on the level, 307 tons up an incline of

1 in 100 (1%) and 85 tons up an incline of 1 in 33.3 (3%).

The twelve engines supplied by Egestorff in 1874/75 to the Baden State Railroad also belong to this family of eight-coupled engines. They were designed as mountain engines for the Black Forest Railroad.

The Creusot-Engerth locomotives were not suitable for mountain lines with sharp curves, as the Est Railroad's experiences had shown. Edouard Beugniot, engineer at the André Koechlin Works in Mulhouse (Alsace), attempted to create a suitable type for this purpose. After studying the problem for two years, he built a demonstration model, on the basis of which the Marseilles-and-Lyons Railroad ordered two experimental locomotives: "La Rampe" (Ills. 189, 190), completed in November 1859 and "La Courbe" in the following year. Beugniot did not think he could dispense with the supporting tender. It was supposed to stabilize the reciprocate and rotating motion of the engine especially on downhill runs where speeds were higher. The front axle of the tender had two axle journals per side: one outside and one inside the wheels. The outer ones, on the tender frame, took a very small part of the tender weight. The inner ones were gripped by two special hornplates on the frame of the locomotive and were sprung, and the driver was able to vary the tension by a screw.

To lessen the disturbing forces caused by the reciprocating masses due to the large cylinders, Beugniot located the latter inside, as close as possible to the front coupled axle. He thus made the cylinders work

189. "La Rampe", tender supported locomotive of the PLM (Paris-Lyon-Méditerranée) Railroad, Edouard Beugniot, 1859.

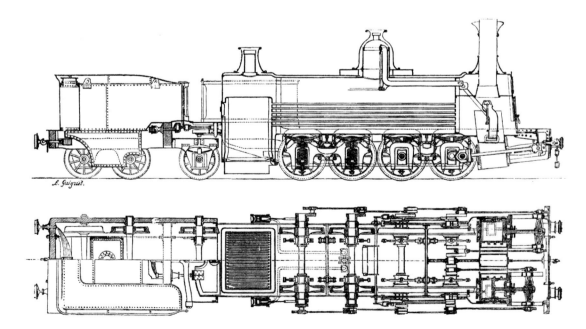

190. "La Rampe", sectional diagram.

153

forwards, with two connecting rods on each cylinder mounted on the crosshead attached to the piston rod. But the main point of the Beugniot engines was the way in which they achieved a better way of traversing curves than the eight-coupled type. As he himself admitted, it was a variation of the old flexible beam truck of Baldwin, which was described in section 5.7. The flexible beams were not pivoted on the axle boxes, but on supplementary duplicate bearings inside the wheels. The two axles thus linked had 13/16 in. play on either side. In this way curves of as little as 100 yards radius could be taken with ease. On the Swiss test runs made by "La Courbe" on the Hauenstein line in March 1860, it pulled 90-125 tons up an incline of 1 in 40 (2.5%) to 1 in 36.5 (2.7%) at a speed of about 10 m.p.h.

Later, probably on the six locomotives of the same type which André Koechlin supplied for the Giovi line to Italy, Beugniot simplified the truck in order to include only a strong lever swinging around a central pivot, which gripped the centrally positioned axle boxes with forks and thus guided them. This Beugniot lever was forgotten until Richard von Helmholtz, longtime chairman of the Krauss Company's drawing office in Munich, remembered them and used them successfully in 1905 on metre gauge tender supported locomotives for Spain, which we shall consider later. But even then the Beugniot lever was not used by anyone else outside Spain, until the German National Railroad* fitted them at the front of three ten-coupled freight locomotives of the 57 class (formerly Prussian G 10) and ten-coupled tender locomotives of the 94 class (formerly T 16). The lever was successful and was used on the forty-one 0–10–0 tender locomotives 82 class of 1950. Even diesel locomotives have on occasions been fitted with it.

9.3 Mountain Locomotives with Kinematic Linkage Drive

Attempts continued to couple more than three axles without adversely affecting performance round curves. The Jassenova, Oravicza and Steierdorf Railroad in South-East Hungary had inclines of 1 in 50 (2%) and curves of only 114 yards radius on its 10 miles of track. Wilhelm Engerth, in charge of traction, and with substantial help from Pius Fink, an engineer, found a new solution for a flexible linkage between the axles on the locomotive and on the supporting tender. The essential feature of this linkage was the insertion of a blind-shaft above the front axle of the tender, which rested on this axle with two swinging rods. Further inclined rods between the blind-shaft bearings and the axle-boxes on the third coupled axle kept both parallel with one another. The blind-shaft cranks drove the coupled tender axles via vertical coupling rods. The first Fink-type locomotive, the "Steierdorf" (Ill. 191), was exhibited at the International Exhibition in London in 1862, where it was subjected to very critical scrutiny. But as it proved successful in service, another three were built by 1867 and all four lasted until 1885.

The solution discovered by Fink spurred many inventors to develop similar drives, as, for example, Heinrich Kirchweger and Josef Anton Maffei in Germany, Ernest-Alexandre Gouin and Rarchaert in France and Gredge and Stein in England. But their systems were never put into practice. This type of kinematic linkage drive was resurrected in the 1880s. On the Bosnia Railroad built by the Austrians, with its 3 ft. 6 in. gauge, long-wheelbase six-wheeled cars were employed, with axles radially adjustable to curves, on the basis of a patent held by Klose, then engine inspector of the United Swiss Railroads. Thus it was appropriate to attempt something similar for locomotives, where, despite the narrow gauge and the severe curvature, powerful locomotives became necessary. A solution came about as a result of collaboration between Adolf Klose, Richard von Helmholtz of the Krauss company, and Julius Kraft, in charge of traction on the Bosnia Railroad. This was to connect the axle boxes of the end axles by prong-shaped guide rods which gripped them, allowing radial adjustment of the locomotive axles on curves. The consequent lengthening and shortening of the coupling rods on each side of the locomotive was effected by a so-called differential head, pivoted on the driving pin of the middle wheels, which was connected to intermediate rocking levers via two parallelogram connections and to the guide rods gripping the axles. Krauss supplied the first engines fitted with this kinematic linkage to the Bosnia Railroad and they entered service in 1885/86. They proved so successful that, once the Bosnia Railroad and the Bosnia and Herzegovina State Railroad had merged, they were followed by ninety-nine such engines by 1904, with various wheel arrangements including one rack locomotive. A large number of these engines were still in service in the 1960s with the Yugoslavia State Railroads.

* Reichsbahn.

154

In 1887, Adolf Klose was appointed Engine Superintendent on the Württemberg State Railroads. This railroad had severe curvatures on its secondary and branch lines. Since they needed a mixed traffic locomotive, but faster than the normal six-coupled engine, Klose introduced his own six-coupled system in 1893, on compound locomotives with long wheelbase, initially with outside cylinders. A year later, inside simple expansion cylinders were substituted (Types F1c and F1). The latter proved more successful, and as a result, twenty-eight of them were ordered (Ill. 192). Including the six Type F1c and a few narrow gauge 0–6–0 and 0–8–0 tank engines, forty-seven Klose-type locomotives entered service with the Württemberg State Railroad. In addition there were ten-coupled engines which will be considered in another section. These types were not taken up in countries other than the two mentioned.

The last version of the kinematic linkage drive came from Christian Hagans, owner of a locomotive works in Erfurt, who was granted a patent on January 11, 1891 for his "swivelling bolster locomotive". In his small factory he himself built no more than eleven engines of this type, all narrow gauge, some of which went abroad, to Tasmania for example, but were not taken up there. By contrast, this system did well with the Prussian State Railroads. In the 1890s,

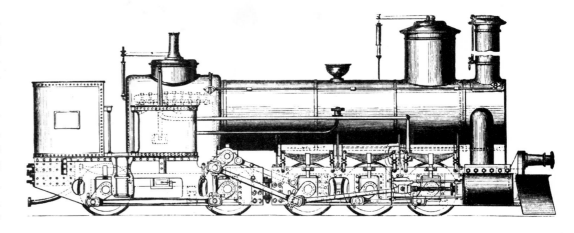

191. The "Steierdorf", Pius Fink, 1862.

the Erfurt Railroad Region was faced with the problem on the hilly lines at Thüringen of having to operate 200-ton trains at a minimum speed of 9½ m.p.h. and 110-ton trains at a minimum of 18½ m.p.h. where there were inclines of up to 1 in 30 (3%) and curves of 200 yards radius. Only five-coupled engines could match these requirements, and apart from the "Cantal" engine on the Paris-and-Orléans Railroad, which will be discussed later, there were no patterns to follow. Moritz Lochner, chief engineer with the Railroad Board at Erfurt, decided in favour of the Hagans type and charged the firm of Henschel to design and build such an engine, later the Type T 15 (Ill. 193). As usual the three

192. Locomotive of the Württemberg State Railroad, Group F1, Adolf Klose, 1893.

front axles were mounted in the main frame. The rear two were mounted in a swivelling bolster, which was linked at the front with the main frame through a pivot pin. The piston rods were linked to a single-armed swing lever mounted vertically, which also took the connecting rods of the front three axles. A second identical swing lever was used to drive the two axles mounted in the swivelling bolster. Both swing levers were linked via a coupling rod attached to their centres (hidden by the auxiliary frame in the illustration). The upper bearing of the front swing lever was fixed on the main frame, that of the rear, on a yoke. The latter was mounted in its middle on the main frame and its position was adjusted by means of a centrally located rod running to the truck. According to the movement of the bolster when taking a curve, the distance between the rear fixed axle and the front bolster axle was increased or decreased and there was a corresponding forward or backward movement on the upper bearing on the yoke of the rear swing lever. These locomotives fully lived up to expectations, and no fewer than ninety-five were acquired. By 1925 they had been broken up.

One T 15 was fitted with a Köchy linkage system, which had a blind-shaft to alter the length of the coupling rods, the position of the shaft being controlled by the swivelling bolster. In contrast, the Prussian State Railroad acquired another twenty-nine eight-coupled tank locomotives built on the Hagans principle, from 1899 on, which later became Type T 13 and were used on lines in Thüringen and on the Mosel Railroad. The firm of Henschel supplied two lighter, almost identical engines to the Baden State Railroad. The last two Hagans engines, which

were built in 1901 by the Vulkan Works in Stettin for the Lentz Light Railroad Co., had the swivelling bolster moved forward, located in front of the cylinders.

The Hagans engines were born too late. We shall see how this type of complicated driving gear had meanwhile been made redundant.

9.4 The Eight-Coupled Locomotive

In the same year as the "Creusot-Engerth", an eight-coupled locomotive family was developed, which was outnumbered only by the "Bourbonnais" and which was used as extensively as that type. Yet again, a light track meant finding new solutions. The Vienna-and-Raab Railroad, with a track which ran through flat countryside where inclines were only between 1 in 200 (0.5%) and 1 in 400 (0.25%), had a very light permanent track with a permissible axle loading of only 9 tons. Today the solution which John Haswell succeeded in applying appears so logical that it is surprising nobody thought of it earlier. It was simply to lengthen a normal "Bourbonnais" in order to insert a fourth coupled axle underneath the boiler. But fears over its ability to negotiate curves were still so pronounced that Haswell adopted the very small wheel diameter of 3 ft. 10 in., and placed the axles as close to one another as possible. This was the origin of the first European eight-coupler with separate tender, two versions of which were supplied to the railroad in question in 1855, the "Wien-Raab" and the "Comorn" (Ill. 194). The axle boxes did not have guiding hornplates on each side, but to negotiate curves and to enable easy adjustment to the cant of the curve, they were joined to one another by cross-plates, which were pivoted at the centre on a pin mounted on a frame stretcher. This arrangement also allowed the rear axle $^{13}/_{16}$ in. side-play. Since these Haswell-type "balanced wheels" soon proved superfluous, they very quickly disappeared. The other notable features of the "Wien-Raab" were the wheels of cast-iron solid discs, the connecting and coupling rods, which had a round cross-section, the return cranks on the Crampton model for operating the valve gear instead of eccentrics, and the valve chests, mounted vertically outside to be readily accessible.

The "Wien-Raab" was taken to the Semmering track to be tried out. On March 21, 1855, it pulled 1,060 tons at 14 m.p.h. along the level run between Vienna and Gloggnitz. The next day it made the entire Semmering run, pulling 112 tons at 12 m.p.h. up the 1 in 40 (2.5%) incline. Haswell then sent it to the International Exhibition in Paris in 1855. The consequences of this will be considered later.

The Vienna-and-Raab Railroad was merged into the Austrian State Railroad Company which immediately acquired twenty-three more locomotives of this type, slightly more powerful, and supplied by Haswell by 1858. Desgranges, then chief engineer on the Southern Railroad, which had taken over the Semmering Railroad in the meantime, designed a more powerful version in 1870. As Series 35, it not only caught on in Austria and was built in large numbers there; more than 318 were to be found on the railroads in Northern Italy until 1905. The final stage of development of the Southern Railroad type was Series 73 of the Austrian State Railroad, which was introduced in 1885 (Ill. 195). This was intended originally for the Arlberg Railroad, where it was able to pull 500 tons up a gradient of 1 in 100 at 9.5 m.p.h. and 180-200 tons up 1 in 40 (2.5%) at 6-7.5 m.p.h. Inside valve gear was used on this engine. The engine crews and maintenance men were particularly keen on this engine because of its uphill performance and its solid simplicity. No fewer than 453 had entered service by 1909. It was logical to introduce a version also of the eight-coupled engine with outside frame and Hall cranks which were so popular in Austria at that time. This version, also by Haswell, was supplied in 1867 for the first time to the Austrian Southern Railroad for the Brenner line. It was not used very extensively, but it was in this version that Germany's first eight-coupled engines were supplied by Kessler in 1869–72

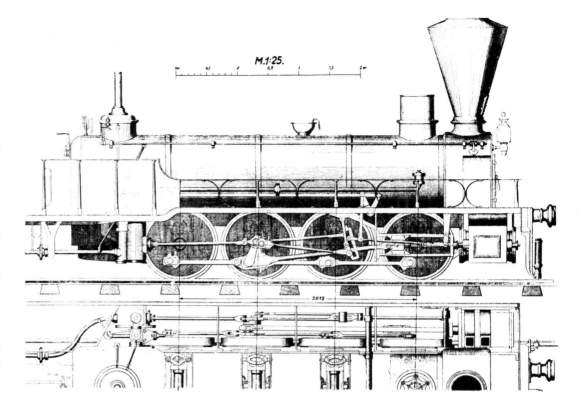

to the Ludwigs Railroad in Hessen for the Odenwald track. Large numbers of this version were acquired in Hungary as a standard type between 1869 and 1891, and a few reached Russia as well.

The "Wien-Raab", which was exhibited in Paris as mentioned previously, was bought as an experiment by the Midi Railroad. It was used only for service trains, since it hardly performed any better than the six-coupled engines already in service there. In May 1895, it was rebuilt as a tank locomotive and it served in this form as a switcher in Bordeaux and Toulouse.

194. 0–8–0 locomotive of the Vienna-and-Raab Railroad, John Haswell, 1855.

195. 0–8–0 locomotive of the Austrian State Railroads, Series 73, 1885.

In 1895 it was sold to the Carmaux Mine Company, which passed it on to the Société Métallurgique du Périgord of Fumel in 1909, where it was in service until the mid-1920s.

When the Midi needed powerful engines for the incline between Capvern and Tournay on the Bordeaux to Sète track, with gradients of 1 in 30 (3%), the old "Wien-Raab" was remembered and a more powerful eight-coupled engine was designed. Between 1863 and 1868 ten such engines, built by the firm of Le Creusot, Series 751–760, entered service. Together with the Series 901–913 (later 1103–1113) introduced by the Paris-and-Orléans Railroad the same year, but not as successfully, they formed the second family of French eight-coupled engines, of which 198 successively improved examples were acquired by the end of the 1880s by the Midi, PO (Paris-and-Orléans), and State Railroads.

The first Midi type, to Le Creusot's design but somewhat more powerful, was accepted by the Norte Railroad in Spain as early as 1864 as Series 2501–2537 (Ill. 196). These were actually built by Le Creusot, and the engines had all the hallmarks of French practice of that time. They are illustrated here because, with their coming, the difficult problem of braking on steep downhill runs was finally solved.

It has been mentioned already that the Semmering locomotive "Vindobona" used a reverse pressure braking system. Bergué had attempted a similar system, with air compressed by the cylinders being forced into a special container, on the steep Saint-Germain incline. At that time Louis Le Chatelier was consulting engineer to the Norte Railroad which included some long, steep gradients. There was an urgent need to solve the problem of how to brake trains on their downhill runs into the valleys. He examined the Bergué system, but found it unsuitable for long downhill runs. He remembered that as early as 1858, the foreman of the Alicante Works of the Madrid, Zaragoza-and-Alicante Railroad had experimented with a controlled inlet of boiler steam into the cylinders. But after an accident, which had nothing to do with the apparatus being tested, the experiments had been abandoned. Le Chatelier arranged for the Norte Railroad's chief engineer, François Ricour, to carry out new tests on this basis on the long inclines in the Guadarrama Mountains north of Madrid. Because of the many tunnels, cuttings and the strong wind, it often happened that the brakemen did not hear the whistle signals given by the engineer. After some preliminary tests, a braking system was developed. It was built into engine No. 527, and on April 30, 1867 was subjected to a variety of running tests.

Notable of these tests was the fact that a dynamometer coach was already being used. To brake, the controls were set for reverse. Boiler steam was introduced into both exhaust pipes on the cylinders via an adjustable valve mounted on the wall of the firebox, which prevented any ash from the smokebox getting into the system. Since the cylinders became

196. 0–8–0 locomotive of the Spanish Norte, Series 2501–2537, built at Le Creusot, 1864.

very hot during the compression process, a second valve linked to the first one sprayed in water (from the boiler) to act as a coolant. Both valves were operated by a common manual lever and this was set so that a light stream of smoke continued to escape from the chimney while braking was going on. This method of braking, which was later the subject of an acrimonious dispute between François Ricour and Louis Le Chatelier as to who had invented it, became well known under Le Chatelier's name. It was so effective and reliable that it was immediately introduced on mountainous routes in the other parts of Spain, France, Italy and Austria. It only declined in importance when the automatic compressed air or vacuum brakes came into being. But even then it was often retained, sometimes in its original form, sometimes in the Riggenbach variant, since it reduced the wear on the wheels and brake blocks and also prevented the tyres from becoming loose as a result of overheating on long downhill runs.

The overhanging firebox was common to all eight-coupled engines of the second French school. When some Spanish engineers visited him, Jules-Alexandre Petiet, who will be discussed in the next section, showed them the plans for a 0–8–0 freight locomotive planned by the Nord Railroad, which were based on the 0–8–0 tank engine (also to be discussed later). The innovation with this was that the firebox was supported on the rear coupled axle, thus minimizing the overhang which affected the running. Petiet's plans seem to have prompted the eight-coupled engines ordered by these engineers from Avonside, intended for the Zaragoza-and-Barcelona Railroad (Ill. 199). The boiler is still pitched very low. In contrast to the French eight-coupled engines, the valve motion is placed inside. As on the "Wien-Raab", the connecting and coupling rods are round in section. The engines were delivered in 1865 and were numbered 91–102 by the railroad. They were the first eight-coupled engines with separate tender to have been built in England. Once the Zaragoza-and-Barcelona Railroad had merged with the Zaragoza-and-Pamplona Railroad, Le Creusot supplied a further eight identical engines, Nos. 317–324. All of them were passed on to the RENFE (the Spanish National Railroads).

The fourteen eight-coupled engines which Sharp supplied in 1878 to the Tarragona, Barcelona and Francia Railroad in Spain (Ill. 198), finally overcame the fear of having a high-pitched boiler, which was evident on every type considered until now. The

overall impression is now far more modern for the first time, with axles a little more spread out and not bunched so closely together. When a subsequent order for eight locomotives was supplied in 1889, the boiler was even higher. The crews thought very well of these simple, sturdy engines and RENFE did not scrap them until the 1960s, with the exception of one being kept for the Railroad Museum.

This seems to have been a model which Sharp reserved for export, or at least repeated several times, for in

197. Train of Gotthard Railroad drawn by three engines, before 1909.

198. Sharp's 0–8–0 locomotive of the Tarragona, Barcelona and Francia Railroad, 1878.

1888 he built identical engines for the Sweden-and-Norway Railroad, but they were not actually despatched. The Barry Railway in Britain acquired two of them in 1889, and in 1897 had two more similar engines built. These were the first eight-coupled engines used in regular service in Britain. The Baden State Railroad also took the opportunity of acquiring ten of the Norwegian engines, and the Palatinate Railroad received five. These Sharp locomotives may be regarded as the predecessors of the similar-type

199. Ironside's 0–8–0 locomotive of the Zaragoza-and-Barcelona Railroad, 1865.

engines acquired from 1902 onwards by Britain's Great Central Railway and from 1901 onwards by the North Eastern Railway. Between 1913 and 1921 the North Eastern fitted a much more powerful version with superheaters, and between 1919 and 1924 even developed them further into three-cylinder locomotives.

There was no requirement in Germany for eight-coupled engines apart from the Black Forest Railroad, the Odenwald Railroad and the Palatinate Railroad. Thus large scale acquisition did not begin until comparatively late, in fact in 1893 with Type G7 for the Prussian State Railroads. These engines seemed very old fashioned, with their low-pitched boilers, as opposed to the Sharp type. But it will be seen that the simple eight-coupled engine with no carrying wheels was in fact retained longest in Prussia.

A preference for inside cylinders would lead one to expect England to have constructed the eight-coupled engine of this variety, and indeed Sharp did so in 1862. He built tank locomotives for India, reverting to the old intermediate driving shaft. Sharp placed the blind-shaft between the two middle axles, which were thus spaced well apart from each other. From 1866 normal "saddle tank" locomotives were built for the Great India Peninsula Railroad. They were

intended for the steep climbs into the Ghat mountains. Designed by James Kitson, a total of eighty-six engines of this type were supplied by various works.

In Britain itself the first inside cylinder eight-coupled engine with separate tender was introduced in one example by Francis Webb on the London and North Western Railway in October 1892. He built the subsequent engines, which will be discussed later, first as three- and then as four-cylinder compound locomotives. It was not until 1910 that this railroad company reverted to the two cylinder simple engine, more than three hundred of which entered service. In 1901 Henry Ivatt followed on the Great Northern Railway with fifty-five similar engines, which were ordered until 1906, and can be regarded as characteristic of this British type. These engines, called "Long Tom" because of their length, were used to pull heavy coal trains (Ill. 201). Other railroads with considerable coal and ore traffic used this type of engine, as, for instance, the Lancashire-and-Yorkshire Railway, which kept faith with this type of engine until 1920. It ordered 245 locomotives, twenty of which had corrugated flue fireboxes. When the London, Midland and Scottish Railway was founded, it inherited a considerable number of eight-coupled engines from the Lancashire and Yorkshire and the LNWR (London and North Western Railway), and added to these another 175 slightly modified examples between 1929 and 1932.

9.5 Jules Petiet's "Colosse" and Victor Forquenot's "Cantal"

As we have seen, the Nord had the 0–8–0 Creusot-Engerth engines for its heavy coal trains. The rolling countryside in France's north-eastern coal-mining area had secondary and branch lines with quite frequent inclines of 1 in 100 to 1 in 55. This was where an eight-coupled locomotive was needed. Since the branch lines for these engines were seldom more than 19 miles long, fuel could be stored on the engine itself and thus the frequent turning at the end of the run could be avoided.

Jules Petiet dared design the locomotive planned for this purpose with the boiler high enough to accommodate the grate above the upper edge of the frame. (Petiet was in charge of engines for the Nord at that time.) In this position, the boiler could be made of large diameter and short length, thus considerably reducing the rear overhang. But to lower the engine's

160

centre of gravity, Petiet arranged the water tanks like an inverted saddle underneath the boiler barrel. This arrangement has often been adopted more recently. The first locomotives built on this principle by Ernest-Alexandre Gouin in 1859 as Series 551–556, proved very successful, but it became apparent that the boiler was too small to enable these engines to run on the principal tracks.

A more powerful type followed, Series 566–605, built between 1862 and 1866, that had other significant innovations besides those already mentioned (Ill. 202). The firebox was built on the Belpaire pattern, to enable fine coal to be burned — a question that will be discussed later. The most significant feature was the steam-drier invented by Petiet. This consisted of a 20 in.-diameter tube running along the back of the boiler, permanently connected at the front with the steam chamber. Two sections inside this tube enclosed a bundle of pipes, through which steam passed before entering the cylinders. The whole assembly was contained in a large tube which received the combustion gases from the smokebox, which penetrated between the tubes and finally passed out of a horizontal chimney directed to the rear. Petiet's steam-drier may be regarded as a predecessor of the superheater which came later, but its heating surface was not large enough to achieve more than moderate drying of the steam. These locomotives, designated *"machines uniques"*, pulled between thirty-two and thirty-four cars weighing about 460 tons in all at 15 m.p.h. up 1 in 200 (0.5%) gradients. The first version of Petiet's steam-drier was altered several times, with the horizontal chimney being replaced by a vertical one. Most of the engines survived the First World War.

At the same time, Petiet took a bold step forward.

His aim was to increase the number of wagons or cars hauled and thereby reduce the number of train journeys required. He needed locomotives with a higher tractive effort for this. Instead of including the tender weight by coupling it up, as Engerth had intended originally, Petiet decided to store the fuel on the locomotive itself, and thereby to use the extra weight to provide adhesion. A powerful boiler was needed for the high performance aimed at. Because of the axle-loading limits, he had to provide six-coupled axles. It seemed too risky to drive these with the use of

200. Japanese freight train with a pusher at the end, ascending mountains.

201. Ivatt's 0–8–0 locomotive of the Great Northern Railway, "Long Tom" type, 1901-06.

161

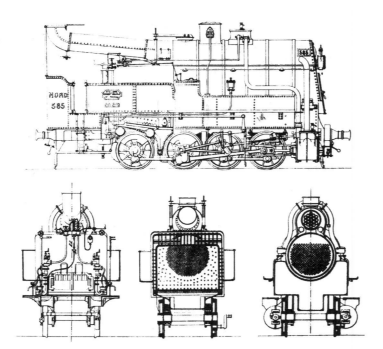

202. 0–8–0 freight locomotive of the French Nord Railroad, Petiet system, Series 566–605, 1862-66.

Ernest-Alexandre Gouin and entered service in mid-1862, i.e., about a year before the 0–12–0 tank locomotive on the Philadelphia-and-Reading Railroad described in section 8.3. This is considered the first twelve-coupled engine, since all its six axles were driven by a single pair of cylinders. Petiet's "Colosse" ran to the same timetable as the Creusot-Engerth engines, but it only hauled four or five more cars than the latter. Although the transport costs are said to have fallen by 40 per cent, helped by the use of cheap, fine coal, they were dismantled after Petiet's death in the Seventies, and the cylinders and gear were used for 0–6–0 tank locomotives. No. 605 was thoroughly tested on the Saint-Gobain line, where it was able to pull eighteen cars weighing 250 tons at 13-17 m.p.h. up inclines of up to 1 in 77. It was able to take a curve of 125-yard radius, but not the works branch track which was laid out with a radius of only 80 yards. It was thus fitted with Beugniot levers on the outer and inner axle of each driving group, which allowed 1¾ in. lateral play: in this way it was able to negotiate any such severe curves. It ran along straight and level track at 16 m.p.h. very smoothly. The next ten engines, Nos. 611–620, shared the same fate as the first ten; they dated from 1867. Two similar engines ordered by the Zaragoza-and-Pamplona Railroad in Spain did not enter regular service because of continual derailments.

Victor Forquenot of the Paris-and-Orléans Railroad tried other, much more conventional, ways of creating a locomotive with adequate adhesion for the Murat

two large cylinders only, so that Petiet split the drive into two groups of three coupled axles each. Thus Petiet's "Colosse" (Ill. 203) took shape, as the British called this type of engine. The boiler and steam-drier had been retained from the 0–8–0 locomotive already mentioned. With a total overall wheelbase of 19 ft. 6 in., each end axle had to have ⅝ in. side-play in each direction to take curves of as little as 150 yards radius. In addition, the flanges on the driving wheels were made thinner. There was a regulator valve for each pair of cylinders, but all four were operated together. The first ten locomotives, Nos. 601–610, were built by

203. Freight train tank locomotive with two groups of three-coupled axles, J.A. Petiet, 1862.

to Aurillac run in the Massif Central in France. This section of the line runs up long gradients of 1 in 33 (3%) to cross the Lioran Pass, 3,780 ft. above sea level. Again a tank locomotive was preferred because of its increased adhesion (Ill. 204). To accommodate a wide, and therefore short firebox, the two rear axles were mounted "in the German style" in a short outside frame. This had the advantage that the four rear axle boxes were not so close to the hot firebox; for Forquenot, in contrast with Petiet, was an adherent of the low-pitched boiler, as is shown by all the locomotives he designed. The negotiating of curves with this engine was achieved by having the middle driving axle as the only rigid one. The end axles had 11/16 in. and the second and third ¼ in. each lateral play in both directions. The "V"-shaped inclined plans which have already been described were used as centering devices along straight sections of track. These three engines, known by the name of the first one as "Cantal", Nos. 1201–1203 (later 2201–2203), were not destined to be a success. They were just able to perform as planned, pulling 150 tons at 9-12½ m.p.h. up a 1 in 33 (3%) gradient, but this was hardly any better than the performance of the company's eight-coupled engines. Thus they were not developed any further.

204. 0–10–0 tank locomotive of the PO (Paris-and-Orléans Railroad), "Cantal" type, Victor Forquenot.

10. THE DEVELOPMENT OF TRUCKS, RADIAL AXLES AND PONY TRUCKS IN EUROPE

205. The "Rauhenstein", Austrian Southern State Railroad, 1857.

10.1   The Four-Wheeled Radius Bar Trucks

In view of the poor running of the short trucks which came over with the Norris locomotives, there were attempts in Europe as well to devise better constructions. For the same reasons as Bissel, Haswell designed simultaneously a similar radius bar truck and anticipated the idea of the swing links centering device realized by Alba F. Smith. The locomotive equipped with Haswell's radius bar truck, the "Rauhenstein" (Ill. 205) of the Austrian Southern State Railroad, was fitted with a quite differently arranged motion from that of the American locomotives. Because the wheelbase could be extended owing to the radial play of the truck, Haswell located the cylinders at the centre of gravity so that they drove the rear axle. Since there was no rear overhang, it was assumed that the motion would be steady, but this was not the case, since the swing links were arranged vertically and thus on the straight they did not provide any centering effort.

Kamper, a member of the general inspectorate of the Austrian Railroads, returned to this Haswell radius bar truck with eight locomotives supplied by the firm

164

of Floridsdorf in 1871 to the Crown Prince Rudolf Railroad. The arrangement was improved many times. Thus Kamper put two swing links slightly inclined towards one another, suspended from a spherical pivot in the middle, which equalized the load and also achieved the necessary centering effort on the straight. The centering was increased by two more draw pendulums which were attached to the front buffer beam on the left and right side so that the radius bar was not pushed but pulled. This Kamper truck was so popular with other Austrian railroads at times, that the classification "Kamper Locomotive" was wrongly extended to embrace all 4–4–0 engines with outside frames. In a slightly different form this kind of truck was used by Fredrik Almgren from 1886 onwards on the standard 4–4–0 locomotives of Swedish State Railroads.

H.J. Vaessen, technical director of the Saint-Léonard works near Liège, proposed two types of mountain engine equipped with a radius bar truck designed by him for the Isabel II Railroad (Spain), running from Santander via the Reinosa Pass in the Cantabrian coastal mountains, 3,215 ft. above sea level, to the Castillian plain near Alar. One of these, a 4–4–0, was intended for passenger traffic, the other, a 4-6-0, was for freight trains. This was the first time that this latter wheel arrangement had been used in Europe. The truck was connected with the locomotive frame through a "T"-shaped radius bar. Apart from these Spanish engines there were only a few built for Belgian Railroads.

The locomotives built for the line crossing the Cantabrian coastal mountains leading from Bilbao over a large loop and up an incline of 1 in 70 to Tudela were to become especially important. The firm of Beyer Peacock supplied twenty-one 2–4–0 locomotives with separate tenders for this purpose in 1862/63 and eight 4–4–0 tank locomotives which used Bissel trucks for

165

the way of the lateral swing of the truck. They were not attached to the smokebox itself but to the main frame extended upwards at the side of the smokebox. The firm of Beyer Peacock subsequently adopted this type of construction with two- or four-wheeled Bissel trucks and inclined outside cylinders and he supplied many engines with various wheel arrangements. Although the two-wheeled Bissel truck remained important right to the end, the four-wheeled version did not prove as successful as the normal truck with centre pivot and thus disappeared from the scene at the end of the 19th century.

207. Beyer Peacock's 4–4–0 tank locomotive for the Bilbao-Tudela Railroad in Spain, 1862/63 fitted with Bissel pony truck.

the first time in Europe on a new engine. Both types were broadly similar. The tank engine (Ill. 207) was equipped with the four-wheeled Bissel truck in order to compensate for the increased weight of the fuel carried. "V"-shaped incline plans were still used as centering devices. The cylinders were inclined steeply over the four leading axles so as not to be in

10.2 The Four-Wheeled Truck with Centre Pivot

The four-wheeled truck with centre pivot became a characteristic feature of the express locomotive thanks to its excellent guiding characteristics. As described in section 8.1, these characteristics were first discovered in North America. In Europe there was opposition to this truck for a long time, although there was no lack of early attempts to apply it. As in America, the ability to negotiate curves was the main

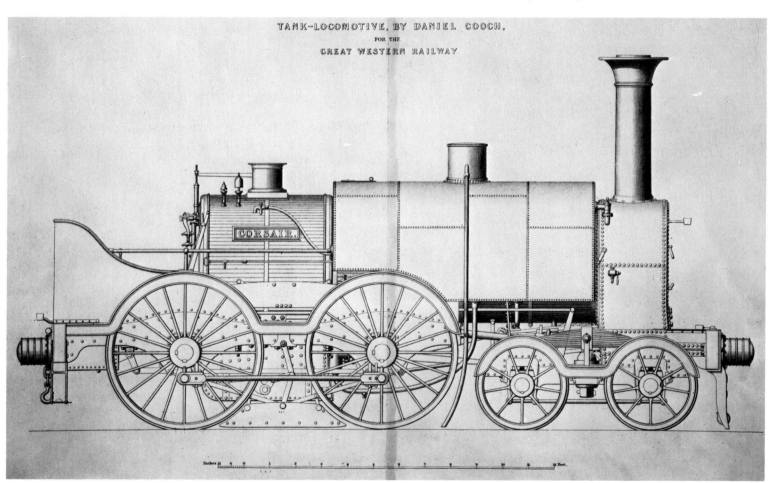

TANK-LOCOMOTIVE, BY DANIEL GOOCH,
FOR THE
GREAT WESTERN RAILWAY

CORSAIR.

208. The "Corsair", 4–4–0 locomotive of the South Devon Railroad, Daniel Gooch, 1854.

166

reason for its introduction. This can be seen in the first 4–4–0s built in England in 1849 to English designs (Ill. 208). These were designed by Daniel Gooch and intended for the South Devon Railway, originally conceived for atmospheric haulage, which consisted of a tube laid alongside the track in which a pump created a vacuum. Inside this tube was a piston fixed to the vehicles. Activated by the atmospheric pressure behind, it hauled the vehicles coupled to it. The South Devon Railway, which connected with the Great Western, had the Brunel broad gauge but, because of its hilly territory, its curves were much sharper than those of the Great Western. As a result the latter's engines with rigid wheelbase could not be used. The truck swivelled on a ball and socket joint, the socket being connected with the horn plates by four strong forgings. The pivot or ball was riveted to the bottom of the boiler. A single inverted spring transmitted the load to the two axle-boxes on each side. The other details of these engines were similar to those of the Great Western Railway.

We have mentioned already that locomotives with separate tenders did not have brakes on the engine wheels themselves in order to spare the expensive

the wheels. There were various other unsuccessful attempts at trucks. C. Hamilton Ellis, the noted English locomotive authority, considers that the true precursor of the classic English 4–4–0 locomotive with inside cylinders was the group of six engines supplied by Slaughter and Grunning to the Barcelona-and-Granollers Railroad (Ill. 209) in Spain in 1859–61. The truck is similar to that of the Gooch locomotive already mentioned, but it has a stronger outside frame. They survived the turn of the century, having been transferred meanwhile to the Madrid, Zaragoza and Alicante Railroad as Nos. 23–28. The last two were scrapped in 1911.

We find the next step forward in perfecting the truck on the twenty-four 4–4–0 tank engines William Adams had built at the Bow Works of the North London Railway between 1863 and 1869. The outside frame was retained but the wheelbase was extended to 6 ft. The frame plates were joined in the centre by two iron cross-beams faced with steel on their upper surfaces. The pivot passed through a bush arranged to slide laterally on the steel faces. On the truck, the load was transmitted through round plates surrounding the truck pivot first to the centre of the

209. Slaughter & Grunning's 4–4–0 for the Barcelona-Granollers Railroad, 1859.

tyres. However a tank engine had to be provided with a brake, so Gooch fitted a sledge brake. A horizontal brake shoe, between the two coupled axles, was pressed against the track. There have since been many attempts to use this type of running sledge brake, in Saxony among other places. It is not until recently that the use of electro-magnetic brakes has resulted in satisfactory operation of this system without leading to derailments because of the release of pressure from

truck and then via the channel irons to the springs on each side, which pressed directly on the axle boxes. William Adams continually improved on his truck. He inserted a thick rubber ring between the two swivelling plates. The pivot was made in a concave shape which acted inside a convex bush so that the truck could swivel both laterally and vertically. He then added rubber pads on each side for centering, that had been lacking up until then. However, escaping oil soon made these rubber blocks hard and brittle so he replaced them by spiral springs. The normal stiff, heavy plate supporting springs could be reduced in size when he inserted a shorter one between the two equalizers of the American swan-neck type. Thus the outside frame of the truck disappeared. In this way, one of the most extensively used trucks was created, a type which was used in various slightly different forms until the end of the steam era.

In Britain the truck was still distrusted. The main

twelve engines supplied between 1870 and 1875 were followed by twenty-five more with the water jacket across the firebox replaced by a bridge of refractory bricks. The exterior difference between these and the earlier examples was the smooth wheel-splashers without slits (Ill. 210). They showed what they were capable of when the first race to Scotland took place between the East Coast and West Coast routes in 1888. At that time they pulled a daily train between London and York, changing engines at Grantham

210. Patrick Stirling's 4–2–2 locomotive of the Great Northern Railway, 1870.

drive for change came from Patrick Stirling who has already been mentioned in section 7.1. But he did not use the truck to obtain a flexible wheel base, for the Great Northern main line did not have any sharp curves, as could have been deduced from the earlier description of how the long-wheel base 2–2–2 engines were used. As he put it, the truck was "because it gradually laid down the road so that the driving wheels laid hold of it." The inside cranks needed for 8 ft. driving wheels led Patrick Stirling to adopt outside cylinders to avoid a boiler pitched too high. A characteristic of all Stirling locomotives was the lack of a dome and the comparatively small boilers. The low firebox resulted in a very effective heating surface exposed directly to the fire.

These 4–2–2 engines proved so efficient that they pulled the main express trains on the Great Northern Railway for more than twenty-five years. The first

with a mean average speed of 55 m.p.h. Stirling's "Masterpiece", as British historians like to call these engines, had two consequences. Firstly the advantages of the truck for express trains and locomotives were finally recognized; and secondly, there was the preference for an uncoupled express engine, supported by the invention of the steam sanding gear which could prevent the driving wheels slipping on starting.

One 4–2–2 engine similar to the Stirling type was introduced on the Great Eastern Railway by the firm of Massey Bromley in 1879 and twenty were built by 1882 (Ill. 206).

The competition between English engineers to produce increasingly attractive locomotives was mainly evident with the 4–4–0 engines. M. Demoulin wrote in 1898: "The question of appearance shows, as long as the other essential conditions are met, that engine-building can develop a certain degree of perfection

168

211. The "North Stafford", 4-4-0 Express engine, John H. Adams, 1910.

into a true art." Illustration 211 may serve to give an impression of those richly painted 4-4-0s with their fine matching cars. The locomotive belongs to a series of four built in 1910 at the Stoke Railroad Works by John H. Adams for the North Stafford Railway. They usually had inside cylinders. Apart from the Scottish 4-4-0 locomotives belonging to the Allan-Crewe school, we only find a significant number of them with outside cylinders on the London-and-South Western Railroad, culminating in the "High Fliers" introduced in 1890 by William Adams, whom we have already met.

One thing was common to almost all of these early 4-4-0 engines: the boiler was too small in relation to the cylinders. This was not changed until John Farquharson McIntosh introduced his famous "Dunalastair" from 1896 onwards, which was successively improved. This set the pace for the further development of the 4-4-0 locomotive in Britain.

On the Continent, the truck was initially developed further in Austria. These 4-4-0 engines may be regarded as a cross between the old Norris and Forrester schools (sections 7.4 and 7.5). Norris initially provided the model for the truck and Forrester the model for the frame construction. The initiative came from the North Eastern Railroad in Switzerland which, as we know, possessed Kessler locomotives built on the Norris pattern. It is possible that their frames were too weak, for the engines acquired from Maffei in 1854 were given outside frames, and cylinders and valve motion on the Hall pattern. The truck still had the short Norris wheelbase. This type of construction died out on the North Eastern Railroad in 1857, for the locomotive superintendent Georg

169

middle of the 1870s, the outside frame 4–4–0 with the Elbel truck replaced the earlier 2–4–0 locomotives on all Austrian railroads, with the exception of the State Railroad Company, whose chief locomotive superintendent Ernest Polonceau came from the Paris-and-Orléans Railroad and introduced its 2–4–2 engines. When the K.u.K. State Railroad* was engaged in 1884 in replacing the many types acquired through the nationalization of several different companies and introducing standard types, it shows the outside frame construction with Elbel truck for passenger trains that

212. The "Rittinger", Austrian North West Railroad, 1873.

213. 4–4–0 locomotive, standard type on the Austrian State Railroad, Series 4.

Krauss developed a completely different type of locomotive on this railroad in the shape of a quite simple four-coupled engine. In 1861 the Baden State Railroad adopted the same 4–4–0 type, and Austria then proceeded with its further development.

These first 4–4–0 Hall-type engines with their short trucks and overhanging fireboxes were not suitable for fast running. At his own expense, Georg Sigl built two locomotives in 1872, avoiding the rear overhang by locating the firebox between the coupled wheels. One of these, the "Rittinger" (Ill. 212), was shown as the "Express Engine of the Future" at the World Fair in Vienna in 1873, but this was only a transitional type, for the wheelbase of the truck was only 4 ft. 3 in. The performance record showed a load of 200 tons up a gradient of 1 in 300 at 18½ m.p.h. and 90 tons on the level at 32 m.p.h. The "Rittinger" was bought by the North West Railroad in Austria and Anton Elbel then developed it further in that country. In the two locomotives ordered from the firm of Floridsdorf in 1874, "Foucault" and "Livingstone", he not only avoided the front overhang by placing the cylinders behind the truck, but he also used a type of truck which proved successful until very recently in various slightly different forms. We shall soon return to this construction. From the

had by now become traditional. It did, however, abandon the very solid but also very expensive "filled" frame in favour of single plates. Apart from that, the picture remains the same, with the exception of the new shape of the spark arrester, the *Kobel*. This spark arrester form, so typical of Austria, was introduced in 1873 when it was decided that the lower section of the old Klein-type conical chimney (called *Stanitzel*) was superfluous and wind resistant. In about 1904, Johann Rihosek improved the *Kobel*.

The first Series 2, which was very similar to the engines on Crown Prince Rudolf's Railroad, followed the Series 4 standard type on the State Railroad between 1855 and 1897 (Ill. 213), which was supplied by all Austrian factories in 230 examples. The following load capacities were quoted:

On gradients of	1 in 100	1 in 66	1 in 44
Expresses at 25 m.p.h.	185 tons	110 tons	60 tons
Local trains at 18½ m.p.h.	245 tons	155 tons	90 tons

This Austrian type of outside frame construction naturally caught on in Hungary and went as far as the

Balkans. Similar engines were also introduced as a standard type on the narrow gauge railroads of former British India.

Further developments came also from Switzerland. On the mainly short lengths of branch line a tank engine could carry sufficient fuel. The first 4–4–0 tank engines to enter service were twelve supplied in 1861 by Emil Kessler to the Fribourg-and-Lausanne Railroad (Ill. 215). They are noteworthy because the widespread truck as had already been introduced in America was being used in Europe for the first time. There is no literature on the method of construction of this truck. The water supply was carried in a saddle tank above the boiler, as was the English custom. Because of its striking appearance, the crew nicknamed this engine "The Turtle". The loads pulled were between 160 and 231 tons up inclines of 1 in 84 (1.2%). In Switzerland, the 4–4–0 remained a tank engine for a long time. The crowning development of this type were the three express tank engines supplied by Maffei in 1890 to the Gotthard Railroad; intended for the southern section in the Tessin valley, they thus had the largest driving wheel diameter ever used in Switzerland, 6 ft. 1½ in.

This same basic arrangement, with inside frame, outside cylinders and motion but with a separate tender, appeared at the World Fair in Vienna in 1878. The engine was built by the firm of Floridsdorf for the Alta Italia Railroad. The truck construction followed Elbel with a rigid ball and socket joint, probably taken from the Austrian engines. This Floridsdorf type proved so successful that the further development of the 4–4–0 locomotive took place in Italy.

214. 4–4–0 locomotive of the Italian Mediterraneo Railroad, "Giovanna d'Arco", Cesare Frescot, 1889-1900.

215. Kessler's "Romont", 4–4–0 tank locomotive Fribourg-Lausanne Railroad, 1861.

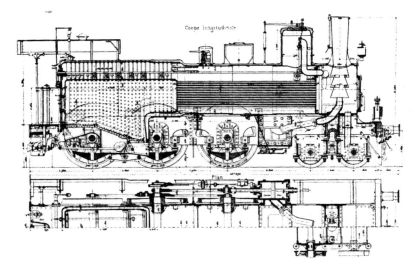

216. 4–6–0 locomotive of the Italian State Railroad, "Vittorio Emmanuele II" type, Group 650, Cesare Frescot.

known as Group 560 on the Italian State Railroads. These had the ball and socket joints with 1 in. lateral play to each side. It can be said that the "Giovanna d'Arco" brought the 4–4–0 locomotive on the European Continent to full maturity. The only remaining item to complete the picture of the 4–4–0 development was the replacement of the Gooch valve gear by the Heusinger-Walschaert gear, as was done earlier by 1888 on Sicilian Railroads.

Cesare Frescot also created the first European 4–6–0 engine with separate tender. At this point, we may revert to the Elbel truck with its ball and socket joint, visible in the illustration (Ill. 216). Later the ball and socket were attached the other way round to prevent the oil being forced out under pressure. It is not clear why Frescot chose such a short wheelbase for the truck, although the 4–4–0s already had a wide-spread truck. Possibly he did not want to run the risk of providing the long connecting rod that would have resulted from placing the cylinder between the truck wheels. Two elements are clear from the sectional diagram: the combustion chamber in front of the firebox, which has been mentioned several times, and the blast pipe with the petticoat jets.

This "Vittorio Emmanuele II" was intended to pull

From 1889 onwards, on a design by the locomotive superintendent of the Mediterraneo Railroad, Cesare Frescot, a considerably more powerful engine, "Giovanna d'Arco" (Ill. 214), was built in the company's works at Turin. It was intended to pull fast trains of 160 tons at 50 m.p.h. on the level or of 120 tons at 31 m.p.h. up a 1 in 100 (1%) gradient. The next ten were the first locomotives built by the subsidiary company established by Kessler in Saronno. By 1900, thirty-one engines entered service, later

217. 4–4–0 locomotive of the French Nord Railroad, No. 2874, "Outrance" type, with a mixed train, 1877-82.

172

loads of 120 to 130 tons at 25 to 31 m.p.h. on the new Giovi line with maximum inclines of between 1 in 40 and 1 in 29, and to travel with the same train load at 37.5 m.p.h. on the subsequent level stretches. Fifty-five engines of the "Vittorio Emmanuele II" type were built by 1895, later the FS Group 650.

C.H. Couche, the noted French author, wrote in 1874: "In general the American locomotive is not recommended for high speeds, not even on good track, because of the lack of load on the truck and the swivelling around the pivot." Thus it is not surprising that the first 4–4–0 engines were not used in France until 1877 when their introduction became a necessity. When the Cramptons had to be replaced on the Nord Railroad around 1871, a 2–4–0 was introduced which was based on an experimentally procured Sturrock 2–2–2 locomotive, similar to the "Jenny Lind" express engine (Ill. 116) on the Great Northern. Built subsequently more powerful, these engines performed perfectly on the old lines belonging to the Nord Railroad. But it was a different matter on the track which had been acquired, partly newly built and partly purchased in the coal mining area of northern France,

where the terrain meant more severe curves. There were doubts about operating these 2–4–0s with their long rigid wheelbase in this area, and it was decided to replace the front carrying axle by a truck. The first of these new 4–4–0 locomotives was supplied on June 29, 1877 by the Belfort works of the Alsace Locomotive Works. It had outside frames on the truck as well (Ill. 217). The truck was loaded with two ball and socket joints located on the sides of the truck cross-stretcher, which could move radially on a slide guide. The pivot did not take the load and had no lateral movement. This 4–4–0 type, which became known as "Outrance", had forty-nine engines built by 1882, but in 1885, however, the last series of twelve reverted to the 2–4–0 arrangement.

It was not until comparative runs were made in 1889/90, following a severe railroad accident near Dijon, that the value of the truck in fast-running locomotives was realized in France. A 2–4–2 locomotive had become derailed when running at full speed downhill. It was decided to discover the behaviour characteristics of other high-speed express locomotives then in use. All seven large French rail-

173

road companies sent their latest models for these test runs, all 2–4–0 or 2–4–2 engines. Only the Ouest Railroad sent a newly introduced 4–4–0 locomotive of a completely English construction with inside motion. From these test runs it emerged that the 2–4–2 engines, which had been praised so highly hitherto, caused severe strain on the track at the speeds under test of up to 75 m.p.h. The 4–4–0 ran the smoothest. Consequently all locomotives were converted, the large 2–4–2s on the PLM (Paris-Lyon-Méditerranée) Railroad, which we will discuss later, the latest Polonceau engines on the Ouest Railroad and the latest "Outrance" series on the Nord Railroad. Furthermore, the general introduction of the truck was soon necessary when the four-cylinder compound system was introduced.

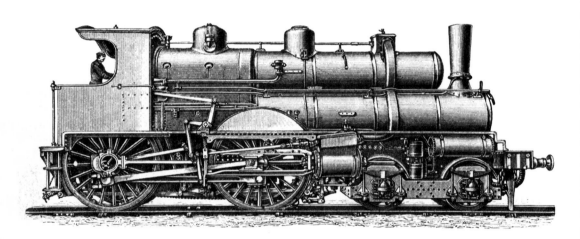

219. 4–4–0 locomotive of the French Est Railroad with Flaman boiler, 1890.

The Est Railroad had also sent one of its Cramptons for these test runs fitted with a new type of boiler. It ran away from all the others, with a much lighter train load, however. The conclusions drawn by Salomon, engine superintendent of the Est Railroad, are further proof of rooted prejudice against a high-pitched boiler. This new boiler type by Flaman, whom we have already met, bowing to this prejudice, was built into a 4–4–0 engine (Ill. 219). It consisted of a very low-pitched boiler, the barrel of which was completely filled with fire tubes, and a second barrel mounted on top, half filled with water and acting as the steam chamber. Further common features with the old Crampton were the coupled axle located behind the underhung firebox and the arrangement of the cylinders near the centre of gravity. Forty engines in this Flaman version were built by 1894, Series 801 to 840.

10.3 The Two-Wheel Guiding Trucks

Designers found themselves in a quandary with six-wheeled locomotives: if the engines were to run smoothly at high speeds they had to have a long wheelbase; but if they had to negotiate severe curves, there was a limit to the wheelbase unless the front axle were given lateral play. But as has been mentioned several times, this in itself was not sufficient because running on the straight was then not properly controlled.

The oldest method of satisfying both requirements were "V"-shaped incline plans on the axle boxes which have already been described. Section 6.4 mentioned how Forquenot saw himself forced to smooth the running of his 2–4–0 express locomotives by the addition of a rear carrying axle. The 2–4–2s thus produced performed as well as the 4–4–0 locomotives but were of simpler construction. This type became popular on the PO, the State and above all on the PLM Railroads. On the PLM, the 2–4–0 engines were also first rebuilt on the PO lines from 1876, but were newly rebuilt with certain modifications: the firebox, notably, was built on the Belpaire pattern, enlarged and supported on the rear axle (Series 51 to 110). The engines of the final Series 111 to 400 (Ill. 218), acquired from 1879 until 1884 in large numbers, were the most powerful 2–4–2 locomotives in France. Their ability to take curves was ensured by ½ in. play to each side on the carrying axles, but several engines had radially swivelling front axles. On test runs these engines pulled 257 tons at 50 m.p.h. on an incline of 1 in 250. With only one car they reached 82 m.p.h. On the basis of the comparative runs already mentioned and the knowledge acquired, ninety-six were converted into 4–4–0 engines between 1891 and 1898, while others were converted into 2–6–0s and the remainder were finally metamorphosed into 0–8–0 tank engines after 1925.

The exclusive use of side-play in the axles was an incomplete solution to negotiating curves. We have seen that Bissel solved the problem in a much better way. But there was a whole series of other proposals and two systems soon clearly emerged: axles swivelling about a rigid pivot and, secondly, axles swinging about an imaginary fulcrum point. In 1870 a simpler construction of the radius bar belonging to the first system was discovered by S.S.W. Novotny, engine superintendent on the Saxon State Railroad. The lines running into the Ore Mountains in this area had curves down to as little as 180 yards radius. Novotny moved the pin to the centre of the leading axle and fixed it to the frame without lateral play. The axle boxes were fixed to a special rectangular frame which moved with the axle. The two main springs were suspended on the frame at the rear and joined at the front by a cross-beam. This three-point suspension ensured that the load on the wheels remained constant. So that the auxiliary frame could follow the play of the springs, the pin had a ball and socket joint. The centering effort was created by "V"-shaped slide plates, whose inclined plans were parallel to the track. This Novotny guiding truck was used very successfully from time to time on the Saxon State Railroad and on other German railroads. Illustration 220 shows such an engine, as supplied by Gustav Hartmann in 1872. Despite the guiding truck and the location of the cylinders close to the coupled wheels, the whole wheelbase is kept cautiously short and as a result the firebox overhangs. But these engines are said to have had very smooth running qualities.

Several designers were involved in the second system, that of guiding trucks swinging radially around an imaginary fulcrum. In France, Edouard Roy developed a graphic method during his work in this matter which helped to establish how a given locomotive would negotiate curves. The principle of this type of guiding truck is that the axle boxes slide in guides curving as the radius of an imaginary fulcrum. Roy's first version in 1856 was still imperfect, and it was not until the 1880s that an improved version proved successful with the Nord Railroad in France. The Swede, Widmark, developed a similar system about the same time as Roy, but the method of centering was too complicated mechanically. But it can be regarded as the predecessor of the most extensively used system, that of the Englishman William Bridge Adams. His radial axle was used for the first time on a 2–4–2 tank engine, the "White Raven", built by Cross & Co., entering service in November 1863 with the St. Helens Railway. The radial axles had no controlling arrangement, so the locomotive ran

with a pronounced swaying movement. Francis Webb of the LNWR (London and North Western Railway) undertook the final improvements to the Adams axle. While Adams had collars on the journals in the middle of the axle boxes, to push them individually, Webb joined both axle box cases to one another by means of parallel plates. The axles boxes were jointly displaced by the journals in the curved hornplates on the main frame. Later the connecting plates were replaced by

220. The "Weipert", 2–4–0 locomotive of the Saxon State Railroad, 1872.

a hollow curved casting. Resetting was effected by horizontal spiral springs, as the final Adams models had worked. The Adams radial axle, as modified by Webb, was used extensively all over Europe, especially on 2–6–0 and 2–8–0 locomotives, but were less suitable for fast trains.

An express engine fitted with Adams radial axles gives us the occasion to consider the work done by Alfred Belpaire on the Belgian State Railroads. It has already been mentioned that the rising price of coke resulted in a change to coal as fuel. This had to be sieved, and much fine coal was left over, which was therefore sold off cheaply. In order to be able to use this fine coal, Belpaire had to design large grate areas; we have already discussed similar instances in connection with North America, but he adopted a completely different construction. Of course, an outside frame was used, so that the grate could be made

221. Belpaire's 2–4–2 express locomotive of the Belgian State Railroads, Series 12, 1888-97.

somewhat wider than normal. For the firebox he returned to the method of construction used for the old "Vindobona" of the Semmering contest. He made the crown flat, which resulted in a larger steam chamber, and the flat walls simplified the insertion of the staybolts and roof staying. Initially these were naturally 2–4–0 and 0–6–0 locomotives with long, flat grates above the rear axle (Ill. 223). Once these engines built after 1861 were no longer sufficient, he created two new, considerably more powerful types. These were a 2–6–0 locomotive — imposing by the

expected to pull a load of 150 tons up a 3-mile gradient of 1 in 200 (0.5%) at 56 m.p.h. Of this Series 12, 109 engines were built between 1888-97, with slight variations and increasing weight. The complicated firebox was difficult to maintain, and, from 1910, new boilers with a narrower but longer firebox were added, once fine coal was no longer being used. The engines survived in this form until 1931 (Ill. 221).

Outside Belgium, Belpaire engines were to be found only once in the early Nineties, with eight on the Main-and-Neckar Railroad, with normal grates and chimneys. On the other hand the original Belpaire firebox with flat roof had been adopted extensively and it was never decided right up to the end whether it was better than the Crampton or not.

Let us return to the swing axles, as Professor Felix Meinecke (1949) calls them. Another variation came from members of the Directorate of the Saxon State Railroads, Ewald Richard Klien and Heinrich Robert Lindner. The problem was to design a powerful freight locomotive for a track with many curves. But the weight had to be spread over as long a base as possible because of the limited capacity of the permanent way. Thus two contrary requirements had to be fulfilled. They were met by the Type IX V engines (Ill. 222). The front carrying axle was made after the Adams radial system. The second coupled axle had ¾ in. side play in either direction. Of necessity, the fourth coupled axle located far back had to be radially adjustable. This was achieved by having the cranks mounted on a shaft whose axle boxes as usual were in an outside frame. The middle of this solid axle had a spherical enlargement. Diametrically opposite pins on this sphere bore an outer hollow sphere forming the middle part of a cast-iron hollow axle surrounding the solid axle. The wheels were mounted on the hollow axle. Thus they could adjust radially to the curves, with the angular displacement and the resetting for straight running being controlled from a steering linkage running from the tender. The rear outer frame needed for the solid axle was very suitable to take a large grate. Despite their long wheelbase, these locomotives easily took curves of only 170 yards radius. To maintain the water level high on inclines, a large steam collection pipe was placed on the boiler instead of a dome. Another individual feature was the drive of the Heusinger-Walschaerts valve gear from the middle of the connecting rod, similar to the English Joy gear. The two cylinders were compound. The locomotives of this Series IX V pulled 1,310 tons on the level at 31 m.p.h. and 605 tons up a slope of 1 in 100

222. 2–8–0 locomotive of the Saxon State Railroads, Group IX V, Ewald Richard Klien and Heinrich Robert Lindner, 1902-08.

standards of the time — built in 1889 and intended for the hilly Luxemburg run, and a 2–4–2 express engine. Both had a great deal in common, as, for example an outside frame, inside valve gear, main springs which were inserted without tension and therefore bent downwards, and an Adams radial axle, with "V"-shaped inclined plans to reset it. The 2–6–0 had room for the grate between the 5 ft. 7 in. coupled wheels, but this was not possible with the 6 ft. 10.5 in. driving wheels on the 2–4–2, without pitching the boiler very high and this was not then at all favoured. Thus the firebox was made in two parts, a wider section above the rear axle and a narrower and deeper one between the coupled wheels. Since the fine coal might have been sucked out unburned by the strong blast, Belpaire inserted rectangular chimneys narrowing towards the top, which were later replaced by round, inverted, tapering chimneys. These engines were

at 15½ m.p.h. They were later built as super-heated steam locomotives and the existing engines had their Klien-designed steam drier replaced by the Schmidt-type superheater. Between 1902 and 1908 a total of fifty of these engines entered service.

The Klien-Lindner hollow axle was very popular on narrow gauge locomotives. The 0–8–0 tank engines of 1 ft. 11½ in. gauge are probably the best known, built in large numbers, as they were, for army field trains during the First World War. Acquired for the German railroad corps brigade, they became known as "brigade locomotives".

10.4   The Krauss-Helmholtz Truck

The swivelling axles described could not compare in terms of guiding qualities with the normal, centre pivot truck. Richard von Helmholtz, son of the famous physicist and chief draftsman at Krauss & Co. in Munich from 1873 on, made a scientific study of the running ability of the locomotive when taking curves. It was he who came up with a successful solution for a swivelling truck, thereby realizing Baldwin's old aim of coupling the second truck axle while retaining the excellent guiding of the centre pivot truck. The free-carrying axle is mounted in a radius bar, like the Bissel arrangement, with the fulcrum located approximately midway between the front axle and the first coupled axle. The latter is moved laterally by a casting which supports it in the middle. Originally the fulcrum was a rigid pin but it was later also given lateral play with a resetting device. In this way, as with the centre pivot truck, on entering a curve the lateral pressure was distributed between the two leading axles.

This Krauss-Helmholtz truck was fitted for the first time in 1888 on a 0–6–2 tank engine Class D VIII of the

223. *Railroad Station in the Woods*, Paul Delvaux (detail), showing 2–4–0 Belpaire locomotive at a Belgian station.

224. 2–4–4 tank loco motive of the Bavarian State Railroads, Group D XII, 1897–1907.

Bavarian State Railroads, the engine being intended for the very twisting stretch of line between Reichenhall and Berchtesgarten. The excellent guiding characteristics were especially noticeable on the fast downhill run, where the engines were running backwards.

There was then a subsequent order for a series of similar 0–6–2s, initially for use on branch lines. It was again the Bavarian State Railroad that took the next step towards the main-line engine in 1897, when high-speed locomotives were required for local passenger services in the Munich area.

This Class D XII (Ill. 224) was designed as a 2–4–4 locomotive, since the weight of the fuel and water supply rested mainly on the rear bogie and consequently adhesion of the coupled wheels was not significantly affected as the supplies were gradually used up. This would be an inconvenience on a locomotive which has to keep stopping and starting. The two front axles were combined into a Krauss-Helmholtz truck. The pivots of both trucks and also the first coupled axle, mounted on the main frame, were given lateral play. Only the second coupled axle was rigid. As a result, this engine had no rigid wheelbase, as had hitherto been considered an indispensable arrangement. Instead there was a long guided length between the two pivots and despite the nonsymmetrical axle layout, the running performances were the same in both directions. These locomotives

set the pace in having the Krauss-Helmholtz truck adopted on a very large scale. By 1907 the Bavarian State Railroad, the Palatinate Railroad and the National Railroad in Alsace/Lorraine acquired a total of 174 such engines.

The metre gauge lines running along the Biscay coast of Spain in rugged mountainous regions met with especially difficult operational conditions. High performance locomotives which could run well through the frequent curves and constantly varying gradients were needed. The types of locomotive that Von Helmholtz designed for this purpose are among the masterpieces of locomotive construction. He commenced work on long-wheelbase 2–6–2 tank engines in 1902. These were then built with a shorter wheelbase — not rigid however — as in the Bavarian Class D XII coupled wheels. The most remarkable of all were the 2–6–0 tender supported locomotives, supplied for the first time simultaneously to the San Sebastian-and-Elgoibar Railroad (later Vascongados) and the Cantabrian Railroad. The last version, in 1920, had the Schmidt superheater (Ill. 225). To keep the overall wheelbase short, taking into account the turntables in use at that time, they were built with supporting tenders and the cylinders were located inclined over the front axle. The supporting tender also allowed a well-supported, large firebox, despite the overall small dimensions. The carrying axle was

225. 2–6–0 supported tank locomotive for the North Spanish Coastal Railroads, Von Helmholz.

combined with the second coupled axle into a Krauss-Helmholtz truck. The first coupled axle was given simple lateral play; the rear axle was the only rigid one, as the tender was also able to swivel radially. These engines, built for the Vascongados Railroad, were intended to pull 300 tons up a gradient of 1 in 38.5 (2.6%) round curves of 100 yards radius at 18½ m.p.h. They ran at 38 m.p.h. on the level, entering the curves smoothly. In all, Krauss supplied these North Spanish Coastal Railroads with twenty-seven similar 2–6–0 tender supported locomotives. In addition six engines came from Maffei. When the Vascongados Railroad switched to electric traction, these engines were eagerly snapped up by other railroads, and only finally changed to diesel traction a few years ago. The Ponferrada-and-Villablino Railroad was so satisfied with the six engines it acquired that, in 1950 and 1956, four more were ordered from the Spanish firm MACOSA. Since this railroad, serving mainly a coal carrier, has no intention of switching to diesel traction, steam locomotive enthusiasts will be able to see ten of these interesting Helmholtz creations in full service for a good number of years to come.

As is often the case when a good design catches on, copies soon followed. This time it was the Italian, Zara, who made a complete frame to link the carrying and coupled axle, instead of the radius bar. Pendulum links were used for the resetting. The Zara chassis completely replaced the normal centre pivot truck in Italy, with the result that the latter was only used on one other occasion: for 4–6–2 engines. Locomotives with this Zara truck will be considered later.

11. NEW DEVELOPMENTS IN HEAT UTILIZATION

11.1   The Compound System

11.1.1   The Two-Cylinder Compound Locomotive

In the 1870s, boiler pressures gradually increased from 40-70 lb. to 110 lb. per sq. in. A high boiler pressure has economic advantages, as power is achieved with a much smaller expenditure of heat, i.e., of coal consumption. The higher pressure does more work in the cylinder, but, on entry, the steam temperature is higher and thus there is a much larger temperature difference accompanying the expansion between the entry and exit of the steam. As a result the loss of steam through condensation on the cylinder walls is greater. If the expansion process is divided by partially introducing the steam to one cylinder and then admitting it to a second cylinder for further expansion, the drop in temperature in each of the two cylinders is less and thus there is less condensation on the cylinder walls. In this so-called compound system, steam and fuel are both therefore saved. Of course, the low-pressure cylinder has to be made larger than the high-pressure if they are both to perform equally, and the

180

low-pressure cylinder also has to be larger to take the larger volume of steam at low pressure.

The compound system had been commonly used on stationary engines and ships' engines since the 1860s. The first to realize a practical solution for its application to locomotives was the Swiss engineer Anatole Mallet, who was granted his first patent for this on October 10, 1874 in France. Mallet did not succeed in persuading the large railroad companies to hold experimental tests, but he did succeed with the small line then being constructed between Bayonne and Biarritz. Mallet designed for them a 0–4–2 tank engine and the firm of Schneider of Le Creusot built three of them, the first successful compound locomotive in the world (Ill. 227). He had to build them however so that they could be easily converted into two-cylinder simple engines.

The first difficulty Mallet had to overcome in construction was that of the starting device. If the engine was in a position whereby the high-pressure cylinder valve shut off the steam inlet, obviously the engine could not start. If the low-pressure cylinder valve was in that same position, only the high-pressure cylinder was in the starting position and the steam issuing from it set up a strong back-pressure. Thus an intermediate container (called the receiver) had to be inserted. This was also necessary in view of the fact that because the cranks were placed at 90°, the timing of the release of the high-pressure steam was not synchronized with the inlet to the low-pressure cylinder.

Mallet overcame this difficulty with a starting device, housed in a cast-iron case on the smokebox. It consisted of a slide valve by which the driver could divert the steam from the high-pressure (HP) cylinder, either into the low-pressure (LP) cylinder or directly into the chimney, as required. An intervening automatic pressure reducing valve prevented steam at too high a pressure from entering the LP cylinder.

These first three compound locomotives entered service in 1873. Compared with traditional two-cylinder locomotives, there were fuel savings of about 25 per cent. They regularly pulled trains of 50 tons at between 20 and 25 m.p.h. along the 5-mile track with gradients of 1 in 80 (1.2%) to 1 in 66.7 (1.5%). The cars were double-deckers, which explains the very tall chimneys.

In 1878, another three more powerful 0–6–0 tank engines followed, capable of pulling 100 tons. At the World Fair in Paris in 1878, one of these was not considered especially noteworthy, but Victor

Forquenot nevertheless decided to make an experiment on the PO (Paris-and-Orléans) Railroad by replacing a 16.5 in. diameter cylinder by one of 22 in. diameter on one of his 2–4–2 express engines, No. 210, in 1877. When this engine had covered about 59,000 miles, it was converted in 1881 back to a normal two-cylinder engine, as neither its performance nor the fuel savings had lived up to expectations. The reason for this was the unsatisfactory ratio between the volumes of the HP and LP cylinders.

227. The "Anglet", 0–4–2 tank locomotive, first compound locomotive, Anatole Mallet, 1873.

Two men immediately recognized the importance of the compound system: in Germany, the locomotive superintendent of the Hanover State Railroads, August Von Borries, and in England Francis W. Webb, locomotive superintendent on the LNWR (London and North Western Railway); but each took a quite different approach.

We shall firstly consider that of the former, whose steps were soon followed by Thomas W. Worsdell of the North Eastern Railway in England.

Like Mallet, Von Borries had to be content with small branch line engines for his initial experiments. These were two 2–2–0 tank engines which had been supplied in 1880 by Ferdinand Schichau and were intended to pull so-called "light omnibus trains" between Hanover and Kreiensen and between Northeim and Ottbergen. A baggage compartment was included behind the driver's cab (Ill. 226), to reduce the weight of the train to be hauled. To ensure an exact comparison, two identical two-cylinder simple-expansion engines were also ordered from Schichau. While Mallet had considered a hand-operated starting valve as has been described, Von Borries thought differently, asserting that "the driver cannot possibly know whether he is better off with the old system or the compound system"

For this reason, Von Borries developed an automatic starting device consisting of a ½ in. port in the

228. 2–4–0 compound locomotive of the Prussian State Railroads, Series P 3², Von Borries, 1887.

regulator valve slide surface which conveyed live steam through a pipe into the LP cylinder when the valve was fully pushed for starting, and which shut when the valve was partially pulled back. Ever since, there have been countless patents for hand-operated valves and for automatic starting valves, and whole pages of contemporary technical journals were filled with descriptions of them. The optimum steam ratio between the HP and LP cylinders had not yet been completely realized. At Von Borries' suggestion, the reversing shaft was divided on the 0–4–0 tank engines supplied by Schichau in January 1881 to the Royal Prussian Eastern Railroad, so that there was independent control over the cut-off on each cylinder. These engines were also intended for branch line operation. Since these small engines proved more economical in fuel consumption than normal two-cylinder engines, at Von Borries' suggestion Henschel in 1882 experimentally built two normal Prussian 0–6–0 locomotives with the compound system (Royal Railroad Region of Hanover, Nos. 1121–1122). The cranks of the reversing rods of the inside Allan valve gear on the

LP side were set towards the HP side so as to give the LP cylinder 40-50 per cent longer cut-off than the HP cylinder when moving forwards. This meant that with a slightly reduced LP cylinder diameter, the effort on both cylinders could be equalized. This arrangement became a characteristic feature of all locomotives with the Von Borries compound system from then on. Both engines, later Class G 3, entered service on flat and in hilly regions working to the same schedule as the otherwise identical two-cylinder simple expansion engines. The coal saved was between 9 and 20 per cent, according to operating conditions. This opened the way and the compound system could now be introduced on a large scale with the Prussian State Railroads.

By 1899, 768 of these 0–6–0 compound engines had entered service, and in 1903, fifty-eight more modern six-coupled engines of a more powerful design with high-pitched boilers were acquired as Class G 4³.

Under the steady influence of Von Borries, the two-cylinder compound engine was systematically developed in Prussia, with the same type of engine being built also as a two-cylinder simple, especially for industrial areas where stations were closer together, and there was much switching. In such circumstances the fuel saved by the compound system was not so noticeable. Nonetheless, of the 2–6–0 goods engines introduced in 1892, the compound variety were in the majority, and this was also true of the four-coupled Class G 7.

The use of the compound system on the Prussian 2–4–0 standard locomotives had resulted in too great a loading on the front axle because of the large LP cylinder. To prevent this and to improve the running performances, Von Borries located the cylinders behind the front carrying axle, which was rigid with no lateral play. Since there was now not sufficient distance between the cylinders and the firebox for an Allan inside valve gear — standard in Prussia — the Prussian State Railroads employed for the first time outside Walschaerts valve gear. Equally, because of lack of space, the reversing shaft had to be curved round the boiler.

These engines, which were first supplied by the firm of Hanomag in 1884, proved their abilities in express train service, but the era of engines with only three axles was coming to an end, with the result that only fourteen were built.

In 1887, similar engines were acquired to pull expresses on the Frankfurt/Main to Bebra run, which had long grades, but they had the more suitable wheel diameter of 5 ft. 9 in. rather than 6 ft. 2 in. The grate area and heating surface were enlarged somewhat. The connecting pipes between the HP and LP cylinders ran through the smokebox initially, as on the engines already described, but eventually they were taken outside the boiler. The smokebox was also made longer. This engine is shown in this final version, and was fitted with the later standard driver's cab (Ill. 228). Although it was conceived as an express for hilly terrain, it emerged as an excellent local passenger train engine. Thus, by 1903, 128 engines had been acquired, their life being one year longer than the later 4–4–0 Class P 4.

These Von Borries Class P 3² engines were the models for similar engines on the Saxon State Railroads, Class VI b *V*, which Hartmann supplied in 1886. These engines had a Novotny-swivelling leading axle. Similar machines ordered from Krauss by the Bavarian State Railroads in 1889, which were nicknamed "Empire Camels", had a front Krauss-Helmholtz truck. By 1891 only fourteen of this Type B X had entered service.

Despite the distrust of the truck, still strong in North Germany, it was now no longer possible to give up the 4–4–0 engine. In November 1890, with Von Borries playing a part, the first two 4–4–0s were supplied experimentally to the Prussian State Railroads. The truck was based on the American pattern, with a swan-neck equalizer. Without involving the truck, the load was taken directly via lateral rubbing plates to the leaf springs suspended from the swan-necks. The pivot, fixed rigidly on the main frame, moved in a guide block mounted on the stretcher of the truck frame and was reset initially by spiral springs and later by horizontal leaf springs. The advantages of this so-called "Hanover truck" were its unsurpassed simplicity and clear load distribution, as well as its good guiding ability. It became the model for all later Prussian trucks, even for those of the German National Railroad* as it was later to become.

After some temporary use of a slightly more powerful 4–4–0 locomotive, designed by Moritz Lochner in 1892 for the Erfurt Railroad Region, and which soon proved unsatisfactory, the Von Borries engine returned in 1893 (Ill. 229). It was now much more powerful and improved in detail, for the permanent way had been renewed and a higher axle loading was permitted. In addition the new turntables which had been installed allowed longer wheelbases. In this way, the Class S 3 express compound locomotive was developed, which for its time, was powerful and

economical. It was also built as Class P 4 with the smaller driving wheel diameter of 5 ft. 9 in. for local passenger trains from 1893 on. In hilly country, it proved very suitable as an express train engine. The last batches had the various early starting devices replaced by the intercepting valve of the Dultz construction that was finally accepted. The 1,072 Class S 3 and the 1,191 Class P 4 engines dominated practically all passenger traffic on the Prussian State Railroads

229. 4–4–0 compound locomotive of the Prussian State Railroads, Series S 3, 1893.

for nearly a decade and a half. Both types were also made as two-cylinder simple expansion engines for trains with frequent stops and for use in populous industrial areas. The S 3, for example, pulled 320-ton trains with ten cars at 47 m.p.h. on the level. In the Nineties, the maximum speed normally permitted was only 50 m.p.h. Up a gradient of 1 in 200 (0.5%), it pulled 205 tons at 31 m.p.h. The P 4, with its smaller driving wheels, was a better performer at lower speeds. Under the same conditions, it could pull 285 tons up this gradient.

The example of the Prussian State Railroads paved the way for the almost forgotten (except in Baden) 4–4–0 engine which was to be used throughout Germany. It was obvious that once again the smaller railroad companies were going to adopt yet another Prussian standard type of engine. But the Saxon State Railroads built various types of very similar engines from 1891 on, and the Bavarian State Railroads followed from 1892 with two-cylinder simple and compound engines, but with a different truck construction. Outside Germany, there were very

* Reichsbahn.

183

230. Carl Gölsdorf's 4–4–0 compound locomotive of the Austrian State Railroads, Series 6, 1893.

similar engines to the Prussian S 3 on the Warsaw-and-Vienna and the St. Petersburg-and-Warsaw Railroads. Another member of this school was the Series 101–130 on the Swiss Jura-and-Simplon Railroad, between 1892 and 1896. The Swiss North-Eastern Railroad preferred the rare choice of compound inside cylinders for its Series 101–120 of 1898. The 4–4–0 compound locomotives, designed in 1893 by Carl Gölsdorf, is remarkable in many respects, and a landmark in the development of locomotive construction in Austria. They proved that even tracks with lightly made permanent ways could take locomotives which matched the performance of those designed for heavier track (Ill. 230). Gölsdorf placed the truck further to the back, so that it could take a larger proportion than usual of the weight of the locomotive. It also had the unusually long wheelbase of 8 ft. 10 in., and with the pivot so far back and mounted 3.5 in. behind the centre of the truck, there was no need for its lateral play. The load was taken by ball sockets on each side. Gölsdorf then dared to mount the boiler high enough to bring the firebox above the frame, thus allowing a wider grate. The truck, as stated already, was intended to take more of the weight than usual, so despite the low permitted axle loading, Gölsdorf was able to provide a considerably larger boiler than that of the Prussian Class S 3. Running ability was excellent, thanks to the high centre of gravity, the wheel arrangement and the large coupled wheels.

These locomotives made perfectly smooth test runs at 81 m.p.h., pulling 210 tons up 1 in 500 (0.2%) to 1 in 333 (0.3%) gradients at 62 m.p.h. and up 1 in 100 (1%) at 36 m.p.h., and making it possible

to reduce the time taken by the *de-luxe* train between Vienna and Karlsbad from twelve to eight hours.

There was another Gölsdorf feature in the starting device: it had absolutely no moving parts, which were always prone to give trouble. The valve slide face of the LP cylinder had small apertures before and after the inlet ports, which fed live steam of reduced pressure from the inlet pipe to the valve chest. This happened only when, for starting, the valve was in full gear, i.e., more than 60-65 per cent cut-off. When the cut-off was reduced, the apertures remained covered by the slide valve.

Sixty-eight Class 6 engines were built and entered service by 1898, and then, with certain improvements, another ninety-nine entered service as Class 106, followed between 1903 and 1907 by another seventy of a further improved and more powerful type, the Class 206. For this latter class, Gölsdorf altered the appearance of the engine, for he had been very impressed by the beautiful designs he had seen on a trip to England. But he did not copy these, choosing to create his own unmistakable style. Finally another three engines with Schmidt superheaters were added in 1908 as Class 306. The Austrian Southern Railroad acquired forty-eight engines of the three State Railroad types.

Even more influential than his 4–4–0 engine was the 2–8–0 two-cylinder compound engine introduced by Gölsdorf in 1897, which may be regarded as the forerunner not only of the modern European mountain engine but also of the present-day general freight locomotive. The Prussian State Railroad was indeed in 1893 the first in Europe to introduce a 2–8–0 Class G 7[3] but, since the boiler and motion on these engines were mounted low as on the G 7 eight-coupler, they were no more powerful, nor, despite the added Adams radial axle, did they run any more smoothly. Only fifteen engines of this type were acquired. The 2–8–0 Class E 1 designed by Von Helmholtz for the Bavarian State Railroads in 1895 represented some progress inasmuch as they were fitted with his truck system. But its use, in practice, with overhanging cylinders and small coupled wheels of only 3 ft. 10 in. diameter, restricting the possible speed, was very limited, and only twelve entered service.

On the other hand, Gölsdorf's 2–8–0s were intended to pull expresses and heavy passenger trains over the Arlberg. In contrast with the German engines described above, Gölsdorf pitched the boiler so high that the firebox could be set above the rear coupled wheels (Ill. 232). Thus it was easy to accommodate a grate

of 42 sq. ft. At the time, this surface area was only exceeded by the Belgian Belpaire engines. As he had done with the 4–4–0 engines, Gölsdorf again succeeded in fitting a much larger boiler than was on the German types, despite the limitation on axle loading. He also had a new way of solving the problem of negotiating curves. Apart from the lateral play on the fourth coupled axle which had often been used by the old eight-coupled engines, he put into practice for the first time the newly developed theories of Von Helmholtz on the negotiating of curves by locomotives with several coupled wheels. He gave lateral play to the coupled axle that followed the first rigid axle. Thus, including the front Adams radial axle, there were three flanges operating, and the lateral shifts were spread over them in such a way as to create a smooth and steady entry into the curve.

The first two engines of this Class 170 were naturally subjected to thorough test runs, which took place between May 19 and 22, 1897 between Purkersdorf and Rekawinkel. This stretch had long inclines of 1 in 100 (1%) and constant curvature. Pulling a train weighing 550 tons, the engines achieved an average speed of 16½ m.p.h. and with 702 tons they still managed 13.7 m.p.h. On their official acceptance runs, they ran at speeds of 52½ m.p.h. very smoothly. These results were not considered feasible for eight-coupled locomotives at that time. Initially only nine engines were ordered, used partly on the express run between Salzburg and Wörgl, which had two watersheds with a maximum incline of 1 in 44 (2.3%). They

231. Prussian State Railroads, Kaiser's Imperial train with an S5 locomotive, c. 1910.

232. Carl Gölsdorf's 2–8–0 locomotive of the Arlberg line.

185

233. Carl Gölsdorf's 0–10–0 locomotive No. 180.01, for the Austrian State Railroad, 1900.

234. Wilson Worsdell's 4–4–0 compound locomotive of the North Eastern Railway.

regularly hauled 230 tons on this line. Thanks to compounding, these engines were also very economical. When, shortly afterwards, there was a need to haul heavier freight trains at higher speeds than usual on level track, this type was again adopted, and proved so successful that it became the most numerous type of locomotive in Austria. No fewer than 796 had entered service by 1919. The Austrian Southern Railroad also had another fifty-four built between 1898 and 1908. After the First World War, the Czechoslovakian State Railroad acquired another fifty-eight engines of this type by 1921. Similar types of 2–8–0 two-cylinder compound locomotives were also extensively used in Russia as standard units.

After this Class 170, Gölsdorf made another important step forward. The 0–10–0 locomotive, Class 180, now designed by him, proved that it was perfectly feasible to drive five axles with the normal coupling rods and, without using very complicated motion or without having to divide the frame, it was possible for such locomotives to take curves as severe as 180 yards radius.

As with the 2–8–0 already mentioned, Gölsdorf started with Von Helmholtz's theoretical work but, being the first to apply the data in a practical way, the technical literature normally refers to this system as the

Gölsdorf system. The first engines of this Series 180 entered service in the spring of 1900 (Ill. 233). There was lateral play on the first, third and fifth axle, and, owing to this, the connecting rod drove the fourth axle. To shorten the connecting rod, the piston rod was extended towards the rear and the slide bars were located next to the second, rigid axle. This time, the boiler was mounted high enough to accommodate the grate above the rear wheels. In trial runs this locomotive pulled 700 tons up a slope of 1 in 100 (1%) at 12½ m.p.h., and up 1 in 27 (3.7%) it managed 180 tons at 9½ m.p.h. Although it was originally intended for the heavy coal-carrying trains on the Bohemia lines, it soon became popular on Alpine routes as well. By 1910, the Austrian State Railroad had ordered 239 engines with only minor variations, and twenty-seven of this type entered service with the Southern Railroad. From 1909, their performance was improved by the provision of a Schmidt superheater while the compound system was retained. About 560 engines of this new Class 80 were acquired.

The fall of the Austro-Hungarian monarchy spread these engines over the railroads of the various states that came into existence in its place and also took them over onto the railroads of France, Italy, Rumania, Poland and Greece as war indemnities. From 1916, four hundred and twenty-one 0–10–0s were also built as two-cylinder simple Class 80 locomotives, and they met the same fate as the others. It should be stressed that the PLM (Paris-Lyon-Méditerranée) Railroad in France had fifty engines of this type built at the State Railroad Company Locomotive Works in 1921/22, that were mainly in service with success in the mountainous regions of Cévennes in southern France. All of them were still surviving in 1935.

Gölsdorf's Series 180 and 80 became the model for the further development of the ten- and even twelve-

coupled locomotive. It therefore fully deserves the place of honour reserved for one such engine now in the Vienna Technical Museum.

As previously mentioned, Thomas W. Worsdell very soon followed in Von Borries' footsteps. While still chief engineer on the Great Eastern Railway, he had eleven two-cylinder compound 4–4–0 locomotives built in 1884. In the English tradition, they had inside cylinders, but in other respects they corresponded to the principles of Von Borries, who was in constant touch with Worsdell. In 1885, Worsdell became chief engineer of the North Eastern Railway, which meant that his engines were not continued on the Great Eastern. From 1886, he continued his efforts in his new surroundings. He first developed two 2–4–0 engines with two inside cylinders arranged with the compound system. Instead of the normal slide valves, they had piston valves in line with Smith's patent — we shall soon meet him again. As both engines used about 15 per cent less coal, between 1887 and 1891 there followed another twenty-five two-cylinder compound 4–4–0s, as well as ten two-cylinder simple engines. One of these compounds took part in the race to Scotland.

At that time, as has been mentioned, there was a renaissance in England of the uncoupled express locomotive. Worsdell followed this trend and was the only person to bring twenty such engines into service there between 1888 and 1890, all working on the compound principle.

Thomas Worsdell retired and gave way to his younger brother, Wilson. The latter only built one more compound locomotive, No. 1619 (Ill. 234). He did not base this on the large-wheeled two-cylinder engine but on the previous 4–2–2s designed by his brother. It has outside — not the traditional inside — valve chests. No. 1619 had no special advantages. The complicated transmission from the inside valve gear to the outside valves caused trouble, as on the foregoing 4–2–2 engines, with the result that it was rebuilt. This heralded a new phase in English compound locomotive construction, that we will come onto in due course.

Wilson Worsdell gradually converted all the engines mentioned, and the 171 0–6–0 compound freight engines built by his brother, to two-cylinder simples because of constant trouble with sluggish starting, compared to the normal simple expansion engines. Thus the short interlude of two-cylinder compound locomotives in England was soon over.

In Italy there was a completely peculiar type of two-cylinder compound locomotive. It was built in 1904 by the firm of Ansaldo for the Adriatico Railroad for mixed traffic, as a replacement for the large wheeled six-coupled engines used hitherto. Both cylinders were inside and the corresponding valve motion was outside (Ill. 235). As a result, the combination lever

235. Compound locomotive of the Italian Adriatico Railroad. Series 380, later Series 600 of the Italian State Railroads, 1904.

of the Walschaerts gear which was normally attached to the cross-head, had to be driven by a second return crank on the crank pin. The Zara truck, described in section 10.4, was used for the first time on these locomotives, Group 380. It became a decisive factor in Italian locomotive construction. Upon nationalization, they were adopted without substantial alteration as versatile, multipurpose locomotives. In all, 230 were built, Group 600.

From 1910, there were a further 108 two-cylinder simple superheated locomotives. In 1906, similar express locomotives, Group 630, were derived from them, with a driving wheel diameter of 6 ft. 1 in., and these were also acquired as a standard type in large quantities. They may be regarded as a rival to the 4–4–0 express engines which were customary in other countries. They had the advantage of a higher adhesive weight, highly suitable for the mountainous tracks common in Italy.

11.1.2 The Three-Cylinder Compound Locomotive

Francis Webb, the other pioneer of the compound system, came to choose this method not only expecting fuel economy but for a second reason which seems rather odd to us today. As he explained in a lecture given in 1883, he intended avoiding coupling rods, and creating a locomotive with two driven axles which could, nonetheless, run as freely as the 4–2–2 engines which had just come back into fashion.

Webb began his work in 1879 with the rebuilding of an old 2–2–2 Allan-Crewe-type engine, and replacing one of the two 15 in. diameter cylinders by a smaller one of 9 in. It was used on light passenger trains on the LNWR (London and North Western Railway) branch line from Ashby to Nuneaton, and served to give him experience of the compound system. In early 1882, Webb's first locomotive of his unique and never repeated system, the "Experiment", appeared. The two HP cylinders were outside, located very close to the first driving axle, and they drove the rear axle. Their exhaust was led into a single large inside cylinder which drove the first pair of driving wheels. For the

head slide bar extended to the rear. The Joy valve gear, which had been generally introduced by the LNWR (London and North Western Railway), had the valve rod moved up and down by another rod inside the fixed radius link, vertically connected to the middle of the connecting rod. The radius link could be set at various angles and the valve stroke was thus increased or decreased.

After tests with other batches of this type, in 1889 the definitive "Teutonic" class appeared (Ill. 236). Webb thought that this had overcome the faults in the earlier engines which had proved disappointing in actual service. The Joy gear for the inside cylinder was omitted completely. The LP valve was operated with a loose eccentric which was kept in position for forward or reverse movement by stops. This, of course, prevented cut-off adjustment for the LP cylinder. On starting, this loose eccentric sometimes

236. The "Jeanie Deans", 2–4–0 three-cylinder compound locomotive of the "Teutonic" class for express train, Francis Webb, 1889.

reasons quoted initially, both driving axles were uncoupled. Unlike the normal English custom, the leading axle of Webb's radial system was fitted.

Another curious and unique feature of Webb's construction was that the firebox had double walls both underneath and on the sides. The space between the grate and the bottom walls served as ash pan which could be emptied underneath through a manhole. There were openings with adjustable dampers in the lower part of the firebox for the inlet of the combustion air. Each cylinder had its own Joy valve gear. The LP cylinder valves were above and those of both HP cylinders below. The radius link of the outside gear was encased and the casing hung on the cross-

created a scene which was the despair of the driver and which amused the travellers in the vicinity enormously: for, if the locomotive had backed up to the train waiting to depart, the inside eccentric obviously remained in the reverse position. On starting, it then often happened that both HP cylinders caused the wheels to slip. The LP cylinder was given a lot of steam and sent the axle it drove backwards, for that was the position of its gear, while the other driving axle tended to go forwards. Despite this, the "Teutonics" were the best of all Webb's three-cylinder compound express engines. The most famous was the "Jeanie Deans" which for years hauled the 14.00 express from London (Euston) to Scotland and returned with a

train from Crewe at 1938. This train consisted of fifteen to sixteen cars with a total weight of 210 tons and covered the journey at an average speed of 50 m.p.h.

By the 1890s, all English railroads had long since adopted 4–4–0 locomotives. Not even the LNWR (London and North Western Railroad) could avoid the introduction of eight-wheel engines. Webb tried to create something equivalent while retaining his three-cylinder compound arrangement. He extended the "Teutonic" by adding an additional carrying axle at the rear. He was now able to put the firebox far enough back without basically altering the motion, thus making room for the eccentrics of Stephenson link gear, which replaced the loose eccentric with its faults. The outside HP cylinders were also operated by a Stephenson gear, placed inside. Webb also thought of producing more steam in the following peculiar way; with a grate area of the same dimensions, an extended boiler would have resulted in the fire tubes being too long, so that he divided the boiler barrel by an intermediate chamber midway, 2 ft. 10 in.

in length. The 5 ft. 10 in. boiler tubes from the firebox opened into this chamber. It served to allow the unburned exhaust gases to burn before entering the smokebox via the front fire tubes 10 ft. 1 in. long. But since the exhaust gases had cooled down too much before entering the intermediate chamber, the arrangement did not live up to its purpose. The first engine of this "Greater Britain" class (Ill. 238) entered service on November 4, 1891 and was tested with a train consisting of twenty-five six-wheeled cars weighing 350 tons in all, with which it reached a speed of some 75 m.p.h.

Webb had high hopes of this 2–2–2 engine. He sent one, the "Queen Empress", together with a few of the newly introduced cars for the West Coast express service, to the World Fair in Chicago in 1893. He subsequently demonstrated the entire train on the Lake Shore and Michigan Southern. On the occasion of the Silver Jubilee of Queen Victoria, someone had the idea of painting one of these engines white, one red and one blue, the British national colours. Only the first two were so treated. The crew never really

237. 4–4–0 three-cylinder compound locomotive for an express train on the Midland Railroad, No. 1000.

189

took to these engines, which eventually proved hardly more powerful than the "Teutonic" class. The driver's footplate had so little room that the fireman had to stand on the swaying running board between the engine and tender while firing. The next ten engines, in the "John Hick" class, were even less of a success, being intended for the difficult stretch of track between Crewe and Carlisle and having smaller driving wheels of 6 ft. 3 in. as a result. Most of these 2–2–2–2s ended their career on modest branch lines where they pulled light local passenger trains.

As mentioned in section 9.4, in 1892 Webb had introduced the first eight-coupled engine to be used by a large English railroad company. Apart from this first example, he used his three-cylinder compound system on 111 engines built between 1894 and 1900 (Ill. 239). For the heavy freight engine, obviously, all the axles had to be coupled. Apart from the intermediate chamber, which was omitted, the boiler was identical to that on the "Greater Britain". All three cylinders were steeply inclined and all drove the second axle.

Three cylinders had certain advantages over two. There was a better balancing of the revolving and reciprocating parts, which on compound engines were especially unequal on the left and right sides. While Webb built uncoupled three-cylinder compounds, the first three-cylinder compound engine with coupled axles was developed in 1887 by Edouard Sauvage, then foreman at the La Chapelle works of the Nord Railroad, in France. This was a 2–6–0 engine with a radial front axle of the old French Roy system (Ill. 240). All three cylinders were under the smokebox in the same vertical plane. Much more logically

than with Webb, the larger volume of LP steam was introduced in two cylinders located horizontally outside, whereas the inside cylinder, inclined to pass over the first coupled axle, received the boiler steam. All three cylinders drove the same axle. The inside cylinder had a peculiar double valve arrangement like the old Meyer expansion system which served to prevent any excessive compression. To do this, the upper valve would be operated manually. In one position, this allowed the steam to enter the LP cylinder freely and thus serve also as a starting device. This locomotive, No. 3.101, with its comparatively large coupled wheels for a 2–6–0 engine (it later became 3.395), was suitable for passenger trains but was used for freight traffic together with eight-coupled engines. A test run on April 4, 1889, between Lens and La Chapelle saw it achieve 17½ m.p.h. up a slope of 1 in 200 (0.5%) pulling a coal train of 549 tons and 30 m.p.h. up 1 in 333 (0.3%). It was subsequently sent to the World Fair in Paris in 1889 where, together with two other compounds belonging to the Nord Railroad, three different ways of constructing compound engines with several cylinder arrangements were demonstrated. Of course, the 2–6–0 had no advantages over the 0–8–0 freight train engine. Thus there were only two other similar engines built in 1892/93, Nos. 3.102–103.

In Switzerland, three-cylinder compound locomotives were very successful. The 2–6–0 locomotive had caught on and proved versatile. From 1889, it was also built as a two-cylinder compound engine. It was time to smooth its running by using three cylinders so that it became suitable for express trains over moun-

238. Webb's "Greater Britain", 2–2–2–2 three-cylinder compound locomotive for express trains, 1891.

239. Webb's 0–8–0 three-cylinder compound freight locomotive of the London and North Western Railway, 1893.

tainous routes. With these considerations in mind, Rudolf Weyermann, locomotive superintendent on the Jura-and-Simplon Railroad, designed such a successful three-cylinder compound 2–6–0 that it was subsequently ordered up to 1907 as Class B 3/4, once he had been appointed the first locomotive supervisor on the Swiss Federal Railroads. It became the most numerous locomotive built in Switzerland, with 147 examples (Ill. 241), all coming from the Winterthur works. The HP cylinder was inside, inclined, well set at the front, and drove the first coupled axle. The two outside LP cylinders were horizontal, set a little towards the rear, and drove the second coupled axle. The three crank pins were set at 120°. Each cylinder had a separate Walschaerts valve gear but these could only be adjusted together. The inside gear was set to give 10 per cent greater cut-off than the two outside ones. For starting, the two LP cylinders were given boiler steam at reduced pressure. The front axle had Adams radial boxes. The performance chart quoted a load of 200 tons up a constant gradient of 1 in 50 (2%) and of 160 tons up 1 in 40 (2.5%) at 12½ m.p.h. The maximum permitted speed was 59 m.p.h.

Outside Switzerland, there were not many three-cylinder compound locomotives. Two remarkable types, both designed by Adolf Klose, were to be found on the Württemberg State Railroads. These were a 2–4–2 express engine and an 0–10–0 freight engine (Ill. 243), both three-cylinder compounds. All three cylinders were identical and drove the same axle.

Their cranks were set at 120°, the HP cylinder being inside. An intercepting valve which admitted live steam into the LP cylinders served both to start and also to continue simple expansion working. The express engines had the inside HP cylinder actuated by a Walschaerts gear, that of the outer LP by Allan gear, located outside. In contrast, the freight engine had inside Allan gears, permitting separate adjustment for the HP and LP cylinders. Both types negotiated curves with the Klose system described in section 9.3, the outer axles being radially swung out by the tender. This was a simple arrangement for the carrying axles on the express engines, but obviously a kinematic

240. 2–6–0 three-cylinder compound locomotive of the French Nord Railroad, Edouard Sauvage, 1887.

191

linkage coupling had to be provided for the coupled axles of the freight engines. These first ten-coupled engines on German tracks were supposed to achieve twice the load of the existing six-coupled types, and therefore the Württemberg State Railroads renounced eight-coupled types in adopting them. They could pull 300 tons up a gradient of 1 in 44.5 (2.2%) at 8 m.p.h. and 680 tons up 1 in 100 (1%) at 11 ½ m.p.h.

241. 2–6–0 locomotive, No. 1310, Series B 3/4, of the Swiss Federal Railroads, Rudolf Weyermann system.

They ran smoothly but the many components used in their construction turned out to be costly to maintain, so that there were only these five Class G engines, which were replaced from 1904 by the simpler Gölsdorf type. Together with the 2–4–2 Class E express engines, which were also acquired in 1892, they were the only three-cylinder compound locomotives on German railroads, with the later addition of the two Wittfeld express engines mentioned in a chapter to come. Elsewhere in Europe, three-cylinder compound locomotives were only built here and there, for example in Austria and Italy. The three-cylinder compound locomotive had its most lasting success in England, where it was least to be expected after the discredit attached to Webb's compound system.

Rarely have locomotives given rise to as much debate and to such a volume of literature as the Midland compounds.

Walker MacKerie Smith, chief draftsman of the North Eastern, suggested that No. 1619 (Ill. 234) already mentioned be converted into a three-cylinder compound engine with a system he had developed. But this was the only such conversion, because the 4–4–0 two-cylinder simple expansion locomotives introduced at the same time had such a decisive success that they overshadowed the experimental engine. Without neglecting the advantage of the lower fuel consumption, Smith wanted to use his system to develop a locomotive better adaptable to the chang-

ing conditions of the track and that could be loaded even more heavily where necessary than was the case with two-cylinder simple engines.

This was exactly what the Midland Railway were after. As train weights had become heavier, it was no longer possible to use properly the 4–4–0s fitted in the old English manner with boilers far too small for the line between Leeds and Carlisle, which had long 1 in 100 (1%) gradients — especially on the approach from each direction to the Blea Moor tunnel. Excellent relations existed between the two chief engineers of the North Eastern and the Midland — Wilson Worsdell and Samuel White Johnson, respectively — and this led the Midland to build as an experiment two three-cylinder compound 4–4–0s, Nos. 2631–2632 using the Smith system, entering service in January 1902. They were arranged so that all three cylinders received live steam on starting; in normal operation, double expansion could be used and also, to increase tractive power, boiler steam could be additionally introduced into the LP cylinder. Finally, all three cylinders could receive live steam if even greater power were needed, and the locomotive then ran for sprints as a three-cylinder simple expansion engine. These various operations were controlled by an intercepting valve operated by the driver, and by the independently adjustable reversing gears for the HP and LP cylinders. The engines fully lived up to their purpose but required skilful operation by the driver. During very extensive trial runs, pulling the heavy load — for those days — of 250 tons up the inclines already mentioned, they maintained speeds of 37 and 43 m.p.h. By November 1903, three more engines were built, but these were without independent reversing gears.

In 1903, S. W. Johnson retired. His successor, Richard Mountford Deeley ordered ten more similar locomotives in 1905, Nos. 1000–1009, built to the same dimensions as the two-cylinder engines ordered at the same time, with the exception of the cylinders. In contrast to the prototype the appearance of the engine was improved (Ill. 237). Apart from an increased grate area the main technical difference was in the starting device.

The throttle valve housed in the dome consisted of a main slide-valve with a jockey-valve sliding along it. This jockey-valve opened first on the initial movement of the regulator handle, while the main slide-valve stayed firm. A small port on the jockey-valve coincided with another port on the main slide-valve so that steam could enter both LP cylinders. When the

regulator handle was opened further, both valves moved, and the small port was then closed. Thus the way for the steam to the HP cylinders was opened and the cylinders worked as compound.

This was the definitive starting method on the Midland compounds; in all forty-four such engines had entered service by 1909, including the first batch of 1902. When in 1923 the amalgamation of British railroad companies took place, and the Midland became part of the London, Midland and Scottish Railway, the Deeley compounds as they were also known were subjected to comparative tests with other engines now belonging to the new company. In the meantime some of the compounds had been fitted with superheaters, and they performed so well that the LMS (London, Midland and Scottish Railway) included them in the selection of types for further construction. By 1927, a further ninety-nine engines had been built with some slight modifications, the last of which survived until 1961.

The Midland compounds had an influence on other British railroads. In 1905, the Great Central placed a trial order for four 4–4–2 engines, and the North Eastern, where Smith's influence had once been felt, even built fifty "Atlantics" on his system between 1911 and 1916; these were among the heaviest of their type and were used on all the crack expresses until this railroad lost its independence.

11.1.3 The Four-Cylinder Compound Locomotives with Divided Drives

The four-cylinder compound locomotive was undoubtedly a high spot in the development of the steam locomotive. It came just at the right time when train weights were increasing rapidly with the rise in passenger traffic, and the introduction of truck cars with side corridors and vestibules, together with the addition of restaurant cars, sleeping cars and saloon cars.

The "Outrances" on the Nord Railroad in France had reached the limit of their capabilities. The chief engineer of this company, Gaston Du Bousquet, therefore tested more powerful engines which could

243. Klose's three-cylinder compound engine, the "Brenner", 0–10–0 freight locomotive, Group 9 of the Württemberg State Railroads.

193

244. 0–4–2 locomotive of the French Nord Railroad, No. 2301, for express trains 1886.

replace the "Outrances". As before, he first viewed how matters had been treated in Britain. As we saw in section 7.7, the Nord Railroad had a large number of well-proven 0–4–2 engines with relatively large driving wheels, so that it did not seem too ambitious to follow William Stroudley's example on the London, Brighton and South Coast Railway (cf. section 7.7), and in 1886 La Chapelle Works produced a similar engine, No. 2.301, to be tested with the express trains to Calais and Belgium (Ill. 244). With its 6 ft. 5 in. driving wheels in front, it derailed in 1889 at full speed, which put an end to its career. It was converted into a 4–2–2 engine but its low adhesion of only 14.5 tons made it difficult to use in practice, and it was scrapped around 1894.

Another British prototype was used for the second trial locomotive: Webb's 2–2–2–0 three-cylinder compound locomotive as one can see by comparing the illustration 236 and 245. But there was a considerable difference in the way the compound system was applied. Alfred De Glehn, then technical director of the Alsace Locomotive Works and responsible for design, avoided Webb's unusually large inside LP cylinder by replacing it with two HP cylinders driving the first pair of large wheels, and added two outside LP cylinders. These acted on the second pair of large wheels. For the same reasons as Webb, he did not couple the two driving axles. To enable as exact a comparison as possible, the new engine was made similar to the last "Outrance" series which, as mentioned, had also omitted the truck. Thus the boiler

pressure of 155 lbs. was retained. The cut-offs in HP and LP could be adjusted either independently or together by means of the same reversing screw. To aid starting, live steam was fed into the receiver. This locomotive, No. 701, came out in January 1886, and in March was subjected to thorough test runs with ten cars weighing 105.5 to 152 tons. There was about 1.5 lb. per mile less coal burnt than with the "Outrance", but the engine was not completely satisfactory. The volume ratio between HP and LP cylinders was too small and pressure built up in the receiver, as the LP side was not able to absorb the volume of steam it received and this affected performance. Equally, the long outlet pipes caused an undesired back-pressure, and like Webb's engines, they tended to slip when starting. This engine was later fitted with a four-wheel truck and is now preserved in the Mulhouse Railroad Museum.

The third trial locomotive, also built in La Chapelle, was the No. 2101, again built on the English pattern as an inside cylinder 4–4–0, but the valve chests were mounted vertically outside the frame (Ill. 246). On test runs in July 1890, it proved superior to the other engines in terms of performance since it was able to pull sixteen to seventeen cars (282 to 293 tons) at the same speeds as they had managed. On the other hand, above 56 m.p.h., it did not run smoothly, probably because the pivot pin had no lateral play. When cracks appeared in the frame after running 39,800 miles, this was attributed to overloading the crank axle.

On the basis of the results achieved by the latter two trial locomotives mentioned, Alfred De Glehn and Gaston Du Bousquet now worked together on a design which was to combine the advantages of both engines and eliminate their faults (Ill. 249). The running characteristics were improved by giving lateral play to the truck pin. The two driving axles were coupled, but for purposes of comparison, one of the engines was fitted with special balance weights to enable it to travel without coupling rods. It was immediately recognized that this threw away one important advantage of the four-cylinder arrangement, namely the good balance of the moving masses, since the two uncoupled driving wheels did not run in phase. The cylinders exchanged positions. The HP cylinders were now outside, the LP cylinders inside, below the smokebox, resulting in shorter exhaust pipes. Although the solution of setting the cranks of HP and LP at 180°, with 90° between them, offered the best balancing of masses, the cranks in each group were arranged at an angle of 162° so that at least one cylinder would always be receiving live steam. The divided drive was retained since, compared to a two-cylinder locomotive with inside cylinders, the crank shaft is placed under only half the load. The cylinder volume ratio of 1.95 to 1 which had been too small on No. 701 was increased to 2.42 to 1. As with No. 701, HP and LP reversing gear could be operated independently or together. The former allowed precise adjustment of the cut-off ratios to whatever

operational conditions existed at the time. The starting device consisted of a large three-way tap in the exhaust pipe of the HP cylinder, enabling the engine to be driven in several ways: firstly, as a normal compound engine; secondly, on starting on live steam, all four cylinders, the HP side with full, the LP side with reduced boiler pressure; and furthermore if there was any damage to one of the two sets of motion, the other could be used on its own. These two engines, Nos. 2.121–122 were built by the Alsace Locomotive Works and entered service in August 1891. Pulling 209 tons behind a tender, they ran between Paris and Amiens at an average speed of 54½ m.p.h. and ran smoothly even at 66 m.p.h. They pulled 140 tons up a 1 in 200 (0.5%) incline at 53 m.p.h. and 200 tons at 47 m.p.h.

245. 2–2–2–0 four-cylinder compound locomotive No. 701 of the French Nord Railroad, De Glehn, 1886.

246. 4–4–0 two-cylinder engine of the French Nord Railroad, No. 2101.

This was the first of a type of locomotive which represented the beginning of an epoch in the development of the steam locomotive — unaware to its creators.

The Nord Railroad subsequently ordered fifteen engines, Nos. 2.123–137, which differed from the prototype only in the extended smokebox and the ribbed tubes on the Jean Serve pattern which were henceforth a standard feature. The ribs were on the inside and were intended to catch the heat of the hot gases passing through the middle. Other batches followed, becoming gradually more powerful. As once with the Crampton, the Nord Railroad again achieved the peak speeds for the Nord Railroad's express trains. For example, the fastest express in 1892 between Paris and Calais took 4 hours and 33 minutes for the 174 miles, reaching an average speed of 43 m.p.h.; by 1896 the travelling time was only 3 hours 41 minutes, with an average speed of 50 m.p.h., including stops. The "Nord-Express" even reached a mean speed of 55½ m.p.h. between Paris and St-Quentin.

The performances of these engines aroused considerable interest in the technical world. Other French railroads immediately began to build engines of this type, with the exception of the PLM which created its own version, which will be discussed later. The Prussian State Railroads which were still hesitating between the 4–4–0 engines of the Von Borries and Lochner varieties (cf. chapter 11.1), were the first foreign company to order in 1894 an engine identical to the Nord's Series 2.123–137, which was taken by the Erfurt Region as No. 37. It remained the only such engine for a time.

The Swiss Locomotive Works at Winterthur chose a similar locomotive to exhibit at the 1900 World Fair in Paris. It was bought by the Swiss Central Railroad*, which then ordered another fourteen, Nos. 251–256 (Ill. 251). Unlike the French type, the inside valves were operated by the compact Joy valve gear. The crank setting on each side was 180°, but in 1902, when a further batch was supplied to the Federal Railroad, a setting of 162° as on the Nord Railroad's engines was adopted. These locomotives were intended to pull expresses of 260 tons up a 1 in 100 (1%) gradient. They were abandoned in favour of the less complicated two-cylinder construction because of their involved assembly and numerous components.

Baden had also begun to take notice. Powerful engines were needed here to pull expresses and slow trains up the long inclines of the Black Forest Railroad, and this meant three coupled axles. For this purpose, they adopted the locomotive suggested by the Alsace Locomotive Works, of the De Glehn system. Thus arose the first 4–6–0 De Glehn engine (Ill. 252), the forerunner of a highly successful type which was to extend practically all over Europe. In accordance with the use intended for this engine, the diameter of the coupled wheels was 5 ft. 3 in. But thanks to the good balance of masses, a permitted speed of 56 m.p.h. was achieved with the result that the engine

*Centralbahn.

247. Main station Frankfurt-am-Main, arrival platform hall, 1888.

could be successfully used both on mountainous lines and on the flat. Between 1894 and 1901, a total of eighty-three engines of this Class IVe were acquired. The performance chart showed them pulling 150 tons up 1 in 500 (0.2%) at 47 m.p.h. and 165 tons up 1 in 50 (2%) on the Black Forest Railroad at 18½ m.p.h. Some of them were handed over to the German National Railroad as Class 38.70, but they were scrapped by 1932. No. 38.7001 (the old No. 38) is on show at the Museum of the Technical University in Karlsruhe.

Following shortly after these Baden engines, the Winterthur Works supplied the St. Gotthard Railroad with two engines built deliberately to be compared with them. One of them, No. 202, was identical with the De Glehn four-cylinder types, and the other, No. 201 was the same, with the exception of the motion, which was arranged on the three-cylinder compound system. No. 201 was to run as a compound engine in the valleys, and as a three-cylinder simple in the mountains. It was not as successful as the other, which, with slight modifications, became the famous St. Gotthard engine. By 1905, thirty

such engines, Nos. 201–230, were acquired (Ill. 248). This time the HP cylinders were inside and the LP ones outside. The cranks of both cylinder groups were set at an angle of 135°. The last five engines omitted the inside valve gear and the slide valves operated from the outside by means of rocking shafts. The performance chart envisaged a load of 250 tons on the level at 56 m.p.h. and 140 tons over the mountain routes at 25 m.p.h. This was to shorten the travelling time on the whole Gotthard run by two hours.

248. The Gotthard express with locomotive No. 202, 1893.

249. 4–4–0 four-cylinder compound locomotive of the French Nord Railroad, No. 2121, Du Bousquet and De Glehn. 1891.

When the Swiss Jura-and-Simplon Railroad found itself forced to use heavier locomotives as express engines, they decided to use a locomotive that was very similar to the Gotthard Railroad type mentioned previously. The most important difference was the driving wheel of 68.9 in. because this new locomotive was to be used on less difficult lines. Besides this, the

250. International train with the SBB (Swiss Federal Railroads) locomotive 737, A 3/5, on Wettinger Bridge near Baden, Switzerland.

LP cylinders were outside and the HP inside, like on the French De Glehn engines. The sliding valve of the inside cylinders were also different from the Gotthard locomotives in their Joy gear. The engine was to draw 300 tons at 31½ m.p.h. up slopes of 1 in 100 (1%). These first two engines, Nos. 231–232, were the models for the well-known and very handsome A 3/5 of the Swiss Federal Railroads, 109 slightly more robust examples of which were built from 1904-09, and from 1907 to 1915, fifty-one examples as superheated locomotives with all four cylinders in line (Ill. 250).

Maffei had also exhibited a 4–6–0 locomotive at the Industrial Exhibition in Nuremberg in 1896, with the four cylinders located as on the Gotthard Railroad engines. But the HP and LP gear could only be adjusted together. The Bavarian State Railroad acquired this exhibition locomotive, after which it built forty-three of a slightly more powerful design, Class CV, between 1899 and 1901.

Further development of the De Glehn type took place after 1900 and thus belongs to a different chapter.

At about the same time as Du Bousquet, his colleague Adolph Henry of the PLM (Paris-Lyon-Méditerranée Railroad) held trials with four-cylinder compound locomotives. He did it on a big scale, for in 1888 he had three prototypes built simultaneously in the Railroad Works in Paris, one for expresses, one for freight and one for mixed traffic. The two express engines, Nos. C 1 and C 2 were similar in terms of general construction to the preceding 2–4–2s, Series 111–400. All four cylinders were in line in front of the leading axle. The inside HP cylinders drove the first coupled axle, the outer LP cylinders the second. There were four sets of Heusinger-Walschaerts gear. No. C 1 (Ill. 253) had the inside links operated by parallel linkage attached to the connecting rods, while No. C 2 had only a single eccentric on each side. Both valve motion sets were adjusted together, their weight balanced by a steam cylinder for lighter operation. For starting, live steam was fed into the HP cylinders, whose cranks were set at 198° to ensure that there was never a piston in the "dead" point. Thus both HP pistons could receive live steam in every position. No. C 1 entered service in 1889/90 on the same timetable as the existing 2–4–2s on the Paris-Laroche run. It kept up a speed of 51-59 m.p.h. pulling trains weighing 294 tons. On a speed trial on July 1, 1890, pulling only one car, it

254. 4–4–0 De Glehn locomotive of the Swiss Central Railroad, No. 254.

252. 4–6–0 De Glehn locomotive of the Baden State Railroad on Black Forest line, Group IV e.

travelled at a sustained speed of between 64 and 84 m.p.h. In 1889 No. C2 was shown in Paris at the exhibition. Both engines pulled regular expresses until 1900, together with the 2–4–2 engines of Series 111–400. They then ran local trains, until they were scrapped in 1923/24.

Henry's next prototype consisted of two eight-coupled engines, Nos. 4301–4302, which were to enable a comparison with the standard locomotives using this wheel arrangement of the Series 2500. The compound arrangement was the same as that on Nos. C1 and C2 already described. The inside HP cylinders were inclined and mounted higher at the front, to clear the leading axle, as they drove the second axle. The outside LP cylinders drove the third axle. On the test runs made in 1892, these compound engines burned 10-13 per cent less fuel than the normal two-cylinder simples and pulled a 5 per cent heavier train weight. No. 430 was also shown in Paris in 1889. The excellent results achieved by these two prototypes led to the building of a further 140 similar four-cylinder compound eight-coupled engines from 1892, using various

parts from old "Bourbonnais" which needed new boilers (Ill. 254).

Henry's third experimental locomotive was new in that it was an eight-coupled engine for mixed traffic, that was to haul express freight trains on the level and heavy passenger trains over mountainous lines (Ill. 255). Because it had to achieve 38 m.p.h., it was fitted with driving wheels of 4 ft. 11 in. diameter, which were large for eight-coupled locomotives at that time. The inside HP cylinders were inclined and

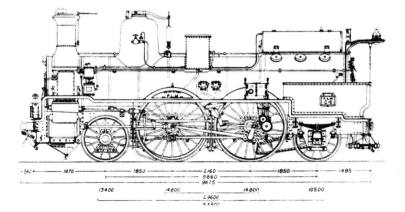

253. 2-4-2 four-cylinder express compound locomotive of the French PLM (Paris-Lyon-Méditerranée) Railroad, No. C1, 1888.

199

set between the two first coupled axles, because otherwise the connecting rods, which drove the third axle, would have been too long. The cranks were set at 225° on each side. It was fitted with the Le Chatelier reverse steam brake for service on mountain tracks. In service, these two locomotives, Nos. 3201 and 3202 gave fuel savings of between 10.5 and 15 compared with the same wheel diameter 0–6–2s used previously, despite the fact that they normally did not pull maximum loads. One of the prototypes was also on show in Paris in 1889. The heating surface was different on each of them; No. 3201 had 1,650 sq. ft. and No. 3202 had 1,744 sq. ft. Between 1892 and 1896, with certain modifications — notably the use of 9 ft. 10 in. Serve-type heating tubes — a further 112 engines entered service. Forty of them were converted into 4–6–0s in 1898/99, so that their maximum speed could be increased from 41 to 50 m.p.h.

254. 0–8–0 four-cylinder compound freight locomotive of the French PLM (Paris-Lyon-Méditerranée) Railroad, No. 4521.

When the comparative runs already described proved the superiority of the truck for fast-running engines, Henry decided to draw up a new design. In 1892 he had two 4–4–0 engines built, Nos. C11 and C12. But he was never able to free himself completely of his old ideas that a truck was an unnecessary complication incurring an increase in weight. He thus had the third locomotive, C51 (later C3) built as a 2–4–0. Both types had the same motion and boiler. This time the HP cylinders were outside and the LP ones inside in the same arrangement as De Glehn. In 1892, Henry died before completion of his work, and Charles Baudry, his successor, carried it on. The 2–4–0 engine was abandoned because of its poorer running, and the 4–4–0 engine was improved slightly. Its external appearance was striking because of the streamlined surfaces used to lessen wind resistance from the Mistral wind which often blew in the Rhône valley. More important was the fact that, after tests held by Privat, an engineer on the railroad, the Gooch type inside LP cylinder valve gear from 1894 was set at a fixed 60 per cent cut-off. When the reversing screw was turned, it carried the inside valve gears to their end position and they were then firmly held by a notch there, so that the reversing screw could now be turned back independently to other cut-off points. This type of combined valve gear was a special feature of the PLM (Paris-Lyon-Méditerranée) four-cylinder compound locomotives for the next twenty years. As it resulted in less tractive power in reverse, tank engines were an exception. The first forty Baudry locomotives, Nos. C21–60, known as the "Small C", were followed between 1895 and 1902 by 120 more powerful "Big C", Nos. C61–180 (Ill. 256). They became famous outside the world of the technical experts, for

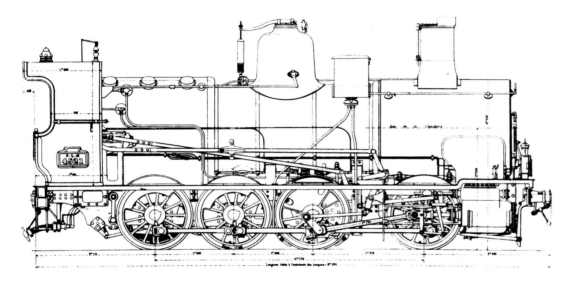

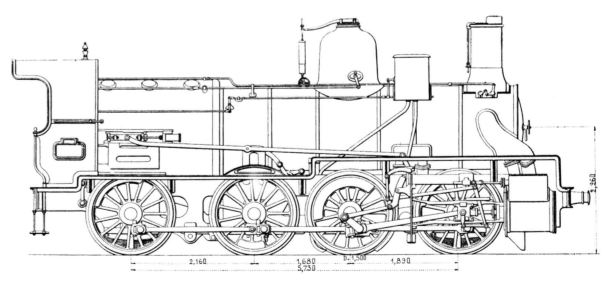

255. 0–8–0 four-cylinder compound locomotive of the French PLM (Paris-Lyon-Méditerranée) Railroad for mixed traffic (Series 3200).

they hauled the "Côte d'Azur Rapide" luxury train for years and were very noticeable because of their appearance, which gave them the nickname "Coupe-vent" (wind-cutter).

This "Côte d'Azur Rapide", sometimes also called the "Nice Express", was one of the fastest trains in the world in its day. Still hauled by this engine in 1906, it ran between Paris and Marseilles at an overall speed of 52 m.p.h. or, excluding stops, at 54¼ m.p.h. Between Valence and Avignon, it even reached the average speed of 57½ m.p.h. The normal weight of the eight-wheeled cars was 230-235 tons. Pulling the "Rome Express" which weighed only 170 tons, one of these "Coupe-vent" engines reached an average speed of 74 m.p.h. on the 25.7 miles between Tonnerre and Laroche, with a top speed of 81 m.p.h. The "Big C" was gradually replaced on express runs after 1911, when the "Pacific" type was introduced, and it was scrapped in 1938/39. No. C115 is exhibited today at the Mulhouse Railroad Museum in Alsace.

11.1.4 The Four-Cylinder Compound Locomotive with Single Axle Drive and Four Cranks

Francis Webb — an authoritarian person who did not take kindly to criticism — finally had to recognize that the bitter complaints from all sides of his three-cylinder compound arrangement were all too justified. His reputation was at stake. He thought matters over,

and in 1897, had two trial engines built at Crewe — remarkable examples at first glance, in that they were the first long-distance locomotives on the LNWR (London-and-North Western Railway) to have a front truck (Ill. 257). One of these engines, No. 1501, the "Jubilee", was built as a four-cylinder simple expansion engine with 14 × 24 in. cylinders; the other, No. 1502, "Black Prince" was a four-cylinder compound engine.

But Webb simplified the De Glehn motion arrangement. He arranged for all four cylinders were lined up together under the smokebox, with the HP cylinders outside and the LP inside. Since the cranks on each pair of cylinders were set at 180°, the gear of the four slide valves was very easy to arrange. The inside LP valves were driven by two sets of Joy gears. Their slide valve spindles emerged at the front and were attached to one end of a horizontally rocking lever, the outside ends also forward extended by HP valve spindles at the other end. The space Webb created by using Joy gear allowed the crank axle to be supported by a central frame plate, a measure which was retained on the LNWR with its later twin inside cylinder engines. Another individual feature was the balancing of the inside revolving masses by extensions of the crank web slabs. The outside revolving masses were balanced in the large wheel bosses which were bored out and filled with lead. This is another detail which often occurred later on the LNWR.

Nothing is now known about the comparative runs

256. 4-4-0 four-cylinder compound express train engine of the French PLM (Paris-Lyon-Méditerranée) Railroad, No. C74, "Big C".

made between the four-cylinder engine and the compound engine. But since the four cylinder simple engine "Jubilee" was modified as compound, it must have consumed more fuel. When modified it was renumbered No. 1901, and was used to signify the whole class of forty engines derived from it. These engines did not, however, prove very successful. The ratio between the cylinder volumes, 1.69 to 1, was insufficient. For this reason, the LP cylinders were increased to the maximum permissible diameter for inside ones — 20½ in. — but even so, the ratio of 1.87 to 1 was unsatisfactory. The boiler pressure was also increased to 200 lbs. There was no starting device: if the HP cylinders were in the wrong position, the driver had to wait for the LP cylinders to fill with steam which leaked past the valves. Despite all these faults, Webb again persevered on his design. His original intention was undoubtedly to build an engine comparable with the "Greater Britain" while avoiding its faults, as can be guessed from the fact that the two boilers were of the same dimensions.

In 1901, however, he was forced to bring out a more powerful version, the twenty engines of the "Alfred the Great" class. Neither this nor the other class proved as successful in service as had been hoped. The old "Bloomer" and "Lady of the Lake" engines were always having to be coupled on as pilot engines. Webb had to resign. His successor, George Whale, tried to salvage what was possible. He altered the valve gear on the compound engines and converted some of them quite radically into twin inside cylinder simple engines. All the earlier three-cylinder compounds were completely abandoned. Thus one of the most individual chapters in the history of the locomotive came to a sorry end. The only ones to survive were the eight-coupled, three-cylinder compound engines and the subsequent four-cylinder compound

engines, modified to a greater or lesser degree, some into 2–8–0s.

De Glehn's 4–4–0 engines, mentioned in the preceding section, which had been ordered on a trial basis by the Prussian State Railroad, ran more smoothly and, above all, more powerfully uphill than the standard class S 3 types. But they asked more in return from the drivers and the maintenance men. For this reason, the Locomotive Committee was instructed to examine the possibility of building an equivalent engine with four-cylinders, which would be easier to operate. A request by the Hanover Locomotive Works (later named Hanomag) to the Ministry of Public Works to build a locomotive which matched the ideas of the Locomotive Committee and which was to be shown at the World Fair in Paris in 1900, was granted. The design was by Von Borries (Ill. 258).

Unfortunately Von Borries was instructed to keep as close as possible to the standard class S 3 engine. The motion matched his former 1897 project: one outside LP and the corresponding HP cylinder formed a single cast block. Both blocks were bolted together and formed a saddle on the American pattern, which supported the smokebox. The front frame was built by bars, also on American lines, which gave easier access to the inside motion. All four cylinders drove the first coupled axle; the cranks on each side were set at 180°, those on both sides at 90°. The four slide valves were operated on each side only by a single inside Walschaerts gear, with its spindles linked to rocking shaft. The combination levers, for control for both the HP and LP valves, were hung on this rocking shaft. The length of the links and the location of the pins of the combination levers were calculated to always give 20 per cent greater cut-off on the LP side than on the HP.

In general, the locomotive exhibited proved satisfac-

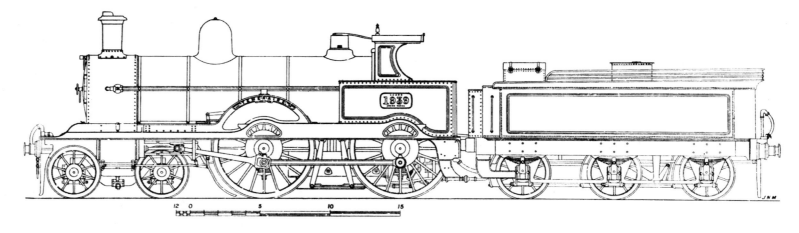

257. The "Temeraire", 4–4–0 four-cylinder compound locomotive of the LNWR (London and North Western Railway, No. 1939, Jubilee Class.

202

258. 4–4–0 four-cylinder compound loco-motive Class S5, of the Prussian State Railroad, Von Borries type, for the Paris World Exhibition, 1900.

tory in service. It was able to pull a regular service of forty-three axled express trains on the Berlin-Hanover-Cologne run. The instruction to adhere to the S3 class had resulted in a good engine in itself, but not in a sufficient improvement in performance. That was one reason why only sixteen engines were ordered. From 1902, seventy-seven somewhat more powerful 4–4–0 De Glehn locomotives entered service. Von Borries's four-cylinder compound arrangement proved so successful that it became the basis for further development of the four-cylinder compound engine in Germany. It was the only one that could be retained, rivalizing with the De Glehn system.

The four-cylinder compound locomotives designed by Plancher for the Adriatico Railroad in Italy were remarkable in many respects (Ill. 259). They were intended to pull express trains between Rome and Milan via the Appennine Pass separating them. Plancher accommodated the large grate he needed for this purpose by turning the boiler the other way round, so that the firebox lay unhindered over the front truck. However, the cylinders were arranged to overhang at the other end. He fitted four cylinders for better compensation of masses. Unlike the types already described, both HP cylinders, one inside and

one outside, were joined in a single casting, and the same was the case with the two LP cylinders. Thus there were two identical cylinders on each side and a common valve for each pair feasible, operated by outside Walschaerts valve gear. The cranks of each pair of cylinders were set at 90° mutual to the other pair. As with the De Glehn system, HP and LP gear could be controlled independently. The driver's cab was at the front. This fact, and the enclosed super-structure, meant that the crew were less troubled by smoke in the many tunnels. The front wall was tapered to reduce air resistance. The coal was stored in a tank mounted at the side, and a six-wheel tank wagon accommodated the water supply.

The first engine, built at the Florence Railroad Works, No. 3701, was shown in Paris in 1900. When the exhibition was over, the Ouest Railroad asked for comparative runs to be held against a De Glehn 4–6–0 engine, No. 2516, on the Ouest's tracks. However the driving wheel diameter of the other engine was only 5 ft. 9 in. and its boiler was smaller. The Ouest's engine had, nevertheless, better fuel consumption figures, so that Ouest kept to the De Glehn type and introduced the first 4–6–0 express engines of this type. On the Adriatico line, the first exhibition engine was

259. 4–6–0 locomotive of the Italian Adriatico Railroad, No. 3701, 1900. The driver's cabin is up in the front.

followed by fourteen more, Nos. 5002-17, some supplied by Borsig, and they later formed Group 670 on the Italian State Railroads.

11.1.5 *The Four-Cylinder Compound Locomotive with Two-Crank Drive*

Since the 1850s, stationary and ships' engines had often used cylinders placed in front of one another, connected to a single crank with a common piston rod, called "Tandem engines". In the United States, H. O. Perry, Director of the Shepherd Ironworks, was the first to think of using this type of steam engine for a locomotive. The Erie Railroad placed its 4–4–0 engine No. 122 at his disposal for trials — it had been built in 1851 by Hinkley Drury of Boston and had been modified in 1868 (Ill. 260). This was one of the classic American engines of its time with inclined outside cylinders of 16 × 26 in. These were replaced by two pairs of HP and LP cylinders arranged one in front of the other. Vertical rotary valves controlled steam inlet and outlet. The cylinder volume ratio of 1:4 was too great. The quantity of steam entering the LP cylinders could not fill them and there was thus

too little pressure in the blast pipe. The locomotive was withdrawn from service owing to poor performance. Even if the attempt was unsuccessful, No. 122 was nonetheless the first locomotive actually to use the compound system and therefore deserves to be rescued from obscurity.

The Boston-and-Albany Railroad built a locomotive at its Springfield Works in 1883, on a patent held by Henry Dumbar, with normal slide valves. After a bare seven months of trials, however, this was converted back into a two-cylinder simple engine, as it had no advantages over others.

Spurred on by Webb's attempts, Matthew Holmes in England converted the 4–4–0 locomotive No. 224, which had plunged into the water at the Firth of Tay Bridge disaster of 1879 and had subsequently been recovered, into a tandem compound engine. The four cylinders were mounted inside, the LP cylinders replacing the original cylinders and the HP ones in front of them. The slide valves for both groups could be adjusted individually by their own Joy valve gear. Neither the results with this engine, nor those with the Great Western's two 2–4–0s built by William Dean in 1886 at the Swindon Works, justified further use of this system.

204

Section 11.1.3 described the efforts by the Nord Railroad in France to create a locomotive to meet the more demanding operational conditions which had arisen. Du Bousquet even extended these attempts to freight engines. He chose the tandem layout, and, like Dean, joined both cylinders in the form of a single casting to save on length (Ill. 261). The LP piston at the front had a piston rod above and below which emerged next to the HP cylinder walls and ended in a common crosshead for all three piston rods. A common valve served as steam inlet and outlet, with an exterior part for the HP steam and an internal one for the LP steam. For starting, boiler steam was passed into the LP cylinder via a spring valve. There was also an air intake valve for running with the throttle closed, which closed automatically when boiler steam was introduced for starting. The short overall length of the tandem cylinders allowed them to be added easily to two standard eight coupled "180 Unités" type engines, Nos. 4.729 and 4.731, in 1887.

Another modified engine, No. 4.733, was sent to the World Fair in Paris in 1889. The first two had trial runs pulling coal trains on the Lens-Logneau line, with gradients of 1 in 167 (0.6%). These engines could pull 886 tons as against the 663 tons hauled by the standard eight-coupled engines. The trip between Fives-Lille and Hirson, with a 1 in 83 (1.2%) gradient saw trains hauled with a weight of 513 tons as against 454 tons. The fuel saving was 11 to 13 per cent. On the basis of this performance, the Nord Railroad ordered from Fives-Lille in 1889 twenty locomotives of this type, Nos. 101–120, most of which were con-

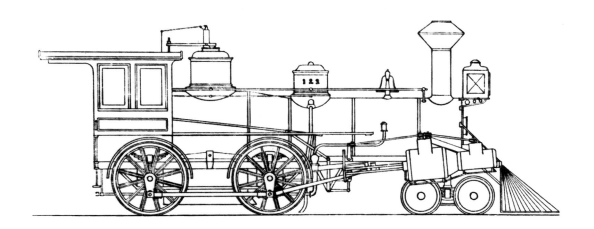

260. Tandem locomotive of the Erie Railroad, 1868, first compound locomotive in the world.

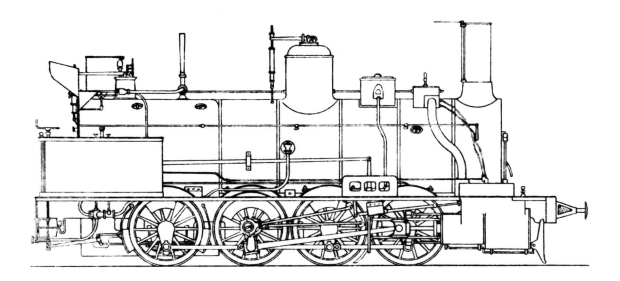

261. Du Bousquet's tandem freight locomotive of the French Nord Railroad, 1887.

205

verted into two-cylinder simple engines between 1912 and 1923.

Because of its heavy reciprocating masses, the tandem arrangement was not very suitable for express engines. But Sigismund Kordina, chief designer at the Hungarian Locomotive Works in Budapest, considered them the best solution in the very difficult conditions he met with, where engines were needed with an axle loading of no more than 14 tons. Indigenous brown coal was to be burned, necessitating a large grate; this in turn, meant an outside frame construction, which was often used in Hungary, for the 4–4–0 wheel arrangement. The locomotives were to be compounds, thereby utilizing the steam better. In view of the outside frames, the LP cylinders had exceeded the loading gauge because of the diameter required. There were some justifiable reservations about crankshafts. These considerations led to the Category I e locomotive (later 222) of the Hungarian State Railroads, with tandem cylinders and outside frame, which allowed the truck to be pushed far back so that it could take a larger share of the load (Ill. 262).

The first such engine, No. 733, was supplied on December 11, 1890. Unlike the Nord Railroads engines already described, the HP and LP cylinders were separate castings, so that their stuffing boxes were easily accessible from the outside. For the first time, the Walschaerts valve gear was fitted in Hungary. It was outside and operated the pairs of slide valves, also arranged in tandem. Initially the Lindner-type starting device was used. Later groups had a special starting valve operated by the driver, and finally there was a semi-automatic valve which was opened by the driver and which closed automatically once the wheels had made one half-turn. The volume ratio between the HP and LP cylinders was altered several times and was finally set at 1.32 to 1. By 1903, ninety-three such engines had been acquired. Thus Category I e outnumbered all other tandem compound locomotives used in Europe. They pulled 160 tons at 37½ m.p.h. up 1 in 1.49 (0.7%), using Hungarian brown coal as fuel. There was a 12 per cent saving in steam compared with two-cylinder simple engines.

Other European railroads did not have conditions as unusual as those in Hungary, so that only a few tandem compound locomotives were built, for expresses in Russia. De Glehn, Mallet and Borodin together designed an engine for the Russian Southern Railroads. It had a normal inside frame. The HP cylinder

262. Locomotive Category I e (later 222) of the Hungarian State Railroads, tandem type, Sigmund Kordina, 1890.

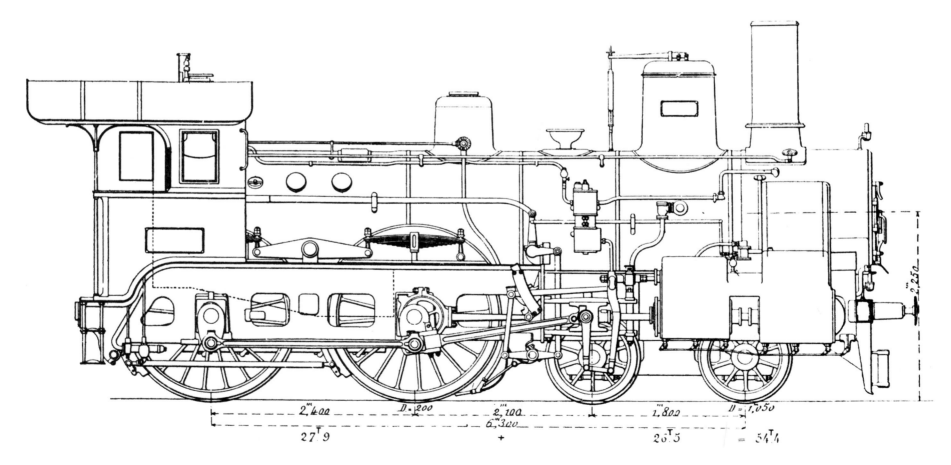

was in front of the LP cylinder, and both were slightly inclined. The first such engine — No. 101 — was built by the Alsace Locomotive Works, and the others — Nos. 102–106 — were built in Russia. Although there were very good results within the permitted speed limit — 37 ½ m.p.h. — the engines were not followed up by others.

In 1898, Russian State Railroads again reverted to the tandem type. On data supplied by the Transport Ministry, sixty-seven engines were built at the Putiloff Works in St. Petersburg, which, apart from the inside frame, were very similar to the Hungarian types (Ill. 263). They were used on the St. Petersburg-Warsaw run, and several were used on the Trans-Siberian Railroad. They really brought to a close the use of 4–4–0 engines in Russia, which had first entered service there in 1845. As in Italy, the 2–6–0 was preferred because of its higher adhesion weight — a factor that mattered more in Russia owing to snow and ice than to sharp inclines.

The tandem compounds were used most of all in the United States. If the compound system was to be retained, the LP cylinder on the two-cylinder version would have had to be so large that it would have projected beyond the loading gauge of the locomotive. In view of the aversion to the less accessible inside

cylinder with its crank axle, the tandem system meant that the standard motion and smaller LP cylinders could be used to obtain the necessary performance. At the same time the tandem system offered equal efforts on both sides with respect to the two-cylinder compound system, known as cross-compound.

It is a curious fact that the introduction and development of the tandem engine in North America is connected with two men bearing the same name, John Player. The first John Player made his plans in 1886, to convert a 4–4–0 into a tandem compound when he was locomotive superintendent of the Iowa Central Railroad. He could not carry these out either in that post or in his next position, with the Wisconsin Central Railroad. However, on June 1, 1890, he made his final move to the Atchisson, Topeka and Santa Fé Railroad, and he was at last able to put his plans into effect on a grand scale. But his namesake preceded him, because the Santa Fé Railroad was in a financial crisis.

The second John Player was chief draftsman at the Brooks Locomotive Works which was merged in 1902 with the American Locomotive Company. His designs, No. 499 and No. 515, which were shown at the Columbia World Fair in Chicago, were delivered to the Great Northern. They were based on the 2–8–0 engine which had been built for the same railroad shortly beforehand. To keep the construction short, both tandem cylinders were located very close to one another. The HP cylinders were governed by piston valves with inside admission. The LP cylinders kept the normal slide valves with outside admission. As both valves thus moved reciprocally, a rocking shaft lever had to be provided to achieve the opposite motion of both valve rods. These were the only two engines built for the time being.

When the first-mentioned John Player was at last able to execute his plans, he built five 2–8–0 locomotives in 1898, which were also based on existing two-cylinder engines. The cylinders on each side were separate castings and each formed a saddle, so that the very elongated smokebox was supported in two places. Both pairs of cylinders were operated in conjunction with two piston valves each, which were mounted on a common valve rod and were driven by the standard inside Stephenson link gear.

No. 999 was compared with a standard sister engine on the difficult mountain track over the Raton Pass in New Mexico. The gradients to the west are up to 1 in 28 (3.5%) and to the east 1 in 30 (3.3%). The tandem compound engine needed 18 per cent less fuel and 14 per cent less water. Player then had two experimental 4–6–0 express engines with tandem cylinders built at the Topeka Railroad Works. They did not prove very suitable, and this type was not repeated, but the two 2–8–0s led to a certain spread of this type to other railroads with difficult mountainous routes. The only such 2–8–0 tandem compound locomotives in Europe were in Russia, where they were

built in large numbers between 1899 and 1910 for various railroads, at home and foreign locomotive works, as, for example, by the Alsace Locomotive Works for the Moscow, Vindau and Rybinsk Railroad (Ill. 264).

On the Santa Fé Railroad, there was meanwhile intense competition between Baldwin and the American Locomotive Company (ALCO) which had been formed as the result of a merger between several locomotive works. The aim was to conquer the Raton Pass with the world's most powerful locomotive. In late 1901, ALCO supplied two 2–10–0 tandem engines with dimensions which surpassed anything supplied previously. Baldwin thereupon immediately delivered a somewhat larger 2–10–0 engine. All three were used as pushers and were very powerful. But when the train was uncoupled at the crest, they had to run tender first downhill and they often became derailed. To provide better guidance for this purpose, Baldwin fitted the engines ordered after 1903 with an additional rear Bissel truck (Ill. 265). Thus arose the Santa Fé type, named after the line of its origin, eighty-six engines of which were built by 1904, Nos. 900–985. Although they have often been written about and illustrated, nothing has been published about this Santa Fé type in respect of its performance.

For the sake of completeness, two other attempts at tandem compound locomotives in Europe must be mentioned briefly. For the trains running on the circular Inner Circle in Paris, fifteen 4–6–0 tank engines were built on plans by Du Bousquet, Nos. 51–66, in the Nord Railroad's main works at La Chapelle. The tandem layout was adopted because they wished to exploit the advantages of the compound

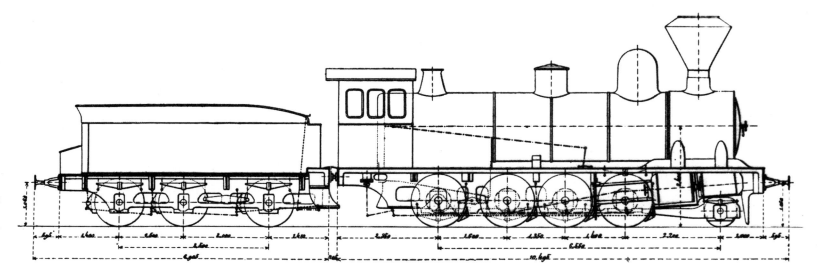

264. 2–8–0 tandem locomotive built by the Alsace Locomotive Works for the Moscow-Vindau-Rybinsk Railroad.

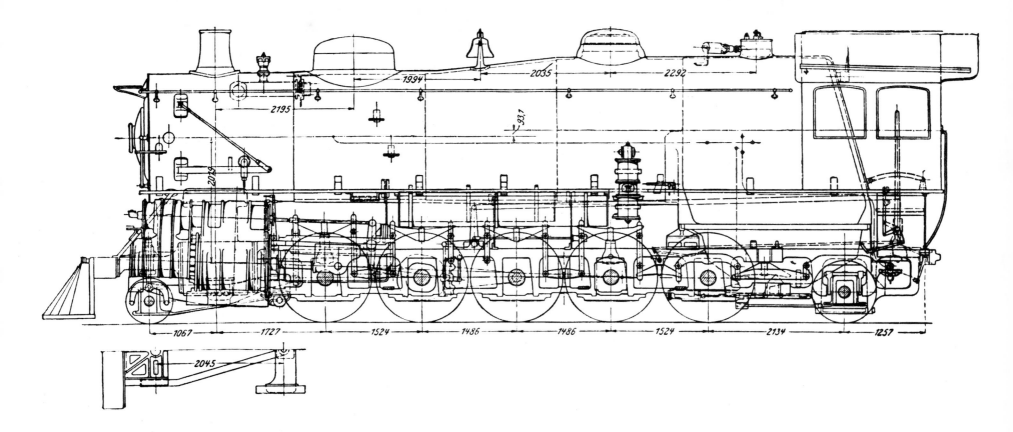

265. 2–10–2 tandem locomotive, Santa Fé type, Baldwin Works, 1903/04.

system and also because the identical motion on both sides enabled faster starts to be made from the frequent stops on the Circle line than those possible with the unequal starting moment of a normal two-cylinder compound.

The second attempt was that of the four 2–8–0 locomotives built with the Sondermann system by Krauss for the Bavarian State Railroads (Nos. 2063–2064) and Palatinate Railroad (Nos. 200–201) in 1896/97. These engines had both cylinders made in a single casting in such a way that the HP side partially projected at the rear and the LP part at the front was arranged around a hollow sleeve extended forwards. The single piston was stepped — the smaller diameter serving for the HP part and the larger one for the LP. This type of construction gave trouble at maintenance, and all four engines were soon converted into two cylinder engines. Another way of arranging the four cylinders while maintaining the twin crank drive was to mount them one above the other. As with the tandem layout, identical cylinder efforts resulted on both sides. The disadvantages of the extra length and the difficult removal of the pistons were avoided, and instead, extremely large and heavy crossheads were to be provided. A single piston valve was sufficient for each pair of cylinders. As was normal in America, both

pairs of cylinders and the valve chests were manufactured as a single casting with a half-saddle for the smokebox. For starting, the steam was passed from one side of the piston to the other via a turning cock, so that steam could always be let into the LP cylinder. Running light, air from outside was admitted through automatic valves.

This system, by Samuel Matthew Vauclain, then chief draftsman and later President of the Baldwin Works, was made for the first time in 1891. It was quickly adopted for both express and freight engines. In April 1894, a locomotive of this type supplied by Baldwin to the Central Railroad of New Jersey (Ill. 266) was submitted to thorough comparative trials with a similar two-cylinder simple engine. It consumed 19.86 per cent less coal and 18.7 per cent less water. A heavy freight engine with Vauclain cylinders was built for the New York, Lake Erie and Western Railroad (later the Erie Railroad). This was the heaviest locomotive shown at the Columbia World Fair in Chicago (Ill. 267), and a good example of the contemporary trend towards the "Colossal". A remarkable feature was the enormous grate area of the huge Wootten anthracite-burning firebox.

There was an attempt to introduce the Vauclain system into Europe as well. In 1899 Baldwin supplied five

209

such 4–4–0 engines to France (Nos. 2801–05), as well as the same number of conventional simples (Nos. 2851–56) at the same time to the French State Railroad. The thorough comparative tests did not result in any special advantages for the Vauclain type which was therefore not introduced in France, where the De Glehn type had meanwhile become standard.

In order to get to know the much heralded advantages of American construction methods at first hand, the Bavarian State Railroads acquired two 4–4–2 and two 2–8–0 Vauclain-type locomotives at about this time. In many points of detail the engines were not satisfactory. Their significance for Bavarian and then for all German locomotive cnstruction, which in turn influenced many other countries, was the introduction of the American bar frame. This became a European feature, although constructed in a different manner.

11.2   The Introduction of Superheated Steam

The compound system had lessened the losses through condensation in the cylinders by dividing the fall in temperature. But the more radical solution to the problem was to heat the steam before entering the cylinders to such an extent that it still remained above condensation point after expansion. Hirn in Alsace made the first tests with superheated steam in the 1850s, using stationary steam engines. He was able to raise the entry temperature of the steam by only 122-212°F (50-100°C) because at that time the only lubricating oil known was organic, which degenerated at higher temperatures. Nevertheless, up to 23 per cent savings in steam were made.

When an engineer, Wilhelm Schmidt of Kassel took up Hirn's idea, he had at his disposal mineral oils which would still lubricate at a temperature of 660°F (350°C). He was thus able to bring the steam to a much higher temperature. Schmidt had such good economic results on stationary steam engines with this "superheated steam" as he called it, that the time was ripe to use its advantages on the most common type of steam engine then prevalent, that of the locomotive. Superheated steam had other specially good characteristics for locomotives, apart from the prevention of losses through condensation. Movement while running kept the boiler water in a state of constant turbulence; this meant that the steam took away thousands of water droplets with it which subsequently evaporated during expansion and further cooled down the cylinder walls. Whereas the specific volume of the saturated steam (i.e., the volume occupied by the unit of weight of steam) diminishes with the increase in pressure, the specific volume, on the contrary, if sufficiently overheated (i.e., superheated), increases. The result is then that when the same amount of water is evaporated in the boiler, with superheating a bigger volume of steam enters

266. 4–4–0 express train engine with Vauclain cylinders, Central Railroad of New Jersey, No. 450, 1893.

267. 2–10–0 freight train locomotive with Vauclain cylinders, New York, Lake Erie and Western Railroad, No. 805.

the cylinders and they can therefore do more work. Obviously an additional form of heat is needed to superheat the steam, but only a small percentage of that needed to vapourize the water. This extra expenditure is more than balanced by the improved performance in the cylinder.

Robert Garbe, engineer and member of the Berlin Region of the Prussian State Railroads, immediately recognized the advantages of superheated steam when Schmidt approached him with the idea of using his invention for locomotives. Garbe and Schmidt, working together, succeeded after unrelenting efforts in overcoming the countless difficulties involved with this pioneering, and they paved the way for the superheated steam locomotive. This represented the greatest step forward in locomotive design since Stephenson. The Prussian State Railroad administration deserves praise for supporting these endeavours in every way. From the outset, Schmidt was aware that an effective superheater had to be created as an integral part of the traditional Stephenson boiler, taking up little space in the confined boiler area without any substantial increase in the weight, and that it should be simple to maintain.

On the basis of a preliminary draft made by Schmidt and Garbe for a superheater, the Henschel firm in March 1897 applied to the Berlin office for permission to install it experimentally in a locomotive. On August 25, 1897, approval was given for two locomotives, then under construction, to be fitted with superheaters. One of these was Class S3 type ordered from the Vulkan works in Stettin, one of a series of fourteen engines with works number 1643. On

April 13, 1898, it left the factory as the first superheated steam locomotive in the world and was designated the No. 74 by the Hanover Railroad Region. This engine was soon transferred to Kassel as No. 20 (later 401), and was compared there with the second superheated steam locomotive supplied by Henschel on July 29, 1898, Class P4, No. Kassel 131 (later 1846). The only existing illustration of the Vulkan engine is a poor amateur photograph taken later, but there is a Works' photograph of the Henschel engine (Ill. 268). The superheater initially consisted of a 17¾ in. flue placed in the middle of the boiler, which contracted to 8 in. near the firebox tube plate to lessen the effect of the impinging flame. The front end which entered the smokebox had slits, and was closed at its end with a special wall with a collector, taking up the free ends of the "U"-shaped superheater elements. The steam passed from the regulator valve into the inner chamber of the collector, then through the elements, returned to the outer chamber and was fed from there into the cylinders. The hot gases flowing through the flue entered the smokebox via the slits mentioned. The flow of the hot gases was controlled by a rotary valve fitted outside in the flue. Slide valves were not suitable with these high steam temperatures as they became distorted, so that only piston valves were suitable. But it took a long time for a type to be found suitable for the high operating temperatures.

Various faults appeared with the boiler and superheater of these first two superheated steam locomotives, as is always to be expected with innovations. Nonetheless the engines remained in service until the

268. One of the two first superheated steam locomotives, Kassel No. 131 (later 1846), 1898.

end of the First World War, and proved that the promoters were on the right track. One of the main faults was that the large superheater flue took up the space of nearly a third of the fire tubes and reduced the boiler heating surface by that amount. Additionally the caps on the elements burned away very quickly as they came too close to the firebox.

Schmidt then produced a new design in which the superheater was entirely arranged outside the smoke-box. The hot gases were fed to the superheater tubes via a flue of only 12 in. diameter running through the lower part of the boiler. The superheater tubes were arranged in three concentric rows around the smoke-box wall. The upper ends of the ring-shaped rows of tubes were bent and expanded into the bottoms of two oblong cast-steel headers which were arranged on the right and left of the chimney. The two inner row tubes were bent in such a way as to constitute an arched continuation of the flame flue with a radius decreasing towards the front of the smokebox and thus forming a passage facilitating uniform distribution of the gases in the superheater. All three rows of ring tubes were surrounded by a sheet metal cover which was arranged concentrically round the smoke-box wall and which reached above the height of the exhaust pipe. The hot gases coming out of the fire tube passed between the rows of dampers inside their cover and left through adjustable dampers at the top.

269. 4–4–0 locomotive with smokebox super-heater, Prussian State Railroads, Berlin No. 74, for the World Exhibition in Paris in 1900.

212

The steam entered first the right-hand header, flowed several times in opposite directions through four rows of tubes between the right and left header and finally entered the cylinders superheated. This superheater type meant making the diameter of the smokebox larger than the boiler and this enlarged smokebox was a characteristic feature on all Prussian superheated steam locomotives, except at the end of their history. In mid-1899, the Prussian State Railroads purchased four engines with this smokebox superheater. Two 4-4-0 tank engines intended for the Wannsee Railroad in Berlin were ordered from Henschel, Nos. Berlin 2069-2070 (later 6682-83). In suburban operation with frequent stops, they did not prove very much better than the standard two-cylinder Class T5, and were thus not continued. The other two engines were again similar to the standard express engine Class S3. One was supplied by the Vulkan Works, No. Hanover 86; Borsig supplied the other, No. Berlin 74 (Ill. 269). After several trial runs, the latter was sent to the World Fair in Paris in 1900 where it appeared quite insignificant between the other large 4-4-2 and 4-6-0 locomotives shown; it was noted, but criticized by the experts.

No. Hanover 86 was put between early 1900 and 1902 on the same timetable runs as the standard two-cylinder compound locomotive Class S3 and the Von Borries-type four-cylinder compound locomotives Class S5. Precise details exist of the coal consumption, which amounted to .038 lb. per mile for the superheated locomotive, with .037 and .038 lb. for the others. The smaller value for the S3 lcomotives is explained by the fact that they needed a pilot engine more often than the other two types. In such cases one half of actual consumption was counted. Lubricating oil consumption by the superheated locomotive was clearly less.

At first, there was no convincing proof of the superiority of the superheated engine as opposed to the normal. Thanks to the particular interest shown by Dr. Müller, a senior engineer in the Prussian ministry of transport, tests were continued. Initially no one knew exactly how large to make the cylinders on superheated locomotives with regard to the greater volume of the superheated steam. The 18 in. of the first engines had given way to 19 in. and 20 in., and 21 in. diameter was chosen for the six engines Nos. Halle 435-440 supplied by Borsig. The heating surface of the superheater was also increased by about 21½ sq. ft., since otherwise no temperature above 570° F (300° C) could be reached. These alterations soon made things look different. The tests held in the summer of 1902 between the two locomotives in question, with a compound Class S3 engine and the Von Borries four-cylinder compound engine resulted in an average performance of 911 h.p. for the superheated engine, 734 h.p. for the S3 and 865 h.p. for the Von Borries, the trials being held on the 77 miles between Berlin/Grunewald and Block 191 near Stendal.

But what aroused the interest of more than just the technical experts was the amazing result of the trials held on the military line between Marienfelde and Zossen in the period January 19-April 19, 1904. The comparison was between a 4-4-4 three-cylinder compound locomotive designed for fast running, to be described in fuller detail later, and the most recent Prussian engines of the time. These were a 4-4-0 two-cylinder compound engine Class S3, a 4-4-0 De Glehn compound Class S5 and a 4-4-2 four-cylinder De Glehn compound, and a 4-4-2 four-cylinder Von Borries compound. Both 4-4-2s were classed as S7. At the last moment, it was decided to also include the Schmidt superheated locomotive which had meanwhile been perfected, and now classed as S4 (Ill. 270). The following maximum speeds were reached:

Train weight	Locomotive type					
	S3 two-cylinder compound	S5 De Glehn compound	S4 superheated	S7 De Glehn compound	S7 Von Borries compound	4-4-4 Express Engine three-cylinder compound
6 eight-wheel cars 221 tons	70	68	80	70	74	74 m.p.h.
3 eight-wheel cars 109 tons	74	75	85	77	79	86 m.p.h.

It was like the fairy tale story of the ugly duckling becoming a magnificent swan. The small and rather odd superheated locomotive not only out-performed its larger more elegant 4–4–2 counterparts, but even achieved the performance of the large engine. It had been built with great anticipation of high speed travel with its streamlined casing, and was 63 per cent heavier, with a 155 per cent larger evaporating surface and it consumed twice as much coal. It was only a short test track but the fact the the superheated locomotive could also perform well on long runs was evident on the further tests between Spandau and Hanover. With a train load of 318 tons, the S4 produced a continuous power of 1,585 i.h.p. as against 1,544 i.h.p. for the second best engine, the 4–4–2 Von Borries locomotive Class S7. Thus began the unchallenged rise of the superheated locomotive throughout the world. Garbe exerted a decisive influence on the further development of the locomotive in Prussia.

As soon as the first favourable results with superheated engines were available, the Prussian State Railroad had three designs made for new standard locomotives intended to last for a long time. These were an eight-coupled goods engine, later Class G 8 replacing the

old standard Class G 7, a 2–6–0 for mixed traffic (later P 6) and a 2–6–0 tank engine, later the T 12, which was intended especially for service in the Berlin city and suburbs. Garbe, of course, influenced these designs. The freight engine was planned by the Vulkan works in Stettin and built in 1902. It entered service on the Mosel Railroad. Its performance was better than that of the old G 7 by 10 per cent, with a considerable saving of fuel and water. It marked the advent of the later Prussian freight engine.

Garbe also had great hopes of the 2–6–0 mixed traffic locomotive, later the P 6. It was to replace no fewer than four types. Firstly a local passenger train engine was required, to replace on hilly routes the 4–4–0 Type P 4, which was no longer adequate. The Prussian State Railroads did in fact have nineteen 4–6–0 De Glehn compounds, Class P 7, but they were not very satisfactory. Their performance was only slightly better than that of the P 4 and the new locomotive was to replace them as well. It was also to replace the large number of 2–6–0 goods engines which were mostly used on fast freight trains. Finally there was a requirement for an express engine on hilly routes, for the existing four-coupled engines were no longer powerful enough. The Hohenzollern Engine Works in

270. 4–4–0 express locomotive with smoke-box superheater of the Prussian State Railroads, Group S 4.

Düsseldorf was given the design for this multi-purpose locomotive. In accordance with Garbe's desire for as much standardization as possible, the boiler of the superheated freight engine already mentioned was adopted. The two front axles were mounted in a Krauss-Helmholtz truck (Ill. 273).

With the first locomotive supplied in 1902, "Cologne 21", very stringent test runs were made on the steeply graded track between Cologne and Jünkerath, which had inclines of up to 1 in 60 (1.7%) in comparison with 4–6–0 De Glehn locomotives Class P 7, the dimensions of which were about the same as those of the French engine of this type of the mid-1890s. Two of the P 7s used became badly damaged and had to be replaced by a third. The P 6 lasted without a fault. It consumed less fuel but, as with the other superheated locomotives built at that time, the cylinder diameter of 20½ in. was too small. It was increased to 21¼ in. and the driving wheel diameter of 5 ft. 1 in.

271. 4–6–0 superheated two-cylinder engine passenger locomotive, formerly Prussian Class P 8, later German National Railroad, Series 38, 1906-20.

272. 4–6–0 locomotive of the Prussian State Railroad, Group P 8. Sectional view, showing the Schmidt fire tube superheater.

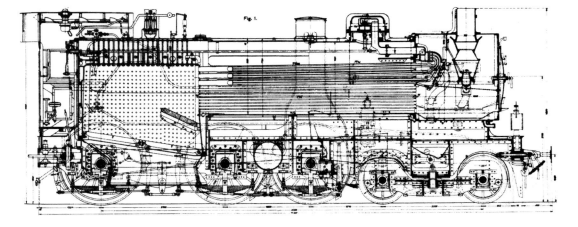

273(a). The "Düsseldorf", 2–6–0 multipurpose locomotive of the Prussian State Railroad, Series P6.

was changed slightly to 5 ft. 3 in. In 1905, another locomotive, fitted with the now standard superheater smoke or fire tube (both names are used), underwent new tests between Berlin, Grunewald, and Güterglück, and the P6 then proved superior to even the De Glehn 4–4–2 locomotives. The P6 also had a higher performance with less fuel consumption than the standard compound 0–8–0 Class G7.

Garbe seemed to have achieved his goal of a versatile locomotive, but unfortunately it was too late. The weight of expresses in hilly country and of freight trains in general had risen so much that the boiler performance was not sufficient for express work and the era of the six-coupled freight engine was over. But the P6 proved very suitable as a local passenger train engine.

Garbe decided to make maximum use of the increased performance of the superheater engine by building a two-cylinder simple 4–4–0 with the same performance as the more complicated 4–4–2 engine. He was helped by the fact that the improved permanent way on main lines now allowed a loading of 16 tons per axle. Thus

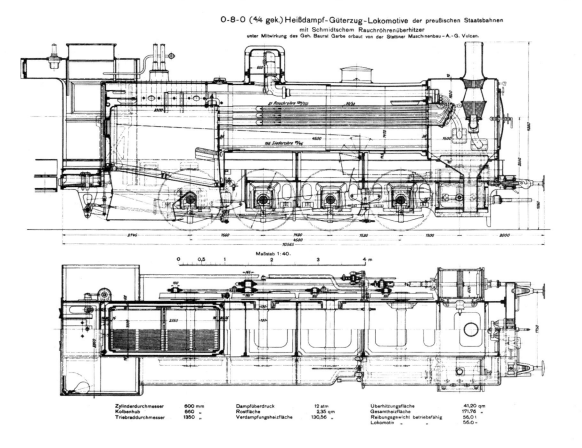

273(b). 0–4–0 freight locomotive, Class G8 of the Prussian State Railroads.

216

the S6 Class was developed, first built in 1905 by the Breslau Works, a remarkable engine in many respects (Ill. 274). The driving wheel diameter was increased to 6 ft. 10½ in., which was unusual in Prussia. By setting the truck back, as Gölsdorf had done with the Austrian Series 6, Garbe was able to mount the boiler of the G8 and P6 with their high-steaming capacity. The most daring and consequential innovation was to omit balanceweights on the wheels to equalize the reciprocating masses. Since this relieved some of the centrifugal forces which hammered the rail, Garbe succeeded in achieving permission for a static axle weight on the engine of 17.35 tons. Garbe envisaged using the tender to take up the recoiling motion which the balanceweights would have equalized, and for this reason he coupled it more tightly to the locomotive than usual. Indeed with this S6, Garbe succeeded in surpassing the performance of the 4–4–2s used in

274. Locomotive Class No. 230 K of the SNCF (French National Railroads), formerly Series 4200 of the Paris-Orléans Railroad, 1915.

217

275(a). 4-4-0 locomotive of the Prussian State Railroads, Series S6, Robert Garbe, 1905.

Prussia at that time. But it eventually emerged that, to save weight, too many pieces had been built too weak and that there was still a pronounced recoiling motion. From 1911, various parts were strengthened therefore and the balanceweights reintroduced. The Class S6 proved very suitable for pulling fast trains of moderate weight in the flat north German regions, with the result that 584 engines had entered service by 1913. These were the last 4-4-0 locomotives in Germany and the most powerful in Continental Europe. Only the Dutch Railroad Company acquired 4-4-0s of similar dimensions as late as 1914, but these had inside cylinders.

As often happened when standardization was introduced, events got out of hand. The traction department urgently required a powerful locomotive which could manage the load that had become essential for express trains over hilly territory. Garbe and his colleagues had meanwhile acquired a lot of experience in building superheated locomotives which could therefore be used to design an engine of these specifications. The order went to the firm of Schwartzkopf in Berlin. Thanks to the bogie, it was possible to mount a much more powerful boiler than that of the previously mentioned Class P6 locomotives. Garbe was fortunate in his choice of boiler dimensions and size of superheater: this engine, Class P8 (Ill. 271), had the fire tube superheater fitted right from the beginning (Ill. 272). An individual feature attributable to Garbe was the dimension of the flanges, which he

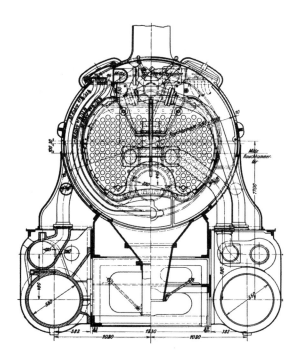
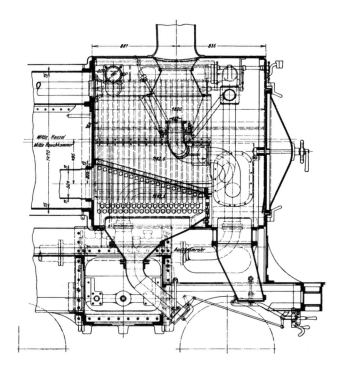

275(b). Sectional views of the Schmidt smoke-box superheater.

218

had turned $5/8$ in. smaller on the first coupled axle, and $3/16$ in. smaller on the driving axle, so that the truck alone guided the engine entering a curve.

The results of the trials made in August 1906 by the locomotive "Cologne 2401" on the 123 miles between Grunewald and Sangerhausen caused a justifiable stir in the technical world. The long incline of 1 in 100 (1%) had been easily taken at up to 31 m.p.h. pulling a 450-ton train. The engine delivered its maximum performance on the trips pulling 520 tons, where 1,845 to 1,980 h.p. had been measured in the cylinders while climbing at speeds of 47 m.p.h. These were unheard of results for a 4–6–0 locomotive at that time, and meant that Garbe's creation was a complete success. However the motion did not measure up to the requirements of express operation over long distances at high speeds. As a result, in time, elements of the P 8 were continually improved and strengthened in places. To spare the motion, the cylinder diameter was reduced from $23^3/16$ to $21^1/2$ in. without affecting the performance. From 1914, the superheater heating surface was increased by about 108 sq. ft., and the knocking of the die block in the link was avoided by fitting the so-called Kuhn sliding loop. Simple, economical and hard-working, it performed so excellently in passenger service and express operation where top speeds were not needed, that the Prussian State Railroad alone had acquired 3,370 engines by 1923. In addition, there were about three hundred engines with other domestic and foreign railroad companies, so the number of P 8s purchased has never been exceeded by any other type of passenger locomotive. It also provided the prototype for a large number of similar engines to be built in many other countries. As an example, we have in illustration 274, Series 4200 of the Paris-and-Orléans Railroad. Under the circumstances imposed by the World War, a break was made with the De Glehn system, and these locomotives were built as superheated two-cylinder engines. From 1914 to 1922, 170 examples were built; they all went to the French SNCF, apart from some that were sold to the Moroccan Railroads. On the SNCF, they were classed as Series 230 K of the Ouest Region. Many P 8s found their way all over Europe as part of the 1919 War reparations and as seized stock after the Second World War; they were so well thought of everywhere that they even survived more modern native products. In Germany, the last was scrapped a short while ago, and in some Eastern European countries it is still running.

12. THE BELLE EPOQUE

276. The "Inn", first
4–4–2 express loco-
motive with wide fire-
box of the Palatinate
Railroad, Series P3[1].

12.1 The "Atlantic" — An Engine for the "High Society"

Around the turn of the century, travelling had become a fashionable craze. The "High Society" met in Paris and on the Riviera or in the large Spas. They wanted an ever-increasing degree of comfort on their long journeys, so that not only did the cars become heavier but a large number of restaurant and sleeping cars entered service. There was an attempt to speed up the international expresses. As a result, considerably more powerful locomotives had to be used and the

most suitable were the 4–4–2 engines, which became constantly better-looking and matched those crack trains which carried the members of the "High Society" of the "Belle Epoque", themselves herald-ing the "Belle Epoque" of locomotive construction. This wheel arrangement occurred at about the same time in Europe as North America. In America, it was the Atlantic Coastline which first introduced it in 1894 and gave it its name. In Europe, it was Kaiser Ferdinand's Northern Railroad in Austria. In both cases, the basis was a 4–4–0 with a rear axle to take a larger boiler with an extended firebox. The

Atlantic Coastline engines had the standard sectional bar frame of the United States. In contrast, the Austrian ones still had the outside frame and outside cylinders of the Hall system. Neither of them yet foreshadowed what was soon to develop from the "Atlantic".

This was more the case with the next European 4–4–2 locomotive. The Palatinate Railroad, which was then still independent, was in intense competition with another Rhine State Railroad. The 2–4–2 express engines ordered between 1891 and 1896 — a wheel arrangement which only the Main-and-Neckar Railroad still had in Germany, but on the Belgian Belpaire pattern — were no longer adequate. Staby, chief locomotive engineer with the Palatinate Railroads since 1897, decided on a 4–4–2 engine which was offered together with a 2–4–4 with a front Helmholtz truck by the Krauss Locomotive Works. For the first time in Europe, it was built with a wide firebox (Ill. 276), pointing the way to which the constructors of the other German "Atlantics" would soon be heading. No one yet dared mount the boiler high enough to accommodate the firebox above the frame. Thus the front part of the frame stopped short behind the second coupled axle. An outer frame running from the first coupled axle to the rear end allowed the rear carrying axle to be mounted with outside bearings. The tapered boiler ring inserted between the round boiler shell and the firebox was new to Europe.

The twelve locomotives of Class P3[1], introduced in 1898 and ordered until 1904, were intended to pull 220-ton trains at 56 m.p.h. on the level and at 37½ m.p.h. up 1 in 100 gradients.

What was merely suggested with these Palatinate locomotives was fully developed with the engines of the Baden State Railroad. The firm of Maffei won a competition to produce a much more powerful engine than the existing 4–4–0s, which was to be capable of pulling 200 tons up 1 in 300 gradients at 62 m.p.h. and attaining a maximum speed of 75 m.p.h. Working closely together, Alexander Courtin, Superintendent for the Baden State Railroad and Anton Hammel, Chief Draftsman at Maffei, created the IId type locomotive (Ill. 277), which was the start of the modern South German school. Characteristic features since retained by the modern locomotive were the high boiler with the unimpeded wide firebox and long smokebox. As with Webb and Von Borries, the four compound cylinders were mounted in one plane and jointly drove the front coupled axle. The valves of the inside HP cylinders were operated by a rocker from the outside Heusinger-Walschaerts gear on the LP cylinder. Special cocks were used for starting, which fed boiler steam into the receiver when cut-off exceeded 65 per cent. These engines reduced the time taken for the 37½ miles between Mannheim and Karlsruhe by between nine and twelve and a half minutes, despite the heavier trains of 300 tons. This amounted to an average of 63½ m.p.h. The highest speed reached on a trial run was about 90 m.p.h. The first twelve Maffei engines of 1902 were followed in 1905 by six from the Karlsruhe Locomotive Works. When ten engines had to be handed over to the Allies after the First World War, the few that remained were scrapped before the Baden State became incorporated into the German National Railroad. In 1905 the Palatinate Railroad acquired five similar locomotives,

277. 4–4–2 express locomotive of the Baden State Railroad, Series IId, Alexander Courtin and Anton Hammel, 1905.

221

Class P4, from Maffei. Their main différence was in the use of the bar frame.

Even the Prussian State Railroad saw itself compelled around the turn of the century to consider more powerful engines than the 4–4–0 standard type S3 (cf. section 11.1.1) and the Von Borries S5 (cf. section 11.1.4). There were two possibilities: either the famous De Glehn type, shown at Paris in 1900, could be adopted — as had happened on a trial basis a few years earlier — or the Baden Type IId could be chosen.

278. 4–4–2 express train locomotive of the Prussian State Railroads, Series S9, 1907-10.

Grafenstaden was given an order for two locomotives of the first-mentioned system and Hanomag was asked for a locomotive of a type proposed by Von Borries with a motion and frame construction derived from the earlier S5. However the boiler was reminiscent of the Palatinate's first P3[1] engine, but somewhat higher pitched. This so-called Hanover type proved more successful than the Grafenstaden engines, both being classified as Type S7 (cf. section 11.2). Thus between 1902 and 1906, a total of 159 Hanomag engines entered service as opposed to only seventy-nine Grafenstaden ones. Even when these latter engines were fitted with a wider firebox from 1904, they were poor steamers and they were also more expensive to maintain than the Hanomag type.

It appeared initially that the 4–4–2 engines might be eclipsed by Garbe's 4–4–0 class S6 which had been introduced in the meanwhile (cf. section 11.2). But improvements in the permanent way and enlarged turntables removed the restrictions which had hampered the S7s until then. The engines could be made more robust and powerful than the S6. Von Borries

died while working on this project with Hanomag, but the new locomotive bore his hallmark. Unfortunately superheated steam, which was not yet quite ready for satisfactory operation, was not attempted. Externally this Prussian Type S9 (Ill. 278) has much in common with the Baden Type IId (Ill. 277). But there are a few differences in construction. Retained from the previous Von Borries engines were the operation of the inside valves, the front of the main frame built by a bar and the slightly tapered boiler ring connecting with the wide firebox. In May and June 1909, several comparative runs were made on the Wustermark-Hanover run by engines of the S9 and S6 classes pulling identical trains of 224 tons to 502 tons. As was to be expected, the smaller S6 used less coal and less water with the lighter train loads because it was operating in its economic range. But 500 tons was the limit of its capacity, while it was only the beginning of the S9's favourable range. This had the same coal consumption figures as the S6, though with higher water consumption. It also beat the fuel consumption figures of the smaller 4–4–0s in regular heavy express service. In 1914, when two of these engines had been fitted with superheaters and Knorr feed water heater, they were reckoned to be the most economical of all Prussian express engines, and explain, among other reasons, why Prussia later on turned to the four-cylinder compound superheated engine. These S9 engines, ninety-nine of which entered service between 1907 and 1910, were undoubtedly the most powerful of the Atlantic type in Continental Europe. They were the first to haul non-stop express trains of 520 tons and sometimes 570 tons on the Berlin-Hanover run (159 miles). They may be regarded as a highspot in the Continental development of 4–4–2 locomotives.

Two different "Atlantic" type De Glehn locomotives were on show at the Paris World Fair in 1900. The one built by the Alsace Locomotive Works for the Nord became world famous, the other, showed by Hartmann in Chemnitz, had no success, for subsequent developments in Germany were affected by the introduction of superheated steam.

The Nord Railroad's engine was basically an extended version of the previous 4–4–0 type, designed by Du Bousquet and De Glehn (cf. section 11.1.3). The long, narrow Belpaire firebox and the Serve corrugated tubes were retained, but the motion had the cranks set at an angle of 180° to improve the balancing of masses. The engine was intended to pull 200-ton express trains up the 1 in 200 incline between Saint-

Denis and the 27.5 km post near Survilliers at 62½ m.p.h. At the trials held there in June, it reached 66 m.p.h. pulling a train weighing 200 tons, and with 285 tons it still managed 60 m.p.h. From 1910 onwards, the engines were fitted with superheaters. Their performance improved to such an extent that they were often given the 350-ton train between Paris and Aulnoye which was scheduled to run at an average speed of 60 m.p.h. Pulling this kind of train — among the fastest in the world — they continued running until the Thirties, and could still be seen pulling medium-weight express trains such as the "Oiseau Bleu" and the "Nord Express" in 1939. Apart from the first two, the slightly modified Nos. 2643–2675 (Ill. 280) were also commissioned, with a longer truck wheelbase as their main modification. Fortunately No. 2670 (SNCF 221 A 30) still exists at the Mulhouse Railroad Museum in Alsace. It is understandable that these De Glehn 4–4–2s were promptly taken on by other French railroads, but only ninety-one were built in the whole of France. The Paris-and-Orleans Railroad had a more powerful version and the Paris-Lyon-Méditerranée changed the motion for a system of its own. Apart from the seventy-nine Prussian engines already mentioned — which gave the Prussian State Railroad second place — there were ten on the Egyptian State Railroads,

seventeen on the Bengal and Nagpur Railroad and four on the Eastern Bengal Railroad in British India. Even the Pennsylvania ordered one of the more powerful PO engines on a trial basis. The 4–4–2 only had a short reign as a "luxury engine"; it was to have its greatest successes in England.

The first 4–4–2 engine introduced in England was by Henry A. Ivatt in 1898 on the Great Northern Railway, and represented a complete break with the previous Stirling tradition and with the use of his small boilers. On the Great Northern, there were only

279. 4–4–2 express train locomotive of the Great Northern Railway, No. 990, "Klondyke" class, Henry A. Ivatt, built from 1898 on.

280. 4–4–2 express locomotive of the French Nord Railroad, No. 2.674.

223

281. Engineer greasing the locomotive.

a few small 4-4-0 engines. It was thus a bold step from the light, uncoupled 4-2-2 Stirling locomotives (cf. section 10.2) to the large 4-4-2s. Ivatt retained the outside cylinders, as the second coupled axle was driven and it was thus easy to make long enough connecting rods. For reasons already discussed, the rear axle was mounted in a short, outside auxiliary frame (Ill. 279). When No. 271 was built as an experiment in 1902 as a four-cylinder simple engine, it emerged that they were under-boilered. Both out-

of the axle layout. To English eyes, used to small, narrow inside cylinder locomotives, the new engine, with its large boiler and wide firebox, was an absolute sensation (Ill. 282). Hardly any other locomotive has been pictured as many times as this one, even on picture postcards and in childrens' books. For twenty years the ninety-one "Large Atlantics" by Ivatt, later Class C1 on the LNER, pulled all main-line trains between London and York, until they were superseded from 1922 on by the "Pacifics" of his successor,

282. 4-4-2 express locomotive of the Great Northern Railway, No. 251, "Big Atlantic" type, Henry A. Ivatt, 1902.

side cylinders had to be removed because the boiler was not producing enough steam. Within their limitations, the twenty-one "Klondykes" built by 1903 — thus called because they were built at the time of the Alaskan gold rush — were very useful engines, and some of them lasted until the 1930s. They began the British school of the 4-4-2 locomotive.

The next "Atlantic" engines were acquired in 1899 by the Lancashire-and-Yorkshire Railway. They were simply longer versions of the previous 4-4-0s, and, like these, had inside cylinders and a long, narrow firebox. They are remarkable in that they had the first superheater to have been fitted in England, of a type developed by the locomotive superintendent Aspinall, who had made several experiments with various superheaters fitted in the smokebox. Aspinall's system was eclipsed by the simpler and more effective Schmidt fire tube superheater, and there were no copies made of his forty inside cylinder 4-4-2 engines built between 1899 and 1902.

Also in 1902, when the unfortunate four-cylinder simple engine appeared, Ivatt produced his masterpiece. With his new 4-4-2, he utilized every possibility

Gresley. The last ten engines, built from 1910, were fitted with superheaters. It was not until then that they showed their paces. During the First World War, they were given train loads of up to 480 tons, although their timetable was not as tight as that in peace time. And more than once, they had to be used without the aid of a pilot when one of Gresley's Pacifics, still suffering from teething troubles, broke down en route. The first "Atlantic" by Ivatt, No. 251, is preserved at York.

Similar engines were also used on other railroads: on the London, Brighton and South Coast Railway, in a more powerful form by the North British and with several modifications by the Great Central, whose engines were given narrow fireboxes.

After the Great Northern, the nearby North Eastern had the largest number of 4-4-2s in England. All of these also had long, narrow fireboxes. After the first twenty, ordered by Wilson Worsdell between 1903 and 1906, with two cylinders, and after two experimental four-cylinder compound engines, Vincent Raven, who succeeded Worsdell, finally adopted the three-cylinder drive. In the Newcastle coal mining area, fuel savings

225

were not as important as the simplicity traditionally preferred. All three cylinders together with their valve chests formed a single casting and drove the first coupled axle. Each cylinder had its own inside Stephenson link motion. The first ten Class Z locomotives of 1911 used saturated steam but the ten Class Z1 engines ordered simultaneously were given Schmidt superheaters, which were subsequently added to the others as well. The last thirty engines of 1914-16 also had these superheaters. These were the most powerful English 4-4-2 engines, and normally pulled expresses of 350 to 375 tons. Together with eighteen "Atlantics" on the Great Western, which will be considered later, 311 engines of the "Atlantic" type entered service in Britain, the highest number in Europe.

12.2 The Birth of the Superheated Three- and Four-Cylinder Locomotive

Apart from unsuccessful isolated examples, England may be regarded as the progenitor of the four-

quite different from the normal way of building new types, to meet the conditions of the moment. Churchward's importance is shown by the fact that he actually succeeded in living up to his aims in an exemplary way, and he figures among the most prominent locomotive engineers of all times.

The first factor in a locomotive's performance is its boiler, and Churchward concentrated on this initially. Probably because of his influence, in 1897 the Great Western introduced the Belpaire firebox on the 4-4-0 "Badminton" class. This was subsequently retained. Inside the narrow British loading gauge, it had the advantage of an enlarged steam chamber. Churchward initially retained the normal cylindrical boiler barrel, but from 1903 he adopted the American pattern of a tapered boiler shell — the bottom of the boiler being horizontal — to improve the restricted vision past the firebox which filled nearly all the width of the engine. The components for this boiler were designed to fit several boiler sizes. The large opening for the dome was a weak point in the boiler. Churchward omitted it and replaced it by the safety valves, where there was the least movement of the water in

283. The "Alliance", 4-4-2 express locomotive of the Great Western Railway, No. 104, De Glehn type, 1905.

cylinder engine, i.e., of locomotives with four cylinders working with normal simple expansion. George Jackson Churchward can be said to be their father, one of the few British engineers who carefully observed what was happening abroad. Of the locomotives running on the Great Western at the end of the 19th century, hardly any six were alike. Under his ageing and very conservative chief William Dean, Churchward began his efforts to create some order out of this chaos. He fully realized that 15-20 years would elapse before the standard types which were to be designed would have their full effect. The new standard types had therefore to match the likely operating requirements at that time. This "forward planning" was

the boiler. As on the old French Crampton, steam was led away via a long slotted tube mounted at the top. Initially Churchward retained the outside frame which the Great Western had always favoured. When boilers became bigger and thus heavier, he abandoned it in favour of the lighter, and simpler inside frame. He was now able to mount outside cylinders and abandon the crank axle. This was a further simplification.

Thus by 1902 Churchward had come step by step to a two-cylinder simple expansion express engine, which was far-sightedly made as a 4-6-0. In honour of his former chief he named it "William Dean". On the trial runs with this No. 100, Churchward realized that the traditional slide-valve travel and steam passages were too small. On the basis of tests made on a stationary steam engine, he almost doubled the valve travel on his next 4–6–0, the "Vanguard" of 1903, No. 98, and he enlarged the steam passages accordingly. He once said on this question: "You can always get steam into a cylinder, the problem is to get it out." Although the Great Western locomotives soon had the reputation of being very free runners and very economical, the significance of Churchward's maxim was not recognized for a long time and it was not until the Thirties that Chapelon used this maxim with amazing success.

By 1900, the famous 4–4–2 De Glehn engines had appeared on the Nord Railroad. For England, Churchward took a very unusual step. In 1903, as the Prussian State Railroad had done, he bought an identical engine to those on the Nord from the Alsace Locomotive Works, and this was adopted by the Great Western as No. 102, and christened "La France". To make exact comparisons he had a 4–4–2 engine built at the railroad's works at Swindon, No. 171, the "Albion", which was on the same lines as the "Vanguard". The comparative tests had no clear results. Thus, in 1905, Churchward ordered

284. Fireman at work.

285. The "Caerphilly Castle", 2–6–0 four-cylinder locomotive of the Great Western Railway, first engine in the Castle Class, 1923.

227

another two engines from the same firm, this time the more powerful Paris-and-Orleans type, No. 103 "President" and 104 "Alliance" (Ill. 283). Long series of test runs with these three De Glehn locomotives and the fourteen Albion class built at the same time resulted astonishingly in equally good fuel consumption for the Albion engines as for the compound ones. This was because one of Churchward's improvements had achieved a smaller back-pressure in the cylinders of the Albion. But there was no question that the De Glehn engines with their well-balanced four-cylinder motion ran much more smoothly than the two-cylinder engines.

Because the Great Western directors wanted to increase the speed of their expresses, Churchward adopted the four-cylinder staggered layout of De Glehn in his new design, but omitted the compound system. He also simplified the valve operation by operating each pair of cylinders by a single Walschaerts gear on the inside, which was linked to the outside valves by horizontal rocking levers. As with the De Glehn engines, he set the boiler pressure at 225 lbs. The first of these new four-cylinder engines, No. 40 "North Star", was built as a 4–4–2 in 1906. But since the seven 4–6–0 engines built meanwhile had proved to be as smooth running as the "Atlantics", Churchward immediately adopted this wheel arrangement, with its higher adhesion weight. There thus arose the famous "Star" class, of which the first engines to enter service in 1907 were Nos. 4001–4009. They fully deserved

their name, for they were indeed stars among British express engines. Churchward's farsightedness is shown by the fact that seventy-two engines were built up to 1923 with only trivial modifications. From 1908 on, they were fitted with a fire tube superheater developed by Churchward himself, and this was subsequently also fitted to the first engines. Despite the small increase in temperature, this resulted in savings with coal and water of 12 per cent and 20 per cent respectively; they were the most powerful 4–6–0 locomotives of their day. In 1907/08, no other British engines were able to pull 480 tons up a slight gradient at a steady 64 m.p.h. and to run at a constant 70 m.p.h. on the level. No. 4003, "Lode Star", is preserved at Swindon Museum.

In 1921, Churchward retired. His successor, Charles B. Collet, found a stock of locomotives which was so up to date that he scarcely had to make any alterations, but merely to increase the dimensions of the "Stars" a little, to bring them up to date with the latest requirements. Before 1939 and then between 1946 and 1950 a total of 164 engines of this "Castle" class were built (Ill. 285), a time record for one type, exceeding even the Prussian P8.

Churchward introduced the age of the four-cylinder locomotive in Britain, a type which was needed because the restricted loading gauge did not allow the large cylinders for a 4–6–0 to be mounted either outside or inside. But since none of these locomotives was built on Churchward's structural principles,

286. 4–6–0 four-cylinder locomotive of the Belgian State Railroads, Class 9, 1905/06.

228

their performance was far inferior, and almost all of them were subsequently modified.

Churchward's four-cylinder simple engines were noted on the Continent. B. Flamme, chief engineer on the Belgian State Railroads, was another pioneer of superheated steam. Under his auspices, there was a complete change in locomotive policy. The unwieldy Belpaire engines disappeared, and were replaced by British types with inside cylinders. He was the first to fit a Schmidt fire tube superheater to a 4–6–0 engine of this type. Initial tests resulted in very good economies using this system. But the De Glehn type 4–4–2 and 4–6–0 four-cylinder compounds ordered on trial had also such good consumption figures that Flamme considered it fair to hold large-scale tests before deciding on the introduction of a more powerful type. For this purpose the following variants on a powerful 4–6–0 locomotive were ordered:

a four-cylinder compound saturated steam locomotive, No. 3301, with 6 ft. 6 in. driving wheels and single axle drive:

a four-cylinder simple expansion saturated steam locomotive, No. 3302 with identical driving wheel diameter and drive;

a four-cylinder simple superheated steam locomotive, identical to the others apart from the Schmidt superheater (No. 3303);

a four-cylinder compound superheater locomotive, No. 3304, with 5 ft. 11 in. driving wheels, single axle drive and a combined superheater — made in two sections, one half superheating the steam for the HP cylinders, the other the steam for the LP cylinders; it could also be connected so that only steam for the LP cylinders passed through the superheater;

eight four-cylinder compound superheated steam locomotives, Nos. 3293–3300, with divided drive, 5 ft. 11 in. wheels and a Cockerill type superheater. In the thorough tests, No. 3303 performed best but its cylinders were too small. Thus, in the standard Class 9 version, they were increased from 17⅛ to 17½ in. (Ill. 286). In this form, sixty-four engines were ordered between 1908 and 1910.

Thereafter, while Flamme was in charge, all heavy locomotives were built as superheated four-cylinder simple types, the 4–6–2 Class 10 engines, which will be discussed later, the 2–10–0 Class 36, and the 4–6–4 tank engine Class 13.

The results of the Belgian tests seemed to confirm Garbe's view that the compound system was superfluous with superheated steam. As the P8 (cf. section 11.2) proved unsatisfactory at high speeds, the

Prussian State Railroads asked Schwartzkopf of Berlin for a design for a 4–6–0 express engine with 6 ft. 6 in. driving wheels. It was made as a four-cylinder simple engine for smooth running. In other respects, it followed the features of the P8 as closely as possible, but with a somewhat larger boiler. One of the first two built, Nos. Erfurt 801–802, could be seen in Brussels at the same time as the Belgian Class 9 already mentioned. On the test runs, these engines did not fully live up to expectations, and the Vulkan Works in Stettin were asked to revise the original design. As with the Von Borries four-cylinder compound engines the frame was made in bar form at the front, to allow easier access to the inside motion, and the surrounding running board was mounted high. The boiler, which was further enlarged, was fitted with

287. 4–6–0 locomotive of the Prussian State Railroad, No. 1207, Class S10², 1915.

a larger superheater. Initially its performance was satisfactory, but fuel consumption was rather high. This was attributed to the unequal distribution of the steam between the HP and LP cylinders, for the inside valves were operated, as on the Belgian engines, via horizontal rocking levers at the front. While running, the valve rods on the outer valves expanded as a result of the heat and the setting which had been made in the cold state was lost. Thus from the second batch onwards, the inside valves were operated from behind the cylinders. In all, 202 engines of this Class S10 were acquired.

Despite the modification, steam consumption did not drop noticeably. When, in time, cracks appeared in the crank axle, the Prussian State Railroads decided to adopt the three-cylinder engine which allowed a better-shaped crank axle, cheaper to manufacture. The revised plans were made by the Vulkan Works in Stettin under the supervision of its chief draftsman, E. Najork. In May 1914, the Vulkan Works supplied

sumed less steam than the four-cylinder simple engines and their performance was superior. According to the Prussian State Railroad performance charts, they pulled 850 tons at 50 m.p.h. or 650 tons at 56 m.p.h. on the level, 415 tons at 43½ m.p.h. or 345 tons at 50 m.p.h. up 1 in 200.

When the private railroads in Italy were nationalized in 1905, as always happens in such cases, standard locomotive types were designed. Based on the 2–6–0 Group 600 (cf. section 11.1.1) in 1907, a 2–6–2 express engine, retaining the Zara truck, had been developed as four-cylinder compounds Group 680. Good results had been achieved, with the Schmidt superheater fitted, in the 2–6–0s, and the omission of the compound system in the 640 Group, so that, as an experiment, two 680 Group engines were fitted with superheaters. These superheated engines gave significantly better consumption figures than saturated steam engines in trial runs but they did not perform quite as well. This was because the cylinder dimensions had not been increased, as was needed for the superheated steam. Instead of altering the dimensions, it was decided to replace the heavier compound cylinders by simple expansion ones. In addition, the superheater was altered in order to take up less evaporating space in the boiler. As often happened with conversions to superheated steam in those days, the pressure was reduced to spare the boiler. The common slide valve gear for each pair of cylinders was retained. A four-cylinder locomotive built in this way in 1912, Group 685 (Ill. 288), was submitted in June 1914 to thorough tests on the Bologna-Roveredo run (130 miles) with gradients of up to 1 in 200, where it pulled 243-293 tons with average speeds of 53½-55½ m.p.h. and peaks of 66-71 m.p.h., which correspond to 1,118-1,230 i.h.p.

288. 2–6–2 four-cylinder express locomotive of the Italian State Railroad, Group 685, 1912.

289. 4–6–2 De Glehn express locomotive of the Paris-and-Orléans Railroad, No. 4541, Series 4500, first series of "Pacific" locomotives in Europe.

the first seven of this new Class S 10², and subsequently 127 were built (Ill. 287).

All three cylinders drove the first coupled axle with cranks set at 130°. The inside valve was operated by two swinging levers mounted horizontally, one on each side, linked to the head of the combination levers and their inner arms were attached to a third floating lever by rods. This third lever was also horizontal and moved between the other two. Its fulcrum was pivoted on the inner valve spindle. The two outer lever arms were in a 1:2 ratio, so that the two movements combined to operate the inside valve spindle in accordance with the corresponding crank setting. From the start, these three-cylinder locomotives had the Knorr feed water heater. They con-

12.3 The "Pacific" Locomotive, Queen of the Rail

One of the main disadvantages of the "Atlantic" was its lack of adhesion weight, while the boiler performance of the 4–6–0 engine was not enough to pull heavy expresses at sustained high speeds. Both difficulties were overcome with the "Pacific" locomotive. There is so much recent literature about this type that we shall only consider the main types briefly.

The first 4–6–2s on European tracks were the two famous Paris and Orléans engines Nos. 4501–4502 which entered service in July and September 1907. They had been produced in a collaboration between E. Solacroup, chief engineer of the PO's drawing office, and the Alsace Locomotive Works under De Glehn. They were a further development of the existing 4–4–2 Series 3000 and the 4–6–0 Series 4000, and their De Glehn four-cylinder compound motion was retained. The coal used demanded a low-lying grate. For this reason, there was a compromise between the wide frame overhanging and the deep narrow firebox: the rear of the firebox was wide and the front narrowed to such an extent that it fitted between the frame plates. Thus at the front, the grate could be mounted low: trapeze-shaped, with stepped sides, it rose at the rear above the frame. It was thus a simpler variant of the form used already by Belpaire for his 2–4–2 engines. In fact it was not an easy firebox to manufacture, but its advantage was that the centre of gravity of the long boiler was further

forward. It also provided a larger heating surface, exposed directly to the fire, than the short and wide grate. As a result, this type of firebox was often used later.

These first Class 4500 "Pacifics" were intended for service between Paris and Toulouse, where they were to pull expresses of 300-400 tons on long 1 in 100 gradients at an average speed of 47-50 m.p.h. On test runs on these stretches, they achieved a performance of 2,050 i.h.p. (Ill. 289).

The first engines, Nos. 4501–4570, were still saturated steam locomotives, but their HP cylinders were fitted with piston valves so that superheaters could be fitted later, as did in fact happen. The next series, Nos. 4571–4580, supplied from 1910 onwards, had superheaters from the outset. In 1909 serial Nos. 3501–3510, fitted with a larger driving wheel diameter of 6 ft. 5 in., came into service for the level run between Paris and Bordeaux — they were still saturated steam engines, and were followed by Nos. 3521–3589 with superheaters. This was the beginning of the Alsace "Pacific" school, which caught on with all railroads in France and in some other European and overseas countries, with various derivations. On the pattern of the 4–6–2s built for the National Railroad in Alsace-Lorraine, the Nord Railroad's engines had long, narrow fireboxes (Ill. 290). We shall consider these engines again later.

It was only the PLM Railroad which again went its own way. In 1908 it initially ordered two prototypes:

291. 4–6–2 four-cylinder compound express locomotive of the Paris-Lyon-Méditerranée Railroad, No. 6017, built at the Henschel Works, 1911.

No. 6001, a saturated steam engine with four-cylinder compound system on the Baudry pattern, only with staggered cylinders and divided drive; the other a superheated four-cylinder simple engine, No. 6101, with all cylinders in line but nonetheless divided drive. Both had wide frame overhanging fireboxes. The compound locomotive had a boiler pressure of 228 lbs., whereas the superheated four-cylinder engine adhered to Garbe's theory, and had a boiler pressure of only 176 lbs. sq. in. The comparative trials were held with a train weighing 445 tons on the test track between Laroche and Blaisy Bas, the track rising gently and then having 1 in 200 and 1 in 125 gradients over the last 8 miles. The superheated four-cylinder simple engine used less fuel than the saturated steam compound engine. So the PLM ordered more four-cylinder engines of the same type between August 1910 and May 1911 (Nos. 6102–6172). In this way the PLM differed from the other railroads in France. By 1907, the PLM had taken on a series of 4–6–0 express engines with a four-cylinder compound system, and ten of these were fitted with superheaters. They showed fuel savings of 10-16 per cent. Thereupon the railroad made further tests with the "Pacific" locomotives. In 1911, Henschel was given an order for twenty four-cylinder compound superheated steam locomotives, Nos. 6011–6030 (later 6201–6220) (Ill. 291). All four cylinders were in line but with divided drive. To make an exact comparison, in 1912 twenty four-cylinder simple engines identical to the prototype were also ordered, (Series 6172–6191), and like the compound engines had a boiler pressure of 200 lbs. sq. in. Both types shared the same schedules. The superheated engines had an average fuel consump-

292. 4–6–2 four-cylinder compound express locomotive of the Baden State Railroad, No. 753, Series VI f, Anton Hammel, 1907.

232

tion of 9.6 per cent lower. Other comparative tests with 2–8–0 locomotives also gave favourable results for the four-cylinder compound superheated locomotives. This served to persuade the PLM Railroad to favour this system, so that subsequently all saturated steam engines were fitted with superheaters. On the test route mentioned, trials with a 646-ton train resulted in values of 2,425 i.h.p. These "Pacifics" and their followers pulled the main line expresses between Paris, Lyons and Marseilles for over thirty years.

Very shortly after the PO Railroad, the Baden State Railroad in August/September 1907, brought out the first German "Pacific". Whereas the Class IId 4–4–2s (cf. section 12.1) pulled 200 tons, the "Pacifics" were expected to haul 300 tons under identical conditions. The design was complicated by the fact that the same engine was to be used on the Black Forest line to pull 185 tons at 31 m.p.h.; consequently,

the driving wheel diameter was fixed at only 5 ft. 11 in. Of the designs submitted, that by Maffei was chosen, once more made by Anton Hammel (Ill. 292). A comparison will show that this new Class IVf was a development of the previous 4–4–2 Type IId (Ill. 277). The motion was identical, but the inside cylinders were set higher and inclined to allow the connecting rods to clear the front coupled axle. For the same reason, the piston stroke was smaller than that of the outside cylinders and thus the play of the connecting rods was reduced. The main modification was in the use of the bar frame, which went back to the American Vauclain engines ordered experimentally by the Bavarian State Railroad in 1900. It had proved successful and had the advantage of a readily accessible inside motion. To bring the centre of gravity further forward, despite the wide firebox, and without making the boiler tubes unnecessarily

293. The "Rheingold" with the Bavarian S3/6 locomotive No. 18.529.

233

294. 4–6–2 four-cylinder compound express locomotive of the Swedish State Railroad, Series F, 1914. These engines were passed on to the Danish State Railroad in 1937.

long, the lower front wall — called the waist or throat plate — was raked backwards for the first time. To reduce the load on the trailing axle still further the whole rear wall of the firebox was also inclined. Both devices, which were also included on the PLM "Pacific" mentioned earlier, were often used later.

295. Driver's cabin of a S3/6 locomotive of the Bavarian State Railroad, built by the firm of J. A. Maffei, A.G., Munich, 1914.

296. 4–6–2 four-cylinder express locomotive of the Belgian State Railroad, No. 10.042, Series 10.

On test runs, an engine of this type pulled 460 tons on the level at 69½ m.p.h., and on the Black Forest Railroad, with a mean gradient of 1 in 60 it pulled 194 tons at 34½ m.p.h. Thirty-five had been commissioned by 1913. As stated already, the contradictory operational requirements had led to the adoption of a driving wheel diameter of only 5 ft. 11 in. However this proved to be too small for the sustained fast running in the Rhine flatlands and led to too much stress on the motion. Moreover as the steam

production was not completely satisfactory, all these locomotives were broken up shortly after being taken over by the German National Railroads. Nevertheless they were the pioneers of the South German "Pacific" school.

By 1906, the Bavarian State Railroads had decided to develop a similar locomotive which was to be capable of pulling 400 tons at 59 m.p.h. up a 1 in 500 (0.2%) gradient and the same load at 40 m.p.h. up 1 in 100 (1%). Hammel was again responsible for the design and he produced his masterpiece, the world-famous S3/6 (Ill. 293). This locomotive has been the subject of so many articles that we can restrict ourselves to observing that the faults still attaching to its predecessor in Baden were now eliminated. The engine proved so extraordinarily successful that it was still ordered after the German National Railroads were founded. It was one of the most economical engines of its day. But the main factor in its fame was its striking appearance. Even the English, who were very keen on this point, count it among the most beautiful locomotives ever built. In all, the Bavarian State Railroads and the German

234

National Railroads had ordered 159 engines by 1931, of which the eighteen supplied in 1912/13 had 6 ft. 7 in. driving wheels as they were intended for the express runs between Munich and Nuremberg and Würzburg, where the maximum speed was 71½ m.p.h.

In Spain, the Madrid, Zaragoza and Alicante Railroad had four descendants of the S 3/6; the eighty built in Rumania between 1913 and 1922 were, unusually, four-cylinder simple engines.

The "Schöne Württembergerin"* (Ill. 297), as the Class C of the Württemberg State Railroads was often called, did in fact look quite different but, despite its plate frame, it belonged completely to the South German school. In exterior appearance, it anticipated many details of the later part-streamlined locomotive. This was partially due to the frame construction. Apart from the main inside frame, a blind frame was provided as a reinforcement outside under the running

board, which ran from the cylinders to the rear end of the locomotive. The single axle drive and the valve gear were similar to those of the Bavarian S 3/6. These engines were intended to pull 350 tons up 1 in 100 gradients at 37½ m.p.h. and to run at 62 m.p.h. on the level. Test runs far exceeded these requirements, and up to 1,900 i.h.p. was reached. However, in normal service, these engines proved inferior to the Bavarian S 3/6. All forty-one engines built between 1909 and 1921 by the Esslingen Locomotive Works came to the National Railroad** and a few were even passed on to the Federal Railroad, where they disappeared in the early 1950s.

The Class F "Pacifics" introduced in 1914 by the Swedish State Railroads are an interesting derivative of the South German school. They had plate frames. The truck had an outside frame. All four cylinders drove the second coupled axle, and each pair had a

297. 4–6–2 Class C four-cylinder compound express locomotive of the Württemberg State Railroads, "Die schöne Württembergerin" (The Pretty Maid of Württemburg), 1921.

* "The Pretty Maid of Württemberg".

** Reichsbahn.

common valve gear. The LP outside cylinders had to be inclined in order not to impede the swing of the truck. Because of electrification, all eleven locomotives were passed to the Danish State Railroads in 1937, where they served long years before diesel traction was introduced (Ill. 294). One is still preserved. The Belgian State Railroad's "Pacifics", Class 10, form a class of their own. Since they were intended for the Luxemburg run, with its long inclines of 1 in 62½, their boilers had to be very powerful. Flamme designed a tapered boiler shell on Churchward lines. As the high permitted axle loading of 20 tons allowed the weight of the boiler to rest exclusively on the rear four axles, he had no need to move it forward. Thus the four cylinders were located in front of the smokebox centrally over the truck. This gave the impression that these engines were pushing their own cylinders along in front of them. Unlike the fore-

going 4–6–0 Class 9, these had divided drive. The test runs between Rhisnes and Namur, with constant gradients of 1 in 62½ saw 381 tons pulled at 31 m.p.h., which amounts to a maximum performance of 2,390 i.h.p. These Belgian "Pacifics" were the heaviest and most powerful of their day in Europe (Ill. 296). On the first twenty-eight locomotives, which entered service in 1910, it emerged that the trailing axle was in fact overloaded. This was avoided on the thirty supplied between 1912 and 1940 by shortening the firebox.

From 1938, these "Pacifics" were improved on the Chapelon pattern (cf. section 15.4), so that they were able to haul a regular 500-ton service on the Luxemburg run with no pilot engine.

When the Austrian State Railroad also had to adopt a twelve-wheel express engine, Gölsdorf was again confronted by the light permanent way and the poor quality coal burned. This prevented the weight of a sufficiently large firebox being placed on only one trailing axle. Carl Gölsdorf therefore inverted the "Pacific": he placed a four-wheel swinging truck at the rear and a Krauss-Helmholtz truck at the front. In this way, in 1908 he produced a locomotive with a good weight distribution, which ran smoothly in curves, helped by its large guided length of 19 ft. 1 in. The name "Adriatic" was suggested for this first 2–6–4 express locomotive in the world (Ill. 299). All four cylinders drove the second coupled axle. One HP and LP cylinder with its corresponding valve chest

298. 2–8–0 four-cylinder compound locomotive of the Gotthard Railroad, No. 2807, Anton Hammel, 1906.

299. 2–6–4 four-cylinder compound express locomotive of the Austrian State Railroad, No. 210.01, 1908.

236

formed a single casting. Two piston valves arranged behind one another in tandem worked in the valve chest. These engines were intended to pull 360 tons at 37½ m.p.h. over sinuous lines with gradients of up to 1 in 100. This corresponds approximately to 1,570 i.h.p. On the trial runs this value was exceeded. The first ten Class 210.01–11 which were fitted with the Clench type steam drier, then very popular in Austria, were followed from 1911 by Nos. 310.01–90 with Schmidt superheaters. When another ten engines were ordered during the First World War, because of the copper shortage, they were fitted with "Brotan" fire-boxes, which will be discussed later. After the War, the Austrian Federal Railroads were no longer able to use these engines on its much reduced network. Three went to Poland, the Prussian State Railroads acquired seven and also passed these on to Poland in 1922. Nos. 310.23 (DR 16.08) has been preserved and is to be given to the Technical Museum in Vienna as soon as there is room for it. The Czech State Railroads have put No. 310.15 on display at the National Technical Museum in Prague.

300. Locomotive No. 110.507 of the Austrian Federal Railroads with a train near Schwarz-bach, 1927.

12.4 Express Engines for the Mountains

Efforts were always being made on the difficult mountain routes, used by important expresses, to run the trains without dividing them if possible, and without the help of pilot engines, as far as such could be avoided.

The Gotthard Railroad's 4–6–0 four-cylinder compound engines (Ill. 248) could only manage 280 tons double headed up the steep inclines of the line. If this load was exceeded, a third pusher had to be added. It was worth trying to create a locomotive which could pull 180 tons at 25 m.p.h. and thus omit the third locomotive but on the other hand it also had to be capable of 40 m.p.h. through the adjacent valleys. The Gotthard Railroad decided on a 2–8–0 locomotive designed by Hammel of Maffei. It bore

301. 2–8–0 twin-cylinder locomotive of the Spanish Norte Line, Series 400, 1909.

237

302. 4–8–0 two-cylinder compound locomotive of the Mediterraneo Railroad, later Italian State Railroad, Group 750, 1906.

all his design hallmarks: four-cylinder compound motion, bar frame, high pitched boiler with wide firebox unhampered by the wheels (Ill. 298). The eight engines ordered, Nos. 2801–2808, entered service in 1906. Superheating had still not quite overcome its teething troubles. Initially a Clench steam dryer on the Austrian model was fitted, but this was replaced between 1913 and 1916 by the Schmidt superheater. The front was carried by an Adams radial axle. When the Gotthard Railroad was taken over by the Swiss

Federal Railroad, no more engines of this type were acquired because they had a similar type of their own. They were scrapped in 1925 when the line was electrified.

In accordance with Jahn's law on the progression of every type, similar locomotives entered service as freight engines on level terrain with the Baden and Bavarian State Railroads. But nevertheless they may be regarded as the start of mountain express locomotives.

The next step came from the Norte Railroad in Spain, where the existing 4–6–0s were also proving unsatisfactory for the line running through the Guadarrama Mountains (cf. section 9.4). Once again, the 2–8–0 arrangement was adopted, but was used for the first time in Europe with the large driving wheel diameter of 5 ft. 1½ in., so that the engine could run comfortably at 38 m.p.h. over the subsequent level stretches (Ill. 301). Whereas in general four-cylinder compound systems were adopted for this type of engine, the Norte dared choose a two-cylinder

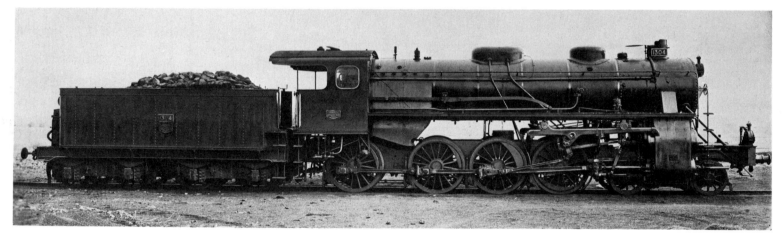

303. 4–8–0 four-cylinder compound locomotive of the Madrid-Zaragoza-Alicante Railroad, Hanomag, 1914.

304. 4–8–0 twin-cylinder locomotive of the Austrian Southern Railroad, Series 570, on the Payerbach-Reichenau stretch.

238

305. 0–8–0 superheated twin-cylinder freight train locomotive of the Prussian State Railroad, Series G 8[1], first built 1912 at Schichau (Elbing), Germany.

simple expansion system. The front axle was mounted in a Bissel pony truck with inclined plans resetting and the superheater was on Schmidt's pattern. These engines succeeded in pulling 275 tons up the Guadarrama inclines and 260-ton passenger trains and 360-ton freight trains over the Cantabrian coastal mountains. The design and the first examples came from St. Léonard. The engines soon proved suitable for universal use, with the result that the first ten were followed by no fewer than 412 between 1909 and 1943 for the Norte Railroad, and a further twenty-three for RENFE (Spanish National Railroads). This engine was numerically Spain's most popular type.

As on the level, twelve-wheeled locomotives soon had to be adopted for mountain work, a process started before the 2–8–0 engines were developed, in 1903, with the Mediterraneo Railroad in Italy. This railroad was the first in Europe to introduce the 4–6–0 locomotive with separate tender (cf. section 10.2) and it was now again the first to put 4–8–0 engines into service. These were not yet true express engines because they were intended for the extension of the Giovi line between Ronco and Alessandria, where there were still long inclines of 1 in 84.5 to 1 in 62.5. On the one hand, they had to pull 500-ton freight trains at a minimum of 12½ m.p.h., while on the other hand they were to reach 28 m.p.h. with passenger trains and even reach 37½ m.p.h. on subsequent level track. Thanks to the truck it was possible to fit a very powerful boiler and with the small driving wheel diameter chosen it was possible to make the rather flat firebox wide-spreading. To increase the steam chamber a tapered ring was included on the boiler barrel. The two cylinders worked as compounds. The first thirty engines, Nos. 4501–4530 — from 1902 built exclusively by Italian factories — were followed by another ten in 1906, this time for the Italian State Railroad, Group 750 (Ill. 302). Twenty-five engines were fitted with a new, higher-pitched boiler, from 1905.

The final arrangement of a 4–8–0 locomotive as a pure express engine was not achieved until 1912 with a De Glehn locomotive for Spain, once again for the Norte Railroad. Apart from its driving wheel diameter, it was identical with the 4–6–2 supplied simultaneously for level terrain. Both came from the Alsace Locomotive Works and had trapeze-shaped grates like those of the PO's "Pacific" engines.

The possibilities in the 4–8–0 arrangement were fully exploited in 1914 with Hanomag's eight locomotives for the Madrid, Zaragoza and Alicante Railroad. At the time they were among the most powerful engines in Europe (Ill. 303). The layout of the four-cylinder motion was very Bavarian, but there was a common piston valve for each pair of cylinders. In contrast, the frame was on the Von Borries pattern, being made of plates at the rear and bar at the front. To allow the large grate area required, the wide firebox was made as on the Bavarian 4–6–2 engines and the distance between the last two-coupled axles was increased to make room for it. The balanced four-cylinder compound system was chosen because the locomotives were to run both through the steep mountain passes and over the subsequent level tracks. The performance chart required 280 tons at 31 m.p.h. up a gradient of 1 in 67, 310 tons at 37½ m.p.h. up 1 in 100, and 340 tons on the level at 62 m.p.h. On test runs, the engines far exceeded these requirements and proved very economical in terms of fuel and water consumption. Owing to the outbreak of the First World War, the next twenty-five engines were ordered from ALCO in the USA. These Hanomag engines were the basis for Spanish locomotive building which started in Spain after the First World War. In 1914 the Southern Railroad Company in Austria ordered two 4–8–0 locomotives from the State Railroad Works in Vienna, with larger-than-usual driving wheels of 5 ft. 9 in. They were intended to pull expresses up to 400 tons on the stretch of track between Trieste and Laibach (Ljubljana today) rising steadily at 1 in 70 from sea level. Thanks to the higher Austrian loading guage, the centre line of the boiler was pitched at the unusual height of 10 ft. 8 in. and thus the firebox could easily be located above the coupled wheels.

On test runs, these locomotives pulled 449 tons up a 1 in 100 gradient at 31 m.p.h. As a result of the War, they did not enter service on the line planned but were transferred to the Semmering Railroad. They proved so good in comparison with the 2–8–2 four-cylinder compound locomotives introduced a year before by the State Railroad that another forty engines, Series 113, were acquired by the Austrian Federal Railroad between 1923 and 1928. Poland also had another sixty engines of the Southern Railroad type, meanwhile slightly modified, between 1926 and 1929. Descendants with a smaller driving wheel diameter were to be found in Hungary and the Soviet Union.

Another possibility of the eight-coupled express engine was the 2–8–2 arrangement. This was made simultaneously in Austria and France in 1913 and 1914 in the form of four-cylinder compounds. As stated already, it was abandoned in Austria in favour of the much simpler 4–8–0. On the PLM, however, it was extremely successful. It was a further development from the 2–8–0s which had been acquired for passenger trains on mountainous routes. To achieve a better performance, the boiler of the "Pacific" type (cf. section 12.3) was to be used, and as a result a rear carrying axle was required to support the wide firebox. A Bissel pony truck was provided at the front, having proved successful with the 2–8–0 engines. Of course, the now standard PLM four-cylinder compound motion was retained. Thus the heavy "Mikado", Series 1000 (Ill. 306), was evolved with a

306. 2–8–2 four-cylinder compound express locomotive of the Paris-Lyon-Méditerranée Railroad, Series 1000, 1913-36.

240

307. Austrian loco-
motive with inter-
national train on the
Semmering line above
Breitenstein.

maximum speed of 59 m.p.h. With certain alterations, a total of 709 were acquired between 1913 and
1936 and they proved so useful as "jack of all trades"
that the SNCF (French National Railroads) continued with them after the First World War. The
performance chart given below provides various data:

Gradient	Freight Trains		Fast Trains	
	m.p.h.	tons	m.p.h.	tons
level	25	2070	56	500
1 in 200	25	978	50	444
1 in 100	25	613	37½	370
1 in 67	18½	490	31	337

12.5 Heavy Freight

The continuing industrialization of Europe and the
growth of consumer cities resulted around the turn
of the century in an unforeseen increase in freight
traffic. Initially the railroads met this by increasing
the number of 20-ton cars, but this meant that train
weights increased considerably.

The Prussian State Railroads tried for as long as
possible to make do with full-coupled simple locomotives whose improved performance depended solely
on the fitting of the Schmidt superheater. Thus
eight-coupled engines were satisfactory at first, the
first type of which, G 8, had been introduced by Garbe
as the standard locomotive of the future as already
stated. At first, this was developed further into the
ten-coupled G 10. When the most important main
lines increased the permitted axle loading to 17 tons,
there was a return to the simpler 0–8–0 engine designed by Schichau in Elbing, and in 1912 the compact freight locomotive G 8[1] was created (Ill. 305).

241

No other type of locomotive had so many examples commissioned in such a short time: 4,948 between 1912 and 1921. Additionally there were 153 for other German railroads, the Swedish State Railroads bought twenty-five, the Rumanian eighty-one and the Polish fifty. With a total of 5,260 locomotives, the G8[1] is one of the most numerous types ever. As a consequence of both World Wars, a large number were dispersed all over Europe, from Russia to the Pyrenees as war reparations or were seized. This robust and powerful locomotive was popular everywhere. It was not scrapped until very late. While this is being written, there are still a large number in service in the east of Europe and in the Balkans.

Other railroad companies without permanent ways of the same quality as those in Prussia preferred the 2–8–0 arrangement. In Austria (cf. section 11.1.1) and Saxony (cf. section 10.3), were two-cylinder compounds; in Bavaria and Baden they were part of the South German four-cylinder compound school; and in France, of course, part of the De Glehn school.

It was also time in England to change from the insufficient classical six-coupled engine for heavy coal trains. Some railroads made do with eight-coupled engines made both with inside motion and with outside cylinders (as the Great Central, North Eastern). Churchward of the Great Western showed himself more far-sighted than his colleagues in this respect. He was the first in England to introduce the 2–8–0 arrangement. In building this, he used various standard parts, such as the boiler from the 4–6–0 engine. After a first prototype of 1903, No. 97, the definitive version came after two years' careful observation of it in actual service, Nos. 2801–2820 (Ill. 308). Consequently the boiler was made higher, allowing the grate to be deeper, and the front axle was in a Bissel pony truck. These first twenty engines were followed by another sixty-three between 1907 and 1913, now with superheaters and consequently with larger cylinders of 18½ in. diameter, Churchward's successor built another fifty slightly altered engines between 1938 and 1942.

A light permanent way was the reason for the introduction of the first 2–10–0 locomotive on the Empire Railroads in Alsace-Lorraine in 1905. This was the first in Europe. This Class G11 (formerly C33) was hardly superior to the French 2–8–0s which also had De Glehn motion. However, it was the model for the considerably larger 2–10–0 engines of Series 6001–6070 which the Paris and Orléans Railroad acquired in 1910 and which introduced this wheel arrangement

308. 2–8–0 freight locomotive of the Great Western Railway, No. 2803, 1915.

309. 2–10–0 freight locomotive of the Belgian State Railroads, Series 36, Flamme, 1921-26.

310. 2–12–0 locomotive for the Austrian Tauern Railroad, No. 100.01, Carl Gölsdorf, 1911.

This engine achieved the maximum performance possible from 0–8–0 engines. Because of the feed water heater, which was now standard, it performed better than the G10 class at higher speeds, as the performance chart shows:

Gradient	Train load in tons	
	9 m.p.h.	12½ m.p.h.
1 in 200	1550	1420
1 in 150	1230	1140
1 in 100	870	810

242

to France. At about the same time in 1913 the Swiss Federal Railroad and the Bulgarian State Railroad started operating 2–10–0 engines. In Switzerland these were four-cylinder compounds of the South German school, in Rumania they were engines with only two compound cylinders.

Flamme designed the most powerful 2–10–0 locomotive at that time, for the Belgian State Railroads. Its close similarity to his 4–6–2s is immediately apparent (Ill. 296). The front axle and the nearest coupled axle were combined in a Zara truck. On test runs this engine pulled 443 tons on the mountainous line between Pepinster and Spa with its long slopes of up to 1 in 40, whereas the six coupled Series 32 engines working in pairs could only manage 400 tons. But their main operational area was the Luxemburg run, where they regularly pulled 600-ton trains at 22 m.p.h. up 1 in 62.5, equivalent to a performance of rather more than 2,000 i.h.p. By 1914, 136 such engines entered service, Nos. 4365–4500, and a further seventeen of this Class 36 were added between 1921 and 1926, Nos. 4348–4364 (Ill. 309). From 1925 on, their boiler tubes were rearranged for the superheater and they were given a double chimney of the Legein type; Legein was Flamme's successor. These modifications increased the performance to 2,300 i.h.p. All these engines survived the Second World War.

One year after the Alsace 2–10–0, Gölsdorf had built a locomotive with the same wheel arrangement but not as a freight engine, but intending it to pull expresses on the Arlberg Railroad. However, neither the performance of this Class 280 nor its adhesion weight was sufficient for the Tauern Railroad. Gölsdorf then made the bold move of making a twelve-coupled engine for this railroad which was able to take sharp curves despite so many axles (Ill. 310). He achieved this by giving the front Adams radial axle boxes 2 in. side play, the third and sixth axle 1 in. each and the seventh, 1½ in. side play in each direction. The side play on the last axle forced him to make the coupling rod as universal joints. The construction of the four-cylinder compound motion

and the boiler was the same as the 2–6–4 express locomotives of Class 210 and 310. This 2–12–0 engine supplied by Floridsdorf in 1911 pulled 300 tons on the Tauern Railroad at 25 m.p.h. up a gradient of 1 in 35.5 but according to the timetable, it was able to manage 360 tons.

As a result of the change in traffic due to the First World War and the improved permanent way, there remained but a single example, No. 100.01, of this remarkable locomotive which was unfortunately also scrapped in 1927. But Gölsdorf had proved that it was perfectly possible to couple six axles with driving rods in a simple manner. He soon led others to do this and the famous 2–12–0 engine in Wurttemberg, Type K appeared. In Bulgaria, the first twelve-coupled tank engine appeared in 1922, reaching its highest state of development as a 2–12–4 locomotive (cf. section 15.1).

311. The last engine of the Swiss Federal Railroads type, Group C 5/6, No. 2972, 1913, 2–12–0, four-cylinder compound locomotive.

243

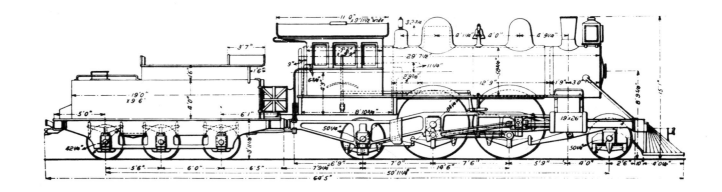

13. NORTH AMERICA STRIVES FOR EVER BIGGER LOCOMOTIVES

312. 2–4–2 express locomotive of the Chicago, Burlington and Quincy Railroad, 1895.

13.1   From the "Columbia" to the "Mountain"

1895 is often regarded as the year of the birth of the modern American express locomotive, when the Chicago, Burlington and Quincy Railroad started operating a 2–4–2 express locomotive, No. 590 (Ill. 312). It was not the first with this wheel arrangement. It had been preceded in 1880 by a locomotive with a wide Wootten firebox on the Philadelphia-and-Reading Railroad and at the Columbia World Fair in Chicago in 1893, Baldwin had exhibited a four-cylinder tandem compound locomotive with a narrow

grate which gave the name "Columbia" to the 2–4–2 wheel arrangement. However the Burlington No. 590 was the first to have all the features which were to become initially characteristic of the America express locomotives and eventually in general, once the 4–4–0 and 4–6–0 arrangements had disappeared: carrying axles front and rear, bar frame, a cylinder casting forming a smokebox saddle, simple expansion, wide firebox mounted above the trailing axle and built with a large deep grate to burn coal. Even the combustion chamber, much used later, had already been fitted. This locomotive was intended to pull expresses of five

244

to six cars between Chicago and Galesburg at an average speed of over 50 m.p.h. With the short boiler, the combustion chamber proved more of a hindrance than a help and steam production was not satisfactory. The guidance of the Bissel truck was not very effective, and with its short wheelbase, the engine tended to sway violently. It was therefore soon converted into a 4–4–2.

This 2–4–2 was adopted by a few railroads instead of 4–4–0s as a compact engine which could easily take a large grate, but because of its rough running it was soon dropped. In all, only about 120 "Columbia" type engines were built.

It was time to change the unsatisfactory Bissel pony truck for a normal truck — the more so to enable a more powerful boiler to be mounted than that on the 4–4–0 or 4–6–0, where the large coupled wheels hampered the firebox. The Atlantic Coastline Railroad operated the first 4–4–2 locomotive in the world in 1894; it was named "Atlantic", and had been supplied by Baldwin. It was simply a 4–4–0 extended at the rear. The rear axle served to take the extra weight of the narrow firebox which was mounted better despite the low-pitched boiler.

The definitive shape of the Atlantic as derived from the "Columbia" appeared on the Chicago and North-Western Railroad in 1900. It spread quickly to other railroads. The Pennsylvania type serves to illustrate its development. After an initial Class E1 with a wide Wootten firebox, the "Mother Hubbard" type, this railroad acquired in 1901 a Class E2 with a normal width firebox for coal burning and with a radius bar truck at the rear instead of a rigid trailing axle. Both ran on the Camden-and-Atlantic City line. Shortly afterwards the more powerful Class E3 followed for the lines running inland. Classes E2 and E3 had the flat Belpaire firebox crown which has almost invariably been used subsequently on the Pennsylvania Railroad. There was an unsatisfactory trial with four-cylinder compound locomotives, including one De Glehn engine of the Paris-and-Orléans type which was bought in Alsace, so that in 1906 the E class was readopted, this time fitted with outside Walschaerts valve gear instead of the inside standard Stephenson link motion fitted previously.

In 1911, the Pennsylvania Railroad tried a superheater for the first time. Because of the very favourable results, all subsequent E3 class engines were so fitted from then on. When the permanent way finally allowed an axle loading of 31 tons, this was utilized to the full by the locomotive superintendent Alfred

W. Gibbs in the last class, E6. Although the first engines which entered service in 1911 still used saturated steam, they proved not to be inferior to the superheated 4–6–2 locomotive of Class K2. They were thus subsequently fitted with a superheater in 1912.

Thus was developed the last and most powerful Atlantic type in North America, Class E6, eighty engines of which were built from 1914 at the railroad's own works in Altoona (Ill. 313). Using all the possibilities created by the high-axle loading, 2,488 i.h.p. was achieved. These engines pulled the heaviest expresses on the main line to the east of Altoona, among them the famous "Twentieth Century Limited", and were operated to the same timetable as the Class K2

313. 4–4–2 express locomotive of the Pennsylvania Railroad, No. 1710, Class E6s, built from 1914 on.

"Pacifics", surpassing them at high speeds. The trains between New York (Manhattan transfer) and Washington consisted of twelve to sixteen all-steel cars: between New York (Manhattan transfer) and Fort Wayne (Indiana), they travelled the 750 miles with no change of engine. They were the best of the North American "Atlantics" but they also represented the brilliant end of this type. In all about 1,900 "Atlantic" engines were built in the United States.

From the 2–6–0 locomotives extensively used on the railroads of the mid-West a 2–6–2 had been developed by the addition of a trailing axle to enable the boiler performance to be increased; it was built almost simultaneously with a driving wheel diameter of 5 ft. 1 in. for fast freight and 6 ft. 8 in. for express passenger trains. The main exponents of this "Prairie" type was the Atchisson, Topeca and Santa

Fé Railroad, which possessed 235, outnumbering even its "Pacific" engines. Some were even built as four-cylinder tandem compound locomotives. Although the "Prairie" type was only ordered in the United States until around 1910, nevertheless about a thousand such locomotives were built for main line use, although no more than a hundred of these can be regarded as true express engines.

As the front Bissel pony truck again proved unsuitable for high speeds, the logical development was the 4–6–2 locomotive. This arrangement was not new in itself. We have already seen it on the Strong engine (Ill. 178) and it occurred again in 1889 with an extended 4–6–0 engine on the Chicago/Milwaukee and St. Paul Rail-road. Both can only be regarded as predecessors of the real "Pacific" which appeared for the first time with a wide firebox in 1902 on the Missouri-and-Pacific Railroad, which gave it its name. Like the earlier "Prairie", it was intended as a locomotive for mixed traffic with a driving wheel diameter of 5 ft. 9 in. It soon caught on with many railroads for this pur-pose, and soon also began to wrest domination of the express field from the "Atlantics". When the New York Central Railroad, whose line was not as easy as that of its competitor the Pennsylvania, fitted its first Class K "Pacific" with 6 ft. 3 in. driving wheels

in December 1903, it began to develop into a true express engine. These first five engines were followed between 1908 and 1910 by the more powerful Class K 2, ninety-seven examples of which existed, and the period 1911 to 1925 produced 281 of the final version, Class K 3, with modified forms (Ill. 314). They were influenced by an ALCO demonstration locomotive, No. 50000, were fitted with a Schmidt superheater and no longer had the traditional Stephenson inside link motion but, instead, had outside piston valves operated by Heusinger-Walschaerts gear. Among other trains, they pulled the famous "Twentieth Century Limited" which then took eighteen hours travelling time between New York and Chicago. One of these engines pulled a 735-ton train on the Michigan line at 68 m.p.h.

Among the improvements gradually introduced, the first to be mentioned should be the use of bar frame sides made of cast vanadium steel. This eliminated troublesome breakages in the old forged and welded bar frames. Some of them were fitted with the so-called "Booster" to aid starting. This consisted of a small pair of cylinders which drove the trailing axle via a spur gear drive which was automatically disengaged once a certain speed had been reached. It was an improved version of the arrangement which

246

the Bavarian State and Palatinate Railroads had, at the turn of the century, unsuccessfully tried to use. When the Chesapeake-and-Ohio Railroad prepared a programme to modernize its fleet, the 4–8–2 arrangement was chosen for the Virginian mountain routes, as the 4–6–2 had insufficient adhesion and the 2–8–2s could not pick up enough speed for passenger trains. Despite the driving wheels of only 5 ft. 2 in. the front truck of the 4–8–2 ensured sufficiently smooth running with the speeds attainable in the mountains. Thanks to the trailing axle, a large enough grate could be mounted which, because of its size, could only be fired by an automatic stoker. The first two locomotives delivered in 1911, which were called "Mountain" engines after their application, fully lived up to expectations.

Initially these "Mountains" were not very highly thought of. But, in 1914, the Chicago, Rock Island and Pacific Railroad ordered two such engines on trial from ALCO. Nos. 4000–4001 but with 5 ft. 9 in.

driving wheels which made them suitable for higher speeds. After a pause during the First World War, ALCO supplied another ten engines in 1920 with a driving wheel diameter of 6 ft. 2 in. This was the breakthrough of the "Mountain" into an express engine (Ill. 315). The firebox incorporated the Nicholson thermic syphons which were then being introduced for heavy locomotives and served to increase the direct heating surface which, with wide fireboxes, was relatively small compared to that of the boiler tubes, and to improve the water circulation. The Baker valve gear was adopted, which was an American version of the Walschaerts gear with its reverse link replaced by combined bell cranks and radius bars.

13.2 From the "Consolidation" to the "Santa Fé"

We mentioned earlier that the "Consolidation" had become the most widespread standard freight engine

315. 4–8–2 express locomotive of the Chicago, Rock Island and Pacific Railroad, No. 4002, 1920.

316. 2–8–0 locomotive of the Toledo, St. Louis and Western Railroad.

in North America (cf. section 8.2). Of course it was constantly being improved. The boiler centre was pitched higher, the narrow firebox crammed between the frame gave way to the wide firebox. The good ratio between tractive effort and steam production resulted in a performance which satisfied most operational requirements for a long time. The popularity of this "workhorse" of American railroads is shown by the fact that about 21,000 2–8–0 locomotives of this type were produced for domestic companies alone. This is by far the highest number of any single type and there were additionally about 12,000 more which were supplied by the North American Locomotive Works principally to railroads in South America. A number of them also reached Europe, some being brought by the USA Expeditionary Corps in both World Wars. The way that the "Consolidation" altered its appearance from its beginnings can be seen from a comparison between the earlier engine (Ill. 171) and a medium heavy version supplied by Lima to the Toledo, St. Louis and Western Railroad (Ill. 316).

The first 2–8–2 locomotives were designated "Mikado", following an export order to Japan in 1897. They were initially operated in 1903/4 in the United States on mountain routes, pulling express freight trains which were hauled on the level by the "Prairie" but which the 2–8–0s could not manage through the mountains.

For this reason the North Pacific acquired "Prairie"

and "Mikado" engines simultaneously in 1904, and was one of the first to do so. In 1907, its 150 "Mikado" locomotives was the largest number of this type in the United States. Of course, the "Mikados" were continually being made more powerful and technical details were altered to keep pace with developments. A locomotive supplied by ALCO in 1920 to the Northern Pacific is an example of an improved "Mikado" (Ill. 317). The cylinders visible under the driver's cab serve to assist the engineer operating the reversing gears. The "Mikado" was one of the best-selling locomotive types in North America. More than 14,000 entered service before it was withdrawn from production around 1930. It always remained a freight engine during its life in the USA.

Despite individual versions, such as the "El Gobernador" (cf. section 8.3) and the "Vauclain" compound engines (cf. section 11.1.5), the ten-coupled locomotive was relatively late in coming to the United States. The high axle loadings permitted meant that eight-coupled axles normally sufficed and the Mallet type was used for difficult mountainous stretches, as we shall see later. Both the 0–8–0 and 0–10–0 arrangements without trucks were used exclusively as switchers. They only occurred as 2–10–0s on a few railroads, for example the "Vauclain" engines on the Sante Fé and those ordered by the Pennsylvania between 1916 and 1926, then the heaviest engines of their type in the world. Their total numbers were hardly more than seven hundred.

317. 2–8–2 freight locomotive of the Northern Pacific Railroad, "Mikado" type, 1920.

The 2–10–2 engines were different, for the reason already mentioned, having to accommodate large fireboxes. As stated in section 11.1.5, the Santa Fé Railroad had made a start in 1904, but the ability of these engines to negotiate curves left a lot to be desired. It was not until the resetting of the Bissel truck was improved by the use of heart-shaped roller (in 1912) that the 2–10–2 type was readopted, in the first place by the Chicago-and-Burlington Railroad.

When the high maintenance costs of the large Mallet engines became evident during the First World War, many railroads only used articulated locomotives as auxiliaries on steep inclines, and ordered the much simpler two-cylinder 2–10–2s of the type supplied by Baldwin to the Union Pacific in 1917 (Ill. 318).

318. 2–10–2 locomotive of the Union Pacific Railroad, 1917.

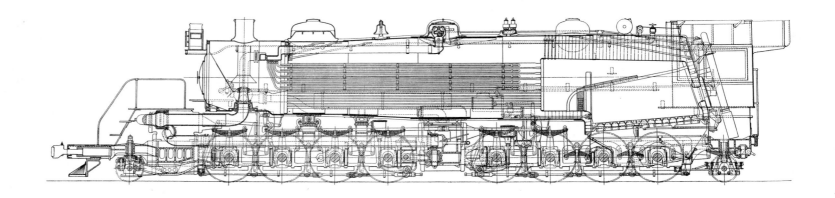

14. LARGE LOCOMOTIVES FOR SHARP CURVES

14.1 The Fairlie Locomotives

In the 1860s and 1870s, when remoter areas were opened up with the construction of railroads, investment costs had to be kept down by accepting steep inclines and sharp curves in mountainous areas. The current locomotives of that time were not very suitable in this respect. Four-coupled engines had too little adhesion weight while six- and eight-coupled types did not take the curves well enough. Two designers tried, at about the same time, to reconcile the contrasting conditions. One, the Englishman

Robert Fairlie, worked on the "Seraing" (Ill. 181) of the Semmering contest, while the other, Jean-Jacques Meyer of Alsace, to whom reference has already been made, reverted to the "Wiener Neustadt".

Let us initially consider Fairlie's activites. After his patent of May 1864, in December 1865 the first Fairlie locomotive was supplied by the James Cross & Co. Sutton Engine Works of St. Helens to the Neath-and-Brecon Railway in Britain. Like the "Seraing", it was an 0–4–4–0 but with outside cylinders. The draw and buffer gears were attached to the trucks. This locomotive was not successful, nor

250

was the second one, supplied in 1866 by the same firm to the Anglesey Central Railway. He only overcame the teething troubles with the "Little Wonder", built for the 1 ft. 11½ in. gauge Ffestiniog Railway in Wales in September 1869 in collaboration with George England, owner of the Hatcham Ironworks in New Cross. James Spooner, the railroad's engineer, had worked on the plans together with Fairlie. It did indeed prove to be a "little wonder", for on several test runs in February 1870, it pulled a 180-ton train of seventy-two cars at 5 m.p.h. up a 1 in 85 gradient. Experts came from far and wide and were amazed how this attractive yet powerful little engine could run lightly and safely through all the many curves. The "Little Wonder" was scrapped in 1883, and was followed by four slightly more powerful engines, of which the "Taliesin", built in 1885 at the railroad's own works at Boston Lodge and restored in 1956, is still active today (Ill. 319).

As a contemporary wrote of Fairlie, he was a past master at "publicizing with pretty pictures". By the mid-1870s, eighty-four engines to his patent had been supplied by various British works, principally the Avonside Engine Co. Most of these had gone to the Andes Railroads then being built in Peru and to Mexico. The "Escalador de Montes"* is typical of the most common 0–6–0 + 0–6–0 type (Ill. 320), one of the three engines supplied by Avonside to the 3 ft.-gauge Chimbote Railroad in Peru. To make more room for the crew, the common firebox was made narrower in the middle than at the tube walls. Both regulator-valves were arranged so that the common regulator handle opened one at first, and then the other when pushed further. This meant that in free running or with light trains, only one driving set needed to be in use. The cylinders measured 13½ × 18 in., the working order weight was 46 tons. The Mexican Railroad had the largest number of

As with all articulated locomotives, ball joints of the steam pipes were the most critical aspect of the Fairlie. To avoid these, F.W. Johnston, the Mexican Central Railroad's engineer, removed the cylinders from the trucks and placed them on the two smokeboxes (Ill. 321). The cylinders worked on a compound system, with the LP cylinder arranged concentrically round the HP cylinder. As a result, the LP piston was ring-shaped and had a piston rod at the top and bottom, joining the one from the middle HP cylinder in a common crosshead. This crosshead had a long, vertical, swinging lever pivoted at the centre, the lower end of which drove the middle coupled axle through a large fly-crank. A similar lever in parallel with this swinging lever linked with a short rod at the top. The connecting rod from this lever operated the main crank of the driving wheels. As in the Hagans system (Ill. 193), these suspended levers could adapt to the lateral swivelling of the trucks. The reversing gear also had this sort of intermediate system. It need hardly be said that a construction as complicated as this did not prove successful on regular schedules. The only three locomotives were built on Johnston's plans in 1892 by the Rhode Island Locomotive Works in the USA.

14.2 The Günther-Meyer Locomotive and its Variants

After selling his locomotive works in Mulhouse to Koechlin, Meyer had set up in Paris as consulting engineer. He succeeded in obtaining financial help from the French government for the construction of a locomotive basically in line with Günther's "Wiener Neustadt" of the Semmering contest (Ill. 180). It can no longer be established whether the French patent for a double locomotive, which Meyer was granted as early as 1843, anticipated the "Wiener Neustadt". Just as he had done with his "riding cut-off" valve locomotives (cf. section 4.5), he found an apt name for the engine now built by Jean François Cail in 1869: "L'Avenir" or "The Future". It was an 0–4–0+0–4–0 tank engine, but, in line with its time, had a round section, parallel boiler and with the very rare (at that stage) Heusinger-Walschaert gear. After works test runs, it was transferred firstly to Switzerland where it was tried on the Jura Industrial Railroad (Neuchâtel to La Chaux-de-Fonds) and the Swiss Central Railroad between Olten and Sissach.

321. 2–6–0+0–6–2 locomotive of the Mexican Central Railroad, F.W. Johnston, 1892.

Fairlie engines in Spanish America. Their last 0–6–0+0–6–0s of 1911, oil-fired, weighed 138 tons. They ran on the extraordinarily difficult line which led at an uninterrupted gradient of 1 in 40 for the 22 miles from the Atlantic port of Vera Cruz up to the interior tableland.

Russia was the country with the most Fairlie engines. In all, more than seventy 0–6–0+0–6–0s were purchased between 1872 and 1887. Apart from that, the Fairlie was not very widespread in Europe. Five-metre gauge 0–4–0+0–4–0s ran on the Saxon State Railroad where a track in the Ore Mountains had gradients of up to 1 in 33 and curves as tight as 50 yards radius.

It performed slightly better than the existing engines, but not convincingly so, so that it moved on to the Belgian Grand Central Railroad, doing no better there, however, than the existing eight-coupled engines. It ended finally on the Charentes Railroad in South-West France where it became No. 0401 when

that the Saxon State Railroads adopted the Meyer type. The firm of Richard Hartmann of Chemnitz supplied the first two 0–4–0 + 0–4–0 tank engines in 1890 as Class MIT V. Exceptionally, they were compounds. Their load of 135 tons up 1 in 40 gradients was not much more than the standard six-coupled

322. 0–4–0 + 0–4–0 tank locomotive of the Saxon State Railroads, No. 98001, Series IT V, Günther-Meyer type, 1910-15.

nationalization occurred. It was not long in service there before it was scrapped in 1886.

Meyer's second design, an 0–6–0 + 0–6–0 tank engine built by the Compagnie Belge (Evrard) in Brussels, did not fare much better. This was exhibited in 1873 at the Vienna World Fair, also failed to improve on the eight-coupled engines on the Grand Central.

It was not until the Nineties that the Meyer locomotive obtained a certain success on lines where conditions were particularly difficult, as for instance those in the Ore Mountains of Saxony. Rigid axles could not be considered because of the tight curves. The Fairlies were difficult to maintain, but there was not enough known about the Mallets, which meant

engine, but they took the curves much better. Their mediocre performance explains why no more Meyer engines were acquired for the time being. It was because of their ability to negotiate curves that they were again adopted in 1910, but in a much more powerful version (Ill. 322). They were now able to pull 195 tons on these same inclines. Nineteen engines of this Class IT V had entered service by 1914, of which the last survivor, No. 98.002, lasted in service until the summer of 1966, being finally handed over to the Transport Museum in Dresden.

The Saxon State Railroads also chose the Günther-Meyer type for their 2 ft. 5½ in. gauge lines. Incidentally, they should be so called to distinguish

253

323. 0–4–0 + 0–4–0 tank locomotive of the Wallücke Railroad, Günther-Meyer type, 1897.

324. 2–8–0 + 0–8–0 locomotive of the Great Southern of Spain Railroad, later RENFE (Spanish National Railroad), Kitson-Meyer type, 1908.

them from other, later versions which will be considered in due course. No fewer than ninety-five engines of this TVK Class, also 0–4–0 + 0–4–0 compound tank engines, were delivered between 1892 and 1916, and one more followed in 1921. Thus the Saxon State Railroads were the only railroad company in Europe to own significant numbers of Günther-Meyer locomotives.

Very similar to these Saxon narrow gauge locomotives were the two 1 ft. 11⅝ in. gauge 0–4–0 + 0–4–0 compound tank engines supplied by Jung to the Wallücke Railroad in 1897. These, undoubtedly the smallest Günther-Meyer engines ever built, weighed only 20

tons (Ill. 323), and were the counterparts of the small Ffestiniog locomotives (Ill. 319). Once the Wallücke Railroad ceased to exist, they were passed on to the Wirsitz District Railroad* in West Prussia.

In England, Kitson of Leeds in particular took to the Meyer pattern. This was brought about by an enquiry from Robert Stirling, who was locomotive superintendent on the Anglo-Chilean Nitrate and Railroad Company. He needed powerful locomotives to convey saltpetre over a track with long inclines of 1 in 40 for nearly three-quarters of its length, and curves of as little as 55 yards radius. Kitson suggested an 0–6–0 + 0–6–0 tank engine, differing from the Günther-

325. 0–6–2 + 2–6–0 tank locomotive of the Grande Ceinture (Paris Outer Circle) Railroad, Du Bousquet-Meyer type, 1910-12.

*Kreisbahn.

254

Meyer type in that the firebox lay between the two sets of motion which were therefore further apart; the cylinders of the rear motion, which were in the way, were overhung at the rear, and exhaust steam had to be led into a second chimney located behind the driver's cab. This Kitson-Meyer type caught on with other saltpetre lines in South America. It only occurred once in Europe, in its largest version. In 1908, Kitson supplied three of these engines, Nos. 50–52, to the Great Southern Spain Railroad, which was then in British hands. They were used to pull trains consisting of twelve eight-wheeled hopper cars, which had to be conveyed empty from the Mediterranean port of Aguilas up gradients of up to 1 in 50 to the iron ore mines. This time the 2–8–0 + 0–8–0 wheel arrangement was adopted, so that the front cylinder overhang was taken by a carrying axle (Ill. 324). All three engines passed to the RENFE (Spanish National Railroads) as Nos. 180.0401–0403, and were scrapped in 1953.

The third variant of the Meyer locomotive came from Du Bousquet — previously referred to — who again

Between 1905 and 1908, the Nord Railroad acquired forty-eight of this type, Series 6121–6128, and the Est Railroad received thirteen at the same time, Series 6101–6113. The Outer Circle Railroad (Grande Ceinture) followed between 1910 and 1912 with another thirty-eight engines, Series 6001–6038. The only other places where similar engines were to be found were on the Peking-and-Hankow Railroad in China and on the Andalusian Railroad, with smaller driving wheels of 4 ft. 5 in. diameter. To decrease weight, the water tanks on this engine were so reduced that a water tender always had to accompany it.

The last examples of the Meyer type were the 0–6–0 + 0–6–0 engines acquired between 1925 and 1928 by South African Railroads, Class FC (Ill. 326). They were in fact known as the "modified Fairlies" but the only thing they had in common with the Fairlie was the articulated layout. They were Kitson-Meyer locomotives with the girder frame extended at the front to take the water tank. A total of fifteen were supplied by the North British and the Henschel Works, representing an attempt by Colonel Collins,

faced his predecessors' problem of creating a new locomotive for the Nord Railroad's increased coal traffic. It was to pull double the weight of the existing engines. The new design was arranged as 0–6–2 + 2–6–0 tank engine (Ill. 325), with the compound cylinders again arranged as originally, in the middle. The rear tank was on a box-shaped girder frame, whereas the front water container rested directly over the front truck.

How far the advent of superheated steam eclipsed this type of complicated engine is shown by the fact that the simple Prussian G 8 (cf. section 11.2) had the same performance as these Du Bousquet engines, which pulled 1,000 tons on the level at 25 m.p.h. and up 1 in 84 at 12½ m.p.h.

then in charge of the engines, to free himself of the Garratt monopoly. In negotiating curves, the pivot pins came under too much stress due to the pronounced lateral sway of the long overhangs. These engines thus proved more expensive to maintain than the Garratt locomotives, and as a result were soon scrapped.

14.3 *The Mallet Locomotive in Europe*

In 1877 Anatole Mallet suggested in one of his writings on compound locomotives that each pair of cylinders of the Fairlie and Meyer locomotives should be operated with double expansion. He was also of the

326. 2–6–2 + 2–6–2 locomotive of the South African Railroads, No. 1388, Class FC, so-called "modified Fairlie" type, 1925-28.

327. 0–4–0+0–4–0
locomotive of the Saxon
State Railroads, No.
1251, Series IV, Mallet
type.

opinion that sufficient flexibility would be achieved if only the front truck could swivel. If the HP cylinders were mounted rigidly on the main frame, the ball joints of the HP steam pipes would be avoided and those in the steam pipes leading to the LP cylinders were easier to keep steam-tight as the steam pressure in them was lower. He was given a French patent for this idea on June 18, 1884.

When Paul Decauville wanted to exhibit the 1 ft. 11⅜ in. (60 cm) gauge portable railroad, easily laid and dismantled, at the World Fair in Paris in 1889, he got in touch with Mallet. Decauville wanted to show that his system was suitable for cheaply constructed narrow-gauge railroads. Mallet was to design a much more powerful locomotive for it than the existing small 0–4–0 for this portable truck. But as with these, it could not have an axle load exceeding 3 tons and had to be able to take curves of 20 yards radius. Mallet made a draft for an 0–4–0+0–4–0 tank engine in line with his patent. It was constructed in five months — being the short space of time avail-

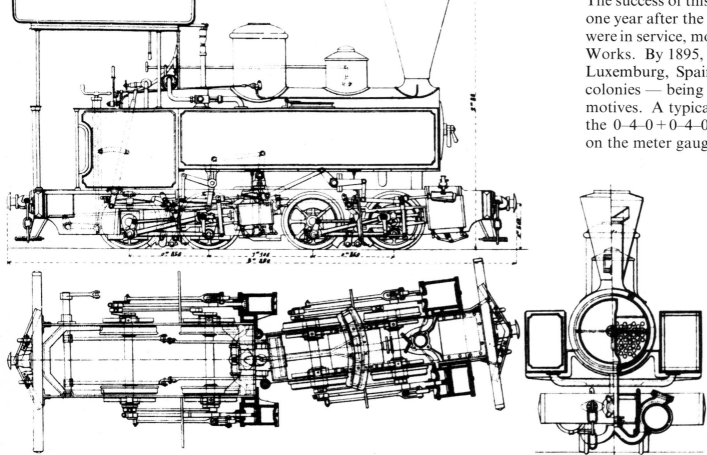

328. 0–4–0+0–4–0
tank locomotive of
Anatole Mallet for the
World Exhibition,
Paris, 1889.

able — by the "Société Belge La Métallurgique" (The Belgian Metallurgical Society) (Ill. 328). The basic layout and the behaviour on curves can be seen in this same illustration. On a quickly laid light track near Laon, with gradients of up to 1 in 16 and 1 in 14, it pulled with ease 10 tons at an average speed of 9 m.p.h. This was the modest beginning of a type of construction which was to lead to the largest locomotives yet built. Along with six sister-locomotives this prototype worked for sixteen hours a day during the Fair and despite the short length of track covered 66 miles a day.

The success of this demonstration was so decisive that one year after the Fair ended, 110 Mallet locomotives were in service, mostly built by the Alsace Locomotive Works. By 1895, they had spread through Germany, Luxemburg, Spain, Switzerland and various French colonies — being almost entirely narrow-gauge locomotives. A typical representative may be taken to be the 0–4–0+0–4–0 and an 0–6–0+0–6–0 locomotive on the meter gauge Zell-and-Todtnau Railroad in the

German Black Forest district (Ill. 329). 0–4–0 + 0–4–0s were supplied in 1896 and 1899 by the Alsace Locomotive Works, while the other type came from Henschel in 1925 and is typical of the type developed during the First World War for the German Military Railroad Headquarters. This type, and a successor, an 0–4–0 + 0–4–0 built by the Karlsruhe Locomotive Works are still in service today on the historical Swiss Blonay-Chamby Railroad.

The first standard-gauge Mallet engines were four 0–4–0 + 0–4–0 tank engines by Cail which entered service 1891 on the Hérault Railroad in France. In the course of a decade, the Mallet was used as an engine with separate tender, in Prussia, Baden, Bavaria, the Swiss Central Railroad and in Hungary. A typical example is the Class IV shown, supplied by Hartmann in 1896 to the Saxon State Railroads (Ill. 327), which can be regarded as a Meyer locomotive (Ill. 322) developed further for main-line service. It was intended to pull 505 tons at 16 m.p.h. up gradients of 1 in 100.

When Gölsdorf proved that sharp curves could be taken with axles with simple lateral play (cf. section 11.1.1), Mallet engines declined somewhat, but continued to be used on lines where conditions were especially difficult. The first larger 0–6–0 + 0–6–0 engines were not very successful. The first heavy 0–6–0 + 0–6–0 Mallet tank engine on the Gotthard Railroad — which had too small a boiler for the weight — was an isolated example. The 0–6–0 + 0–6–0 tank engine by Belpaire, which was enormous for its day, was the first European locomotive weighing more than 100 tons, and was acquired by the Belgian State Railroad but was abandoned in 1905 because of constant trouble. Nevertheless, the way towards the further development of the heavy Mallet had been shown.

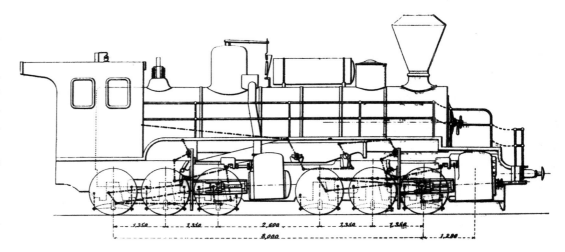

The first country to adopt this type successfully was Russia. In 1899, the Moscow-and-Kazan Railroad ordered 0–6–0 + 0–6–0 engines with separate tenders weighing 81 tons from Briansk, and one was exhibited in Paris in 1900 (Ill. 330). Other Russian railroads — including the Trans-Siberian Railroad — acquired these locomotives, so that by 1910 nearly one hundred had entered service in Russia. The Mallet locomotives were especially suitable for the light permanent way on Russian tracks which were often ballasted only by sand, and therefore only permitted small axle loads.

331. 0–8–0 + 0–8–0 tank locomotive of the Bavarian State Railroads, No. 96001, Series Gt 2 × 4/4, Mallet type.

Apart from Russia, the only large Mallet locomotives were used in Europe by broad and standard-gauge railroads in Spain and Hungary. In Spain, the Central Aragon had already received a series of 0–6–0 + 0–6–0 tank engines from Borsig. However, they had proved too heavy and were converted into 2–6–0 + 0–6–0s with separate tenders. The next were similar to the Russian locomotives, including thirteen for the Central Aragon and three for the Zafra-and-Huelva Railroad.

On the other hand, the Mallet locomotive was systematically developed in Hungary. On the line between Fiume (present-day Rijeka) to Karlstadt (Karlovne), which was then still Hungarian, rigid eight-coupled engines were too demanding on the track. Between 1898 and 1902, thirty 0–4–0 + 0–4–0 Mallets with separate tenders, Category IV d (later 422) were gradually acquired. They pulled 394 tons at about 10 m.p.h. up 1 in 60 gradients. To replace the 4–6–0 locomotives which were no longer powerful enough for passenger trains in 1905 fifteen 2–4–0 + 0–4–0 engines were introduced, Category 40 (401). They had a larger driving wheel diameter of 4 ft. 9 in. instead of 4 ft. because they were required to travel at up to 38 m.p.h. They were able to pull 130 tons at 18½ m.p.h. up a 1 in 40 gradient. A few Cate-

332. 2–6–0 + 0–6–0 locomotive of the Hungarian State Railroads, Cat. 601.017, Mallet type, 1916.

gory IV d engines were used on the coal line between Piski and Petrosény in the Carpathian Mountains but they were not able to run on the subsequent stretch of line between Petrosény and Lupény which only permitted 12 tons axle loading. In 1909 0–6–0 + 0–6–0 engines, Category VI m (651) were introduced on this line. They were so successful that they were also put into service on the Karst line. By 1919 their numbers had increased to fifty-eight. These engines could pull 508 tons at 12½ m.p.h. up a gradient of 1 in 67.

They were soon found to be insufficient on the Karst line, and as the permanent way had now been improved to admit 16-ton axle loading, a much more powerful 2–6–0 + 0–6–0 locomotive, Category 601, was introduced in 1914. This can be regarded as a development from Category 401, being suitable for passenger trains because of the front carrying axle and the same driving wheel diameter of 4 ft. 9 in. (Ill. 332). It was fitted with a superheater and Brotan firebox because of the shortage of copper. This was invented in 1900 by Johann Brotan, who was works foreman at the Gmünd headquarters of the Austrian State Railroads. Its final shape consisted of leg-shaped tubes closely packed together and forming the combustion chamber, entering at each side into an overhead drum as a steam collection chamber. At the bottom end, the tubes extended into a hollow steel casting forming the foundation ring which was in turn linked with the underside of the boiler shell by curved water pipes. The upper steam collector mentioned opened into the principal steam chamber in the boiler shell, the rear shell ring of which was consequently tapered. This was the only firebox differing significantly from the Stephenson pattern which proved successful. It was used on all large locomotives on the Hungarian State Railroad. The fifty locomotives in Category 601 acquired between 1914 and

258

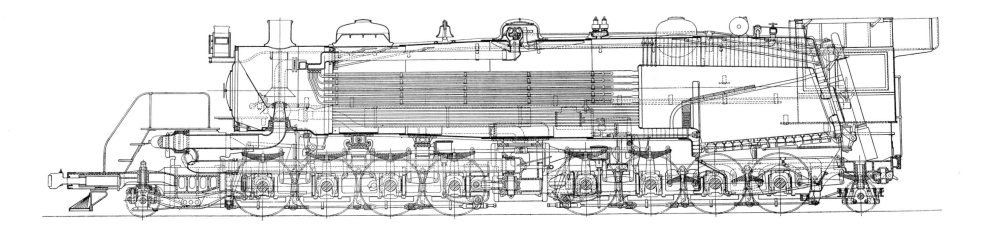

1921 were able to pull up to 396 tons at 12½ m.p.h. up a 1 in 40 (2.5%) gradient and 373 tons at 25 m.p.h. The Hungarian State Railroad had far more Mallet locomotives than any other European railroad with a total of 163, all built in Budapest.

To cross the Fichtel Mountain range with its long 1 in 50 to 1 in 40 gradients, all freight trains had to be divided and, even then, could only be hauled across the mountains with the aid of a pusher engine. The Bavarian State Railroads ordered fifteen 0–8–0 + 0–8–0 Mallet tank engines from Maffei for this line, Class Gt 2 × 4/4 (Ill. 331), which were intended to pull 670 tons up a 1 in 50 gradient and 540 tons up 1 in 40 at 11 m.p.h. Since they were also required to aid expresses, they had to be able to travel at 31 m.p.h. or more. In 1923, another ten engines of this type were added. A comparison with the later 2–10–2 tank engines on the German National Railroad showed that, despite less adhesion weight, the latter achieved the same banking performance because in the Mallet engines, the LP cylinders did not get enough steam at full throttle. The diameter of the HP cylinders was then increased to 23⅝ in. and a larger superheater and improved exhaust were fitted.

Despite a considerable increase in performance the high cost of conversion meant that only twelve engines were modified.

14.4 The Mallet Giants in America

No engine caused a greater stir at the World Fair in St. Louis in 1904 than the huge 0–6–0 + 0–6–0 Mallet locomotive with separate tender, No. 2400, which was built by the American Locomotive Co. and exhibited by the Baltimore-and-Ohio Railroad. It was to replace two Mogul engines on lines in the

Alleghennie Mountains. It soon emerged that, because of the short wheelbase of the trucks, stability was very poor. It was an isolated example and was only used for auxiliary switching, nonetheless surviving in this role for thirty-four years.

It introduced the era of giant locomotives to the United States, for it demonstrated how heavy trains could be hauled over mountain routes without dividing them. On the basis of trials with various wheel arrangements, the two most commonly used basic types were established by 1910. Both had Bissel pony trucks at each end for improved running. The first of these basic types was the 2–6–0 + 0–6–2 engine, first supplied by Baldwin to the Great Northern Railroad. Its performance was approximately that of two Moguls of that time. It was the most numerous type of Mallet, being about 47.7% of the entire range, with about 1,300 locomotives built by 1949.

The second basic type was a 2–8–0 + 0–8–2 locomotive first supplied in 1909 by Baldwin to the Southern Pacific Railroad. Initially it was much used to replace 2–6–0 + 0–6–2 engines on railroads where high axle loads were not permitted because of the permanent way or wooden trestle bridges, but it was soon also used on other, mountainous routes, which carried much coal traffic. About 710 were built by 1950, which was considerably fewer than the 2–6–0 + 0–6–2

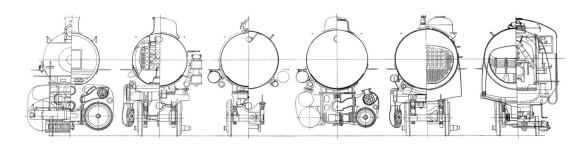

333. 2–8–0 + 0–8–2 locomotive of the Nashville, Chattanooga and St. Louis Railroad, No. 902, Class M 1-99, Mallet type. Cross-sections.

334. 2–8–0+0–8–2 locomotive of the Nashville, Chattanooga and St. Louis Railroad, No. 902, Class M 1-99, Mallet type.

engines, but nevertheless represented 22.5% of the whole range of Mallet locomotives. The example chosen of a heavy 2–8–0+0–8–2 engine is the Class M1–99 locomotive built by Baldwin in 1915 for the Nashville, Chattanooga and St. Louis Railroad (Ills. 333 and 334). The construction is clear from the sectional drawing. These engines were intended to bank heavy trains through the Cumberland Mountains, where there were gradients of 1 in 42½ and 1 in 40. They were able to take curves of only 103 yards radius despite their great length.

The large grates on these locomotives could no longer be fed by hand. In 1905, attempts had begun to devise mechanical arrangements for feeding the coal into the firebox. The first attempt was with plungers pushing the coal into the grate from underneath. Around 1910, a continuous chain was used, running into a broad tube with the coal being spread over the grate by a spray of steam. Then came the final solution with the coal brought in by screw feed conveyors, the coal being spread over the grate by a steam jet. The conveyors were operated by an auxiliary steam engine.

The Virginia Railroad set a first size record with a Mallet. This railroad depended mainly on coal traffic and had to operate its trains west of Roanoke between Elmore and Clark's Gap on a single line which had an 11-mile incline of 1 in 48, and curves down to 148 yards radius. In 1912, four 2–8–0+0–8–2s had been introduced, but to manage the increased traffic in 1918 ten 2–10–0+0–10–2 locomotives, Nos. 800–809 (Ill. 335) were acquired. As the loading gauge of the Virginia Railroad's engines was much larger than usual, these giants had to be taken from the ALCO factory in Shenectady with the cylinders, boiler equipment and driver's cab dismantled. Even so, many detours had to be made, so that in all the journey to Princeton took fourteen days. To convey an idea of the proportions: the smallest diameter of the boiler was 8 ft. 9½ in. at the front, and the largest 9 ft. 10½ in. at the rear. At that time the largest boilers in Europe were about 6 ft. diameter. On a test run on May 21, 1921, 120 freight cars weighing a total of 15,000 tons were coupled up, resulting in a train 1½ miles long! So as not to place too much stress on the couplings when starting, three 0–8–0 switchers were used at the rear until 12½ m.p.h. was attained. The Mallet then

335. 2–10–0+0–10–2 locomotive of the Virginia Railroad, No. 802, Mallet type, 1908.

continued alone reaching 27 m.p.h. This performance represented 6,600 to 7,000 i.h.p., a figure which was not achieved until the electric and diesel locomotives decades later.

Normally two of these giants were used as bankers on the mountain line in question with a 2–8–0 + 0–8–2 Mallet pulling. There were seventy-eight freight cars with a total weight of 5,330 tons. The Virginia Railroad was one of the first to use hopper cars for 100-ton loads. In 1926, the ten giants were used on other lines when this mountain route was electrified, and were replaced by diesel engines between 1948 and 1958.

The Erie Railroad, which had been the first to use the Mallet engines in North America, had similar problems to the Virginia Railroad as we have seen. It solved them by using Triplex Mallet locomotives. Basically this used the same idea of a tender driven by cylinders which had been actually put into practice

Mallet (Ill. 336), which was to better the performance of the 2–10–0 + 0–10–2 locomotives. Following the Erie Railroad's experiences, cylinder and boiler proportions were matched more carefully. To accommodate large stocks of fuel, a four-wheeled truck was inserted at the rear. The engine entered service on the incline between Princeton and Oney Gap Tunnel as a banker, the gradient in question being 1 in 62. It was actually able to pull trains uphill of eighty-five freight cars weighing 6,000 to 7,000 tons, but in the long run it did not prove possible to keep the stuffing boxes of all the articulated pipe joints sealed. Thus the locomotive was surrounded in such clouds of steam that vision was dangerously impeded, and the continual losses of steam led to high water consumption. Thus 1921 saw the tender separated; it was given a boiler and a front running axle which resulted in a 2–8–4 engine with separate tender. The two front

by Verpilleux in 1843 with three 0–4–0 locomotives on the St. Etienne-and-Lyons Railroad in France, and which was revived in 1863 by Sturrock on the Great Northern in England, and later on the Est Railroad in France as well. But the Triplex engines had the tender frame hinged to the main frame of the locomotive in the same way as the leading truck. The engines were 2–8–0 + 0–8–0 + 0–8–2s. All six cylinders were identical, the middle pair worked as HP and the other two as LP cylinders. The exhaust from the rear two issued from a separate chimney. These three locomotives built by Baldwin in 1914 had boilers which quickly ran out of steam soon after starting, and were therefore not followed by further examples. The Virginia Railroad also risked using a Triplex

groups were given new, unequal pairs of cylinders working in compound. Thus the Triplex came to a sorry end, and was converted into a 2–8–0 + 0–8–0 with tender.

The Triplex Mallet engines had already gone beyond the bounds of what was possible at that time. They were the end of the first development stage of the American Mallet.

14.5 The Garratt Locomotive

Herbert William Garratt was neither Australian nor a painter, as is sometimes stated. He was a typical English colonial engineer, working on several rail-

336. 2–8–0 + 0–8–0 + 0–8–4 locomotive of the Virginia Railroad, Triplex Mallet type.

roads in South America and Africa, finally ending up as receiving engineer with the New South Wales Government Railroad in Australia, returning to England in 1906. It is said that he conceived the idea for the type of locomotive named after him by noticing during an inspection how heavy, eight-wheel freight wagons on trucks rode easily through tight "S"-bends. Armed with not much more than a rough sketch, he called on the firm of Beyer-Peacock. His luck was in. This firm, which was going through hard times, had just changed its management. Garratt's proposal was seen as a real opportunity. By chance, an order was in hand from the Tasmanian Government Railroad, which needed a powerful locomotive for the 2 ft. gauge North East Dundas line, 17 miles long. There were a great many tight curves on this stretch of line, which was used for the transport of lead ore.

Garratt submitted his patent which was granted on June 18, 1908. Sam Jackson, a young engineer, was to carry out the plans. Garratt himself was only to be seen a few hours a week, and was not always addicted to temperance. He died in 1913 when very few of his locomotives had been built. Jackson developed this type of construction, and the Beyer-Garratt locomotive is really the production of Jackson much more than it is a child of Garratt.

In 1909, the two engines were supplied to Tasmania. Like the first Fairlie and Mallet locomotives, they were a very modest start (Ill. 337). Unlike the Mallet engines (Ill. 328), the Garratt had a long girder frame which initially was supported in the center of the widely distributed power units and took the boiler and the driver's cab. Thus the boiler and, above all, the firebox could be given all the space they needed. The fuel and water tanks rested on the power units. These two Tasmania locomotives were compound, a system which was not often used on later Garratts. They remained in service until 1930, when the line was abandoned. In 1947, one was bought back by Beyer-Peacock, and when the firm closed in 1966, it was acquired by the Ffestiniog Railway.

Both these first two proved so successful that in 1912 the Tasmanian Railroad acquired two 2–6–2 + 2–6–2 (Class L1) types, and two 4–4–2 + 2–4–4 (Class M1) types for its 3 ft. 6 in. gauge lines. The Class M1 engines were not only the first Garratts for passenger trains but also the first with four cylinders on each unit, this time of the simple expansion type. On trial runs they ran smoothly at 50 m.p.h., an amazing speed for narrow gauge at that time.

By the outbreak of the First World War, only about twenty-two Garratts had been built, all narrow-gauge types. But it was not Beyer-Peacock who achieved the breakthrough on African railroads, where they were easily the most common types later on, but his licensee, the St. Léonard Company in Liège, which introduced this type from 1911 on the Congo's railroads.

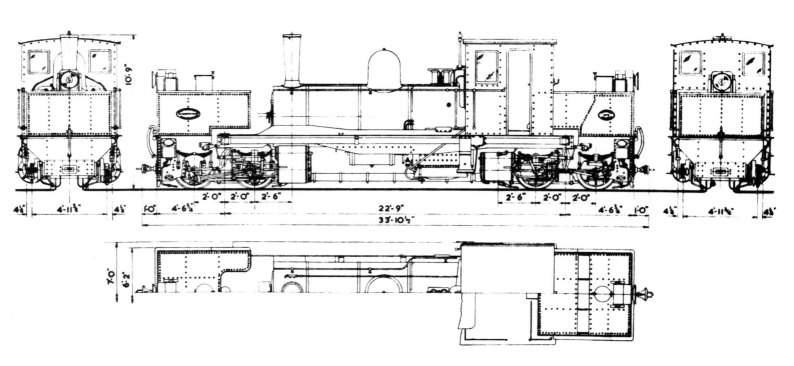

337. 0–4–0 + 0–4–0 locomotive of the Tasmanian Railroad, first Garratt locomotive, 1909.

262

It was not until peacetime that the advantages of the Garratt over all other articulated locomotives were fully understood: it was not only the ability to fit a short, large, well steaming boiler together with an unimpeded firebox, but also the widely separated trucks distributed the weight over a long section of of St. Léonard, Nos. 101–104 to the metre-gauge Catalan Railroad (Ferrocarriles Catalanes), whose main-line ran north from Barcelona up steep gradients and round tight curves deep into the Pyrenees Mountains (Ill. 338). They were examples of the 2–6–0 + 0–6–2 arrangement, the most common, as were built

track, thus reducing the axle loading, so that even where the permanent way was not very strong, powerful engines could run. It also had an excellent ability to negotiate curves and the capability of running at high speeds, thanks to the free-swinging motion of the trucks. The result was that the Garratt even became an express engine. Jackson's skilled hand saw the Garratts achieve the highest performances outside North America, and on narrow gauge too! Practically all possible axle layouts were employed, up to the powerful 4–8–4 + 4–8–4 on the East African Railroad. In Europe, it was only in Spain and England that a significant number of Garratts were used. It is understandable that Spain, with its mountainous countryside, should use them, but very surprising that England should have done so. Spain saw the first and only Garratt express engines in Europe in regular service. The first Garratts were supplied in 1922 by the firm in large numbers and with similar dimensions for Africa, South America and Asia, Nos. 105–108 followed in 1925, and one of these is preserved today at Manresa. The Robla had four similar Garratts, the Sierra Menera, two, and the Rio Tinto Railroad, two. When the Central Aragon Railroad in Spain — mentioned in section 14.2 — opened its newly built branch line from Caminreal to Zaragoza (later part of the main line between Valencia and Zaragoza), it ordered two Garratt types. These were six 2–8–2 + 2–8–2 freight engines, Nos. 201–206, built in 1931 at the Babcock and Wilcox Works in Bilbao on plans by Maffei, for which RENFE (Spanish National Railroad) placed a subsequent order for ten engines in 1960, Nos. 282.0421–0430. At the same time, the only express Garratts were ordered, six 4–6–2 + 2–6–4s, Nos. 101-106 (Ill. 339). They were supplied by Euskalduna of Bilbao on plans from Beyer-Peacock

338. 2–6–0 + 0–6–2 locomotive of the Catalan Railroad, Garratt system, 1922 and 1925.

263

and were intended to pull 300-ton expresses at 24½ m.p.h. up the long incline averaging 1 in 46 to the Escandon Pass, 3,996 ft. above sea level. In all, thirty-eight Garratts ran in Spain. One example of each of the last two types has been preserved for the projected Spanish Railroad Museum.

Even heavier than the Spanish types were the thirty 4–6–2 + 2–6–4s supplied a year later to the standard gauge Algerian network of the PLM, for they had a service weight of 216 tons and a driving wheel diameter of 5 ft. 11 in. They pulled 466-ton trains from the Moroccan to the Tunisian border at an average speed of 60-66 m.p.h. They were scrapped in 1951 and sold to Spain, as scrap metal!

In England, in 1925 Gresley introduced a 2–8–0 + 0–8–2 on the London and North Eastern Railway

replaced by an inclined rotating drum, which was then often used on other big Garratts.

There were thirty-four Garratt engines running in England, almost as many as in Spain. Apart from that the Garratt could only be found in Europe in one example, a 4–8–2 + 2–8–4 supplied by Beyer-Peacock in 1932 to Soviet Railroads.

As mentioned previously, the Garratt was used most of all in Africa, south of the Sahara, where there is a continuous steep rise from the coast inland. It was used by all large railroad companies there, but above all by the South African Railroads (SAR). The first Garratts were ordered in 1914, but because of the War, not delivered until 1919. These were 2–6–0 + 0–6–2s, GA Class, which had the then high-axle loading for narrow gauge of 17.8 tons. After several

339. 4–6–2 + 2–6–4 locomotive of the Central Aragon Railroad, Garratt system.

which was intended as a banking engine on the 2½-mile incline near Worsboro. Both engine trucks were identical to the 2–8–0 three-cylinder freight engine, and thus each had three cylinders. This was the heaviest engine ever used on British railroads. It remained a sole example and was scrapped in 1955.

The London, Midland and Scottish Railway suffered from the policies pursued by the railroads out of which it had been formed: that meant, of their using as small a type of locomotive as possible. The railroad lacked any really powerful freight engines. In 1927, an initial three 2–6–0 + 0–6–2 Garratts, Nos. 4997–4999 (Ill. 340), were supplied by Beyer-Peacock to pull 1,500-ton coal trains on the 127-mile run from Toton to Cricklewood, and the slightly modified Nos. 4967–4996 followed these in 1930. To ease the work of the fireman, a push piston was fitted in the coal bunker. It did not work very well and so was

similar series, in 1927/28 there came GH Class engines built by German firms, which were also suitable for passenger trains and which had bar frames for the first time. In 1942, the 2–8–2 + 2–8–2 Class GE locomotive was introduced, and the ultimate was reached with the 4–8–2 + 2–8–4 engines which were built in several forms until 1956. Shown in illustration 341, a similar engine for the Rhodesian Railroads was designed to pull heavy freight trains of 1,400 tons on a slope of 1 in 64 (1.55%). This Class 20A, Nos. 721–760 was delivered in 1956-57 by Beyer-Peacock. As with all new Garratts, the tanks had rounded edges so that they had a more pleasant appearance.

The largest Garratts ever built for narrow gauge were the Class 59 4–8–2 + 2–8–4s on the East African Railroad, which were almost built to American dimensions. They were built to pull 1,200 tons up a 1 in 66 slope.

340. 2–6–0 + 0–6–2 locomotive of the London, Midland and Scottish Railway, No. 4995, Garratt system, 1930.

To simplify the installation of the mechanical coal-feed, SAR ordered 2–6–2 + 2–6–2 and 4–6–2 + 2–6–4 engines from Maffei in 1927, which had the girder frame extended further back with the coalbunker resting on it. They had the same faults as the "modified Fairlies" mentioned earlier, and were not pursued.

Finally the Garratt variation created in 1928 by Louis Goldschmidt and Weber of the Hain - St. Pierre Works should be mentioned. It was called "Golwé" from the juxtaposition of the first syllables of its two designers' names. The two units were placed as near together as the centrally hung firebox would allow. The purpose of this arrangement was to facilitate dismantling of the boiler tubes and superheater elements without having to remove the water tank in front of the smokebox. All supplies were held in a tank over the rear unit, and this had its cylinders arranged towards the middle, so as to keep the steam connecting pipes short. This Golwé type was first introduced on the Ivory Coast Railroad and a small number were also supplied to other colonial railroads in French West Africa.

14.6 Other Solutions

No normally constructed locomotives could be used on the timber-conveying lines in the American northwest, which had been laid quickly without any real earth works, and which had steep gradients and sharp curves. A former doctor, Ephraim Emmanuel Shay, improvised his own locomotive for his privately owned

341. 4–8–2 + 2–8–4 locomotive Class 20 of the Rhodesian Railroads, Garratt system, 1956.

forest railroad, and received a patent for it on June 14, 1881. He sold it to the Lima Works, which made agricultural machines, sawmill equipment and steam boilers. These Shay locomotives had upright boilers at first, replaced from 1883 by normal, horizontal locomotive boilers. The Shay locomotive was built with two, three and even four trucks, but basically remained the same until the end of its life. Since the cylinders and motion were located on one side, the boiler had to be placed towards the other side to maintain the balance. One of these locomotives entered service with the Greenbrier, Cheat and Elk Railroad (Ill. 342), which had a network of 116 miles where there was hardly a single level section, with gradients of up to 1 in 14.3 and curves of only 54 yards radius.

As always, there were soon copies. The first was the Climax Manufacturing Co. in Corry, Pennsylvania.

342. Articulated engine of Greenbrier, Cheat and Elk Railroad, Shay system, built by the Lima Locomotive Works.

343. 0–6–0 + 0–6–0 tank locomotive of the Saxon State Railroads, Series XV HT*V*, 1916.

To obviate the unsymmetrical mounting of the boiler, the cylinders were arranged inclined on both sides between the trucks. They worked on a counter-shaft, which in turn drove the cardan shafts running in the middle lengthwise via bevel gears. In 1894, Charles Heisler of the Erie (Pennsylvania) Railroad created a different type, with the cylinders set crosswise to the boiler at an angle, so that the driven crankaxle was in the same direction as the cardan shafts, thus eliminating the bevel gears. Neither of these types achieved the popularity of the Shay model.

As already stated, the Saxon State Railroad had various types of articulated locomotives. When their performance was no longer good enough, at Lindner's suggestion the only possible solution was attempted: to build an engine, despite the long wheelbase, without trucks (Ill. 343) and thus without all the stuffing boxes on the joints at the steam pipes, which were difficult to keep sealed. The long wheelbase had to be retained because, as with the Garratt, the weight of the engine had to spread over as great a length of track as possible. A common casting was made for one HP and one LP cylinder, located in the middle. These drove two independent groups of axles, the outer one of which could move laterally 1½ in. in each direction, guided by radius rods on the Klien-Lindner system. As the Klien-Lindner hollow axles had outside bearings, two short outside frames had to be added at the ends of the locomotive. In addition, the two axles facing the cylinders were given 1 in. lateral play. The engine could thus take curves of as little as 170 yards radius. The two locomotives built experimentally by Hartmann as Class XV HT*V* entered service in 1916. The maximum permitted speed was 44 m.p.h. The engines did not live up to expectations, and the hollow axles proved troublesome. Thus these interesting locomotives were restricted to the hump of the Dresden-Friederichstadt marshalling yard and they were abandoned after only ten years of service.

15. NEW PROGRESS BETWEEN THE TWO WORLD WARS

15.1 Standardization and Interchangeable Parts

During the First World War, a blockaded Germany could only build those locomotives that were required for military transport. Just as in the 1870/71 War, the large number of differing types owned by the separate regional railroads posed problems. Urged by the Commander of the Military Railroad Corps, representatives from each region met and worked out a draft, which anticipated many of the standard locomotives of the German National Railroad which came later: they decided on a 2–10–0 three-cylinder engine with superheater, a high-pitched boiler and bar frame of milled heavy steel plates on the South German model. The firebox was of the Belpaire type and was mounted on the frame. But the four-cylinder compound system was not used, preference being given to the simpler three-cylinder arrangement which had proved successful in Prussia on the S10² type (cf. section 12.2). The front axle was mounted in a Bissel pony truck (Ill. 344).

This locomotive, designated G12 in Prussia (later the German National Railroad BR 58), was immediately ordered in large numbers, by the State Rail-

344. 2–10–0 locomotive, Series G12 of the Prussian State Railroads, later German National Railroads, Series 58, 1917-24.

267

345. 0–10–0 freight train locomotive of the Soviet Union, 1922. First locomotive with interchangeable parts.

roads in Prussia, Saxony, Baden and Württemberg and the Alsace-Lorraine railroads. Henschel supplied the first in April 1917, and a total of 1,519 were built by 1924. The load finally determined for them was a train of 1,010 tons on a gradient of 1 in 200 at 25 m.p.h.

From this engine, a three-cylinder 2–8–0 locomotive was developed, with one axle less, Class G 8^2, and finally the simplified two-cylinder engine, Class G 8^3. Thorough tests burning coal dust in the G 12 and G 8^2 were made between 1927 and 1930 but this complicated system was not a success.

The G 12 survived the Second World War and ran with the German Federal Railroads* until 1954. It was fitted with new welded boilers on the National East Railroad**, and there are probably still a few in existence.

In 1922, August Meister, chief draftsman at the firm of Borsig, developed a three-cylinder 2–8–2 on similar lines, intended to be as versatile as the P 8 (cf. section 11.2). This Class P 10 (BR 39) (Ill. 347) had a

French-type Belpaire trapeze-shaped firebox. The two front axles were combined into a Krauss-Helmholtz truck. Two hundred and sixty engines of this type were built before 1927. Between Charlottenburg and Lehrte, they pulled 720-ton expresses on the level at 62-75 m.p.h., and 390-ton trains up 1 in 40 gradients at 28 m.p.h. on the Black Forest line. They lasted longest in the mountainous countryside of South West Germany; the last one was retired in 1967.

Once the political situation had been settled, the Soviet Union began to set about satisfying its urgent need for locomotives, because their stock had been considerably depleted by the War and the Revolution. A commission was appointed to procure them, under Professor George Lomonossov, and the Nohab Co. in Sweden was appointed general contractor for one thousand 0–10–0 freight engines (Ill. 345), undoubtedly the largest single order ever placed. Nohab decided to make three hundred itself, and split the rest between nineteen German factories. The basic condition of this order was that every part supplied

* Deutsche Bundesbahn.

** Reichsbahn-Ost.

346. First standard locomotive of the German National Railroads, 4–6–2 locomotive, Series 02, 1925.

347. Three-cylinder
2–8–2 passenger train
locomotive, Class P 10,
Prussian State Rail-
roads, 1922.

had to be interchangeable with any corresponding part supplied by any of the other firms, with no further machining or adjustment. This concept was based on the experience acquired in arms manufacturing during the First World War, which had led to precision machining of individual components by defining the manufacturing tolerances.

On February 15, 1922, the first locomotive assembled from twenty components made in this way was completed by the Tegel Works of Borsig. These twenty principal components were produced by as many different factories, without any adjustment being necessary.

When the German National Railroad was formed on April 1, 1920, as always with such mergers, the question was whether to continue with the most successful and numerous types among the 210 different types acquired, or to develop completely new basic types. The second solution was adopted once the

Swiss August Meister of the Borsig Works, by presenting a series of designs, had demonstrated how locomotives for any use could be built using interchangeable components. A standardization office was created, with the National Railroad's locomotive superintendent, Richard Paul Wagner, as chairman and engineers delegated from the locomotive building industry.

It is not possible to expose the programme in detail. We would refer the reader to the extensive writings on this subject (see bibliography), and we shall merely consider the first standard locomotive, supplied as Class 02 by Henschel in October 1925, for its historical interest (Ill. 346). It was built experimentally as a four-cylinder compound but as it did not prove markedly superior in comparative trials with the two-cylinder version built in parallel, its higher maintenance costs meant that no further examples were ordered.

348. 4–10–0 locomotive of the Bulgarian State Railroads, Series 11, 1939.

The first standard freight locomotives then emerged as Class 44 (Ill. 351), ordered experimentally as two- and three-cylinder types. Their leading axle and front coupled axle ran in a Kraus-Helmholtz truck. By 1949, more than two thousand of these three-cylinder engines had been commissioned, with many modifications. This type was acquired over the longest period and in the greatest quantity.

The German locomotive industry designed a standardized series which had much in common with those of the National Railroad for Bulgaria, Yugoslavia and Turkey. Some of them were special models for exceptional operating conditions, such as the rare 2–10–0 arrangement of Class 11 with three cylinders, supplied to the Bulgarian State Railroad by Henschel in 1939 (Ill. 348), or the unique powerful three-cylinder 2–12–4 tank engines, the last version of which came from Krupp in 1943, Class 46.13–20 (Ill. 349).

349. 2–12–4 tank locomotive of the Bulgarian State Railroads, No. 4618, 1943.

350. 4–6–2 locomotive of the Erie Railroad, USRA (United States Railroad Administration) standard type.

Because of the War, the railroad companies in the United States were placed under the official control of the United States Railroad Administration (USRA) in 1918 and work was immediately begun to develop standard locomotives in collaboration with the three large locomotive works. The basic range comprised twelve different types, with eight different wheel arrangements and with various axle loads.

About 1,830 were built. A characteristic example is the heavy "Pacific" as acquired by the Erie Railroad, among others (Ill. 350). When the railroads were returned to the companies in 1920, standardization soon collapsed.

15.2 The New Era in Great Britain

On January 1, 1923, the British railroad companies amalgamated into four large groups; Great Western, London Midland & Scottish, London & North Eastern, and Southern Railways. Naturally this soon affected British locomotive construction.

The Great Western Railway (GWR) was least affected, since it only acquired a few small engines chiefly carrying coal traffic. Its chief engineer, Charles B. Collet, thanks to the far-sighted standardization achieved by his predecessor Churchward (cf. section 12.2) was able to continue his work without many

351. 2–10–0 standard freight train locomotive of the German National Railroads, Class 44.

271

changes. This programme was crowned by the "King" Class — so named as each locomotive was named after an English king. Thirty of this class were built between 1927 and 1930 (Ill. 354). The "Kings" were a more powerful version of the previous four-cylinder "Castle" Class of 1923. The use of the "Kings" Class was restricted by its high axle loading of 22.5 tons, which meant it was not able to replace the "Castle" Class entirely. These were the most powerful 4–6–0 engines built outside the United States. The GWR existed until nationalization with these two powerful classes and without a single "Pacific" engine. The single locomotive "Great Bear" once imposed on Churchward for reasons of prestige was converted in 1924 into a 4–6–0 "Castle" Class locomotive, and renamed "Winston Churchill".

The situation on the London and North Eastern Railway (LNER) was not so simple for each of the four major railroads amalgamated had much the same number of engines, and the stock of the North Eastern was twice as large as any of the others. Nigel Gresley was appointed chief engineer, combining the same position which he had held on the Great Northern since 1911 as Ivatt's successor. His policy was to keep the best locomotives in good condition, or to improve them, and also to develop new designs. The basis for this was the Great Northern range already created by him. These were mostly three-cylinder engines. A type which he had introduced in 1921 as a 2–8–0 locomotive was characterized by the operation of the inside valves which had been invented by Gresley. This was effected by a combination of swing levers linked by the outside Walschaerts valve gear. One of the new Gresley type locomotives, which were really transitional types, was the "Sandringham" (or B 17) Class built in 1928. These machines were originally for the East Anglia line of the former Great Eastern, that ran partly through hilly country. During the summer holiday period, they were heavily loaded. Two of them were given a streamlined covering. The last of these machines were named after English football clubs.

The first series of "Pacifics" acquired between 1923 and 1925 introduced a long line of successively improved express engines which became famous on long distance expresses. We shall return to these in a different connection. Gresley created an express freight engine, the "Green Arrow" Class V 2, a three-cylinder 2–6–2 locomotive (Ill. 352), which proved so versatile

352. 2–6–2 express freight locomotive Class V 2 of the London-and-North Eastern Railway, Nigel Gresley.

353. 4–6–0 three-cylinder simple locomotive, the "Royal Scot", express locomotive of the London, Midland and Scottish Railway, 1927.

that it was often even used to replace a "Pacific" during the Second World War, when there was a shortage of engines. Thus by 1944, 184 had been built, the largest number on the LNER apart from the traditional six-coupled engines with inside motion also designed by Gresley. Gresley was not so successful with the six three-cylinder 2–8–2 locomotives, the "Cock o' the North" Class designed for hilly Scottish lines. They proved too cumbersome on severe curvature and were soon converted into 4–6–2s by his successor.

Two of the most important railroads with the largest fleet of locomotives — the London and North Western and the Midland — were merged into the London Midland and Scottish Railway (LMS). After a short period under George Hughes of the Lancashire and Yorkshire Railway, Henry Fowler took over. He had already been chief engineer of the Midland and it was only natural that he decided to continue with these types without substantial alteration. For express service, the Deeley three-cylinder compound locomotives (cf. section 11.1.2) had proved superior in performance and more economical in fuel consump-

tion than other locomotives compared, including even the two-cylinder 4–6–0 "Prince of Wales" Class on the London and North Western Railroad (LNWR). Thus with slight modifications, another 195 were ordered by 1932. But time was passing: none of the four-cylinder 4–6–0 locomotives which had come from the Lancashire and Yorkshire, LNWR and even the LMS's most powerful engines could meet the increasing traffic demands. The situation became so critical that the North British Locomotive Co. was asked to build a three-cylinder 4–6–0 locomotive to fill the gap. This was to be similar to the four-cylinder 4–6–0 "Lord Nelson" Class on the Southern Railway, while giving the same performance as the Great Western's "Castles". Thus in 1927 the famous "Royal Scot" was born (Ill. 353) and fifty engines were built. Apart from the Belpaire firebox, not much had been retained of the Midland tradition. Unlike the Gresley three-cylinder locomotives, the long travel valves on the GWR pattern were actuated by three sets of Walschaerts valve gear.

Fowler retired in late 1930. William A. Stanier was appointed as his successor, coming from the post of

354. The "King George V", 4–6–0 locomotive of the Great Western Railway, "King" Class, 1927-38.

273

types or in modifying existing ones. Even the "Royal Scot" was included. One of his standard types, Class 5P 5F (Ill. 356) called the "Black Five", because of its black paint, was the equally successful counterpart of the widespread Prussian P8 (cf. section 11.2), and, with 842 engines built, was the most numerous British mixed traffic locomotive, even becoming, with modifications, British Railways standard type for mixed traffic. Another equally successful Stanier engine was his 2–8–0 locomotive Class 8F of 1935, with cylinder and boiler measurements almost identical to those of Class 5P 5F. This was the most numerous 2–8–0 type, with 773 engines in service by 1945.

The least standardization was achieved on the Southern. R.E. Maunsell was in charge on this railroad; he had been in charge of the South Eastern and Chatham Railway since 1913. A European influence is evident on his engines. Inside motion was finally abandoned in favour of outside cylinders with Heusinger-Walschaerts valve gear. In 1925, the two-cylinder engines of the 4–6–0 "King Arthur" Class came out, and one year later, the four-cylinder "Lord Nelsons" already mentioned. He followed the 2–6–0 general purpose locomotives he had introduced on the South Eastern and Chatham in 1917 by 4–6–0 versions. All of these were outwardly similar to each other, but they had little else in common. His most remarkable and last creation was the reintroduction of the 4–4–0 wheel arrangement but as three-cylinder engines. This famous "School" Class, with engines named after English public schools, was created because of the restrictions imposed by the bridges and tunnels on the Hastings line. Maunsell succeeded in creating such a compact 4–4–0 that its performance was practically identical to that of the "King Arthur". The forty "School" Class engines (Ill. 357), built between 1930 and 1935 were the most powerful 4–4–0 engines built outside the United States.

355. Part of an English poster for the Southern Railway of the 1920s, showing a "King Arthur" Class locomotive.

deputy chief engineer on the Great Western, and he immediately began to introduce Great Western ideas and methods. After only seventeen months in office, his first engine came out in June, the 4–6–2 "Princess Royal", thereby finally breaking with the old tradition of building locomotives for the needs of the moment. We shall return to this engine. Under Stanier, the LMS began energetically to standardize and systematize. Apart from the Great Western, the LMS went furthest in standardization, whether in developing new

15.3 The 4–8–2, Last Word in Express Locomotives

The Saxon State Railroad had two lines with intensive express passenger traffic where tests with a borrowed Bavarian S 3/6 (cf. section 12.3) had shown that the adhesion of three-coupled axles was insufficient. Based on the Bavarian locomotive, the State's chief engineers, Meyer and Heinrich Lindner developed the first large-wheeled eight-coupled express engine in Europe (Ill. 358). It had a bar frame and compound

274

four-cylinders of the Von Borries type. The two front axles were mounted in a Kraus-Helmholtz truck and the trailing axle was of the Adams radial pattern. Test runs were very satisfactory. This engine pulled 585 tons up a 1 in 100 gradient at 31 m.p.h. and with 275 tons it took the 1 in 40 inclines near Tharand at 25 m.p.h. Despite the promising start, only twenty-three examples of this Type XX H*V* were built by Hartmann between 1918 and 1922, because the foundation of the German National Railroad brought about different developments in engine construction. These engines survived the Second World War as BR 18.001–010 with the Eastern National Railroad and were retired in 1961/62. 18.010 is preserved for the transport museum in Dresden.

This "Sachsenstolz" ("Pride of Saxony"), as the largest German express locomotive of its day was called, caused considerable interest abroad. By 1921 Italy had followed with a similar locomotive which was not quite as large, Group 746.

Both engines were preliminary stages in the final development of the 4–8–2 express locomotive in Europe. Once again the impetus came from the very difficult lines in Spain. There was a desire to eliminate the awkward change of the four-cylinder 4–8–0 De Glehn compound engines on trains hauled over the Guadarrama Mountains by the 4–6–2 De Glehn engines, which continued across the subsequent flat country (cf. section 9.4). Studies undertaken by the assistant chief engineer Armand Flobert showed that it was possible to make do with one 4–8–2 engine over the entire line. Hanomag won the order to supply these locomotives, the design coming from its young engineer Adolf Wolff. The performance chart envisaged a train of 400 tons being pulled up a 1 in 114 gradient at 34 m.p.h. and up 1 in 200 at not less than 56 m.p.h. The De Glehn system was to be used.

356. 4–6–0 locomotive of the London, Midland and Scottish Railway, Class 5P–5F (Black Watch), William A. Stanier.

357. 4–4–0 locomotive of the Southern Railroad, "School" Class, R. E. Maunsell, 1930-35.

358. 2–8–2 four-cylinder compound express train locomotive of the Saxon State Railroads, Series XX HV, 1918-22.

Following a thorough study of operating conditions on the spot and the complicated approval procedures for the detailed plans, actual delivery was delayed and the Norte Railroad was beaten by the French Est Railroad in the use of this type of engine. But the Est's engine was a single prototype, and in no way detracts from the honour of the Norte as the first European railroad company to use a 4–8–2 on regular schedules. The six engines delivered by Hanomag in the spring of 1925 (Ill. 360) were followed by another sixty from Spanish works, with a somewhat larger superheater (Norte Nos. 4601–56 and 4690–99, formerly the Andalusian Railroad). All were passed on to the RENFE as Series 241.4001–4066. They ran the whole 285 miles from Madrid to Miranda, with two firemen. In 1939, No. 4648 was modified on the Chapelon pattern and given Dabeg valve gear and a Kylchap double chimney; as such, it was the model for another twenty-eight locomotives, ordered later by RENFE between 1946 and 1948, Series 241.4067–4094. The Est's 4–8–2 already mentioned was in fact supplied on January 17, 1925, but it must have had some teething troubles because the first systematic test runs did not begin until October and lasted until August 1929. This engine, designed by Mestre and built at the Epernay Railroad Works, also had a De Glehn motion arrangement (Ill. 361). The higher axle loadings permitted a more powerful construction. In test runs, it pulled 600 tons at 25½ m.p.h. up a 1 in 100 gradient and over twelve runs between Paris and Bar-le-Duc (159 miles) it achieved an average speed of 60 m.p.h. with trains weighing between 575 and 690 tons. But it proved that yet more modifications were needed, to enlarge the steam passages and raise the boiler pressure. In 1930, two identical batches of the modified version were ordered, forty for the Est Railroad, Nos. 241.002–041 and thirty-nine for the State Railroad, Nos. 241.001–039. The prototype of these series has been preserved for the Mulhouse Railroad Museum.

In February 1925, the PLM Railroad also brought

359. Clermont-Ferrand-Paris express with a Class 241 P locomotive.

360. 4–8–2 four-cylinder compound express locomotive for the Spanish Norte Railroad, Adolf Wolff, 1925.

276

361. 4–8–2 four-cylinder compound express locomotive of the French Est Railroad, No. 241001, 1925.

out a 4–8–2, No. 241.A.1, which had smaller driving wheels of 5 ft. 10½ in., being intended for more steeply graded lines than those on the Est Railroad. The four-cylinder compound system was of the Von Borries type. A special feature was the parabolic smokebox door (Ill. 362), made according to the form developed by the German physicist from Göttingen, Prandl, to minimize wind resistance. On test runs between 1925 and 1927, this engine developed an average output of 2,180 i.h.p., pulling a 625-ton train between Laroche and Blaisy-Bas. This engine, initially called "Valentin's Folly" by its critics (Valentin of the PLM built it) proved so successful that 144 were constructed between 1927 and 1931, Series 241.A.1–145. It pulled all types of heavy train including freight. Its small driving wheel diameter made it less suitable for high speed work. Thus a new engine, No. 241.C.1, was built with 6 ft. 6½ in. driving wheels — it was an isolated example, but acted as the pattern for Series 241.P introduced by SNCF (French National Railroad) after the Second World War.

The Madrid, Zaragoza and Alicante Railroad (MZA) had the same problem as the Norte Railroad. It adopted a solution which seemed very risky at a time when multi-cylinder types were in general use for large locomotives: the use of two-cylinder 4–8–2 engines (Ill. 363). The first to arrive, on a test run on July 17, 1925, pulled a 535-ton train at an average speed of 26 m.p.h. on the mountainous run between Arcos and Torralba, with continuous gradients of 1 in 131 and a 6-mile section at 1 in 70. These engines, with their

effective boilers and simple construction, proved to be the MZA's most successful locomotive. By 1931, ninety-five had been commissioned, Series 1701–1795. Nos. 1770–1775 were fitted with Lentz gear; Nos. 1776–1795 with the Dabeg type, and one is being preserved for the railroad museum. All were built by the Maquinista Works at Barcelona.

With its eight-coupled express engines, Austria had the same problem as with its six-coupled, and so the 2–8–4 wheel arrangement was adopted. Adolf Giesl-Gieslingen, Floridsdorf's draftsman, had prepared a design for a two-cylinder engine (Ill. 364) which was in fact made. But there were doubts about the high crank pin stresses and an otherwise identical, three-cylinder engine was ordered in parallel. The two-cylinder version emerged first in late 1928, and the three-

362. 4–8–2 locomotive with parabolic smokebox door, PLM Railroad, Series 241 A, 1925.

cylinder version from the Wiener Neustadt Works came out in April 1929. Both met the requirement to pull 500 tons at 31 m.p.h. up a 1 in 100 gradient. The concern over the crank pin pressures proved groundless, and as the three-cylinder type used more coal, it gave way to the two-cylinder version, Nos. 214.02–13 of which entered service between 1931 and 1936.

On a test run, No. 214.13 reached the highest speed ever attained by an Austrian locomotive: 97 m.p.h. No. 214.10 had been preserved for the railroad museum.

The largest 2–8–4 locomotives were those of the "Joseph Stalin" Class in Russia (Ill. 365), which were introduced in 1933 and showed the characteristic American influence, true of all more recent Russian locomotives. These engines were intended to pull 800-ton passenger trains at 25 m.p.h. up 1 in 140 gradients, and pulling 998 tons on trial runs they achieved a performance of 3,172 i.h.p.

15.4 Chapelon's Rejuvenation Treatment

In 1922 the French Nord Railroad had introduced its "Superpacific", Series 3.1201–1240 (Ill. 366). It was a development by De Caso of the previous Series 3.1151–1170 of 1912, and like the latter had long, narrow fireboxes with a grate of the unusual length of 11 ft. 6 in. More important were the very large diameter steam passages and long travel valve.

363. 4–8–2 locomotive of the Madrid-Zaragoza-Alicante Railroad, 1925.

364. 2–8–4 locomotive of the Austrian Federal Railroads, Series 21.402–21.413, 1931 and 1936.

278

365. 2–8–4 locomotive of the Soviet Union, "Stalin" Class, 1933.

This "Superpacific" proved superior in performance to other 4–6–2 locomotives on French railroads.

From 1925, the Paris-and-Orléans Railroad under André Chapelon had held comparative tests with various blast pipe nozzles, the best of which had proved to be the Kylchap, invented by the Finn, Kiläla, and improved by Chapelon. Without affecting exhaust performance it reduced back pressure in the cylinders and thus enabled the performance to be improved. Chapelon was then asked by his superior Maurice Lacoin to consider all the possibilities of improving the performance of the existing "Pacifics". Trials made the following alterations appear possible: doubling the size of all steam ports and passages from the regulator valve to the blast pipe nozzle, streamlining the steam flow through the pipes; providing a poppet valve gear which gave better indicator diagrams; increasing the temperature of the superheated steam from 570° F (300° C) to at least 650° F (400° C), to prevent the steam from entering the LP cylinder at too low a temperature; putting Nicholson thermic syphons in the firebox to increase their heating surface; doubling the vacuum in the smokebox with the help of the Kylchap double chimney and blast pipe system, and fitting an Acfi feedwater heater.

The first "Pacific" modified on these lines, No. 3566, entered service on November 19, 1929. The very first

trips showed a tremendous improvement in performance, with the result that the Series 3501–3520, still using saturated steam, were immediately modified (cf. section 12.3). Several of these modified engines used experimentally on other railroads confirmed that there had been a successful two-fold improvement on their earlier performance. Values of 2,500 to 2,600 i.h.p. and even of 3,400 i.h.p. were recorded with the coal consumption being unusually low at 1.57 to 1.759 lbs./i.h.p. When the main lines began to be electrified there were too many of these engines

366. 4–6–2 four-cylinder compound express locomotive of the French Nord Railroad, Series 31201–31240, 1922.

279

367. 2–6–4 four-cylinder compound express locomotive of the Nord Railroad, 1936.

368. 4–8–0 four-cylinder compound locomotive of the PO (Paris and Orléans) Railroad, modified "Pacific" type by Chapelon.

for the PO Railroad. In 1933 the Nord Railroad took on twenty engines modified at the Tours works, and these were followed in 1936 by another twenty-eight new engines (Ill. 367). The East also followed this example, and acquired twenty-three PO modified "Pacifics".

The "Pacifics" of Series 4500, used on the mountainous lines of the company, proved to be no longer satisfactory, either. A modification was made, but a much more radical one: they were converted to 4–8–0 locomotives to increase their adhesion weight on steep gradients. This conversion necessitated a completely new boiler which was made with a long, narrow firebox on the lines of the Nord's "Superpacific". The results from the converted saturated steam No. 4271, now No. 4701, exceeded expectations. In various test runs undertaken on the level run between Paris and Bordeaux, values of over 3,000 i.h.p. were recorded repeatedly. On the long 1 in 100 gradients between Limoges and Toulouse, it was easily able to pull 550-ton expresses at 53½ m.p.h. the equivalent of over 4,000 i.h.p. This was the first time that this figure had been reached in Europe by a steam locomotive. In all, twelve locomotives were modified in this way, Nos. 4701–4712 (Ill. 368).

In 1940/41, the French SNCF purchased another twenty-five engines of this type, Series 240.P.1–25. They were given different cylinder dimensions and a mechanical coal feed. Both in terms of specific performance and steam consumption, these rejuvenated Chapelon engines represented a peak in the development of the steam locomotive. In one way or another, many railroads followed his example, for both new and existing types. This included the PLM Railroad for the heavy four-cylinder 2–10–2 compound locomotives of Series 151.A.1–10 (Ill. 369), with which it overtook the 2–10–0 types used on other railroads in France. Because of their size, the LP cylinders could not be mounted inside. If the HP cylinders were to be mounted in their place, it was thought that the stresses on the crank axle would have been too great. As a result, all four cylinders were mounted outside. Both sets of motion were linked by inside coupling rods. The valve gear used Dabeg poppet valves which were operated by rotating shafts from the second coupled wheels. The front axle was on the Bissel pattern. These engines were intended to pull heavy freight trains on the Laroche to Dijon run with 1 in 125 gradients and for the St. Etienne coal line with 1 in 59 gradients. On a test run made on May 22, 1933, on the Nord's line between Lens and Le Bourget, 2,599 tons were pulled at an average of 33½ m.p.h. In normal service they pulled 1,250 tons between Laroche and Dijon at 31 m.p.h. Once the SNCF had been formed, these engines were abandoned in favour of future construction programmes.

15.5 The Final Glorious Era of the Steam Locomotive in North America

In North America, various pre-war types — more or less powerful — continued to be built until into the 1920s. The evergrowing competition from canals and

especially from trucking companies had to be met in the first instance by speeding up freight trains which then ran at an average speed of 10 m.p.h. The main requirement was for a higher boiler performance than was achieved by the widespread "Mikados".

The Lima Locomotive Works, until then a relatively modest company, introduced a revolution in the construction of freight engines as a result of its attempts to compete with the firm of Baldwin and ALCO. Under its director, Will Woodward, in 1924 a demonstration locomotive was built, the A–1. This engine had the rear pair of wheels replaced by a four-wheeled truck (Ill. 370). This enabled a grate of 51 per cent larger area and an 11 per cent larger heating surface than on the "Mikados" without hindrance from weight considerations. It was basically the same idea as Gölsdorf had already used with his 2–6–4 (cf. section 12.3). This demonstration locomotive gave such good results on the Berkshire Hills Line of the Boston-and-Albany Railroad that forty-five were immediately ordered and christened "Berkshire". The first of these Lima "Superpower" locomotives had the frame finishing behind the last coupled axle. The truck was hinged to it and supported the ash pan. Later, as usual, the frame was extended backwards and the so-called Delta cast steel swivelling truck was fitted. By 1949, about 750 "Berkshires", some of them supplied by ALCO, had entered service. They succeeded in doubling the average speed of freight trains. The development of the "Berkshire" to a 2–10–4 locomotive occurred naturally, thanks also to the

Lima Locomotive Works, which supplied such an engine in 1925 to the Texas-and-Pacific Railroad, the type being thus known as "Texas". These locomotives still had driving wheels of 5 ft. 3 in diameter, with the result that the centrifugal forces of the heavy masses could not be sufficiently balanced for higher speeds. When the Chesapeake-and-Ohio Railroad acquired these 2–10–4s for 10,000–ton coal trains, the wheel diameter was increased to 5 ft. 9 in. These engines, which also came from the Lima Works, Nos. 3000–3039, in fact ran at speeds of up to 66 m.p.h., pulling long trains consisting of 140 coal cars. The crowning "Texas" type were the engines built by Baldwin in 1938 for the Santa Fé Railroad, with

369. 2–10–2 four-cylinder compound freight locomotive of the PLM Railroad, with divided drive, No. 151 A1.

370. 2–6–4 freight locomotive of the Boston-and-Albany Railroad, from the Lima Locomotive Works and built under the direction of Will Woodward.

6 ft. 2 in. driving wheels. This was the largest diameter ever used for ten-coupled engines. By 1944, about 450 such "Texas" engines entered service.

The enormous piston forces of these engines necessitated a special construction of the connecting rod ends, with so-called floating bushes i.e., mounted loosely in the heads. Another way of lessening the piston forces was to fit three cylinders as on European engines. ALCO chose this method for the rivals to the "Texas" type with a 4–10–2 arrangement. In 1925, it

were the crowning achievement of the American freight train engine with a rigid frame.

As in Europe, there were efforts in America to make locomotives as versatile as possible. Initially the 4–8–2 seemed most suitable, and this was developed from the freight engine (cf. section 13.1) gradually to the multipurpose engine and finally the passenger engine. One example of this is Class 7000 of the Union Pacific of 1922 (Ill. 372).

Just as the "Berkshire" derived from the "Mikado",

371. 4–12–2 locomotive of the Union Pacific Railroad, No. 9000, 1926.

supplied a three-cylinder engine to the Southern Pacific. But in all, only sixty three-cylinder locomotives of this type were built, forty-nine of which were for this railroad alone. All of them had Gresley-type valve gear motion.

The Union Pacific which had acquired on trial in 1925 a heavy two-cylinder 4–10–2, found it unsatisfactory for its operational requirements. It replaced it by a 4–12–2 locomotive built by ALCO which was so satisfactory that by 1930 a total of eighty-eight of this class 9000 entered service (Ill. 371). They were three-cylinder engines. Surprisingly, they ran so smoothly that the maximum permitted speed was raised from 50 to 55 m.p.h. These "Union Pacifics"

the same considerations led the "Pacific" to develop into the "Hudson". The New York Central Railroad started this process. In comparative tests by the first "Hudson", Class J–1, which had been supplied by ALCO on February 14, 1927, it proved superior to a "Pacific" with 24 per cent better performance at the draw bar with a 26 per cent higher speed. As the engines were perfected, these values increased to figures of 38 per cent and 31 per cent for the "Super Hudson", Class J–3a of 1937 (Ill. 373). At 77 m.p.h., the output was 4,770 i.h.p. This was a wonderful success for their creator Paul W. Kiefer, NYC's chief engineer. The last fifty engines were given Timken roller bearings in all axle boxes, on the connecting rod heads and five more on all crank pins. In all, more than 250 Hudsons entered service with the NYC alone. They soon appeared on other railroads where there was a significant express service, with the result that about five hundred engines in all were on the rails. In January 1927, the Northern Pacific brought out a 4–8–4 locomotive as a further development of the "Mountain" type. This engine could exploit all the progress made in American locomotive construction during the last years: outside Baker valve gear, a well-

These 4–8–4s had various names because the railroads introduced their own appellations such as "Northern", "Niagara", "Pocono", "Confederation" and others. The most famous were the NYC's "Niagaras" which were initially multi-purpose in 1945, but which were developed into express locomotives.

These large rigid bed engines seemed to be displacing the "Mallet", and they partially succeeded. But the high performance of "Mallets" made them indispensable on mountainous routes. The highly super-

372. 4–8–2 locomotive of the Union Pacific Railroad, Class 7000, 1922.

373. 4–6–4 locomotive of the New York Central Railroad, Class J-3a, Paul W. Kiefer, 1937.

designed superheater for high steam temperatures, feed water heater, mechanical coal feed, booster, and soon a cast steel frame in one piece which included the cylinders (called locomotive bed), and finally roller bearings. The 4–8–4 locomotive was conceived initially as a multi-purpose engine but soon developed into an express engine, or an express freight engine once passenger traffic diminished. It reached its highest form as an express train engine in the second series built by the Lima Works in 1938, Nos. 6405–6410, for the Grand Trunk Western, an American subsidiary of the Canadian National (Ill. 374). For its part, the Canadian National had already acquired fifty engines of this type.

heated steam allowed the compound system to be dispensed with and thus the cumbersome old "Mallets" could be given improved running characteristics. This idea was realized for the first time in 1924 with the single expansion 2–8–0 + 0–8–2 by ALCO for the Chesapeake-and-Ohio Railroad. As with the rigid frame engines, and for the same reasons, these types also had four-wheeled swing truck at the rear. The Norfolk and Western Railroad built corresponding 2–6–0 + 0–6–4 engines Nos. 1200–1222 (Ill. 378) at its own railroad works. They were intended for express freight trains.

The development of the single-expansion articulated locomotives led to such well-known types as the

374. 4–8–4 locomotive of the Grand Trunk Western Railroad, No. 6405, 1938.

375. The "Cab-Ahead", 4–8–0 + 0–8–2 locomotive of the Southern Pacific Railroad.

376. The "Big Boy", 4–8–0 + 0–8–4 locomotive of the Union Pacific Railroad, 1941.

377. Express freight train of the New York Central Railroad with the 4–8–4 locomotive No. 2823.

Southern Pacific's "Cab-Ahead" (Ill. 375). As once in Italy (cf. section 11.1.4), the driver's cab was at the front so that the crew would not be hampered by smoke and exhaust gas in the tunnels and avalanche sheds. Bunker oil was used for firing, and was carried in the tender together with the feed water.

Finally these "double twins" reached their greatest-ever dimensions with the "Big Boys" 4–8–0 + 0–8–4 locomotives for the Union Pacific in 1941 (Ill. 376). With a performance at the draw bar of 6,290 i.h.p., they could pull up to 4,000 tons at 20-25 m.p.h. on the mountainous route between Ogden and Wasatch which had an average gradient of 1 in 88, occasionally reaching 88 m.p.h. on the level.

16. THE HIGH-SPEED LOCOMOTIVES

379. The "Cornwall", 4–2–2 locomotive of the London and North Western Railway, Francis Trevithick, 1847.

16.1 Initial Ideas

As stated already (cf. section 6.1), from the beginning attempts had been made to create locomotives intended for high speed. While being in accordance with the ideas of the time, they were characterized by a boiler as low as possible and large driving wheels. These were contradictory requirements. As a result, the two components were separated on a locomotive tested by the Great Western, the "Hurricane". The boiler was mounted on a special six-wheeled car and pulled by a 4–2–2 driving truck on which the

cylinders were mounted. The "Hurricane" is said to have reached a speed of 100 m.p.h. on a 28-mile test run in September 1839. These details must be regarded with caution since stop watches were not current at that time.

During the "Battle of the Gauges", Francis Trevithick of the LNWR tried to outdo Gooch's "Great Western" in speed (cf. section 6.1). He was also misled by ideas of the time in fitting an excessively large driving wheel of 8 ft. 6 in. diameter; and as for a low centre of gravity, he out-trumped Crampton by mounting the boiler below the driving axle. His

"Cornwall" (Ill. 379), built in 1847, was exhibited in London in 1851 where it caused a stir. There are also tales that it reached the unlikely speed of 117 m.p.h. but travelling light and slightly downhill. Trevithick's successor, John Ramsbottom, converted this locomotive in 1858 into a 2–2–2 with a boiler mounted normally over the driving axle. It was used as an express engine for light trains between Liverpool and Manchester and later to pull an inspection car. It was finally preserved at the museum in Clapham, London which has since closed.

"L'Aigle", designed on the same principles but with four-coupled wheels by Aimé-Etienne Blavier and Larpent and built by Ernest-Alexandre Gouin in 1855 was shown at the World Fair in Paris the same year (Ill. 380). It was supposed to travel at twice the speed of the Crampton locomotive while avoiding the drawback of insufficient adhesion weight. Again it is said that in test runs on the Ouest Railroad, it travelled at 100 m.p.h. Like its predecessors already mentioned, it did not enter regular service but proved that high speed locomotives could certainly have four-coupled wheels, and the Ouest was the first railroad to do so (cf. section 7.3).

The six-coupled locomotive built in 1889 in Paris by Boulet & Co. and designed by Estrade shows how deeply rooted prejudices can be. It also had over-large wheels, and these were considered necessary for the cars as well. It has already been mentioned how this type of large front wheel led to serious derailments in service (Ills. 381 and 382). The third class passengers travelling on the lower deck cannot have been very comfortable. This engine, "La Parisienne", was shown at the World Fair in Paris in 1889 but it is not certain whether it ever ran. At all events, the disproportion between the boiler and the motion would have produced an operational fiasco.

16.2 The "Wind-Cutter" Locomotives

François Ricour, who has already been encountered in connection with tests on a reverse steam brake (cf. section 9.4), had meanwhile become chief engineer on the State Railroad. In 1883, he fitted a 2–4–0 Orléans Type No. 2071 of his company with wedge surfaces in front of the smokebox and the driver's cab and between the chimney and the dome to establish how far the wind resistance of the moving locomotive could be reduced by this means. This engine ran to the same timetable as the regular locomotives for the thirteen months between June 1884 and June 1885. The "wind-cutter" engine used 12 per cent less fuel. As a result (cf. section 11.1.3), the PLM Railroad fitted its four-cylinder 4–4–0 compound locomotives with this kind of wedge.

380. "L'Aigle", 2–4–0 locomotive, Aimé-Etienne Blavier and Larpent, 1855.

381. "La Parisienne", Estrade, 1889.

382. Two-storeyed express train car with the third-class compartments below and the second-class above.

287

Ricour's successor, Desdouits, tried to build a two-cylinder simple locomotive with this type of fuel-saving surface to compete with the De Glehn four-cylinder compound engines just acquired on a trial basis. The shape of the wedge surfaces was different at the front from that on the PLM locomotives, giving them the nickname "Beaked" locomotives *(machines à bec)* (Ill. 383). In fact these engines, Series 2751–2754 (later 220.011–014), are said to have used the same amount of coal as the De Glehn engines at first. But later, exact tests proved that there was very high back pressure in the cylinders caused by the piston valves made according to a patent held by Ricour. After a short interlude with American loco-motives on the two-cylinder Vauclain pattern, the State Railroad adopted the De Glehn types per-manently.

These "wind-cutter" surfaces were introduced to Ger-

383. "L'Encloître", express train locomotive with so-called "beaked" form, French State Railroad, Series 2751-2754, 1897.

many in 1900 with the last batch of 4–4–0 inside cylinder locomotives, Class IIc for the Baden State Railroad. As the shaping at the front hampered access to the smokebox, it was omitted: in its place, a conical, pointed smokebox door was often fitted. Finally, there was merely a wedge-shaped front to the driver's cab, which lasted longest in Germany in Bavaria and was still visible on locomotives built in France after the Second World War.

Of course, the wedge-shaped surfaces are character-istic of specially high speed locomotives, and it was always used when incorporated into their design. At the International Exhibition in Paris in 1900, a locomotive built to a design by Thuile of Le Creusot was shown (Ill. 384), which was intended to pull a 180-200-ton luxury train on the level at a minimum of 76 m.p.h. The designer still stuck to excessively large driving wheels of 8 ft. 2½ in. diameter; to mount a sufficiently large boiler within the loading gauge, he reverted to the old pear-shaped boiler cross-section of Kessler, but put the narrower section underneath between the large coupled wheels. The wide Belpaire firebox, because of its weight, needed a six-wheeled truck at the rear with a centre pivot. The relatively short boiler barrel allowed enough room at the front for a large driver's cab which also housed a turbo-dynamo for the train's electric lighting.

The very long tender ran on five axles and held enough coal for a 220-mile run. On test runs in May and June 1900 on the State line between Chartres and Thouars, this engine, which was large for those days, was a disappointment. It only just achieved its intended performance and tended to derail; it required a crew of three: a driver and two firemen. On one of these test runs, Thuile leant out too far, was hit by a post and killed. After this, the engine stood around idle and was scrapped in 1904.

Another exhibit with a front driver's cab was the Italian engine (Ill. 259) by Plancher (cf. section 11.1.4), and on this, the front wall of the driver's cab was wedge-shaped.

Soon after the turn of the century, the Prussian study group for electric high speed railroads began its work, and was crowned on October 23, 1903 when an electric railcar reached the remarkable speed of 130.8 m.p.h. Steam locomotive builders put on a new spurt. The association of German mechanical engineers arranged a competition for a design for an express locomotive in 1902/03 which had to pull 180 tons at a steady 75 m.p.h. and also be able to run safely at 94 m.p.h. The design by chief engineer Kuhn of the Henschel Company was chosen, being a three-cylinder compound locomotive of the Wittfeld system. The driver's cab on the two examples built was at the front; one had a second cab at the back for the fireman, and the other had for the first time the whole area above the wheels protected by a box-shaped structure (Ill. 385) which continued over the tender — the first time, that is, if one disregards the steam/electric locomotive of Jean-Jacques Heilman. This engine had a side corridor for the train crew to reach the driver's footplate.

384. Express loco-
motive with wedge-
shaped front, enclosing
the driver's cab, Thuile
system, 1900.

385. Express loco-
motive with entirely
enclosed structure,
Wittfeld design,
1902-03.

With the adopted Wittfeld arrangement, the two parallel LP cranks were in advance of the HP cranks by 90°, resulting in such heavy recoiling motion that the setting of the LP cylinder cranks was altered to place the left inside crank 45° in advance and the right one 45° behind the HP crank. This was only possible with a fly crank arrangement called a "lightning crank" because of its shape. Because of the high costs involved this modification was only made to one of the two engines. Section 11.2 already mentioned that this large locomotive was disappointing in terms of performance. When the front footplates and the casing had been removed, both locomotives ran until 1918 together with the 4–4–2 engines of Class S9.

This attempt in Prussia spurred the Bavarian State Railroads to build a similar express locomotive. The Maffei Works was given the task, and Hammel was the designer. The motion was the same as that on the Class IId 4–4–2 Baden engines (Ill. 277), but he fitted the now-standard bar frame. Whereas the locomotives described earlier looked primitive, Hammel's design is almost modern in appearance. He understood how to make even the wedge-shaped surfaces look attractive, with his excellent feeling for style, even if later aerodynamic science proved that they were incorrect. This engine, No. 3201 (Ill. 386), was exhibited in 1906 in Nuremberg at the Bavarian Jubilee Fair. On test runs in July of the following year on the 39-mile run between Augsburg and Munich, pulling 150 tons, this engine achieved the record speed in Germany at that time of 96 m.p.h.

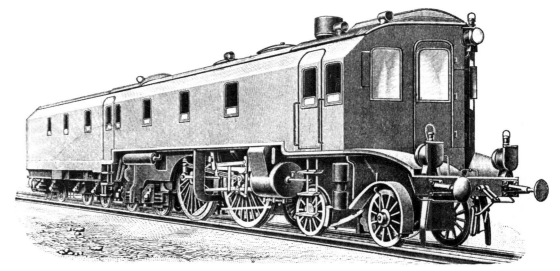

386. 4–4–4 four-cylin-
der express locomotive
of the Bavarian State
Railroad, No. 3201,
Anton Hammel, 1906.

Neither the permanent way, nor the signal arrangements and brakes, permitted such high speeds in normal service in those days. This engine remained a single example, and was handed to the Transport Museum in Nuremburg in 1925.

16.3 The Streamlined Locomotive

In the 1930s, competition from airplanes and automobiles began to rob railroads of their passengers. The best counter to this was to increase train speeds. Initially, high-speed railcars with internal combustion engines were the first step. But to achieve greater

387. 4–6–4 streamlined high-speed express locomotive of the German National Railroads, No. 05.001, 1935.

train moves along the ground, not through the air. There was some concern: would the motion overheat if it were no longer exposed to the cooling head wind? Would the grate still obtain enough air for combustion? To answer these questions the German National Railroads made tests between mid-April and late September 1934 on a three-cylinder standard 4–6–2 locomotive 03.154, whose motion was covered by an apron and whose smokebox front was covered with a Prandl paraboloid to reduce wind resistance. These dire fears proved groundless; the partial covering reduced the wind resistance and effected a gain in actual performance of 9.1 per cent at 75 m.p.h. and of 27 per cent at 87 m.p.h.

Thus the project of building two express locomotives could be continued with confidence, and these were ordered from AEG's Borsig works at Hennigsdorf. The construction work was carried out by the engineer Adolf Wolff whom we already met as the designer of the Spanish 4–8–2 locomotive (cf. section 15.3). To determine the most favourable type of casing, there were tests in the wind tunnel of the Technical High School at Charlottenburg, and later thorough replica tests in the larger wind tunnel at Göttingen.

The performance required — to pull trains of 200–250 tons (five to six cars) at over 94 m.p.h. and to have enough in reserve to make up for lost time — led to the adoption of a 4–6–4 locomotive with 7 ft. 7 in. driving wheels. In view of the better balancing of the masses offered, a three-cylinder drive was adopted. In terms

388. Locomotive with streamlined casing, London, Midland and Scottish Railway, No. 6220, 1937.

speeds in general, faster running steam locomotives had to be developed. Since aircraft construction had meanwhile brought new knowledge in the field of streamlining, this could be applied to railroads where air resistance to the moving train increases to the power of four. Unlike the airplane, however, the

of construction these two engines — No. 05 (Ill. 387) — were similar to the German National standard locomotives. Both were supplied in 1935. No. 05.001 was exhibited in Nuremburg on the occasion of the centenary of German Railroads. Both undertook a large number of test runs. They achieved speeds of

112 to 115 m.p.h. without difficulty and with excellent running characteristics. No. 05.002 made a memorable journey on May 11, 1936, on the 12½ miles straight and level track between Neustadt (D) and Paulinenaue, when 121 m.p.h. was reached soon after starting with a top speed of 124.3 m.p.h., and 124.34 m.p.h. sustained for 1.9 miles. The train weighed 297 tons and the maximum performance achieved 3,400 i.h.p.

A third locomotive, No. 05.003, was fitted for burning coal dust. It had the boiler reversed and the footplate was thus at the front. The outbreak of the Second World War, and the resulting limited time-tables, prevented these three engines from being used as planned, and they stood mostly idle. Since there were no plans for repairing them at the time, in early 1950, they came to the Krauss Maffei Works in Allach where their creator, Adolf Wolff, had become director, and they were stripped of their covering. 05.003 was also converted into a normal 4–6–4. On July 14, 1958 it was decided to discard them. No. 05.001, the best preserved, was ceremonially presented to the Transport Museum at Nuremburg on June 16, 1963, with its designer and the driver of the record-breaking run participating. They were the pattern for further streamlined locomotives on the German National Railroad.

The introduction of the famous diesel fast railcar "Der fliegende Hamburger" ("The Flying Hamburger") led Nigel Gresley to examine whether such railcars could be used for an express service between London and Scotland. But since they could not achieve sufficiently high speeds on the existing lines and also had a restricted number of seats, he decided to retain steam. Following comparative tests with Great Western locomotives, he had made continual improvements to his first three-cylinder "Pacific", Class A1. Initially using this engine and then using the A3 Class, he made various tests between late November 1934 and early March 1935 on behaviour at high speeds. In the course of these, the "Papyrus" reached a maximum speed with 217 tons behind the tender of 108.3 m.p.h. It emerged, however, that certain modifications would have to be made for normal service. For this reason, the A4 Class was created with a higher boiler pressure, smaller cylinders and, above all, completely streamlined. Before the first four engines of this class entered service, Gresley made a trial run with the "Silver Link", pulling a 230-ton train when 112½ m.p.h. was reached. The "Silver Jubilee" express trains between London and

Newcastle began regular operations on September 30, 1935, followed by further similar trains. A Kylchap pipe nozzle was fitted to the last four engines of the A4 Class. One such locomotive, the "Mallard" (Ill. 392), set a world record for steam locomotives, pulling a train of three eight-wheel cars and the dynamometer weighing 240 tons in all on July 3, 1939, with a speed of 126 m.p.h., for only a short period, however, and on a stretch of track with a gentle slope of 1 in 240 downwards. The "Mallard" ended up in the Clapham Museum.

As mentioned already (cf. section 15.2), in June 1933 Stanier brought out the first "Princess" Class "Pacific" on the LMS Railway. This was a four-

389. Locomotive wheels spinning at full speed.

cylinder engine with divided drive, and was entirely in the Great Western tradition. The four sets of Walschaert's valve gear, two inside and two outside were an innovation. Subsequent examples were fitted by Stanier with a combustion chamber and a larger superheater. He also simplified the valve gear by omitting the two inside sets and operating the inside valves from the outside gear.

When Gresley introduced his streamlined locomotives on the LNER there was again a kind of race to

291

390. Locomotive of the "Merchant Navy" Class, Compagnie Générale Transatlantique, No. 21 C 19, 1941.

391. 4–6–4 locomotive of the New York Central Railroad, No. 5453, Class J 3, with the express "Twentieth Century Limited". Design of the streamlined casing by Dreifuss.

Scotland. In 1937 Stanier built five "Duchess" Class engines with a streamlined casing (Ill. 388) to match the LNER's "Coronation" express introduced for the coronation of King George VI, with an equivalent "Coronation Scot". A journey for the press on June 29, 1937 by No. 6220 "Coronation" saw a speed of 114 m.p.h. achieved, breaking the earlier record of the LNER's "Silver Fox". In normal service, these locomotives pulled 470-530 tons. On the Southern, the traditionally-minded Maunsell was succeeded by O. V. S. Bulleid, who was completely the opposite. He saw ahead to the possible operating requirements after the end of the War, and designed a locomotive which was to pull 600-ton trains at 70 m.p.h. It was not to weigh more than

95.5 tons to take account of the existing track conditions. This forced him to build the firebox of welded high-grade steel. This was all the more necessary, since a high boiler pressure of 280 lbs. had been chosen, to achieve the tractive effort required with smaller and therefore lighter cylinders. Bulleid found a new solution for the operation of the valves. They were not operated directly from the driving axle but via two intermediate shafts which were themselves driven by chains running from the driving axle. The eccentric cranks were mounted on the second of these chain wheel shafts. The whole valve gear mechanism was completely encased in an oil bath. The method of operating the piston valves for the three cylinders was also new. These valves had inside admission and no outer stuffing boxes, since they were operated by rocket shafts located outside which were in turn connected to a pushing rod inside the large steam chest. This "Merchant Navy" Class (Ill. 390) could also be used for heavy freight trains. The Southern lacked this type of engine and, despite the War, they were permitted to build a whole class after the first entered service in 1941. The complicated valve drive proved to be very temperamental. But as these and the subsequent "West Country" Class engines were exceptionally efficient they were

converted by British Railways. They were given normal Walschaerts gear, and to spare the boiler, its pressure was reduced to 250 lbs.

Simultaneously with Germany, there were attempts in America to operate high speed trains. Diesel railcars again made a start here. The first was the "Zephir" in 1933, operating on the Chicago, Burlington and Quincy Railroad. Then, in November 1934, the New York Central Railroad fitted one of its Hudson Class J-1c engines, No. 5344, with a streamlined casing, with a shape determined after tests in a wind tunnel. This was the famous "Commodore Vanderbilt" which was offered in various simplified forms on a small scale by the toy industry for many years.

As the Federal Railroad in Germany, which created an entirely streamlined train in the Henschel-Wegmann train with specially matching locomotive and lightly constructed carriages, the Chicago, Milwaukee, St. Paul and Pacific Railroad did the same when they built their "Hiawatha". For the first time, an artist-designer of industrial products,

Otto Kühler, was used to help design the exterior outline of the 4–4–2 engine to be used, and he created the "shovel-nosed" styling. Raymond Loewy created the "balloon shape" for the next four Class K4 engines built by the Pennsylvania Railroad as streamlined locomotives. This was an attempt to impose aesthetic aspects onto the purely physical forms. Henry Dreifuss adopted the same style in creating the streamlined casing for the ten Hudson locomotives, Class J3, Nos. 5445–5454, for the New York Central Railroad (Ill. 391). Instead of covering the entire locomotive with an "inverted bathtub" as he put it, he matched the casing to the natural shape of the engine, leaving the motion completely uncovered. Naturally these engines pulled the best expresses on this railroad, such as the "Twentieth Century Limited". They became the NYC's symbol, and were skilfully exploited for advertising purposes. As was predictable, the other railroads soon realized the advertising potential of streamlining and competed with one another in the creation of striking shapes. Thus what had begun

392. The "Mallard" (world speed record holder), 4–6–2 express engine of the London and North Eastern Railway, No. 4468.

293

393. 4-4-4-4 loco-
motive of the Pennsyl-
vania Railroad, 1940.
Streamlined casing by
Raymond Loewy.

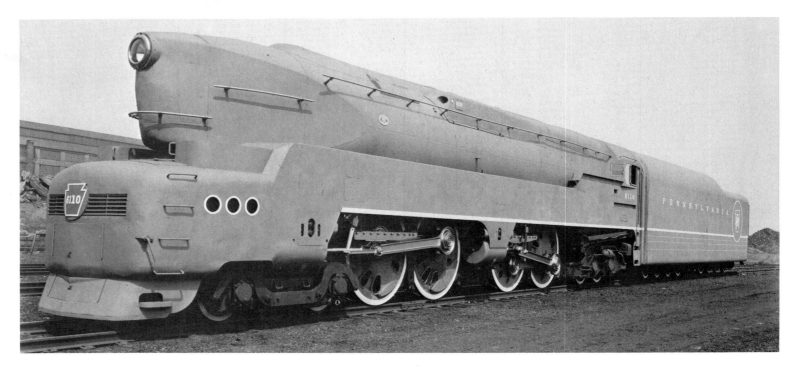

strictly as a technical improvement, went off-course
and became merely a means of advertising.

In 1939, the Pennsylvania had exhibited a 4-4-4-6
engine, No. 6100, at the New York World Fair, and
it was supposed to be the "biggest express locomotive in the world". It was so large that it
could not be used in service at all and posed
many problems so that the design was modified.
The duplex driving gear was retained, because it was
thought to provide a better balancing of masses in
view of the lower weight of the driving and coupling
rods. One is reminded inadvertently of Petiet's
"Colossus" (cf. section 9.5). Baldwin was given
the order for the first two Class T1 engines, now
4-4-4-4, in July 1950. Raymond Loewy designed
the external chisel-nosed appearance (Ill. 393), but it
was more successful as advertising than streamlining.
The ability to negotiate curves of these long-wheelbase engines was ensured by the considerable lateral
play, 2 in., on the first and the third coupled axle.
The performance required was 800 tons on the level
at 100 m.p.h., a speed which was considerably
exceeded in actual service. In the Altoona locomotive test centre 6,552 i.h.p. at 85.5 m.p.h. was
recorded. Initially there was great satisfaction, and
it was thought that a more powerful substitute for
the 4-8-4s so far used had been found, but in time
the engines proved not completely satisfactory. As a
result of weight shifts when starting, they were very
prone to slip and were not easy to drive. Nevertheless, another fifty engines were acquired; they
were all fitted with an unreliable poppet valve gear
with the result that they were not able to be used,
as planned, on long runs. Although they had a higher
performance than diesel locomotives, they soon gave
way to them.

17. SHORT-DISTANCE TRAFFIC

As railroad networks continued to proliferate, there arose a great number of branch lines of varying lengths. In the catchment areas of the large cities there was a real need to link the suburbs with the centre. It was difficult to install turntables which would have been necessary to turn the locomotives of that time which used separate tenders and were thus excessively long. Consequently, locomotives were built which carried their own fuel requirements and were able to run equally well in both directions. Thus the "tank" engine was created. We can divide these into two main groups, apart from those used as switchers and for light freight: those used on inner urban (metropolitan) railroads and those for suburban lines.

17.1. Metropolitan Railroad Engines

On January 10, 1863, the first section of a city railroad was opened by the London Metropolitan Railway Co. between Bishop's Road and Farringdon Street. At first the double track was operated with broad gauge 2–4–0 tank engines from the Great Western

394. London, Metropolitan Railway, Baker Street Station.

295

Railway, but there were soon quarrels between the two companies. Thus, the Metropolitan was forced to obtain its own engines as a matter of urgency. For this, the railroad's constructor, John Fowler, turned to Beyer-Peacock, that went back to the plans for the 4–4–0 tank engines supplied recently to the Tudela-and-Bilbao Railroad (cf. section 10.1), with Bissel pony trucks, and he built a slightly larger version of these (Ill. 207). Since the Metropolitan Railway ran both in underground sections as well as open or partially open cuttings, the engines were fitted with a condensor for the exhaust steam (Ill. 396). This consisted of an adjustable valve controlled by the engineer and fitted in the exhaust pipe which diverted the exhaust steam via tubes into the side water tanks. Thus when the train was in a tunnel, the steam was condensed there by the water instead of being ejected with the smoke into the tunnel. Since the water in the containers became very hot during the underground journeys piston pumps had to be fitted to feed the boiler. In places where the locomotive ended its run, pits were fitted to release the water, which was almost at boiling point, while the tanks were refilled with cold water. The fireman was only allowed to feed the fire on the open sections of track but nevertheless the London underground was notorious for its smoky atmosphere.

On the Metropolitan tracks, which had several slopes of 1 in 100 to 1 in 70, these locomotives pulled trains of five eight-wheeled cars, weighing about 100 tons. By 1885 the Metropolitan Railway Co. had acquired sixty-six engines from Beyer-Peacock. Another fifty-four were also supplied to the Metropolitan District Railway. The two railroads combined to form the Inner Circle Line. Until the underground was electrified in 1905, these 4–4–0 tank engines were a characteristic feature of the London scene.

395. London, Metropolitan Railway, Hampstead Road. From top to bottom: street, water installations, course of Metropolitan Railway. Project for a connection between Hampstead and Charing Cross.

396. 4–4–0 tank locomotive of the London Metropolitan Railway, 1880.

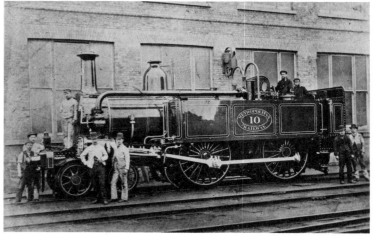

The next city to acquire a metropolitan railroad was New York. Here the long, straight and broad avenues allowed a raised railroad to be built cheaper than an underground railroad through the rocky substrata. But there were curves of as little as 36 and 27.5 yards radius, especially at the loops arranged at the end of each line to avoid the engines being changed. These loops and the limitation imposed by the steel elevated track led to locomotives quite different from those in London. The New York Elevated, which started operations in 1868, tested light 0–4–0 tank engines initially but their performance was inadequate. The Metropolitan Elevated then commenced with more powerful 2–4–2s, which were encased in wooden panelling in the same style as the cars which it pulled. Their ability to negotiate curves was unsatisfactory, until finally a type patented by Mathias N. Forney in 1866 was introduced. These were 0–4–4 tank engines with a frame extended so far at the rear that it was able to take all fuel required, supported on a truck (Ill. 397). In this way the adhesion weight of the engine did not alter as supplies diminished over the course of the journey. This was advantageous for an engine constantly stopping and starting. Rogers Locomotive Works specialized in this type, and offered the "Forney" in the 1880s in two sizes. Until electrification, these small, nimble, flexible engines pulled their three to five light eight-wheel cars of a typical American pattern with open platforms at each end. They were as much a part of the New York scene as the first skyscrapers and the Statue of Liberty.

In Paris, the "Ceinture" or "Circle Line", was not very important for passenger traffic because of its unfortunate location running round the old city centre. The syndicate in charge of this line acquired its own passenger trains for the first time in 1899 for the planned World Fair in Paris. The large-wheeled 0–6–0 inside cylinder engines of the Ouest Railroad were chosen: the so-called "Boers" which had been running since 1883 (Ill. 398), and had been based on the famous "Terrier" of the London, Brighton and South Coast Railway, one of the most successful of Stroudley's creations for suburban traffic in London; some are still to be seen in preserved lines in England. The Berlin City and Circle Railroad*, later called the "S-Bahn" was completed on February 7, 1882 with the opening of the West to East line running between Charlottenburg and Schlesische stations. It was operated initially with 2–4–0 and 0–4–2 tank engines, and later with 2–4–2s of the T5 Class. But the "S-Bahn" locomotive "par excellence" was the T12

Class 2–6–0 tank locomotive (Ill. 399). It was one of Garbe's types (cf. section 11.2). In general construction, it was like the P6 and also had a leading Kraus-Helmholtz truck. The first four were supplied in 1902 by the Union Giesserei in Königsberg. Several comparative runs were made with a similar saturated steam engine of Class T11. This T11 had been built because there was uncertainty whether the T12 would prove successful. The comparison resulted in a 14.6 per cent greater load pulled by the T12, with a reduction in coal consumption of 16 per cent and in water consumption of 37 per cent. The S-Bahn in Berlin was not electrified until much later than the New York and London lines, and as a result no fewer than five hundred T12s had been delivered by 1921 out of the total built of 974. From 1907, they were fitted with a smoketube superheater, and later the Knorr feed-water heater was added and other modifications made. Borsig supplied the third version (Ill. 399) from 1914. These advanced metropolitan railroad engines lasted until the "S-Bahn" was electrified in the 1930s. The last four engines were not abandoned by the Bundesbahn until 1965.

17.2 Extended Suburban and Inter-City Traffic

Powerful and fast-running locomotives were needed for service on the lines leading out of the large cities which had heavier trains than those on the metropolitan railroads and where the distance between stations was greater but travelling times had to be kept as short as possible. A brief review of this type of locomotive is given below.

In England the 0–4–4 tank engine was very popular. Apart from the advantages already mentioned was the fact that these engines almost always ran with the truck in front. Thus the driver's vision was not

397. 0–4–4 tank locomotive of the New York Elevated Railroad, Forney type.

*Berliner Stadt-and-Ringbahn.

hampered by steam and smoke on the congested sections of track. Although the axle layout was the same as on the American "Forney" they were rather a derivation from the classical British 4–4–0 inside cylinder locomotive, but with the boiler the other way round. The most powerful and most modern example of this extensive type is Class M7 of the London and South Western Railway (Ill. 402). Introduced in 1897 by D. Drummond, a total of 105 such engines were built by 1911 and many were passed on to the nationalized British Railways. Some of them were fitted for shuttle service in 1905.

If the locomotive could not or was not intended to be turned at the end of a line, the symmetrical 2–4–2 and 2–6–2 arrangements were adopted. As we know, single radial axles were unsuitable for high speeds. The Nord Railroad in France was the first railroad to use four-wheeled trucks at both ends of the engine. Its 4–4–4 tank engines "Revolver", Series 2.231-2.305, were introduced on the Grande Banlieue line between

398. 0–6–0 tank locomotive of the Paris Inner Circle Line (Ceinture), 1889.

399. 2–6–0 tank locomotive of the Berlin "S"-Bahn, Series T 12.

1901 and 1906 (Ill. 403). All the controls were in duplicate so that they could be used for operation in either direction.

Two trucks also meant that sufficient fuel and water could be carried for longer journeys, extending the application of the tank engine. This was why Maffei made the first 4–6–4 tank engine for the Madrid, Zaragoza and Alicante Railroad for the considerable local traffic in the area around Barcelona, which entered service up to 1911 as Series 620–641 (Ill. 404). In Italy, the Mediterraneo Railroad adopted this wheel arrangement in 1905 but used it for a three-cylinder compound engine which was not very suitable for a locomotive that had to keep stopping and starting. As a result, the six engines were converted by the Italian State Railroad into two-cylinder simple engines.

France gave the most enthusiastic reception to the 4–6–4 tank engine, and here it was built as a four-cylinder compound engine. The first of the De Glehn type was operated by the Est Railroad in 1904, and a year later the National Railroad in Alsace-Lorraine adopted a somewhat lighter engine. The largest number entered service on the PLM, and the two Series 5501–5545 of 1908 and 5301.5350 of 1913 were both the heaviest and most powerful (Ill. 405). They had the standard four-cylinder arrangement for this railroad. The first were used on the Grande Banlieue and subsequent examples in Nice as well. There they even pulled expresses for short runs.

The opening of the railroad ferry between Sassnitz on Rügen Island and Trelleborg in Sweden required a powerful tank engine for the short island line which

400. New York, the Bowery at night, painting by Louis Sonntag.

299

had not yet been connected to the mainland. There was also a requirement for this type of engine on the shuttle service between Wiesbaden and Frankfurt/Main and Wiesbaden and Mainz. As a result, the Prussian State Railroads entrusted the Vulkan Works in Stettin with a design for a 4–6–4 tank engine derived from the proven P8 (cf. section 11.2). Despite its smaller driving wheel diameter, this Class T18 (Ill. 406) was very suitable for express service. On the run between Berlin and Stettin (84 miles) it pulled 350 tons at 56 m.p.h. on the level, and was just as versatile as its predecessor the P8. Between 1912 and 1927, no fewer than 460 engines were put into service; the T18 was also adopted by the National Railroad in Alsace-Lorraine, in Württemberg and in Turkey. In 1970, fourteen were still running in Germany and it was thus one of Germany's longest living engines.

In contrast with the other railroads in France, the Nord had introduced a two-cylinder 4–6–4 tank engine in 1909 for its Grande Banlieue. They were followed in 1930 by two prototypes which were 2–8–2 coupled to increase the adhesion weight. Both the driving wheel diameter of 4 ft. 8½ in. and the boiler dimensions were too small, with the result that the timetable could not be maintained. De Caso, then chief engineer on the Nord, revised the project (Ill. 407). He fitted

the engine for a shuttle service which had been tested by the Nord since 1912. The pneumatic control device originally fitted was converted into an electro-pneumatic system as developed by Aubert, one of the railroad's engineers. This comprised a turbo-dynamo on the locomotive which fed the pneumatic control device with DC power so that switches, relays and electro-pneumatic valves could be operated from the opposite end of the train to operate the regulator and the other controls as required. The Cossart system to operate the piston valves was also new.

The crowning passenger tank engine was the 4–8–4. These were first built for Spain, by the North Railroad in 1913, being closely modelled on the 4–8–0 De Glehn

404. 4–6–4 tank locomotive of the Madrid-Zaragoza-Alicante Railroad, Series 620–641.

405. 4–6–4 tank locomotive of the French PLM, Series 5501–5545, 1908.

406. 4–6–4 tank locomotive of the Prussian State Railroad, Series T 18, 1912-27.

mountain express engine acquired a year earlier. In 1927, the PLM developed a 4–8–4 engine also on a four-cylinder compound system, based on its 4–6–4 locomotives. With various modifications, 351 engines of this type were commissioned by 1933, the highest number for this type of engine.

Finally No. 475.001 is shown as an example of the highly developed locomotive industry of Czechoslovakia (Ill. 409). It had a three-cylinder drive and belonged to the Czech National Railroads' standard range mentioned earlier. The bar frame was a type of cast vanadium steel by the Skoda Works in 1925,

407. 2–8–2 tank locomotive of the French Nord Railroad, Series 1.1201–1272, for shuttle service.

the first of its type made in Europe. Like all modern
Czech locomotives, this one was distinguished by its
pleasing appearance. This prototype was followed
in 1951 by thirty-eight similar engines with a higher
boiler pressure, Series 476.1, and in 1957, another
twenty even heavier models were built, Series 477.0.

409. 4—8—4 tank loco-
motive of the Czech
State Railroad, No.
475001.

303

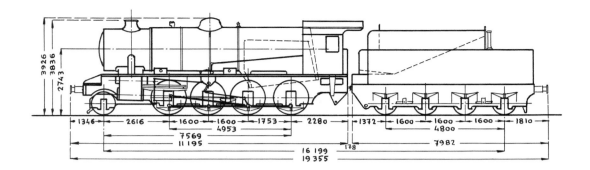

18. THE SECOND WORLD WAR AND THE END OF STEAM TRACTION

The "Austerity"
(see Ill. 411 b).

* Übergangskriegs-
lokomotiven.

18.1 "Austerity" War Locomotives

In Germany, total war, which involved the whole industry in exclusively military production, naturally applied to locomotives as well. Shortages of materials initially led to the process of stripping down to bare essentials, omitting unnecessary parts; substitute materials were used and machine finishing was kept to a minimum. Locomotives built in this way were designated "UK"* (wartime transitional engines) by the National Railroad. This did in fact succeed

in increasing production considerably but nonetheless supply could not match demand from the ever-increasing areas of military operations.

The National Railroad's managers thus realized in December 1941 that they needed to get the industry to construct a locomotive, which, with the absolute minimum use of material and labour, was able to pull 1,200 tons on the level at a sustained 40 m.p.h. The result was the Class 52, 2–10–0 coupled war locomotive (Ill. 410), which abandoned the traditional methods of manufacturing in many respects. For example, the connecting and coupling rods were

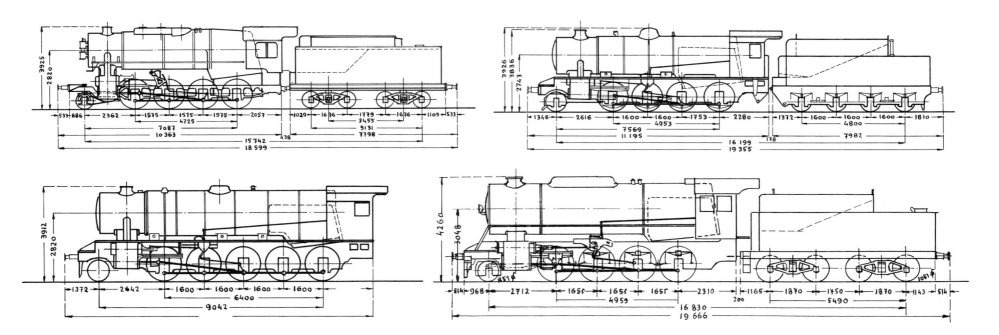

410. 2–10–0 loco-
motive, war type of the
German National Rail-
road, Class 52.

411a. The "Liberty",
2–8–0 locomotive,
British war engine.

411b. The "Austerity",
2–8–0 locomotive,
British war engine, 1943.

411c. 2-10-0 loco-
motive, variation on the
"Austerity", 1944.

411d. The "Libera-
tion", 2–8–0 locomotive
UNRRA, 1946.

simply made by welding two forged heads onto an unprocessed standard rolled section. Many individual components were designed so that they could easily be made by other unspecialized factories, thus releasing the locomotive factories for more essential work. As the thick steel slabs of the normal bar frame were needed for other purposes, there was a return to the plate frame. On the other hand, the engines intended for service in the East had to have special frost-protection devices installed. The first BR 52 standard model was supplied by the Borsig Works on September 12, 1942 and, contrasting with the secrecy then normally in vogue, it was shown off to the public and the press and radio. In time, several structural alterations were tried but none was actually put into real practice, apart from the steam condensing device fitted to the tender. Despite all the simplifications which had been executed, the BR 52 proved a very successful working engine. Six thousand, four hundred engines of this type were built, the highest number of any one type ever built.

Like the Great Central's 2–8–0 in the First World War, in Great Britain an existing engine, Stanier's 1 D twin-cylinder goods engine, LMS Class 8000, was taken into military service in the Second World War, with more than seven hundred such engines being supplied. As the War extended, the Western Allies needed more engines. Thus the British Government decided to order as simple a 2–8–0 locomotive as possible from ALCO in the USA in 1942, and from 1944 this entered service as the "Liberty" (Ill. 411a).

At the same time, as in Germany, a 2–8–0 type the "Austerity" (Ill. 411b) was created by the LMS under R.A. Riddles, and the first engine of this type was supplied on January 20, 1943 by the North British Locomotive Company. More than a thousand engines of this type were built during the War, afterwards spreading to various European countries. In 1944, a 2–10–0 was derived from it (Ill. 411c), with identical motion but with a considerably larger boiler. In fact only twenty-five entered service, but they did at last introduce definitively the ten-coupled locomotive on British tracks.

Because the War had depleted the locomotive stocks of participating countries and these had to be replenished as quickly as possible after the War, the Technical Advisory Committee of Inland Transport (TACIT) was consequently formed with representatives from France, Belgium, Holland, Czechoslovakia, Poland, Yugoslavia and Greece. The aim was to develop a standard European locomotive, which was to satisfy the following general criteria: tractive effort between 39,600 and 49,700 lbs., boiler with large grate between 39 and 48 sq. ft., axle weight below 18 tons, sharpest curve to be taken 100 yards and compliance with the Berne International Loading Gauge. After complicated discussions, the locomotive which emerged was designated the UNRRA or "Liberation" (Ill. 411d). The Vulcan Foundry built 120, all in 1946, divided between Czechoslovakia, Poland, Yugoslavia and Luxemburg.

It should be mentioned briefly that in Britain two

412. Express train of the German Federal Railroad with a Series 10 locomotive.

standardized Garratt types were built for overseas, a 4–8–2 + 2–8–4 metre-gauge engine with a low axle weight, and a 2–8–2 + 2–8–2 cape gauge engine with a higher axle weight. The United States also created a 2–8–2 standard engine for metre gauge, which became known as the "MacArthur" type. This type included eight engines supplied to Greece for the Peloponnese Railroad.

18.2 The Last Steam Locomotives

As the Second World War ended, much design work was begun, to design locomotives which were to be used for future transport. The little, grey clouds coming from the small number of diesel locomotives in the United States gave no clue as to the storm which was to sweep the steam locomotive from the tracks in a very few years.

The busiest country in this respect was France. There the railroads had been nationalized on January 1, 1938 into the "Société Nationale des Chemins de Fer Français" (SNCF). Initially the designs for multi-purpose engines were naturally given priority. To replenish depleted stocks as rapidly as possible, America was approached, where the firm of Baldwin worked together with French engineers to produce a 2–8–2, Series 141 R (Ill. 415). One thousand, three hundred and forty engines were ordered from the large American and Canadian locomotive works.

307

Apart from seventeen lost in a shipwreck, all were supplied in 1945–47. They were a successful combination of the latest American and European practices. They differed in some respects from one another. Nos. 1101–1200 and 1241–1340 had Boxpock wheels of hollow cast steel, and a one-piece cast steel bed instead of the welded bar frame of the others. Six hundred and four engines were gradually converted to burn oil, while the other burned coal and had a mechanical stoker. They could pull 650 tons at 62 m.p.h. on the level and 500 tons up a gradient of 1 in 77. These robust and undemanding engines, used on a shift schedule, were able to perform monthly running miles considered quite impossible in Europe hitherto. They were the last steam locomotives still running in France.

In terms of fuel consumption, however, these 141 Rs proved much less economical than the Series 141–P introduced in 1938, which had been derived from the PLM engine (Ill. 306), which, despite its smaller dimensions, had been superior in terms of efficiency because of its four-cylinder compound system. Urged by the South East Region, which needed more powerful engines than the 4–8–0 Chapelon Series 240–P, used on the Paris-Lyons-Marseilles run; an order for forty 141–Ps then under construction was replaced by an order for thirty-five "Mountain" Series 241–P, an improved version of the PLM–241–C (Ills. 413 and 421) (cf. section 15.3). On test runs between Laroche and Dijon, one of these engines maintained 62 m.p.h. up a 1 in 125 gradient, pulling 600 tons. Some of these engines passed to other regions, where they pulled expresses of up to 800 tons. 241–P–16, one of these last great French express engines, has been preserved for the museum in Mulhouse.

We must mention briefly two notable modifications made under Chapelon's supervision, or rather new constructions using certain components from previous engines: one was the conversion in 1946 of the unsuccessful 4–8–2 four-cylinder compound engine for the State Railroad 1932 into a 4–8–4 three-cylinder compound (Ill. 414). It was the first locomotive

in Europe to achieve a steady output of 5,000 i.h.p. But when the SNCF abandoned steam traction on its main lines in favour of electric traction, this kind of large engine had no application. It remained a sole example, and although it would have been a future pointer in other circumstances, it was unfortunately scrapped in 1962.

The second such engine was also an isolated example, for the same reasons. This was the conversion of a 2–10–0 De Glehn PO Series 6000 locomotive into a 2–12–0 six-cylinder compound, with four LP cylinders arranged in series inside and outside between the front running axle and the first coupled axle and the two HP cylinders inside between the second and third coupled axle.

In Europe, as in America, the 4–8–4 engine was the last development stage of the express steam engine. The first European railroad to introduce this type

had been the National Railroad in Germany in 1936, with its BR 06. As a result of the Second World War, only two of these streamlined engines entered service. The division of Germany split the important through-line Berlin-Bebra-Frankfurt/Main, whose hilly terrain had been the reason for these engines; finding themselves without any useful employment, they were scrapped.

By contrast the 4–8–4 was a success in two countries which were quite different geographically: 1950 in the Soviet Union and 1956 in Spain. As an example of the remarkable American-influenced post-war development of the Russian locomotive, a characteristic of all modern Russian engines even more underlined by the Box-pock wheels, we may cite the P36 Class (Ill. 416). It was to replace the proven and widely used 2–6–2 Su Class engines, where the "Stalin" Class 2–8–4s (Ill. 365) could

417. Locomotive No. 10.001 with the express train D177 at Kassel main station in Germany.

Spain also introduced the 4–8–4, having nationalized all broad-gauge railroads on February 27, 1943 and constituted the "Red Nacional de Ferrocarriles Españoles" (RENFE). These engines used the boiler from the 2–10–2 three-cylinder locomotive, Series 151.3101–3122 of 1942, as had also occurred with the 4–8–2 two-cylinder engines of Series 241.2201–2257. They had a driving wheel diameter of 5 ft. 9 in. and were thus not suitable to pull the heavier trains over the level stretches of track at the requisite speed once the Guadarrama line had been electrified. Nor did the performance of the 4–8–2 De Glehn engine suffice any more. The four-cylinder compound drive was now omitted from the 4–8–4 engine. Instead, 6 ft. 3 in. driving wheels were put in, which

418. 4–8–4 locomotive of the Spanish RENFE.

419. Express train Stockholm-Paris with a French SNCF locomotive, Series 232 S.

not be used because of their high axle load. The rear truck meant that the axle load could be reduced from 20 to 18 tons with no loss of performance. After the prototype built in 1950, about 250 of these successful engines entered service, all built by Kolomna. The Soviet Union then abandoned the steam locomotive in 1956.

required the boiler to be mounted further back where it was supported by the rear truck. Designers Cunill and Augé from the Maquinista Works in Barcelona endeavoured with these ten engines to create a pleasing appearance without adding the fashionable streamlined casings. These locomotives are still in service (Ill. 418).

In Britain, the four large railroad companies were nationalized on January 1, 1948 and reorganized as the British Railways. This naturally resulted in another effort to create standard types. A committee was formed with E.S. Cox as chairman, and six types were established initially. The characteristic feature of all these standard engines, which entered service from 1951, was the return to the simple two-cylinder locomotive of the old days, but now with outside cylinders and with outside Walschaerts gear which made them more similar to Continental engines than before. Some of the new standard locomotives were simple derivatives from existing types, the "Black Fives" (Ill. 356), for example, whose components had been interchangeable from much earlier on. By contrast, both "Pacific" engines in Class 6 and 7 were new and they developed under the chairmanship of the British Railways first chief engineer, R.A. Riddles. After overcoming various difficulties with the "Britannia" Class 7 engine (Ill. 420), especially in connection with the roller bearings, only forty-five examples were built. However, they proved to be good workers rather than very fast runners.

The political division of Germany affected the railroad network as well. The lines under Soviet control retained their old "Deutsche Reichsbahn" (German National Railroads) designation. The others, initially operating independently in each Western zone, were merged under their own management as the "Deutsche Bundesbahn" (German Federal Rail-

roads) on December 13, 1951. Both the East and West introduced standardization programmes mainly embracing tank engines. The National Railroad did not get far with its standardization, since the existing locomotives were rebuilt more or less uniform as "Reko" types. Nor did matters get very far with the Federal Railroads, following the decision to introduce electric and diesel traction. For example, when the old P8 was to be exchanged for a new and more powerful 2–6–2, only fifty-one locomotives were actually built. The last standard locomotive No. 10 (Ills. 412 and 417) only saw two examples built by Krupp in 1956/57, and they were scrapped by 1967. They were based at Kassel and pulled expresses to Frankfurt/Main.

420. 4–6–2 locomotive of the British Railways, Class 7, "Britannia" Class.

421. Express train of the French SNCF with a locomotive of Series 241 P.

422. The "Evening Star", 2-10-0 loco-motive, 1960. The last steam locomotive of the British Railways.

423. Locomotive of the Spanish RENFE, Series 242 F, with an express train from Madrid to Irún.

Great Britain was the country in which the first steam locomotive was built and one could consider that the history of the steam locomotive also ended here with the "Evening Star", built in 1960. This last British steam locomotive was another Riddles design. Initially it was to be built as a 2–8–2, but the usefulness of the 2–10–0 "Austerity" led to the adoption of this arrangement, despite the fact that a multi-purpose locomotive was envisaged. The "Evening Star" fully lived up to expectations and even exceeded them (Ill. 422). It was often used when "Pacific" engines broke down and on two occasions reached a speed of 90 m.p.h. These engines had a Chapelon type double chimney. The last one was fitted with a Giesl ejector, a surprisingly successful Austrian development which replaced the normal blast pipe nozzle and produced a remarkable increase in performance. Unfortunately it came too late to be used generally. Ten of the engines built between 1954 and 1960 were fitted with the Franco-Crosti feed-water heated boiler as an experiment in 1955 — an Italian invention which was tried on several railroads but not adopted anywhere. Two hundred and fifty-one locomotives of this last English type, the "Evening Star", Class 9-F entered service.

CONCLUSION

Two things brought about the decline of the steam locomotive. Contrary to popular belief, the reason for that decline was not in the first place increasing electrification. Electrification not only required new locomotives; it also involved very high installation costs. Apart from visible things such as the overhead catenaries with their innumerable gantries, there were the many invisible factors — power feeding lines, converter and transformer sub-stations as well as re-laying telephone and telegraph lines, sinking the track under bridges and in tunnels to accommodate the catenary plus sufficient safety margin, and so on. Despite the electric locomotive's improved utilization of energy as compared with the steam engine, and even in countries where hydro-electric power was available, these enormous installation costs were economically justifiable only above a certain level of traffic density. Electrification alone would undoubtedly have supplanted the steam locomotive to some extent, but on less busy lines steam could have continued to serve for many years to come.

Then, however, came the diesel locomotive. Originating in Germany, the diesel locomotive first thrived on American soil, which possessed the rich oil fields that Europe lacked. Basically it was simply an electric locomotive that carried around its own, diesel-driven power station. It required none of the expensive fixed plant of conventional electric operation and had the same liberty of movement as the steam locomotive.

Furthermore diesel oil has a much higher calorific power than coal. In fact the diesel locomotive turned out to be so much more economical than steam that it is said to have saved the North-America railroad system from total collapse. Before long almost every railroad had followed the example of the United States. In the face of increasing competition from both road and air transport, economy was and had to be the order of the day for all railroads. For the good, old, highly uneconomic steam locomotive, however, it was the death sentence.

But there was another important cause of that demise, and one that has tended to be overlooked. This was that the steam locomotive had reached the peak of its performance potential. It had to run on a track gauge that had become far too small for it. The clearance gauge set limits of height and width that could not be exceeded. Consequently the boiler — the largest single component — and with it the whole locomotive could only be extended lengthwise. But here too limits were set by the degree of rail curvature the locomotive could take. In the case of those latter-day American giants one already had the feeling that the natural limits had been overstepped. Neither the electric nor the diesel locomotive is hampered by the same limits, or at least not to the same extent, and whereas in the case of the steam locomotive it took colossal and cumbersome monsters to beat the 4,000 h.p. barrier, the other two manage it with no trouble at all.

The age of steam thus came to its inevitable end. Rise followed by decay is an unalterable law of nature, to which the steam locomotive was as subject as anything else. Fortunately there are large numbers of railroad enthusiasts determined, at great expense of time and money, to keep alive here and there the monarchs that once proudly ruled the railroads of the world, in order that generations to come shall still be able to form some conception of a phenomenon that already today belongs to a romantic past — the steam locomotive with its unique aura, made up of steam and smoke and oil vapour, puffing along just as though it were a creature of flesh and blood.

BIBLIOGRAPHY

Ahrons. E.L., The Development of British Locomotive Design, The Locomotive Publishing Co., London 1914

Alexander, E.P., Iron Horses, American Locomotive 1829-1900, W.W. Norton & Co., New York, 1st. ed. 1941

Allen, Cecil J., Locomotive Practice and Performance in the Twentieth Century, W. Heffer & Son Ltd., Cambridge 1949

Barbier, F. et Godfernaux, Les Locomotives à l'Exposition de 1900, Dunod, Paris 1902

Bombe, H., Die alten preussischen Eisenbahnen (unpublished manuscript)

Born, Erhard, Die Regel-Dampflokomotiven der Deutschen Reichsbahn und der Deutschen Bundesbahn, Verkehrswissenschaftliche Lehrmittelgesellschaft, Frankfurt/Main 1953

Born, Erhard, 2Cl-Entwicklung und Geschichte der Pacific-Lokomotiven, Franckh'sche Verlagshandlung, Stuttgart 1964

Bowman, Hank Wieand, Pioneer Railroads, Arco Publishing Co., Inc., New York 1954

Bruce, Alfred W., The Steam Locomotive in America, Development in the Twentieth Century, W.W. Norton & Co., New York 1952

Chapelon, André, La Locomotive à Vapeur, J.B. Baillière et Fils, Paris 1938

Le Chatelier, E. Flachat, J. Petiet et C. Polonceau, Guide du Mécanicien Constructeur et Conducteur de Machines Locomotives, Paul Dupont, Paris, 1st ed. 1851, 2nd ed. 1859, new ed. 1865

Couche, Ch., Voie, Matériel roulant et Exploitation technique des Chemins de Fer, Dunod, Paris 1874

Dambly, Phil., Nos inoubliables Vapeurs (History of the Belgian Locomotive), Le Rail, Brussels 1968

Deghilage, Origine de la Locomotive, A. Broise et Courtier, Paris 1886

Demoulin, Maurice, Locomotive et Matériel roulant, Dunod, Paris, 1st ed. 1896 and 2nd ed. 1924

Demoulin, Maurice, Traité pratique de la machine Locomotive, Librairie Polytechnique Baudry et Cie, Paris 1898

Demoulin, Maurice, La Locomotive actuelle, Librairie Polytechnique Ch. Béranger, Paris 1906

Dendy Marshall, C.F., Two Essays in early Locomotive History, The Locomotive Publishing Co., London 1928

Dendy Marshall, C.F., A History of British Railways down to the Year 1830, Oxford University Press, 2nd ed. 1971

Dewhurst, P.C., The Norris Locomotives, The Railway and Locomotive Historical Society, Boston (Mass.) 1950

Durrant, The Steam Locomotives of Eastern Europe, David & Charles Locomotive Studies, Newton Abbot (Devon) 1966

Durrant, The Garrat Locomotives, David & Charles Locomotive Studies, Newton Abbot (Devon) 1969

Ewald, Kurt, 20000 Schriftquellen zur Eisenbahnkunde, Henschel & Sohn GmbH, Kassel 1941

Ewald, Kurt, Der Erfurter Lokomotivbau 1872-1928 und die Hagans Gelenklokomotive, Jahrbuch für Eisenbahngeschichte 1971

Fenton, William, Nineteenth Century Locomotive Engravings, Hugh Evelyn, London 1964

Fleming, H.M. le, and J.H. Price, Russian Steam Locomotives, John Marshbank Ltd., London 1960

Fournereau, J., Les Locomotives à Vapeur de la SNCF, Editions Loco-Revue, Montchauvet (Set 0) 1947

Gairns, J.F., Locomotive Compounding and Superheating, Charles Griffin & Co., London 1907

Gaiser, F., Die Crampton-Lokomotive, Neustadt a.d. Haardt 1909

Garbe, Robert, Die Dampflokomotiven der Gegenwart, Julius Springer, Berlin, 1st ed. 1907, 2nd ed. 1920

Garbe, Robert, Die zeitgemässe Heissdampflokomotive, Julius Springer, Berlin 1924

Griebl, Helmut, CSD-Dampflokomotiven, Verlag Josef Otto Slezak, Vienna 1969

Hamilton Ellis, C., Four Main Lines, George Allen & Unwin Ltd., London 1950

Hamilton Ellis, C., Some Classic Locomotives, George Allen & Unwin Ltd., London 1949

Hamilton Ellis, C., The Midland Railway, Ian Allan Ltd., London, 2nd ed. 1955

Hamilton Ellis, C., The South Western Railway, Its mechanical History and Background, George Allen & Unwin Ltd., London 1956

Hamilton Ellis, C., The Lore of the Train, Madison Square Press, New York 1971

Hammer, Gustav, Die Entwicklung des Lokomotiv-Parkes bei den preussisch-hessischen Staatsbahnen, Special Edition from «Glasers Annalen», Berlin 1912

Hammer, Gustav, Neuerungen an Lokomotiven der preussisch-hessischen Staatseisenbahnen, Special Edition from «Glasers Annalen», Berlin 1916

Holley, Alex. L., American and European Railway Practice in the economical Generation of Steam, New York 1861

Horn, Alfred, Die Bahnen in Bosnien und Herzegowina, Special Edition of «Die Eisenbahn», Vienna 1964

Horn, Alfred, Die Österreichische Nordwestbahn (mit Geschichte der Dampflokomotiven), Bohmann Verlag, Vienna-Heidelberg 1967

Horn, Alfred, Die Kaiser-Ferdinands-Nordbahn (mit Geschichte der Dampflokomotiven), Bohmann Verlag, Vienna-Heidelberg 1971

Igel, Martin, Handbuch des Dampflokomotivbaus (with the collaboration of Morgenroth and Reder), M. Krayn, Berlin 1923

Jahn, J., Die Dampflokomotive in entwicklungsgeschichtlicher Darstellung ihres Gesamtaufbaus, Julius Springer, Berlin 1924

Kalla-Bishop, P.M., Tandem Compound Locomotives, Kalla-Bishop Books, London 1949

Kilburn Scott, E., The Career of Matthew Murray, Special Edition from «Society of Engineers», 1931

Kinert, Reed, Early American Steam Locomotives, First seven decades 1830-1900, Bonanza Books, Superior Publishing Co., New York 1962

Kitson Clark, Edwin, Kitsons of Leeds 1837-1937, The Locomotive Publishing Co., London 1938

Krauth, Gerhard, Dampflok-Verzeichnis der Kgl. Bayerischen Staatsbahn, VdEF, Wuppertal 1966

Kronawitter, J.B., Die bayerischen S 3/6-Lokomotiven der Baureihen 18⁴, 18⁵ und 18⁶, Krauss-Maffei-Informationen Nr. 213, Separata from «Der Eisenbahner» 1959

Lake, Chas. S., The World's Locomotives, Percival Marshall & Co., London 1905

Lake, Chas. S., Locomotives of 1906, Percival Marshall & Co., London 1906

Lomonossov, G., Lokomotivversuche in Russland, VDI-Verlag, Berlin 1926

Lukas, Walter A., 100 Years of Steam Locomotives, Simmons Boardman Publishing Corp., New York 1957

Maedel, Karl Ernst, S 10¹, Geschichte der letzten preussischen Schnellzug-Dampflokomotiven, Franckh'sche Verlagshandlung, Stuttgart 1972

Mallet, A., Les Locomotives à l'Exposition Universelle de 1878, Paris 1879

Marshall, L.G., Steam on the RENFE, Macmillan & Co., Ltd., London 1965

Marvá y Mayer, José, Tracción en vías férreas, Madrid 1877

Mathias, Felix, Etudes sur les machines locomotives de Sharp et Roberts, Librairie Scientifique-Industrielle de L. Mathias, Paris 1844

Matschoss, Conrad, Die Entwicklung der Dampfmaschine, Julius Springer, Berlin 1908

Mayer, Max, Esslinger Lokomotiven, Wagen und Bergbahnen, VDI-Verlag, Berlin 1924

Meinecke, F. und Fr. Röhrs, Die Dampflokomotive, Lehre und Gestaltung, Springer Verlag, Berlin 1949

Messerschmidt, Wolfgang, 1Cl, Entstehung und Verbreitung der Prairie-Lokomotive, Franckh'sche Verlagshandlung, Stuttgart 1972

Messerschmidt, Wolfgang, 1Dl, Erfolg und Schicksal der Mikado- Lokomotiven, Franckh'sche Verlagshandlung, Stuttgart 1963

Messerschmidt, Wolfgang, Von Lok zu Lok, Esslingen und der Lokomotivbau für die Bahnen der Welt, Franckh'sche Verlagshandlung, Stuttgart 1969

Messerschmidt, Wolfgang, Geschichte der italienischen Dampflokomotiven, Orell Füssli Verlag, Zurich 1968

Metzeltin, G.H., Die Lokomotive, ein Lexikon ihrer Erfinder,

Konstrukteure, Führer und Förderer, Deutsche Gesellschaft für Eisenbahngeschichte, Karlsruhe 1971

Moreau, Auguste, Traité des Chemins de Fer, Fauchon et Artus, Editeurs, Paris, undated, (90th Year)

Moser, Alfred, Der Dampfbetrieb der schweizerischen Eisenbahnen, Verlag Birkhäuser, Basle, 2nd ed. 1938, 4th ed. 1967

Mühl, Albert und Karl Seidel, Die Württembergischen Staatseisenbahnen (mit ausführlicher Geschichte der Lokomotiven), Konrad Theiss Verlag, Stuttgart and Aalen 1970

Nock, O.S., The Midland Compounds, David & Charles Ltd., Strand, Dawlish (Devon) 1964

Nock, O.S., The Premier Line. The Story of London & North Western Locomotives, Ian Allan Ltd., London 1952

Nock, O.S., The Great Western Railway in the Nineteenth Century, Ian Allan Ltd., London 1962

Norris, Septimus, Norris's Handbook for Locomotive Engineers and Machinists, Philadelphia 1853

Oppizzi, Pietro, I più fecenti Progressi della Tecnica nelle Ferrovie e Tramvie, Ulrico Hoepli, Milan 1915

de Pambour, Le Comte F.M.G., Traité théorique et pratique des Machines Locomotives, 2nd ed., Bachelier, Paris 1840

Paulus, Rudolf, Bau und Ausrüstung der Eisenbahnen, Julius Maier, Stuttgart 1872

Pettigrew, William Frank and Albert Ravenshear, A Manual of Locomotive Engineering, Charles Griffin & Co., London 1899

Pierson, Kurt, Dampfzüge auf Berlins Stadt- und Ringbahn, Franckh'sche Verlagshandlung, Stuttgart 1969

Rakow, W.A., Lokomotiven der Sowjetischen Eisenbahnen (in Russian), Moscow 1955

Ransome-Wallis, P., The Concise Encyclopedia of World Railway Locomotives, New Horizon Books, Hutchinson of London 1959

Ransome-Wallis, P., The last Steam Locomotives of Western Europe, Ian Allan Ltd., London 1963

Reder, Gustav, L'initiation de la Traction à Vapeur en France et les Locomotives du Chemin de Fer de Saint-Etienne à Lyon (unpublished manuscript)

Reed, Brian, Modern Locomotive Classes, The Locomotive Publishing Co., London, 2nd ed. 1950

Reed, Brian, Locomotives in Profile, Vol. I, Profile Publications Ltd., Windsor 1971

Rolt, L.T.C., A Hunslet Hundred, David & Charles, London 1964

Sagle, W. Lawrence, A Picture History of the Baltimore & Ohio Motive Power, Simmons Boardman Publishing Co., New York 1952

Sauvage, Edouard, La Machine Locomotive, Librairie Polytechnique Baudry et Cⁱᵉ, various ed. 1894-1941

Sauvage, E. and A. Chapelon, La Machine Locomotive (10th enlarged ed. of the previous one), Ch. Béranger, Paris 1947

v. Schmidt, Adalbert, Mittheilungen über die Vorbereitung der materiellen Mittel zum Betriebe der Eisenbahn über den Semmering, betr. die Preisausschreibung für die geeignetste Lokomotive und den Erfolg der Preis-Konkurrenz, Vienna 1852

Sekon, The Evolution of the Steam Locomotive (1803 to 1898), The Railway Publishing Co., London 1899

Slezak, Josef Otto, Die Lokomotivfabriken Europas, Verlag Josef Otto Slezak, Vienna 1963

Slezak, Josef Otto, Die Lokomotiven der Republik Österreich, Verlag Josef Otto Slezak, Vienna 1970

Smiles, Samuel, The Life of George Stephenson, John Murray, London 1881

Staufer, Alwin F., Steam Power of the New York Central System. Vol. I: Modern Steam Power 1915-1955. Vol. II: New York Central's Early Power 1813-1916. Private edition Medina (Ohio) 1965-1967

Steffan, Hans, Belgische Lokomotiven, Special enlarged edition from «Die Lokomotive», Vienna 1918

Stockklausner, Hanns, Österreichs Lokomotiven und Triebwagen, Zeitschriftenverlag Ployer u. Co., Vienna, 1st ed. 1949, 2nd ed. 1954

Stockklausner, Hanns und Werner Walter Weinstötter, 25 Jahre deutsche Einheitslokomotiven, Miba-Verlag, Nuremberg 1950

Stretton, Clement E., The Locomotive Engine and its Development, Crosby Lockwood & Son, London, 6th ed. 1903

Swengel, F.M., The American Steam Locomotive. Vol. I: The Evolution of the Steam Locomotive 1870-1949, Midwest Rail Publications, Davenport (Iowa) 1967

Troske, L., Allgemeine Eisenbahnkunde für Studium und Praxis. II. Teil: Ausrüstung und Betrieb der Eisenbahnen, Otto Spamer, Leipzig 1907

Tuplin, W.A., Great Western Steam, George Allen & Unwin Ltd., London 1958

Tuplin, W.A., North Western Steam, George Allen & Unwin Ltd., London 1963

Vilain, Lucien M., Les Locomotives à Vapeur françaises à grande vitesse et à grande puissance du Type «Pacific», Vigot Frères, Paris 1959

Vilain, Lucien M., Un Siècle (1840-1938) de Matériel et Traction sur le Réseau d'Orléans, Editions A. Gozlan, Paris 1962

Vilain, Lucien M., Evolution du Matériel Moteur et Roulant de la Compagnie des Chemins de Fer du Midi, Les Presses Modernes, Paris 1965

Vilain, Lucien M., L'Evolution du Matériel Moteur et Roulant de la Compagnie des Chemins de Fer Paris-Lyon-Méditerranée, Editions Vincent, Fréal et Cie, Paris 1971

Vilain, Lucien M., Le Matériel Moteur et Roulant du Réseau de l'Ouest et des Chemins de Fer de l'Etat (incl. Paris-Saint-Germain et Paris-Versailles, Editions Dominique Vincent et Cie, Paris 1973

Vilain, Lucien M., Les Locomotives articulées du Système Mallet dans le Monde, Editions Vincent, Fréal et Cie, Paris 1969

Wagner, Ludwig, Sächsische Lokomotiven, VdEF-Mitteilungen, Wuppertal, several issues, 1971-1973

Warner, Paul T., Locomotives of the Pennsylvania Railroad 1834-1924, Special Edition from Baldwin Locomotives 1924, Owen Davies Publisher, Chicago 1959

Warren, J.G.H., A century of Locomotive Building by Robert Stephenson & Co., 1823-1923, Andrew Reid & Co., Newcastle 1923

White jr., John H., American Locomotives, An Engineering History 1830-1880, The Johns Hopkins Press, Baltimore 1968

Whith, Emile, Nouveau Manuel complet de la Construction de Chemins de Fer, Librairie Encyclopedique de Roret, Paris 1857

Wolff, Adolf, Die 2C2-h3-Schnellzug-Lokomotive 05.003 der Deutschen Reichsbahn, Georg Siemens, Berlin 1947

Wolff, Adolf, Dampflokomotiven der New York Centralbahn für hohe Geschwindigkeiten, Georg Siemens Verlagsbuchhandlung, Berlin-Bielefeld 1951

Wood, Nich., Traité pratique des Chemins de Fer (Enlarged French edition from 2nd English edition), Carilian-Gœury, Paris 1834

Young, R., Timothy Hackworth and the Locomotive, The Locomotive Publishing Co., London 1923

Works of Collective Authorship

Ahrons, E.L., The British Steam Railway Locomotive 1825-1925, The Locomotive Publishing Co., London 1925

Nock, O.S., The British Steam Railway Locomotive from 1925-1965, Ian Allan, London 1966

Die Entwicklung der Lokomotive im Gebiete des Vereins Deutscher Eisenbahnverwaltungen. Bd. I: 1835-1880, R. v. Helmholtz and W. Slaby, R. Oldenburg, Munich, Berlin 1930. Bd. II: 1880-1920, Metzeltin

Histoire des Chemins de Fer en France (with a contribution by Chapelon on the Development of French Steam Locomotives)

Locomotive Superheating and Feed Water Heating, Supplement to The Locomotive, Railway Carriage and Wagon Review. The Locomotive Publishing Co., London, undated.

The Locomotives of the Great Western Railway (Parts one, seven, eight, nine). The Railway Correspondence and Travel Society, 1951-1958

Organ für Fortschritte des Eisenbahnwesens, Supplement Vol. X, 1893

Locomotives à Vapeur de la SNCF, Films documentaires Loco-Revue, Auray 1973

Blum, v. Borries, Barkhausen, Das Eisenbahnmaschinenwesen der Gegenwart. First Paragraph, First Part, Die Lokomotiven, 2nd ed. Wiesbaden 1903

Barkhausen, Blum, Courtin, Weiss, Das Eisenbahnmaschinenwesen der Gegenwart. First Paragraph, First Part, Second Half, First Delivery, Brückmann, Heissdampflokomotiven mit einfacher Dehnung des Dampfes, 3rd ed. Berlin, Wiesbaden 1920

A Pictorial History of the Festiniog Railway, 2nd ed., Festiniog Railway Co., Portmadoc 1958

History of the Baldwin Locomotive Works 1831-1922

Selected Periodicals and Journals

Annales des Mines, 1825-1856
Annales des Ponts et Chaussées, 1834-1847
Baldwin Locomotives
Die Lokomotive, First Continuation, Vienna
Eisenbahn, Vienna
Hanomag-Nachrichten
Henschel-Hefte
La Nature
Lok-Magazin, Stuttgart
Revue générale des Chemins de Fer
Revue de l'Association française des Amis des Chemins de Fer

WHEEL ARRANGEMENTS

Locomotives are commonly classified according to the White system of notation of wheel arrangement into front wheels, driving wheels and rear wheels. Hence a 4-6-2 arrangement denotes a locomotive having 4 carrying wheels, 6 driving wheels and 2 rear carrying wheels. Articulated engines are similarly shown using a + sign to denote the break.

Symbol	White System	Denomination in the USA	Other Denominations
	0–2–2		
	2–2–0		Planet
	2–2–2		England: Single; Germany: Spinnräder
	4–2–0	Jervis	France: Crampton
	4–2–2	Bicycle	England: Bogie Single
	0–4–0	Four-wheel switcher	England: Samson
	0–4–2		France: Lyon
	2–4–0		England: Rear-coupled six-wheeler
	2–4–2	Columbia	France: Orléans
	4–4–0	American	England: Rear-coupled bogie
	4–4–2	Atlantic	
	4–4–4	Reading	
	0–6–0	Six-wheel switcher	France: Bourbonnais; England: Six-coupled; Germany: Dreikuppler
	2–6–0	Mogul	
	2–6–2	Prairie	
	2–6–4		Adriatic
	4–6–0	Tenwheeler	
	4–6–2	Pacific	
	4–6–4	Hudson	Baltic
	0–8–0	Eight-wheel switcher	England: Eight-coupler; Germany: Vierkuppler
	2–8–0	Consolidation	
	2–8–2	Mikado	
	2–8–4	Berkshire	
	4–8–0	Mastodon	
	4–8–2	Mountain (Mohawk)	
	4–8–4	Confederation (Pocono, Niagara, Northern)	
	0–10–0	Ten-wheel switcher	Germany: Fünfkuppler
	2–10–0	Decapod	
	2–10–2	Santa Fé	
	2–10–4	Texas	
	4–10–0	(formerly Mastodon)	
	4–10–2	Union Pacific	
	0–12–0		Germany: Sechskuppler
	2–12–0	Centipede	Gölsdorf
	4–12–2	Union Pacific	
	0–6–0 + 0–6–0	Erie	
	2–6–0 + 0–6–6	Allegheny	
	4–6–0 + 0–6–2	Southern Pacific Cab in Front	
	4–6–0 + 0–6–4	Challenger	
	2–8–0 + 0–8–4	Yellowstone	
	4–8–0 + 0–8–4	Big Boy	

Note:

Locomotives without front carrying wheels were only used in the USA as switchers. Besides being used as tender locomotives for switching, such engines were only rarely used on regular runs and for this reason were not given a particular name.

ABLE OF TECHNICAL DATA

bles listing the leading characteristics of the locomotives illustrated in illustration sequence. (Anglo-American measurements are given in
ics beneath metric measurements).

planation of technical characteristics

ing gear

dimensions are laid out in the tables in the following order:
ylinder-diameter × Piston stroke / Diameter of driving wheels
r compound engines:

umber × Diameter of HP cylinder × Piston stroke / Diameter of
umber × Diameter of LP cylinder × Piston stroke / driving wheels

Dimensions are given in millimeters followed by the equivalent in inches.

Boiler pressure

Kg/sq.cm followed by the equivalent in lbs./sq.inch.

Heating surface (given as evaporating and superheater surfaces [if any])
Sq.metres followed by the equivalent in sq.feet.

Weight

Metric tons followed by the equivalent in lbs.

Wheelbase

Millimeters followed by the equivalent in inches.

Illustration	Name of Locomotive	Wheel arrangement	Year	Builder	Railroad	Driving gear	Boiler Pressure atmospheres	Grate area	Heating surface firetubes and superheater	Weight — Adhesion weight	Weight in Service	Coupled wheelbase	Total wheelbase	Remarks
9	(Trevithick 1)	0-4-0	1804	Trevithick	Pen-y-Darren	210×1372/1092 *8.2×54/43*								First locomotive in the world
9	(Trevithick 2)	0-4-0	1805	John Steel	Gateshead	179×919/965 *7×36/38*								Trevithick system
10	Prince Royal (Regent)	0-4-0	1812	Fenton & Murray	Middleton	203×610/... *8×24*								Rack and pinion locomotive. The first serviceable engine
11	Berliner Dampfwagen 1	0-4-0	1816	Kgl. Eisengießerei, Berlin	Königsgrube (Upper Silesia)	130×314/... *5×12.4*								First locomotive built outside England (in Germany)
12	Puffing Billy	0-4-0	1813	Hedley	Wylam	229×914/991 *9×36×39*	3.3 *48.5*	0.56 *6.0*	7.15 *76.9*			1900 *74.8*	1900 *74.8*	
14	Blücher	0-4-0	1814	G. Stephenson	Killingworth	203×610/914 *8×24/36*								First locomotive by G. Stephenson
19	Dart, Tally-Ho, Star	0-4-0	1822	G. Stephenson	Hetton	229×610/965 *9×24/38*	3.5 *51.4*							
20	Locomotion	0-4-0	1825	R. Stephenson & Co.	Stockton-and-Darlington	254*×610/1219 *10×24/48*	1.76 *26*		5.57 *40*	6.5 *14,332*	6.5 *14,332*	1194 *47*	1194 *47*	* According to other sources 241 mm (9½ ins.). First locomotive built by Robert Stephenson & Co., called Lever or Quadrant engine
	Experiment	0-6-0	1828	R. Stephenson & Co.	Stockton-and-Darlington	229×610/1219 *9×24/48*								
22	Royal George	0-6-0	1827	Hackworth (Shildon)	Stockton-and-Darlington	279×508/1219 *11×20/48*	3.5/3.7 *51/54*	0.52 *5.6*	13.1 *141*					
23	Wilberforce	0-6-0	1833	Hackworth (Shildon)	Stockton-and-Darlington									
24	Derwent	0-6-0	1845	Kitching	Stockton-and-Darlington	368×610/... *14.5×24*								
25		0-4-0	1827	R. Stephenson & Co.	St. Etienne-Lyon	220×660/1219 *8.7×26×48*	3.5 *51.4*			9.43 *20,793*	9.43 *20,793*			
26	No. 1	0-4-0	1829	Marc Séguin	St. Etienne-Lyon	230×590/1213 *9×23/47.7*	3 *44*	0.65 *7*	22.18 *238.7*	6 *12,230*	6 *13,230*			
29,	Lancashire Witch	0-4-0	1828	R. Stephenson & Co.	Bolton-and-Leigh	223×610/1219 *9×24/48*		1.12 *12*	66	7 *15,435*	7 *15,435*	1524 *60*	1524 *60*	
31	Sanspareil	0-4-0	1829	Hackwortli	Liverpool-and-Manchester	198×483/1372 *7.8×19 */54*		0.93 *107*	8.36 *90*	4.86 *10,760*				Rainhill Contest
32,36	Rocket	2-2-0	1829	R. Stephenson & Co.	Liverpool-and-Manchester	203×432/1435 *8×17/56.5*	3.5 *51.4*	0.56 *6*	13.28 *142.9*	4.32 *9525*		2184 *86*	2184 *86*	* according to Wood Built for the Rainhill Contest. Dimensions of the original state
33	Novelty	0-4-0	1829	Braithwaite	Liverpool-and-Manchester	153×305/1270 *6×12/50*		0.17 *1.8*	3.95 *42.5*	3.09 *6,813*				Designed by Ericsson. Rainhill Contest
38	Northumbrian	2-2-0	1830	R. Stephenson & Co.	Liverpool-and-Manchester	279×406/1524 *11×16/60*	3.5 *51.4*	0.58 *6.2*	38.6 *415.3*	4 *8,820*	7.47			
39	Globe	0-4-0	1830	R. Stephenson & Co.	Stockton-and-Darlington	229×406/1524 *9×16/60*								Designed by Hackworth
	Planet	2-2-0	1830	R. Stephenson & Co.	Liverpool-and-Manchester	279×406/1524 *11×16/60*				5 *11,025*	8 *17,640*	1600 *63*		
40	Jackson	2-2-0	1835	Fenton, Murray & Jackson	Paris-Saint-Germain	280×410/1540 *11×16/60.6*		0.65 *7.0*	25.48 *274.2*	9.25 *20,396*	9.25 *20,396*	1530 *60.2*		Dimensions from French sources
41,42	Samson	0-4-0	1831	R. Stephenson & Co.	Liverpool-and-Manchester	355×406/1372 *14×16/54*		0.97 *10.4*	43.46 *467.6*	10 *22,050*	10 *22,050*			
43	Papin	0-4-0	1832	Tourasse	St. Etienne-Lyon	... /1500 *59*								Rebuilt to 0-4-2
44	Bury	2-2-0	1836	Bury	London-and-Birmingham	280×415/1546 *11×16.3/61*		0.66 *7.1*	33.07 *355.8*	5 *11,025*	10 *22,050*			Dimensions from French sources
47	Patentee Type	2-2-2	1837	R. Stephenson & Co.		279×475/1676 *11×18/66*		0.92 *9.9*	33.82 *363.9*	4.37 *9,637*	11.63 *22,644*	3048 *10*	3048 *120*	
57	Sharp Type	2-2-2	1838	Sharp		406×508/1676	5.2 *76.4*	1.17 *12.6*	85.47 *919.7*	21.5 *47,407*				Dimensions from Mathias
49	Hercules	0-4-2	1833	R. Stephenson & Co.	Stanhope-and-Tyne	356×457/1372 *14.3×18/54*			46.49 *500.2*	14 *30,870*				
50	Atlas	0-6-2	1834	R. Stephenson & Co.	Leicester-and-Swannington	406×508/1372 *16×20/4'6"*		0.95 *10*	61 *656.5*	17	17	3543 *11'7½"*	3543 *11'7½"*	

Section	Illustration	Name of Locomotive	Wheel arrangement	Year	Builder	Railroad	Driving gear	Boiler Pressure atmospheres	Grate area	Heating surface firetubes and superheater	Adhesion weight	Weight in Service	Coupled wheelbase	Total wheelbase	Remarks
	51	La Victorieuse	2-2-0	1837	R. Stephenson & Co.	Paris-Versailles (Left Bank)	380×450/1386 15×17.7/54.6	4 58.4	0.95 10.2	48.28 519.5		13 28,665	2100 82.7	3580 14.1	
4.5	53, 55	La Gironde	2-2-2	1840	Le Creusot	Paris-Versailles (Right Bank)	330×460/1670 13×18.1/65.75		1.02 11	50.48 543.2	7 15,435	15.5 34,177			
	54	L'Espérance	2-2-2	1842	J.-J. Meyer	Chemins de Fer d'Alsace	380×460/1829 15×18.1/72	5 73.5		46.6 501.4					With Meyer riding cut-off valve
5.1	58	Stevens's Demonstration Locomotive	2-2-0	1824	Colonel J. Stevens	—	82.5×368/... 3.25×14.5					0.45 992			The first locomotive in the USA
	59	Tom Thumb	2-2-0	1830	Peter Cooper	Baltimore-and-Ohio	89×356/... 3½×14								
5.2	60	The Best Friend of Charleston	0-4-0	1830	West Point Foundry	South Carolina	152×406/1371 6×16/54	3.5 51.4			4.5 9,923	4.5 9,923			First locomotive on regular service in USA
5.4	66	Atlantic	0-4-0	1832	Ross Winans	Baltimore-and-Ohio	305×559/989 12×22/39	5.2 76.4			8.5 18,743	8.5 18,743		1245 49	So-called "Grasshopper"
	67	Mazeppa	0-4-0	1837	Ross Winans	Baltimore-and-Ohio	318×610/914				8.5 18,743	8.5 18,743			So-called "Crab"
5.5	69	John Bull	0-4-0	1831	R. Stephenson & Co.	Camden-and-Amboy	229×508/1372 9×20/54		0.93 10	27.85 300	10.5 23,153	10.5 23,153	1499 59	1499 59	Later fitted with a front axle
	70	Experiment (Brother Jonathan)	4-2-0	1832	West Point Foundry	Mohawk-and-Hudson	241×406/1524 9.5×16/60					7 15,435			
	71	Martin Van Buren	4-2-0	1839	Baldwin	Philadelphia-and-Columbia	229×406/1372 9×16/54	8.4 123.5				7.5 16,538			Measurements taken from the "Lancaster" of similar type
		George Washington	4-2-0	1836	William Norris	Philadelphia-and-Columbia	260×448/1219 10.25×17.6/48	4 60			3.95 6,710	6.77 14,928	1969 77.5	2413 95	Measurements of wheelbase uncertain
	72	Washington Country Farmer	4-2-0	1836	William Norris	Philadelphia-and-Columbia	267×457/1219 10.5×18/48				5.11 11,268	8.94 19,713			
5.6	73	Campbell's Locomotive	4-4-0	1837	James Brooks, Philadelphia	Philadelphia Germantown-and-Norristown	356×406/1372 14×16/54	6.33 93		67.17 722.7	8 17,640	12 26,460			First 4-4-0 locomotive in the world
	75	Gowan & Marx	4-4-0	1840	Eastwick and Harrison	Philadelphia-and-Reading	305×406/1067 12×16/42				9 19,845	11 24,255			
	76	Virginia	4-4-0	1842	William Norris	Winchester-and-Potomac	318×508/1219 12.5×20/48				9.1 20,160	13.7 30,240			
	77		4-4-0	1846	Baldwin	Camden-and-Amboy	349×457/1524 13.7×18/60					16.8 37,000			
	78	Allegheny	4-4-0	1849	Baldwin	Pennsylvania	368×508/1372 14.5×20/54				13 28,665	22.25 49,061			
5.7	80	No. 80	0-6-0	1842	Baldwin	Central of Georgia	381×457/... 15×18								Rebuilt from a 4-2-0 with flexible beam truck
	81	(Atlas)	0-8-0	1846	Baldwin	Philadelphia-and-Reading	445×457/1066 16½×18/42				23.7 52,259	23.7 52,259			With flexible beam truck
			0-8-0		Baldwin		457×510/1016 18×20/40				32.26 71,133	32.26 71,133	5921	5921 233.1	With flexible beam truck. Dimensions of a similar locomoti[ve]
	83	Chesapeake	0-8-0	1847	Septimus Norris	Philadelphia-and-Reading	368×559/1168 14.5×22/46				14.5 31,973	19.98 44,056			
	84	Monster	0-8-0	either 1834	Robert Stevens and Isaac Dripps	Camden-and-Amboy	457×762/1219 18×30/48				27.6 60,858	27.6 60,858			
6.1	87	North Star	2-2-2	1837	R. Stephenson & Co.	Great Western	406×406/2438 16×16/96		1.25 13.5	66.05 710.7		21 46,305		4064 160	Built for the 7-foot gauge
		Great Western	2-2-2	1846	Gooch, Swindon	Great Western	457×610/2438 18×24/102.9	7 102.9	2.1 22.6	151 1624.7		29 63,945			Built for the 7-foot gauge
	88	Lord of the Isles	4-2-2	1851	Gooch, Swindon	Great Western	457×610/2438 18×24/96	7 102.9	2.0 21.5	166.29 1789.3	27,552	79,520			
		Waverley Class	4-4-0	1855	Gooch, Swindon and R. Stephenson & Co.	Great Western	432×610/2133 17×24/84		1.78 19.2	146.2 1574	21.95 46,525	27.24 80,813			
6.2		No. 30 Montgolfier	2-2-2	1843	R. Stephenson and Meyer, Alsace	Paris-and-Orleans	355×510/1720 14×20/67.7	6 88.2	0.35 3.8	68.39 735.9	7.55 16,648	18.7 41234		3338 131.4	Inside connected
	93	No. 5 Sézanne	2-2-2	1847	Hallette	Montereau-Troyes	340×550/1640 13.4×21.65/66.5	6 88.2	0.36 3.9	62.9 1676.8	8.37 18,456	21.1 46,526		2010 79	Outside connected. Later No. 29 of the French Est Railroad
	94	La Tarasque	4-2-0	1846	Le Benet	Avignon-Marseille	380×560/1650 15×22/65				12.7 28,003	27.0 59,535		4050 159.4	Later No. 192 of the French PLM Railroad
	86	Ixion (Firefly Class)	2-2-2	1840-1842		Great Western	381×457/2134 15×18/84		1.21 13	55.93 601.8		21.0 46,305			7-foot gauge
		Great A	4-2-0	1845	R. Stephenson & Co.	York and North Midland	381×610/2007 15×24/69		0.89 9.6	77.18 830.4		23.88 52,655			
6.3	96	Namur	4-2-0	1845	Tulk and Ley (Crampton)	Namur-Liège	406×508/2134 16×20/84	6 88.2	1.35 14.5	91.88 988.6	10.5 23,153	22.0 48,510	—	3962 156	First Crampton locomotive. Later No. 81 of the South-Eastern Railroad
	98	Liverpool	6-2-0	1848	Bury, Curtis and Kennedy	London and North Western (Southern part)	457×610/2438 18×24/96	8.4 123.5	2.0 21.5	212.74 2289	12.2 26,901	35.56 78,410	—	5639 222	
	86	Iron Duke	4-2-2	1847	Gooch	Great Western	457×610/2438 18×24/96	7 102.9	2.1 22.6	151.02 1625		21.0 46,305	—		7-foot broad gauge cf. Ill. 86 (bottom row, centre)
	99	Folkestone	4-2-0	1851	R. Stephenson & Co.	South Eastern	381×560/1830 15×22/72	6 88.2	1.3 14	107.11 1152.5	10.2 22,491	26.7 58,874	—	4871 191.8	Inside connected with countershaft
		Series 122-133	4-2-0	1839	Cail	French Nord	400×500/2100 15.75×19.7/82.7	6.5 95.6	1.42 15.3	98.4 1058.8	12.6 27,783	28.9 63,725	—	4860 191.3	

Section	Illustration	Name of Locomotive	Wheel arrangement	Year	Builder	Railroad	Driving gear	Boiler Pressure atmospheres	Grate area	Heating surface firetubes and superheater	Adhesion weight	Weight in Service	Coupled wheelbase	Total wheelbase	Remarks
	100	Series 134-145	4-2-0	1853	Cail	French Nord	420×560/2300 16.5×22/90.5	7.5 110.3	1.27 13.7	95.63 1029	12.6 27,783	29.8 65,709	— —	4500 177	
		Series 501-510	2-4-0	1878	Epernay Railroad Works	French Est	440×640/2310 17.3×25.2/91	10 147	1.73 18.6	100 1076	28.66 61,196	41.84 92,257	2500 98.4	5350 210.6	
		Series 543-562	2-4-0	1884	Epernay Railroad Works	French Est	440×610/2100 17.3×24/82.7	10 147	2.4 25.8	115.46 1242.3	28.9 63,725	42.8 94,374	2500 98.4	5350 210.6	
		Baude (Series 12-19)	4-2-0	1852	Wöhlert	Prussian Eastern	381×508/1982 15×20/78	6 88.2	1.07 11.5	78.6 845.7	9.6 21,168	24.9 54,905	—	4499 177	With inside cylinders and countershaft
		Die Pfalz	4-2-0	1853	Maffei	Bavarian Palatinate	381×610/1830 15×24/72	7.23 106.3	0.98 10.5	79.83 859	10.5 23,153	27.25 60,086	—	3960 156	
	103	Pölnitz	4-2-0	1863	Esslingen (Kessler)	Bavarian Palatinate	356×610/1830 14×24/72	6.3 92.6	0.98 10.5	68.6 738.1	9.2 20,286	24.2 53,361	—	3962 156	
	104	Series 69-76	4-2-0	1854	Karlsruhe	Baden State	405×560/2130 16×22/83.9	7 102.9	1.07 11.5	81.79 880		28.5 62,843	—	4380 172.4	With leading truck
	105		4-2-2	1849	Baldwin	Pennsylvania	356×508/1829 14×20/72				8.2 68,081	21.3 46,967	—		With four-wheel leading truck
4	106	No. 28 John Stevens	6-2-0	1849	Richard Norris	Camden-and-Amboy	356×965/2438 14×38/96		1.86 20			25 55,125	—	5050 199	Designed by Dripps with six-wheel leading truck
	108	La Hyène	2-4-0	1846	Le Creusot	French Centre	380×600/1600 15×23.6/63	6 88.2	0.84 9	75.05 812.4	16.8 37,044	22.7 50,054	3130 123.2	3130 123.2	Later PO Series 345-359
	109	Herford	2-4-0	1866	Haswell	Cologne-and-Minden	457×610/1581 18×24/62.2	8 117.6	1.58 17	120.11 1292.4	26.15 57,683	34.75 76,624	3308 130.2	3308 130.2	
	110	Series 201-212	2-4-0	1864	Ivry	Paris-and-Orleans	420×650/2026 16.5×25.6/79.8	8.5 125	1.4 15	136 1463.4	29.8 65,709	34.0 74,970	2100 82.6	4000 157.5	Designed by Forquenot, later rebuilt as 2-4-2
	111	No. 246	0-6-0	1858	E. B. Wilson	Madrid-Zaragoza-Alicante	440×600/1430 17.3×23.6/56.3	8 117.6	1.32 14.2	111.13 1196	28.24 62,269	28.24 62,269	3430 135	3430 135	
		Series 1513-1532	0-6-0	1857	Parent-Shaken	French PLM	450×650/1300 17.7×25.6/51.2	10 147	1.34 14.4	115.91 1247.2	35.38 78,013	35.38 78,013	3370 132.7	3370 132.7	Bourbonnais type
	114	Series 0.401-426	0-6-0	1867	Epernay	French Est	440×660/1400 17.3×26/55.1	8 117.6	1.31 14	121.05 1302.5	33 72,765	33 72,765	3580 141	3580 141	Ardennes type
	113	Albmaschine	0-6-0	1848	Esslingen	Württemberg State	447×612/1230 17.6×24.1/48.4	7 1092.9	0.9 9.7	97.0 1043.7	33.5 73,868	33.5 73,868	3210 126.4	3210 126.4	Built for the Geislingen incline, Württemberg
	115	Simplon	0-6-0	1865	Borsig	Cologne-and-Minden	482×610/1372 18.9×24/54	8 117.6	1.43 15.4	123.6 1330	40.8 89,964	40.8 89,964	3296 129.8	3296 129.8	
	112		0-6-0	1885	Vulkan Stettin	Lérida-Reus-Tarragona	460×600/1500 18.1×23.6/59	9 132.3	2.06 22.2	139.4 1500	39.7 85,539	39.7 85,539	3600 141.7	3600 141.7	Spanish Norte No. 1481-1482
1	119	Jenny Lind	2-2-2		E. B. Wilson	London, Brighton and South Coast	381×508/1829 15×20/72	8.4 123.5	1.13 12.2	74.32 799.7	8.7 19,184	24.4 53,802		4115 162	
	116	Several Nos.	2-2-2	1868		Great Northern	470×660/2286 18.5×26/70	11.2 164.6	1.72 18.5	97.08 1044.6	17.68 38,984	41.3 91,067		5816 229	Stirling design
	117	Lüneburg	2-2-2	1853	Egestorff	Brunswick State	381×559/1830 15×22/72	7 102.9	1.19 12.8	91.24 981.7	12.8 28,224	27.7 61,079		4467 175.8	
	118	Series 247-256 Bloomer	2-2-2	1851	Sharp	London and North Western (Southern section)	406×559/2134 16×22/84	10.5 154.4		134.57 1448	12.55 27,673	30.99 68,333			McConnell design
	120	Class DX	0-6-0	1855	Crewe	LNWR	432×610/1575 17×24/62	8.4 123.5	1.39 15	102.9 1107.2	27.4 60,417	27.4 60,417		4724 186	Ramsbottom design
2	123	Vauxhall	2-2-0	1834	Forrester	Liverpool-and-Manchester	279×457/1524 11×18/60			24 258.2					Similar dimensions found on a locomotive of the Dublin-Kingston Railroad
		Allan-Crewe Type	2-2-2	1843	Crewe	LNWR	381×508/1524 15×20/60		1.0 10.76	70 753.2	14 30,870	20 44,100			Allan design
	124	Allan-Crewe Type	2-4-0	1843	Crewe	LNWR	391×610/1524 15.4×24/60		1.0 10.76	70 753.2	13.97 30,804	19.61 43,240	2235 88	8861 348.8	
	125	Sky Bogies Type	4-4-0	1884		Highland	457×610/1600 18×24/63		1.50 16.14	112.97 1215.6			2667 105	6554 258	Jones design
	126	Nos. 1-40	2-2-2	1843	Buddicom & Allcard	Paris-Rouen	318×533/1600 12.5×21/63		0.86 9.3	48.52 522	7.0 15,435	14.5 31,973		3377 133	Later Ouest Railroad Nos. 101-140
	127	Series 17-50	2-2-2	1846	Hallette Cail	French Nord	360×560/1680 14.1×22/66.1	6.5 95.6	0.91 9.8	75.5 812.4	11.2 24,696	23.82 52,523		3190 125.6	Clapeyron design. Wheelbase enlarged to 4,600 mm.
3	128	Series 153-157	2-4-0	1850	Ivry	French PO	440×600/1500 17.3×23.6/59	7 102.9	0.99 10.7	103.98 1118.8	18.98 41,851	26.22 57,815			Polonceau design
	129	Series 658-719	0-6-0	1854	Ivry	French PO	420×600/1350 16.5×25.6/53.1	8 1176	1.1 11.84	89.47 962.7	25.98 57,286	25.98 57,286		4200 165.3	Polonceau design
		Series 720-791	0-6-0	1856	Ivry	French PO	420×650/1350 16.5×25.6/53.5	8 117.6	1.21 13	130.71 1406.4	30.54 67,341	30.54 67,341		3560 140	Polonceau design
		Series 369-380	2-4-0	1857	Gouin	French Ouest	420×560/1910 16.5×22/75	9.5 139.7	1.24 13.3	110.2 1185.7	20.83 45,930	28.73 45,930	2030 80	3750 147.6	Polonceau type. Overhanging firebox
		Series 707-743	2-4-0	1877		French Ouest	420×600/1930 16.5×23.6/76	9 132.3	1.75 18.8	92.0 989.9	24.9 54,905	36 79,380	2250 88.5	4400 173.2	Supported firebox
	131	Series 636-706	2-4-0	1880		French Ouest	430×600/2040 16.9×23.6/80.3	9 132.3	1.64 17.6	107 1151.3	29.0 63,945	22.5 49,613	2300 90.5	4650 183	Supported firebox
		Series 621-623	2-4-0	1886		French Ouest	430×600/2010 16.9×23.6/79.1	10 147	1.64 17.6	118.35 1273.4	27.9 61,520	40.1 88,421	2700 106.2	5050 198.8	Firebox hung between rear axles
4	133		2-2-2	1836	Forrester	Grand Junction	279×457/1524 11×18/60	3.5 51.5		29 312					

Section	Illustration	Name of Locomotive	Wheel arrangement	Year	Builder	Railroad	Driving gear	Boiler Pressure atmospheres	Grate area	Heating surface firetubes and superheater	Weight — Adhesion weight	Weight — Weight in Service	Wheelbase — Coupled wheelbase	Wheelbase — Total wheelbase	Remarks
	134	Group A V	2-2-2	1853	Maffei	Bavarian State	381×554/1676 15×22/66	7 102.9	1.07 11.5	63.7 685.4	9 19,845	22 48,510		3506 138	First Hall type
	136	Series 467-539	2-4-0	1859	Various	Austrian Southern	411×632/1500 16×24.9/59	6.5 95.6	1.38 14.8	180 1936.8	22.5 49613	32.55 71,773		3477 137	
	137	Series 29	0-6-0	1860	Various	Austrian Southern (Graz-Köflach)	429×632/1245 16.5×24.9/49	9 132.3	1.54 17.1	128.5 1382.7	38 83790	38 83,790	2950 116.1	2950 116.1	
	138	Series 445-453	2-4-0	1869	Schwartzkopff	Lower Silesian-March	445×524/1846 17.5×20.6/72.6	10 147	1.47 15.8	107.15 1152.9	25.04 55,213	38.58 85,069	2485 97.8	4525 178.1	Wöhler design
7.5	143	"Kleine Gloggnitzer"	4-4-0	1848	Haswell	Vienna-Gloggnitz	368×579/1422 14.5×22.7/56	5.5 80.9	0.94 10.1	70.6 759.7	15 33,075	22.7 50,054		3872 152.4	
		"Grosse Gloggnitzer"	4-4-0	1845	Haswell	Vienna-Gloggnitz	402×579/1264 15.8×22.8/49.7	5.5 80.9	1.00 10.76	90.6 974.9	15 33,075	21.3 46,967		3818 150.3	
	142	Pribram	4-4-0	1852	Cockerill	Northern State	382×610/1738 15×24/68.4	6.33 93	1.00 10.76	74.79 804.7	15.4 38957	28.1 61,961		5258 207	
	144	Rhein and Reuss Nos. 3 and 4	4-4-0	1847	Karlsruhe (Kessler)	Swiss Northern	362×559/1320 14.25×22/52	6 88.2	0.80 8.6	57.1 614.4	10,0 22,050	10,0 22,050		4451 175.2	
	146	Limmat No. 1	4-2-0	1847	Karlsruhe (Kessler)	Zurich-Baden (Swiss Northern)	362×559/1320 14.25×22/52	6 88.2	0,9 9.6	9 616.5	19,845			2800 110.2	First locomotive in Switzerland
	145	Einkorn Class E	4-4-0	1856	Esslingen	Württemberg State	410×610/1218 16.1×24/47.9	8 117.6	1.63 11.1	85.12 915.9	19.5 23,358	29.6 65,268		5070 199.6	
7.6	147	Borsig	4-2-2	1841	Borsig	Berlin-and-Anhalt	292×457/1372 11.5×18/54	4.4 64.7	0.85 9.1	30.3 326	9.62 21,212	19.2 42,336		4200 165.3	
	148	Beuth	2-2-2	1844	Borsig	Berlin-and-Anhalt	330×558/1525 13×22/60	5.5 80.9	0.83 8.9	46.6 501.4	9.1 20,066	18.5 40,793		3813 150.1	
	150	Oker	2-2-2	1869	Richard Hartmann	Cologne and Minden	381×508/1676 15×20/66	8 117.6	0.9 9.7	84.61 910.4	12.8 28,224	31.9 70,340		4708 185.3	
	152	Perraches Nos. 1-45	2-2-2	1847	Cail	Paris-Lyon	380×600/1800 15×23.6/70.8	6 (8) 88.2 (117.6)	0.92 9.9	79.0 850	11.3 24,917	25.3 55,917		4015 158	Later PLM Nos. 101-145
	151	Problem or Lady of the Lake Class	2-2-2	1859	Crewe	LNWR	406×610/2324 16×24/91.5	8.4 123.5	1.39 15	102 1097.5	11.68 25,754	27.4 60,417		4674 184	Ramsbottom design
	153	Canute Class	2-2-2	1855	Nine Elms	LSWR	381×533/1981 15×21/78		1.49 16	71.44 768.7	9.6 21,168	28.91 63,747			
7.7	154	901 Class	2-4-0	1872	Gateshead	North Eastern	432×610/2134 17×24/84	9.8 144	1.5 16.1	111.56 1200.4	27.5 60,638	40.08 88,376		4902 193	
	155	Precedent Class	2-4-0	1874	Crewe	LNWR	432×610/2019 17×24/79.5	9.8 144	1.59 17.1	100.65 1083	22.86 50,406	32.87 72,478		4774 188	Webb design
	156	Flieger Class	2-4-0	1871	Borsig and Hartmann	Cologne-and-Minden	420×508/1981 16.5×20/78	10 147	1.57 16.9	124.43 1339	26.0 57.330	42.0 92,610	2500 98.4	5690 224	
		Group P3	2-4-0	1884	Several works	Prussian State	400×560/1730 15.75×22/68.1	12 176.4	1.85 19.9	95.35 1026	25.66 56,580	36.78 81,100	36.78 98.4	2500 117.6	So-called Standard locomotive
	157	Type S1	2-4-0		Schichau and others	Prussian State	420×600/1980 16.5×23.6/77.9	12 176.4	2.07 22.3	93.95 1010.9	27.6 60,858	41.3 91,067	2000 78.74	4500 177.6	
		Rhône Type	0-4-2	1851	Gouin	Paris-Lyon	420×560/1850 16.5×22/72.8	8.5 125	1.25 13.5	78.9 849	20.76 35,753	25.45 56,117	2215 87.2	4230 166.5	Later PLM Nos. 301-303 and 351-367
	159	Series 2451-2551	0-4-2		Fives-Lille	French Nord	420×560/1800 16.5×22/70.8	8 117.6	1.52 16.4	82.37 886.3	23.0 50,715	32.4 71,442	2150 84.6	4400 173.2	
	161	Gladstone Class Nos. 172-220	0-4-2	1882		London, Brighton and South Coast	464×660/1981 18.2×26/78	10.5 154.4	1.91 20.6	137.99 1484.8		39.32 86,701		4750 187	Stroudley design
	162	Pluto	0-4-2	1865	Borsig	Berlin-Hamburg	406×560/1516 16×22/59.7	8 117.6	1.48 15.9	80.5 866.2	30.1 66,371	34.95 77,065		4472 176	
8.1	164	South Port	4-4-0	1857	Danforth Cooke & Co.	Delaware, Lackawanna and Western	432×559/1676 17×22/66		1.71 18.4				3134 123.4	4956 195.1	1829 mm (72 in.) gauge
	166	No. 24	4-4-0	1885	Rogers	New York, West Shore and Buffalo	457×610/1727 18×24/68	9.8 144	1.58 17	112.59 1211.5	28.25 62,291	43.47 95,851	2591 102	6944 273.4	
	165	No. 111	4-4-0	1880	Reading	Philadelphia-and-Reading	533×559/1727 21×22/68	8.4 123.5	7.0 75.3	103.77 1116.6	29.14 64,254	43.64 96,226		6426 253	Wootten firebox
	168	Class P	4-4-0	1880		Pennsylvania	470×610/1727 18.5×24/68	9.8 144	3.22 34.6	142.14 1529.4	30.8 67,914	45.6 100,548	2362 93	6921 272.5	
	169	Class L	4-4-0	1895		Pennsylvania	470×660/2032 18.5×26/80	13 191.1	2.99 32.2	176.1 1894.8	42.64 94021	61.01 134,527	2362 93	6934 273	
	170	Rogers Normal Type	2-6-0	1880s	Rogers	Several railroads	406×610/1219 16×24/48				25.85 56,999	31.75 70,009	4521 178	6807 268	Smallest version
			2-6-0	1880s	Rogers	Several railroads	508×610/1372 20×24/54				35.56 78,410	44.61 98,365	4724 186	7061 278	Largest version
	171	Class R (H3)	2-8-0	1885		Pennsylvania	508×610/1270 20×24/50	9.8 144	2.9 31.2	160.9 1731.3	45.63 100614	51.99 114,637	4216 166	6629 261	
	173	Champion	4-8-0	1882	Weatherley	Lehigh Valley	508×660/1219 20×26/48	8.8 129.4			37.39 82,445	46.13 101,717	3972 156.4	7061 278	Hofecker design
	174	El Gobernador	4-10-0	1884	Sacramento	Central Pacific	533×660/1448 21×26/57				67 147,735			7607 229.5	
		No. 100	4-8-0	1898	Brooks	Great Northern	533×863/1397 21×34/55	14.8 217.6	3.36 36.6	307.31 3306.7	78.02 172,034	96.53 212,849	4826 190	8128 320	
	177	Pennsylvania	0-12-0	1863	Reading	Philadelphia-and-Reading	508×660/1092 20×26/43		2.9 31.2	130 1399	50 110,250	50 110,250	5969 235	5969 235	Tank locomotive, Milholland design, first 0-12-0 in the world rebuilt in 1870

Illustration	Name of Locomotive	Wheel arrangement	Year	Builder	Railroad	Driving gear	Boiler Pressure atmospheres	Grate area	Heating surface firetubes and superheater	Adhesion weight	Weight in Service	Coupled wheelbase	Total wheelbase	Remarks
179	Bavaria *	0-4-4-4	1851	Maffei	Semmering Contest *	529 × 764/1080 20 × 30/42.5	6.8 100	1.30 14	157.54 1695.1	44 97,020	44 97,020	6335 249.4	11,992 472 With Tender	
180	Wiener Neustadt *	6-4-4-4	1851	W. Günther	Semmering Contest *	4 × 329 × 632/1120 4 × 13 × 24.9/44	6.8 100	1.66 17.9	175.12 1884.3	44	44 97,020	2 × 2312 2 × 91	8159 321.2	Tank locomotive 9.7 m³ water 3 m³ coal
181	Seraing *	0-4-4-0	1851	Cockerill	Semmering Contest *	4 × 407 × 711/1049 4 × 16 × 28/41.3	5.8 85.3	2 × 1.0 2 × 10.76	2 × 170.95 =341.9 2 × 1839.4 =3678.8	49.45 109,037	49.45 109,037	2 × 2134 2 × 84	82.04 323	Tank locomotive with additional four-wheeled tender
182	Vindobona *	0-4-0	1851	Haswell	Semmering Contest *	421 × 580/957 16.6 × 22.8/37.7	6.8 100	1.45 15.6	159.44 1715.6	45.5 100,328	45.5 100,328	24742 186.7	4742 186.7	
183	Engerth locomotive	0-6-2-0	1853	Esslingen and Cockerill	Semmering (Austrian Southern)	475 × 610/1068 18.7 × 24/42	7.4 108.8	1.28 13.8	140.5 1511.8	390 85,995	56.0 123,480	2292 90.2	5997 236	Later with tender
184	Series 401-436	0-4-0+6	1856	Esslingen (Kessler)	French Nord	420 × 560/1739 16.5 × 22/68.4	8 117.6	1.35 14.5	125.5 1350.4	21.66 47,760	47.66 105,090	2700 106.3	8000 315	
185	Basel	0-4-0+6	1854	Esslingen (Kessler)	Swiss Central	408 × 561/1375 16 × 22/54	9 132.3	0.9 9.7	100.9 1085.7	26 57,330	45 99,225	2250 88.6	6525 257	
187	Series 360-399 (4361-4400)	0-8-0+4	1855	Le Creusot	French Nord	500 × 660/1258 19.7 × 26/49.5	8 117.6	1.94 20.9	197 2119.7	42.3 93,272	62.8 138,474	3950 155.5	8700 342.5	Four-wheel tender; Water 8.3 m³ Coal 2.0 m³
188	Series 4001	0-4-0	1868	Grafenstaden and others	French PLM	540 × 660/1260 21.25 × 26/49.6	9(10) 132.3 (147)	2.08 22.4	199.48 2146.4	51.7 113,999	51.7 113,999	4050 159.4	4050 159.4	
189, 190	La Rampe	0-4-0+6	1859	Koechlin	Marseille-Lyon	540 × 560/1200 21.26 × 22/47.2	3 102.7	1.89 20.3	172.93 1860.7	47.3 104,297	70.85 156,224	3900 153.5	9600 378	Beugniot design PLM No. 1998
191	Steierdorf	0-6-4-0	1862		Jassenova, Oravicza and Steierdorf	461 × 632/1000 18.1 × 24.9/39.4	7 102.7	1.44 15.5	121.5 1307.3	42.5 93,712	42.5 93,712	10500 413.4	10500 413.4	Fink and Engerth design
192	Group F1	0-6-0	1894	Esslingen	Württemberg State	450 × 612/1380 17.7 × 24/54.3	14 205.8	1.40 15	116.7 1255.7	41.6 91,728	41.6	5000 196,8	5000 196,8	Klose design
193	Class T15	0-6-4-0		Henschel	Prussian State	520 × 660/1200 20 × 24.8/47.2	12 176.4	2.37 25.5	137.4 1478.4	69.81 153,931	6860	6981 270	6860 270	Hagans type
194	Wien Raab	0-8-0	1855	Haswell	Vienna-Raab *	461 × 632/1185 18.1 × 24.9/46.6	7.3 107.3	1.2 12.9	86.76 933.5	34.72 76,558	34.72	3815 150.2		First European eight-coupled locomotive Later State Railroad Co
195	Series 73	0-8-0	1885	Floridsdorf	Austrian State	500 × 570/1100 19.7 × 22.4/43.3	11 161.7	2.25 24.2	163.8 1762.5	55.1 121,495	55.1	3900 153.5	3900 153.5	
	Series 34	0-8-0	1867	Haswell	Austrian Southern	500 × 610/1070 19.7 × 24/42.1	8 117.6	1.84 19.8	181.8 1956.2	47.3 104,297	47.3	3450 135.8	3450 135.8	Outer frames
196	Series 2501-2537	0-8-0	1864	Le Creusot	Spanish Norte	500 × 660/1300 19.7 × 26/51.1	8 117.6	1.88 20.2	165.6 1781.9	43.5 95,918	43.5	4130 162.6	4130 162.6	1674 mm (66 ins.) gauge
199	Series 91-102	0-8-0	1865	Avonside	Zaragoza-Barcelona *	483 × 611/1294 19 × 24/51	8 117.6	2.34 25.2	128.4 1381.6	43.3 95,477	43.3	4440 174.8	4440 174.8	1674 mm (66 ins.) gauge. Later Spanish Norte 2571-2582
198	Series 213-226	0-8-0	1878	Sharp	Tarragona-Barcelona-Francia	508 × 660/1388 20 × 26/52.7	8 117.6	2.61 28.1	137.14 1475.6	47.69 105,156	47.69	4615 181.7	4615 181.7	1674 mm (66 ins.) gauge. Madrid-Zaragoza-Alicante, 562-575
	Class T Nos. 2116-2225	0-8-0	1901	Gateshead	North Eastern	508 × 660/1403 20 × 26/55.2	12.3 180.8	2.0 21.5	155.61 1674.3	59.23 130,602	59.23	5232 206	5232 206	William Worsdall design
	Class G7	0-8-0	1893	Several locomotive works	Prussian State	520 × 630/1250 20.5 × 24.8/49.2	12.0 176.4	2.25 24.2	144.15 1551.1	51.65 113,888	51.65	4500 177.2	4500 177.2	First batches
201	Class K Nos. 401-455	0-8-0	1901	Doncaster	Great Northern	502 × 660/1410 19.8 × 26/55.5	12.3 180.8	12.28 132.1	129.93 1398	55.5 122,378	55.5	5385 212	5385 212	Inside connected. Iraff design. First batch
197	Class D4/4 Nos. 101-127	0-8-0	1882	Maffei and SLM, Winterthur	Gotthard	520 × 610/1170 20.5 × 24/46	10 147	2.1 22.6	158 1700	52.8 116,424	52.8	3900 153.5	3900 153.5	
202	Series 566-577 *Machines Uniques*	0-8-0	1862	Gouin	French Nord	480 × 480/1065 18.9 × 18.9/41.9	8.5 125	2.61 28.1	152.9 +12.98 1645.2 +139.7	43.2 95,256	43.2	3800 149.6	3800 149.6	Petiet design Tank engine 5.8 m³ water 2 t. coal
203	Series 601-610 (Colossus)	0-6-6-0	1862	Gouin	French Nord	4 × 440 × 440/1065 4 × 17.3 × 17.3/41.9	9 132.3	3.33 35.8	199.9 +22 2150.9 +236.7	59.7 131,639	59.7	2 × 2280 2 × 89.8	6000 236.2	Petiet design Tank engine 8.0 m³ water 2.2 t coal
204	No. 1201-1203 (2201-2203, Cantal)	0-10-0	1867	Ivry	French PO	500 × 600/1070 19.7 × 23.6/42.1	9 132.3	2.07 22.3	228 2453	60 132,300	60 132,300	4532 178.4	4532 178.4	Forquenot design Tank engine 5.4 m³ water 1.5 t coal
205	Rauhenstein	4-4-0	1857	STEG	Austrian Southern State	395 × 580/1580 15.6 × 22.8/62.2	6.5 95.6	1.1 11.8	94 1011		31 68,355			
	Grimming	4-4-0	1871	Sigl, Wiener Neustadt	Crown Prince Rudolf	435 × 630/1710 17.1 × 24.8/67.3	9 132.3	1.68 18.1	111.6 1200.8	25 55,125	41.5 91,508	2400 94.5	5800 228.3	1700● 67 Kamper design
207	Series 27-34	4-4-0	1863	Beyer-Peacock	Tudela-Bilbao	407 × 610/1524 16 × 24/60	7 102.9	1.37 14.7	87.64 943	26.4 58,212	38.4 84,672	2438 96	5486 216	1024● 40.3 1674 mm (66 ins.) gauge Tank engine Later Spanish Norte 27-34
208	Corsair	4-4-0	1854	Swindon and Hawthorn	South Devon	422 × 610/ 16.6 × 24	123.5				39.1 86,216		5537 218	1524● 60 7-foot gauge, tank engine Gooch design
209	Series 9-14	4-4-0	1859	Slaughter & Grunning	Barcelona-Granollers	420 × 560/1920 16.5 × 22/75.6	10 147	1.35 14.5	95.52 1027.8	22.6 49,833	36.2	2660 104.7	5930 233.5	1370● 54 1674 mm (66 ins.) gauge Dimensions of replaced boiler. Later Madrid-Zaragoza-Alicante 23-28

* these dimensions are reckoned according to Adalbert von Schmidt (1852).

● Dimensions of truck wheelbases.

Section	Illustration	Name of Locomotive	Wheel arrangement	Year	Builder	Railroad	Driving gear	Boiler Pressure atmospheres	Grate area	Heating surface firetubes and superheater	Adhesion weight	Weight in Service	Coupled wheelbase	Total wheelbase	Remarks
	210	Nos. 771-778	4-2-2	1884		Great Northern	$457 \times 711/2464$ $18 \times 28/97$	11.3 166.1	1.64 17.6	108.23 1164.6	15.24 33,604	39.06 86,127		6985 275	Stirling design
	206	245 Class	4-2-2	1871	Dübs	Great Eastern	$457 \times 610/2286$ $18 \times 24/90$	9.8 144	1.59 17.1	112 1205.1	15.34 33,825	42.32 93,316		7036 277	2134 ● Bromley design 84
	211		4-4-0	1910	Stoke Works	North Staffordshire	$470 \times 660/1829$ $18.5 \times 26/72$	12.3 180.8	1.95 21	113.8 1224.5	32.5 71,663	48.8 107,604	2896 114	7049 277.5	1753 ● J. H. Adams design 69
	212	Rittinger	4-4-0	1872	Sigl, Wiener Neustadt	Austrian North-Western	$411 \times 632/1900$ $16.2 \times 24.9/74.8$	10 147	1.64 17.6	107.6 1157.8	23.1 50,936	39.5 87,098	2400 94.5	5370 211.4	1320 ● 52
	213	Series 4	4-4-0	1885	Sigl, Wiener Neustadt	Austrian State	$435 \times 630/1810$ $17.1 \times 24.8/71.25$	11 161.7	2.06 22.2	127.04 136.7	26.5 58,433	44.5 98,123		5900 232.3	1700 ● 67
	215	Romont Series 1-12	4-4-0	1861	Esslingen (Kessler)	Fribourg-Lausanne	$410 \times 612/1374$ $16.1 \times 24/54$	8 117.6	1.2 12.9	103.8 1116.9	27 59,535	41 90,405		6090 239.8	Tank engine 4.0 m³ wate 2.7 t. coal Later Jura-Simplon, 251-262
	214	Giovanna d'Arco	4-4-0	1889	Turin	Mediterraneo	$450 \times 620/2100$ $17.7 \times 24.4/82.7$	11 161.7	2.26 24.3	110.64 1190.5	31.8 70,119	48.6 107,163	2600 102.3	6800 267.7	2000 ● Frescot design. Later 78.74 FS Group 560
	216	Vittorio Emmanuele II	2-6-0	1884	Turin	Mediterraneo (Alta Italia)	$470 \times 620/1675$ $18.5 \times 24.4/65.9$	10 147	2.2 23.6	124 1334.2	37.5 82,688	53.0 116,865	3760 148	7260 285.8	1200 ● Frescot design. Later F 47.2 Group 650
	217	Nos. 2861-2911 Outrances	4-4-0	1877	Alsace Locomotive Works, Belfort	French Nord	$432 \times 610/2130$ $17 \times 24/83.8$	10 177	2.31 24.9	100 1076	26.9 59,315	43.2 95,256	2500 98.4	6230 245.3	1800 ● Engines with differing 70.9 cylinder diameters
	219	Series 801-840	4-4-0	1890		French Est	$470 \times 660/2130$ $18.5 \times 26/83.9$	12 176.4	2.42 26	168.3 1810.9	33.4 73,647	56.77 125,177	3000 118.1	7450 293.3	1900 ● Flaman boiler 74.8
10.3	218	Series 111-400	2-4-2	1879	Several locomotive works	PLM	$500 \times 600/2000$ $19.7 \times 23.6/78.7$	10 (11) 147 (161.7)	2.22 25	142.5 1533.3	28.8 63,504	52.4 115,542	2100 82.7	5800 228.3	Subsequently modified various times
	220	Weipert	2-4-0	1872	Hartmann	Saxon State	$381 \times 559/1390$ $15 \times 22/54.7$	8.5 125	1.13 12.2	88.9 956.6	27.14 59,844	35.52 78,322		357.5 140.7	Novotny radial axle
	221	Series 12	2-4-2	1888	Cockerill	Belgian State	$500 \times 600/2100$ $19.7 \times 23.6/82.7$	10 147	4.71 50.7	124.68 1341.8	26.35 98,102	42.2 93,051	2165 85.2	6565 258.5	
	222	Group IX V	2-8-0	1902	Hartmann	Saxon State	$\frac{530}{770} \times 630/1240$ $\frac{28.9}{30.3} \times 24.8/48.8$	14 205.8	3.17 34.1	180.48 +16.40 1942 +176.5	62.4 137,592	72.0 158,760	5460 (rigid) 2860 215	7760 306	Klien-Lindner hollow radial axles
10.4	224	Group D XII	2-4-4	1897	Krauss	Bavarian State	$450 \times 560/1640$ $17.7 \times 22/64.6$	13.1 191.1	1.96	107.0 1151.3	28.8 63,504	69.0 152,145	2050 80.7	8000 315	Krauss-Helmholtz truck
	225	Series 50-63	2-6-0+2	1920	Krauss	Spanish Vascongados	$450 \times 600/1300$ $17.7 \times 23.6/51.2$	12 176.4	2.0	103.6 +32.5 1114.7 +349.7	37.0 81,585	45.0 99,225	2800 110.2	9760 384.3	1 metre gauge
11.1.1	227	Anglet	0-4-2	1873	Le Creusot	Bayonne-Biarritz	$\frac{240}{400} \times 450/1200$ $\frac{9.4}{15.75} \times 17.7/47.2$	10 147	1.0 10.76	45.1 485.3	15.2 33,516	19.3 42,556	1300 51.2	2700 106.3	First successful compound locomotive in the world, Mallet design. Tank locomotive
	226	Hanover 83-84	2-2-0	1880	Schichau	Prussian State	$\frac{200}{300} \times 400/1130$ $\frac{7.9}{11.8} \times 15.75/44.5$	12 176.4	0.52 5.6	22.79 245.2	9.7 21,389	18.2 40,131		4000 157.5	First compound locomotive in Germany, Von Borries design. Vankengine
		Hanover 1121-22 Group G3	0-6-0	1882	Henschel	Prussian State	$\frac{460}{65.0} \times 630/1330$ $\frac{18.1}{25.6} \times 24.8/52.3$	12 176.4	1.53 15.5	118.8 1278.3	38.5 24,893	38.5	3400 133.9	3400 133.9	Von Borries type
	228	Group P3²	2-4-0	1895	Several locomotive works	Prussian State	$\frac{440}{630} \times 580/1750$ $\frac{17.3}{24.8} \times 22.8/68.9$	12 176.4	1.92 20.7	98.73 1062.3	27.3 60,197	41.1 90,626	2300 90.6	5000 196.9	Last batch, Von Borries type
	229	Group S3	4-4-0	1893	Hanomag and several others	Prussian State	$\frac{460}{680} \times 600/1980$ $\frac{18.1}{26.8} \times 23.6/78$	12 176.4	2.23 24	118 1269.7	30.4 67,032	50.5 111,353	2600 102.4	7400 291.3	Last batch, Von Borries type
	230	Series 6	4-4-0	1893	Floridsdorf	Austrian State	$\frac{500}{740} \times 680/2100$ $\frac{19.72}{29.1} \times 26.8/82.7$	13 191.1	2.70 29	140 1506.4	28.8 63,504	55.4 122,157	2800 287.4	2700 106.3	Gölsdorf design
	232	Series 170	2-8-0	1897	Sigl, Wiener Neustadt	Austrian State	$\frac{540}{800} \times 632/1300$ $\frac{21.26}{31.5} \times 24./51.2$	13 191.1	3.91 42.1	250.3 2693.2	58 127,890	70.5 155,453	4300 169.3	6800 267.7	Gölsdorf design
	233	Series 180	0-10-0	1900		Austrian State	$\frac{590}{850} \times 632/1258$ $\frac{23.2}{33.5} \times 24.9/49.5$	14 205.8	3.0 32.3	182.7 1965.9	65.7 144,869	65.7 144,869	5600 220.5	5600 220.5	Gölsdorf design
	234	No. 1619	4-4-0	1893		North Eastern	$\frac{508}{711} \times 610/2165$ $\frac{20}{28} \times 24/85.2$	14 205.8	1.81 19.5	124.58 1340.5	36.08 79,556	54.61 120,415	2820 111	7163 282	T. W. Worsdell. Wilson Worsd design

	Illustration	Name of Locomotive	Wheel arrangement	Year	Builder	Railroad	Driving gear	Boiler Pressure atmospheres	Grate area	Heating surface firetubes and superheater	Weight Adhesion weight	Weight in Service	Wheelbase Coupled	Wheelbase Total	Remarks
	235	Group 380	2-6-0	1904	Ansaldo	Adriatico	$\frac{410}{650}\times 700/1510$ $\frac{16.1}{25.6}\times 27.6\|59.4$	14 *205.8*	2.3 *24.8*	117.4 *1263.2*	39.9 *67,980*	50 *110,250*	4200 *165.4*	6750 *263.8*	Subsequently FS 600
.2	236	Teutonic Class	2-2-2	1889	Crewe	London and North Western	$\frac{2\times 356}{762}\times 610/2159$ $\frac{2\times 14}{30}\times 24\|85$	12.3 *180.8*	1.9 *20.4*	130.2 *1401*	31.5 *68,906*	46.2 *101,871*	— —	5512 *217*	Webb design
	238	Great Britain Class	2-2-2-2	1891	Crewe	London and North Western	$\frac{2\times 381}{762}\times 610/2159$ $\frac{2\times 15}{30}\times 25\|85$	12.3 *180.8*	1.9 *20.4*	139.88 *1500.1*	31.5 *68,399*	52.93 *116,711*	— —	7214 *284*	Webb design
	239	Class A	0-8-0	1894	Crewe	London and North Western	$\frac{2\times 381}{762}\times 610/1359$ $\frac{2\times 15}{30}\times 24\|53.5$	12.3 *180.8*	1.9 *20.4*	138.33 *1488.4*	50.04 *110,338*	50.04 *110,338*	5258 *207*	5258 *207*	Webb design
	240	No. 3.101 —3.395	2-6-0	1887	La Chapelle	French Nord	$\frac{432}{2\times 500}\times 700/1650$ $\frac{17}{2\times 19.7}\times 27.6\|65$	14 *205.8*	2.09 *22.5*	113.8 *1224.5*	40.6 *89,523*	47.4 *104,517*	4100 *161.4*	6630 *261*	Sauvage design
	241	Series B 3/4	2-6-0	1896	SLM Winterthur	Jura-Simplon (Swiss Federal Railroads)	$\frac{500}{2\times 540}\times 600/1520$ $\frac{19.7}{2\times 21.3}\times 23.6\|59.8$	14 *205.8*	2.3 *24.7*	140.3 *1509.6*	44.5 *98,123*	54.8 *120,834*	3900 *153.5*	6310 *248.4*	Weyermann design. Last batch
	243	Group G (Elephants)	0-10-0	1892	Esslingen	Württemberg State	$3\times 480\times 612/1230$ $3\times 18.9\times 24\|48.4$	12 *176.4*	2.17 *23.3*	215.2 *2315.6*	68.88 *151,880*	68.88 *151,880*	6000 (rigid 2610) *236.2*	6000 *236.2*	Klose design
	237	No. 1000 (1005)	4-4-0	1905	Derby	Midland	$\frac{483}{2\times 535}\times 660/1842$ $\frac{19}{2\times 21}\times 26\|72.5$	15.5 *227.9*	2.64 *28.4*	136.8 *147.2*	39.72 *87,583*	60.86 *134,196*	2896 *114*	7392 *291*	Deeley design
.3	244	No. 2.301	0-4-2	1886	La Chapelle	French Nord	$450\times 635/1950$ $17.7\times 25/77$	10 *147*	2.3 *24.7*	114.5 *1232*	27.45 *60,527*	38.55 *85,5003*	2590 *102*	4840 *190.5*	Du Bousquet design
	245	No. 701	2-2-2-0	1886	Sté Alsacienne	French Nord	$\frac{2\times 320}{2\times 460}\times 610/2100$ $\frac{2\times 12.6}{2\times 18.1}\times 24\|82.7$	11 *161.7*	2.35 *25.3*	103.3 *1111.5*	28.2 *62,181*	39 *85,995*	2500 *98.4*	5500 *216.5*	De Glehn type
	246	No. 2101	4-4-0	1890	La Chapelle	French Nord	$480\times 600/2130$ $18.9\times 23.6/83.8$	12 *176.4*	2.04 *22*	110.8 *1192.2*	26.95 *59,425*	43.25 *95,366*	3000 *118*	7340 *289*	Du Bousquet design
	249	Nos. 2-121-122	4-4-0	1891	Sté Alsacienne	French Nord	$\frac{2\times 340}{2\times 530}\times 640/2113$ $\frac{2\times 13.4}{2\times 20.9}\times 25.2\|83.2$	14 *205.8*	2.04 *22*	112.55 *1211*	30.4 *67,032*	43.5 *95,918*	3000 *118*	7350 *289,4*	De Glehn and Du Bousquet design
	251	Nos. 251-256	4-4-0	1897	SLM Winterthur	Swiss Central	$\frac{2\times 330}{2\times 510}\times 600/1730$ $\frac{2\times 13}{2\times 20}\times 23.6\|68$	14 *205.8*	2.2 *23.7*	129.4 *1392.3*	30 *66,150*	49 *108,045*	2600 *102.3*	7000 *275.6*	De Glehn type Subsequently Swiss Federal Railroads A 2/4
	252	Group IV e	4-6-0	1894	Sté Alsacienne	Baden State	$\frac{2\times 350}{2\times 550}\times 640/1600$ $\frac{2\times 13.8}{2\times 21.7}\times 25.2\|63$	13 *191.1*	2.1 *22.6*	125.93 *1355*	41.7 *91,949*	58.8 *12,654*	3600 *141.7*	7650 *301.2*	De Glehn type
	248	Nos. 203-230	4-6-0	1894	SLM Winterthur	Gotthard	$\frac{2\times 370}{2\times 570}\times 600/1610$ $\frac{2\times 14.6}{2\times 22.4}\times 23.6\|63.4$	15 *220.5*	2.4 *25.8*	166 *1786.2*	47.8 *105,399*	65 *143,325*	3830 *150.8*	7930 *312.2*	De Glehn/Winterthur type
	253	No. C1-C2	2-4-2	1988	Paris	French PLM	$\frac{2\times 310}{2\times 500}\times 620/2000$ $\frac{2\times 12.2}{2\times 19.7}\times 24.4\|78.7$	15 *220.5*	2.34 *25.2*	128.03 *1377.6*	29.6 *6,527*	53.5 *117,968*	2160 *85*	5860 *230.7*	Henry type
	254	No. 4301-4302	0-8-0	1888	Paris	French PLM	$\frac{2\times 360}{2\times 540}\times 650/1260$ $\frac{2\times 14.2}{2\times 21.3}\times 25.6\|49.6$	15 *220.5*	c2.18 *23.5*	157.68 *1696.6*	58 *127,890*	58 *127,890*	4050 *159.4*	4050 *159.4*	Henry type
	255	No. 3201-3202	0-8-0	1889	Paris	French PLM	$\frac{2\times 340}{2\times 540}\times 650/1500$ $\frac{2\times 13,4}{2\times 21.3}\times 25.6\|59$	15 *220.5*	2.45 *26.4*	150.9 *1623.7*	56.9 *125,465*	56.9 *125,465*	5730 *225.6*	5730 *225.6*	Henry design
	256	No. C 61-180 (Big C)	4-4-0	1895	Paris	French PLM	$\frac{2\times 340}{2\times 540}\times 620/2000$ $\frac{2\times 13.4}{2\times 21.3}\times 24.4\|78.7$	15 *220.5*	2.48 *26.7*	189.51 *2039.1*	33.46 *73,779*	55.46 *122,289*	3000 *118.1*	7250 *285.4*	Baudry type
	250	Group A 3/5 Nos. 603-649	4-6-0	1910	SLM Winterthur	Swiss Federal	$\frac{2\times 425}{2\times 630}\times 660/1780$ $\frac{2\times 16.7}{2\times 24.8}\times 26\|70$	14 *205.8*	2.8 *30.1*	177.1 40.7 *1905.6 437.9*	48 *105,840*	73.1 *161,186*	4350 *171.3*	6650 *261.8*	Four cylinders in line

Section	Illustration	Name of Locomotive	Wheel arrangement	Year	Builder	Railroad	Driving gear	Boiler Pressure atmospheres	Grate area	Heating surface firetubes and superheater	Adhesion weight	Weight in Service	Coupled wheelbase	Total wheelbase	Remarks
		A 3/5 Nos. 231-232	4-6-0	1902	SLM Winterthur	Jura-Simplon	$\frac{2 \times 360}{2 \times 570} \times 660/1780$ $\frac{2 \times 14.2}{2 \times 22.4} \times 26/70$	15 220.5	2.7 29	168.8 1816.3	45 99,225	65 143,325	3000 118.1	8100 318,9	De Glehn type
11.1.4		Black Prince No. 1502	4-4-0	1897	Crewe	London and North Western	$\frac{2 \times 381}{2 \times 495} \times 610/2159$ $\frac{2 \times 15}{2 \times 19.5} \times 24/85$	12.3 180.8	1.9 20.4	130 1398.8	36.07 79,534	55.27 121,870	2946 116	7064 278.1	Webb design
	258	Group S5	4-4-0	1900	Hanomag	Prussian State	$\frac{2 \times 330}{2 \times 520} \times 600/1980$ $\frac{2 \times 12}{20.5} \times 23.6/78$	14 205.8	2.27 24.4	118.6 1276	29.07 64,099	61 112,455	2700 106.3	7500	Von Borries type
	259	Group 500	6-4-0	1900	Florence	Adriatico	$\frac{2 \times 360}{2 \times 590} \times 650/1920$ $\frac{2 \times 14.2}{2 \times 23.2} \times 25.6/75.6$	14 205.8	3.0 32.3	150.8 1622.6	43.2 95,256	69.9 654,130	4100 161.4	8350 328.7	Plancher design Subsequently FS 670, final form
11.1.5	260	No. 122	4-4-0	1868	Hinkley & Drury	Eric	$\frac{2 \times 229}{2 \times 610} \times 660/1524$ $\frac{2 \times 9}{2 \times 24} \times 26/60$	— —	1.46 15.7	31.32 337	— —	27.85 61,409	— —	— —	First tandem compound engine
	261	Nos. 4729, 4731 and 4733	0-8-0	1887		French Nord	$\frac{2 \times 380}{2 \times 660} \times 650/1300$ $\frac{2 \times 15}{2 \times 26} \times 25.6/51.2$	10 147	2.14 23	126.45 1360.6	52.8 116,424	52.8 116,424	4250 167.3	4250 167.3	Du Bousquet design Rebuilt from older engines
	262	Category I e	4-4-0	1890	Budapest	Hungarian State	$\frac{2 \times 320}{2 \times 490} \times 650/2001$ $\frac{2 \times 12.6}{2 \times 19.3} \times 25.6/78.8$	13 191.1	2.98 32	134.9 1451.5	28 61,740	54.7 120,614	2400 94.5	6300 248	Kordma design
	263	Series P (= R)	4-4-0	1898	Putiloff	Russian State	$\frac{2 \times 365}{2 \times 547} \times 610/2000$ $\frac{2 \times 14.4}{2 \times 21.5} \times 24/78.7$	13.4 197	2.62 28.2	146.08 1571.8	30 66,150	56 123,480	3000 118.1	7500 295.3	Petoff design
	264		2-8-0	1899	Sté Alsacienne	Moscow-Vindau-Rybinsk	$\frac{2 \times 400}{2 \times 600} \times 600/1270$ $\frac{2 \times 15.75}{2 \times 23.6} \times 23.6/50$	12 176.4	2.54 27.3	155.6 1674.3	49.65 109,478	57.75 127,339	4350 171.25	6550 257.9	
	265	Nos. 900-985	2-10-2	1903	Baldwin	Atchisson, Topeka and Santa Fe	$\frac{2 \times 483}{2 \times 813} \times 813/1448$ $\frac{2 \times 19}{2 \times 32} \times 32/57$	15.8 232.3	5.43 58.4	445.56 4794.2	106.36 234,524	130.29 287,289	6020 .237	10.947 431	
	266		4-4-0	1894	Baldwin	Central Railroad of New Jersey	$\frac{2 \times 330}{2 \times 559} \times 610/1981$ $\frac{2 \times 13}{2 \times 22} \times 24/78$	12.66 186.1	3.57 38.4	158.94 1710.2	38.04 83,878	54.77 120,768	2286 90	6795 267.5	Vauclain type
	267	No. 805	2-10-0	1893	Baldwin	New York, Lake Erie and Western (Later Erie)	$\frac{2 \times 408}{2 \times 586} \times 711/1270$ $\frac{2 \times 16}{2 \times 23} \times 28/50$	12.65 186	8.31 89.4	224.97 2420.7	78 171,990	88.45 195,032	6045 238	8306 327	
11.2		Group S4 Hannover 74 (Kassel 20)	4-4-0	1898	Vulkan, Stettin	Prussian State	$460 \times 600/1980$ $18.1 \times 23.6/78$	12 176.4	2.27 24.4	85.65 18 921.6 193.7	33 71,765	55 121,275	— —	— —	Fluetube superheater
	268	Group P4 Kassel 131 (Kassel 1846)	4-4-0	1898	Henschel	Prussian State	$460 \times 600/1750$ $18.1 \times 23.6/69$	12 176.4	2.3 24.7	65.08 21 750.3 226	31 68,355	49.3 108,707	— —	— —	Fluetube superheater
	269	Group S4 Berlin 74	4-4-0	1900	Borsig	Prussian State	$500 \times 600/1980$ $19.7 \times 23.6/78$	12 176.4	2.27 24.4	108.5 28 1167.5 301.3	32.4 71,442	56 123,480	2600 102.3	7200 283.5	Smokebox superheater
	270	Group S4	4-4-0	1904	Borsig	Prussian State	$540 \times 600/1980$ $21.25 \times 23.6/78$	12 176.4	2.27 24.4	100.7 30.75 1083.5 330.9	30 66,150	54.47 120,106	2600 102.3	7600 199.2	Smokebox superheater
	273 (a)	Series P6	2-6-0	1902	Hohenzollern	Prussian State	$540 \times 630/1600$ $21.26 \times 24.8/63$	12 176.4	2.25 24.2	131.59 31.7 1415.9 341.1	44.5 98,123	58.33 128,618	4000 157.5	6450 254	Smokebox superheater
			2-6-0	1904	Hohenzollern	Prussian State	$540 \times 630/1600$ $21.26 \times 24.8/63$	12 176.4	2.25 24.2	134.92 41.91 1451.7 4.51	45.69 100,746	59.71 131,661	— —	— ---	Firetube superheater. Final form
	275 (a)	Group S6	4-4-0	1911	Linke-Hofmann	Prussian State	$550 \times 630/2100$ $21.7 \times 24.8/82.7$	12 176.4	2.31 24.9	149.03 40.32 1603.6 433.8	34.5 76,073	60.69 133,821	3000 118	8000 315	Firetube superheater. Last batch
	271, 272	Class P8	4-6-0	1906	Schwartzkopff	Prussian State	$590 \times 630/1750$ $23.2 \times 24.8/68.9$	12 176.4	2.6 28	150.6 49.38 1620.5 531.3	47.7 105,179	69.5 153,248	4500 177.1	8350 328.7	Initial form. Firetube superheater

Section	Illustration	Name of Locomotive	Wheel arrangement	Year	Builder	Railroad	Driving gear	Boiler Pressure atmospheres	Grate area	Heating surface firetubes and superheater	Adhesion weight	Weight in Service	Coupled wheelbase	Total wheelbase	Remarks
		Group P8	4-6-0	1914	Schwartzkopff	Prussian State	$575 \times 630/1750$ $22.6 \times 24.8/68.9$	12 *176.4*	2.65 *28.5*	146.28 58.9 *1574* *633.5*	51.9 *114,420*	77.5 *170,888*	4500 *177.1*	8350 *328.7*	Last form
	274	Series 4201-4370 (230 K-401-451 French SNCF, Ouest Region)	4-6-0	1915	Several works	French PO	$500 \times 650/1720$ $19.7 \times 25.6/67.7$	12/13 *17.4/ 191.1*	2.77 *29.8*	132.9 37.1 *1430* *399.2*	48.6 *107,163*	67.8 *149,499*	3900 *153.5*	7700 *303.1*	
.1	276	Series P 3[1]	4-4-2	1898	Krauss	Palatinate	$490 \times 570/1980$ $19.3 \times 22.4/77.9$	13 *191.1*	2.7 *29*	186.6 *2007.8*	30 *66,150*	59.6 *131,418*	2050 *80.7*	8700 *342.5*	Inside connected. Von Helmholtz design
	277	Group II D	4-4-2	1902	Maffei	Baden State	$\dfrac{2 \times 335}{2 \times 570} \times 620/2100$ $\dfrac{2 \times 13.2}{2 \times 22.4} \times 24.4/82.6$	16 *235.2*	3.87 *41.6*	210 *2260*	38.5 *84,893*	75.7 *166,919*	2200 *86.6*	10.420 *410.2*	Four-cylinder compound engine, Courtin/Hammel design
		Group S7	4-4-2	1903	Hanomag	Prussian State	$\dfrac{2 \times 360}{2 \times 560} \times 600/1980$ $\dfrac{2 \times 14.1}{2 \times 22} \times 23.6/78$	14 *205.8*	2.71 *29.2*	162.82 *1752*	30.31 *66,834*	62.9 *138,695*	2100 *82.6*	9000 *354.3*	Four-cylinder compound engine, Von Borries type
	278	Group S9	4-4-2	1909	Hanomag	Prussian State	$\dfrac{2 \times 380}{2 \times 580} \times 600/1980$ $\dfrac{2 \times 15}{2 \times 22.8} \times 23.6/78$	14 *205.8*	4.0 *43*	227.1 *2443.6*	33 *72.765*	74.5 *164,273*	2300 *90.6*	10.750 *423.2*	Four-cylinder compound, Von Borries type
	280	Nos. 2643-2675	4-4-2	1901	Sté Alsacienne	French Nord	$\dfrac{2 \times 340}{2 \times 560} \times 640/2040$ $\dfrac{2 \times 13.4}{2 \times 22} \times 25.2/80.3$	16 *235.2*	2.74 *25.9*	208.52 *2243.7*	32 *70,560*	64 *141,120*	2150 *84.6*	8500 *334.6*	Four-cylinder compound, De Glehn type
	279	Klondykes 990 Class	4-4-2	1898		Great Northern	$476 \times 610/2019$ $18.7 \times 24/79.5$	12.3 *180.8*	2.48 *26.7*	133.97 *1441.5*	31.5 *69,458*	58.93 *129,941*	2083 *82*	8026 *316*	Narrow firebox, H. A. Ivatt design
	282	Class 251	4-4-2	1902		Great Northern	$483 \times 610/2019$ $19 \times 24/79.5$	12.3 *180.8*	2.88 *31*	232.25 *2499*	36.58 *80,659*	69.39 *153,005*	2080 *81.9*	8035 *316.3*	Wide firebox, H. A. Ivatt design
		Class 1452	4-4-2	1910		Great Northern	$508 \times 610/2019$ $20 \times 24/79.5$	10.5 *154.4*	2.88 *31*	187.84 39.67 *2021.2* *426.8*	— —	— —	2080 *81.9*	8035 *316.3*	Wide firebox. Superheated. H. A. Ivatt design
		Class Z	4-4-2	1911	North British Locomotive Company	North Eastern	$3 \times 394 \times 660/2083$ $3 \times 15.5 \times 26/82$	12.7 *186.7*	2.15 *27*	217.39 *2339.1*	40.23 *88,707*	77.93 *771,836*	2311 *91*	8992 *354*	Three-cylinder locomotive. V. Raven design
		Class Z1	4-4-2	1911	North British Locomotive Company	North Eastern	$3 \times 419 \times 660/2083$ $3 \times 16.5 \times 26/82$	11.3 *166.1*	2.51 *27*	138.76 *1493*	41.4 *91,287*	80.52 *177,547*	2311 *91*	8992 *354*	Three-cylinder superheated locomotive. V. Raven design
.2	282	No. 103-104 President and Alliance	4-4-2	1905	Sté Alsacienne	Great Western	$\dfrac{2 \times 360}{2 \times 600} \times 640/2045$ $\dfrac{2 \times 14.2}{2 \times 23.6} \times 25.2/80.5$	16 *235.2*	3.1 *33.4*	256.13 *2756*	37.8 *83,349*	72.85 *160,634*	2150 *84.6*	8700 *342.5*	Four-cylinder compound locomotive, De Glehn type
		Star Class	4-6-0	1907	Swindon	Great Western	$4 \times 362 \times 660/2046$ $4 \times 14.25 \times 26/80.6$	15.8 *232.3*	2.52 *27.1*	199.07 *2142*	56.29 *124,119*	76.81 *169,366*	4496 *177*	8306 *327*	Four-cylinder locomotive, Churchward design
	285	Castle Class	4-6-0	1923	Swindon	Great Western	$4 \times 406 \times 660/2046$ $4 \times 16 \times 26/80.6$	15.8 *232.3*	2.81 *30.2*	190.34 24.4 *2048* *262.5*	59.79 *131,837*	81.13 *178.892*	4496 *177*	8306 *327*	Four-cylinder, Collet design
	286	Series 9	4-6-0	1908	Several works	Belgian State	$4 \times 445 \times 640/1980$ $4 \times 17.5 \times 25.2/78$	14 *232.3*	3.13 *33.7*	146.39 37.8 *1575.2* *406.7*	53.3 *117,527*	81.3 *179,267*	4260 *167.7*	8710 *343*	Four-cylinder, Flamme design
		Group S10	4-6-0	1911	Vulkan, Stettin	Prussian State	$4 \times 430 \times 630/1980$ $4 \times 16.9 \times 24.8/78$	14 *205.8*	2.82 *30.1*	154.25 61.5 *1659.7* *661.7*	51.73 *114,065*	79.55 *175,408*	4700 *185*	9100 *358.3*	Four cylinder locomotive. Definitive form
	287	Group S10[2]	4-6-0	1914	Vulkan, Stettin	Prussian State	$3 \times 500 \times 630/1980$ $3 \times 19.7 \times 24.8/78$	14 *205.8*	2.82 *30.1*	153.09 61.5 *1647.2* *661.7*	51.37 *113,271*	80 *176.400*	4700 *185*	9150 *360.2*	Three-cylinder locomotive, Najork design
	288	Group 685	2-6-2	1912	Breda	Italian State	$4 \times 420 \times 650/1850$ $4 \times 16.5 \times 25.6/72.8$	12 *176.4*	3.5 *37.7*	190.8 48.54 *2053* *522.3*	45 *99,225*	70.8 *156,114*	3950 *155.5*	8451 *332.7*	Four-cylinder locomotive
.3	289	Series 4501-4570	4-6-2	1907	Sté Alsacienne	French PO	$\dfrac{2 \times 390}{2 \times 640} \times 650/1850$ $\dfrac{2 \times 15.3}{2 \times 25.2} \times 25.6/72.8$	16 *235.2*	4.27 *45.9*	257.25 *2768*	52.3 *115,321*	90 *198,450*	3900 *153.5*	10 500 *413.4*	Solacroup (chief engineer), De Glehn type
		Series 3501-3520	4-6-2	1909	Sté Alsacienne	French PO	$\dfrac{2 \times 390}{2 \times 648} \times 650/1950$ $\dfrac{2 \times 15.4}{2 \times 25.2} \times 25.6/76.8$	16 *235.2*	4.27 *45.9*	257.25 *2768*	52.5 *115,763*	90.4 *199,332*	4100 *161.4*	10700 *421.3*	Solacroup (chief engineer), De Glehn type
	290	Series 3.1151-1170	4-6-2	1912	Sté Alsacienne	French Nord	$\dfrac{2 \times 410}{2 \times 600} \times 660/2040$ $\dfrac{2 \times 16.1}{2 \times 23.6} \times 26/80.3$	16 *235.2*	3.22 *34.6*	212.98 +45.0 *2291.7* + *484.2*	49.17 *108,420*	85.57 *188,682*	4300 *169.3*	10350 *407.5*	

Section	Illustration	Name of Locomotive	Wheel arrangement	Year	Builder	Railroad	Driving gear	Boiler Pressure atmospheres	Grate area	Heating surface firetubes and superheater	Weight Adhesion weight	Weight Weight in Service	Wheelbase Coupled wheelbase	Wheelbase Total wheelbase	Remarks
	291	Series 6011-6030 (6201-6220)	4-6-2	1911	Henschel	French PLM	$\frac{2\times440}{2\times650}\times650/2000$ $\frac{2\times17.3}{2\times25.6}\times25.6/78.7$	14 _205.8_	4.25 _45.7_	202.13 64.47 _2174.9_ _699_	55.5 _122,378_	91.21 _201,118_	4200 _165.3_	11230 _442.1_	Four-cylinder compound
		Series 6172-6191	4-6-2	1911	Batignolles	French PLM	$4\times480\times680/2000$	14 _205.8_	4.25 _45.7_	219.30 70.63 _2359.7_ _760_	55.5 _122,378_	93.06 _205,197_	4200 _152.8_	11230 _442.1_	Four-cylinder. Simple expansion
	292	Group IV f	4-6-2	1907	Maffei	Baden State	$\frac{2\times425\times616}{2\times650\times670}\Big/1800$ $\frac{2\times16.7\times24}{2\times17.3\times26.4}\Big/70.9$	16 _235.2_	4.50 _48.4_	208.72 50.0 _2245.8_ _538_	49.6 _109,368_	88.3 _194,702_	3880 _152.8_	11210 _441.3_	Four-cylinder compound. Hammel design
	293	Group S3/6	4-6-2	1908	Maffei	Bavarian State	$\frac{2\times425\times610}{2\times650\times670}\Big/1870$ $\frac{2\times16.7\times24}{2\times17.3\times26.4}\Big/73.6$	15 _220.5_	4.50 _48.4_	218.4 50.0 _2350_ _538_	48.0 _105,840_	86.6 _190,953_	4020 _158.3_	11365 _447.4_	Four-cylinder compound locomotive Hammel design. First batch
	294	Group F	4-6-2	1914	Nydquist	Swedish State	$\frac{2\times420}{2\times630}\times610/1880$ $\frac{2\times16.5}{2\times24.8}\times24.8/74$	13 _191.1_	3.60 _38.7_	190.3 56.7 _2048_ _610.1_	18.0 _105,840_	87.8 _193,599_	3950 _155.5_	11100 _437_	Four-cylinder compound
	296	Series 10	4-6-2	1910	Several works	Belgian State	$4\times500\times660/1980$ $4\times19.7\times26/78$	14 _205.8_	4.58 _49.3_	239.59 62.0 _2578_ _667.1_	57.0 _125,685_	98.0 _216,090_	4100 _161.4_	11425 _449.8_	Four-cylinder, simple expansion, Flamme type
	299	Series 210.01-11	2-6-4	1908	Floridsdorf	Austrian State	$\frac{2\times390}{2\times660}\times720/2140$ $\frac{2\times15.4}{2\times26}\times28.3/84.3$	16 _235.2_	4.62 _49.7_	212.9 43.4 _2290.8_ _467_	44.1 _97,240_	86.0 _189,630_	4440 _174.8_	10450 _411.4_	Four-cylinder compound locomotive, Gölsdorf type
12.4		No. 203-204	4-6-0	1894	SLM Winterthur	Gotthard	$\frac{2\times370}{2\times570}\times600/1610$ $\frac{2\times14.6}{2\times22.4}\times23.6/63.4$	15 _220.5_	2.4 _25.8_	166 _1786.2_	46.8 _103,194_	65.0 _173,325_	3520 _138.6_	7470 _294_	Four-cylinder compound, De Glehn type
	298	No. 2801-2808	2-8-0	1906	Maffei	Gotthard	$\frac{2\times395}{2\times635}\times640/1350$ $\frac{2\times15.6}{2\times25}\times25.2/53.1$	15 _220.5_	4.10 _44.1_	213.15 41.0 _2293.5_ _441.2_	62.4 _137,592_	76.4 _163,462_	4800 _189_	7520 _296_	Four-cylinder compound
	301	Series 400	2-8-0	1909	St. Léonard	Spanish Norte	$610\times650/1560$ $24\times25.6/61.4$	12 _176.4_	3.05 _32.5_	184.5 46.49 _1985.2_ _500.2_	64.49 _142,200_	70.5 _155,453_	5200 _204.7_	7850 _309_	Two-cylinder simple expansion. 1674 mm (66 ins.) gauge
	302	No. 4501-4530 (F.S. Group 750)	4-8-0	1902	Ansaldo and Breda	Italian Mediterraneo	$\frac{540}{800}\times680/1400$ $\frac{21.3}{31.5}\times26.8/55.1$	12 _176.4_	4.80 _51.6_	163.14 _1755.4_	55.2 _121,716_	74.6 _164,493_	4560 _179.5_	7960 _313.4_	Two-cylinder compound locomotive
		Series 4000	4-8-0	1912	Alsace Locomotive Works	Spanish Norte	$\frac{2\times400}{2\times620}\times640/1560$ $\frac{2\times15.7}{2\times24.4}\times25.2/61.4$	16 _235.2_	4.10 _44.1_	184.7 56.0 _1987.4_ _602.6_	61.0 _134,505_	78.7 _173,534_	5100 _200.8_	8950 _352.4_	Four-cylinder compound engine, De Glehn type. 1674 mm (66 ins gauge. First especially built expre engine for mountain lines
	303	Series 1300	4-8-0	1914	Hanomag	Madrid-Zaragoza-Alicante	$\frac{2\times420}{2\times640}\times650/1600$ $\frac{2\times16.5}{2\times25.2}\times25.6/63$	16 _235.2_	4.10 _44.1_	201.13 570 _2164.2_ _613.3_	60.0 _132,300_	88.0 _194,040_	5700 _224.4_	9700 _381.9_	Four-cylinder compound engine. 1674 mm (66 ins.) gauge
	304	Series 570	4-8-0	1914	STEG	Austrian Southern	$610\times650/1740$ $24\times25.6/68.5$	14 _205.8_	4.47 _48.1_	217.9 75.4 _2344.6_ _811.3_	58.4 _128,772_	84.9 _187,205_	5550 _218.5_	9540 _375.6_	Steffan and Prossy design
	306	Series 1000	2-8-2	1913	SLM Winterthur	French PLM	$\frac{2\times510\times650}{2\times720\times700}\Big/1650$ $\frac{2\times20\times25.6}{2\times28.3\times27.6}\Big/65$	16 _235.2_	4.25 _45.7_	219.08 70.63 _2357.3_ _760_	69.5 _153,248_	93.33 _205,793_	5400 _212.6_	11200 _440.9_	Four-cylinder compound engine
12.5	305	Group G8[1]	0-8-0	1912	Schichau	Prussian State	$600\times660/1350$ $23.6\times26/53.1$	14 _205.8_	2.6 _28_	130.5 51.9 _1404.2_ _558.4_	68 _149,940_	68 _149,940_	4700 _185_	4700 _185_	Two-cylinder simple expansion
	308	Nos. 2801-2820	2-8-0	1905	Swindon	Great Western	$457\times762/1410$ $18\times30/55.5$	16.8	2.51 27	199.05 _2141.8_	62.89 _138,672_	69.33 _152,873_	5131 202	7798 307	Churchward design
		Series 6001-6070	2-10-0	1910	Several works	French PO	$\frac{2\times460\times620}{2\times660\times650}\Big/1400$ $\frac{2\times18.1\times24.4}{2\times26\times25.6}\Big/55.1$	16 _235.2_	3.80 _40.9_	201.2 55.4 _2164.9_ _596.1_	76.9 _169,565_	85.2 _187,866_	6400 _252_	8650 _340.6_	Four-cylinder compound engine De Glehn type
	311	Series C5/6 Nos. 2951-2953	2-10-0	1913	SLM Winterthur	Swiss Federal	$\frac{2\times470}{2\times710}\times640/1330$ $\frac{2\times18.5}{2\times28}\times25.2/52.4$	15 _220.5_	3.7 _39.8_	211.3 54.5 _2273.6_ _586.4_	76.1 _167,801_	85.8 _189,189_	6450 _253.9_	8800 _346.5_	Four-cylinder compound locomotive
	309	Series 36	2-10-0	1909	Several works	Belgian State	$4\times500\times660/1450$ $4\times19.7\times26/57$	14 _205.8_	5.1 _54.9_	238.95 62 _2571.1_ _667.1_	87.8 _198,599_	104.2 _229,761_	7616 _299.8_	10116 _398.3_	Four-cylinder simple expansion. Flamme type

Illustration	Name of Locomotive	Wheel arrangement	Year	Builder	Railroad	Driving gear	Boiler Pressure atmospheres	Grate area	Heating surface firetubes and superheater	Adhesion weight	Weight in Service	Coupled wheelbase	Total wheelbase	Remarks
310	Series 100	2-12-0	1910	Floridsdorf	Austrian State	$\frac{2\times450}{2\times760}\times680/1410$ $\frac{2\times17.7}{2\times27.6}\times26.8/55.5$	16 235.2	5.0 53.8	224.1 50.7 2411.3 545.5	82.2 181,251	95.8 211,239	7650 301.2	10100 397.6	Four-cylinder compound engine. Gölsdorf type
	Group K	2-12-0	1917	Esslingen	Württemberg State	$\frac{2\times510}{2\times760}\times650/1350$ $\frac{2\times20}{2\times29.9}\times25.6/53.1$	15 220.5	4.2 45.2	232 80 2496.3 860.8	94.6 208,593	108 238,140	7500 295.3	9900 389.8	Four-cylinder compound
312	No. 590	2-4-2	1895	Baldwin	Chicago, Burlington and Quincy	$483\times660/2140$ $19\times26/84.25$	14 205.8	4.14 44.5	146.78 1579.4	39.1 86,216	62.6 138,033	2286 90	7391 291	
	No. 1015	4-4-2	1900	Schenectady	Chicago and North Western	$508\times660/2032$ $20\times26/8$	14 205.8	4.29 46.2	218.19 2347.7	40.82 90,008	72.57 160,017	2153 84	8153 321	Final form of the "Atlantic"
313	Class E 6 S	4-4-2	1911	Altoona	Pennsylvania	$597\times660/2032$ $23.5\times26/80$	14.4 211.7	5.13 55.2	269 56.95 2894.4 612.8	61.69 136,026	110.5 243,653	2261 89	9068 357	
	No. 1123	4-6-2	1902	Brooks	Missouri Pacific	$508\times660/1753$ $20\times26/69$	14 205.8	3.98 42.8	272.2 2928.9	55.34 122,025	82.55 182,023	3759 148	9652 380	First definitive form of the "Pacific"
314	Class K3q	4-6-2	1923	ALCO	New York Central	$597\times660/2007$ $23.5\times26/79$	14.1 207.3	5.25 56.5	318.43 77.37 3426.4 432.5	88.22 194,525	134.04 295,558	4267 168	11125 438	
315	No. 4002	4-8-2	1920	ALCO	Chicago, Rock Island & Pacific	$711\times711/1880$ $28\times28/74$	14.1 200.1	5.85 63	435.6 115.8 4689 1247	114.8 253,000	167.4 369,000	6045 238	12497 492	
316	No. 203	2-8-0		Lima	Toledo, St. Louis and Western	$559\times711/1448$ $22\times28/57$	13 185	4.30 46.3	192.84 44.13 2076 475	77.34 173,500	90.75 200,500	4878 194	7569 298	
317	No. 1814	2-8-0	1920	ALCO	Northern Pacific	$711\times762/1600$ $28\times30/63$	12.7 180	6.53 70.3	333.23 81.2 3587 874	112.04 247,000	152.86 337,000	5029 198	10744 423	
318	No. 5036	2-10-2	1917	Baldwin	Union Pacific	$749\times762/1600$ $29.5\times30/63$	14.1 200	7.8 84	478.25 108.23 5148 1165	129.86 286,300	167.15 368,500	6858 270	12624 497	
319	Taliesin	0-4-4-0	1869	George England	Festiniog	$4\times208\times330/711$ $4\times8.2\times13/28$	14 205.8	1.02 11	67.8 729.5	19.81 43,681	19.81 43,681	2×1524 2×60	5817 259	Dimensions of the "Little Wonder". 519 mm (20.5 ins) gauge
320	Escalador des Montes	0-6-6-0		Avonside	Chimbote Railroad Peru	$4\times349\times457/ \text{- - -}$ $4\times13.7\times18/ \text{- - -}$	— —	— —	— —	46 101,430	46	— —	— —	914 mm (36 ins) gauge
		0-6-6-0	1911	Vulcan Foundry	Mexican Central	$4\times483\times635/1219$ $4\times19\times25/48$	13 191.1	4.44 47.8	271.64 2922.8	140 308,700	140	$2\times$ 2819	10820	
321	No. 150	2-6-6-2	1892	Rhode Island	Mexican Central	$\frac{2\times330}{2\times711}/1016$ $\frac{2\times19}{2\times28}/40$	— —	— —		90.72 200,038		$2\times$ 2540 100	13952 549.3	Johnston type
	L'Avenir (0401)	0-4-4-0	1872	Cail	Compagnie des Charentes	$4\times340\times550/1300$ $4\times13.4\times21.7/51.2$	10 147	1.68 18.1	152.6 1642	50.5 111,353	50.5	2×900 2×35.4		First Meyer engine
332	Series IT V	0-4-0+0-4-0	1910	Hartmann	Saxon State	$\frac{2\times360}{2\times570}\times630/1260$ $\frac{2\times14.2}{2\times22.4}\times24.8/49.6$	13 191.1	1.6 17.2	99.3 1068.5	60.2 132,741	60.2	$2\times$ 2000 $2\times$ 78.7	7700 303.1	
323	Nos. 1-2	0-4-0+0-4-0	1897	Jung	Wallücke	$—/1700$ 66.9	— —	1.0 10.76	50 538	20 44,100	20	$2\times$ 1100 2×43.3	5000 393.8	600 mm (24 ins) gauge
324	Nos. 50-52	2-8-0+2-8-0	1908	Kitson	Great Southern of Spain	$4\times374\times609/1215$ $4\times14.7\times24/48$	15 220.5	3.21 35.5	176.6 1900.2	92.05 202,970	102.62 226,277	$2\times$ 4510 $2\times$ 177.6	149990 590.2	Kitson-Meyer type
325	Series 6121-6128	0-6-2-2-6-0	1905	B. W. Hellemes	French Nord	$\frac{2\times400}{2\times630}\times680/1455$ $\frac{2\times15.75}{2\times24.8}\times26.8/57.3$	16 235.2	3.0 32.3	188.2 2025	90.37 199,265	106.7 235,274	$2\times$ 3470 $2\times$ 136.6	12590 495.7	Du Bousquet type
326	Class FC	2-6-2-2-6-2	1925	North British and Henschel	South African	$4\times356\times584/1086$ $4\times14\times23/42.8$	12.7 186.7	3.16 34	128.9 26 138.7 280	62 136,710	101.3 223,367	$2\times$ 2438 2×96	17372 684	1067 mm (42 ins.) gauge So called "modified Fairlie"
328		0-2-2-0	1889	Sté Belge "La Metallurgique"	International Exhibition, Paris 1889	$\frac{2\times187}{2\times280}\times260/600$ $\frac{2\times7.36}{2\times11}\times10.2/23.6$	12.0 176.4	0.48 5.2		11.7 25,799	11.7	2×850 $2\times$ 33.5	2800 110.2	600 mm (24 ins) gauge Tank locomotive
329		0-4-4-0	1896	Sté Alsacienne	Zell-Todtnau	$\frac{2\times250}{2\times380}\times450/900$ $\frac{2\times9.8}{2\times15}\times17.7/35.4$	12.0 176.4	0.75 8.1	— —	28 61,740	28 61,740	— —	— —	1 metre gauge. Tank locomotive

Section	Illustration	Name of Locomotive	Wheel arrangement	Year	Builder	Railroad	Driving gear	Boiler Pressure atmospheres	Grate area	Heating surface firetubes and superheater	Weight Adhesion weight	Weight Weight in Service	Wheelbase Coupled wheelbase	Wheelbase Total wheelbase	Remarks
	329		0-6-6-0	1925	Hanomag	Zell-Todtnau	$\frac{2\times400}{2\times620}\times450/900$ $\frac{2\times15.75}{2\times24.4}\times17.7/35.4$	15 220.5	1.85 19.9	130 1398.8	56.4 124,362	56.4 124,362	2× 2500 2× 98.4	7000 275.6	1 metre gauge. Tank locomotive
	327	Group IV	0-4-4-0	1896	Hartmann	Saxon State	$\frac{2\times420}{2\times650}\times600/1240$ $\frac{2\times16.5}{2\times25.6}\times23.6/48.8$	12 176.4	2.08 22.4	141.6 1523.6	60 132,300	60 132,300	2× 1700 2× 67	5750 226.4	
	330		0-6-6-0	1898	Briansk	Moscow-and-Kazan	$\frac{2\times475}{2\times710}\times650/1220$ $\frac{2\times18.7}{2\times28}\times26/48$	12.4 182.3	2.45 26.4	201.8 2171.4	81.5 179,708	81.5 179,708	2× 2700 2× 106.3	8000 315	
		Category IV e (401)	2-4-4-0	1898	Budapest Works	Hungarian State	$\frac{2\times390}{2\times635}\times650/1440$ $\frac{2\times15.4}{2\times25}\times25.6/56.7$	16 235.2	3.55 38.2	235.75 2536.7	65.32 1440,31	75.32 166,081	2× 1850 2× 72.8	7710 303.5	Passenger engine for mountaino sections
	332	Category 601	2-6-6-0	1914	Budapest Works	Hungarian State	$\frac{2\times520}{2\times850}\times660/1440$ $\frac{2\times20.5}{2\times33.5}\times26/56.7$	15 220.5	5.09 54.8	275.9 ×79.7 2968.8 ×857.6	96.94 213,753	109.36 241,139	2× 3400 2× 133.9	11.980 471.7	Boiler on the Brotan system
	331	Group Gt 2×4/4	0-8-8-0	191.	Maffei	Bavarian State	$\frac{2\times520}{2\times800}\times640/1216$ $\frac{2\times20.5}{2\times31.5}\times25.2/47.9$	15 220.5	4.25 45.7	230.89 ×55.39 2484.4 ×596	123.2 271,656	123.2 271,656	2× 4500 2× 177.2	12.200 480.3	Tank locomotive
		No. 2400 Class DD1 No. 7000	0-6-6-0	1904	ALCO	Baltimore-and-Ohio	$\frac{2\times508}{2\times813}+813/1422$ $\frac{2\times20}{2\times32}\times32/56$	16.5 242.6	6.71 72.2	518.94 5583.8	151.73 334,565	— —	2× 3048 2× 120	9347 368	First big Mallet locomotive in America
		Class L-1	2-6-6-2	1906	Baldwin	Great Northern	$\frac{2\times546}{2\times838}\times813/1397$ $\frac{2\times21.5}{2\times33}\times32/55$	14 205.8	7.25 78	525.63 5655.8	142.79 314,852	160.8 354,654	2× 3048 2× 120	18.744 738	
	333, 334	Class M 1-99	2-8-8-2	1915	Baldwin	Nashville, Chattanooga and St. Louis	$\frac{2\times686}{2\times1016}\times762/1422$ $\frac{2\times27}{2\times41}\times30/56$	14.8 210	7.94 85.5	504.73 117.24 5433 1262	195.18 430,300	212.92 469,400	2× 4572 2× 186	16.967 668	
	335	No. 800-809	2-10-10-2	1918	ALCO	Virginia	$\frac{2\times762}{2\times1220}\times813/1422$ $\frac{2\times30}{2\times48}\times32/56$	15 215	10.1 108.7	800.4 192.2 8605 2120	280 617,000	310.5 684,000	2× 6070 2× 238	19.583 771	
	336	No. 700	2-8-8-4	1916	Baldwin	Virginia	$6\times864\times813/1422$ $6\times34\times32/56$	15.1 222	10.0 107.6	679.5 190 7311.4 2044.4	320 725,475	382 842,310	3× 4647 3× 183	27,837 1096	Triplex Mallet locomotive
14.5	337		0-4-4-0	1909	Beyer-Peacock	Tasmanian Government	$\frac{2\times279}{2\times432}\times406/800$ $\frac{2\times11}{2\times17}\times16/31.5$	13.7 201.4	1.38 14.8	58.34 627.7	34.05 75,080	34.05	2× 1219 2× 48	8179 322	First Garratt locomotive. 610 mm (24 ins.) gauge
		Class M1	4-4-2-2-4-4	1912	Beyer-Peacock	Tasmanian Government	$8\times305\times508/1524$ $8\times12\times20/60$	11.3 166.1	3.15 33.9	156.6 30.9 1685 332.5	48.77 107,538	96.27 212,275	2× 1829 2× 72	18.847 742	Eight-cylinder passenger train engine. 1067 (42 ins.) gauge
	338	No. 101-104	2-6-6-2	1922	Sté St. Léonard	Catalan	$4\times430\times500/1000$ $4\times16.9\times19.7/39.37$	12 176.4	2.75 29.6	134.25 24.47 1444.5 263.3	65 143,325	78 171,990			1 metre gauge
	339	No. 101-106	4-6-2-2-6-4	1931	Euskalduna Bilbao	Central Aragon	$4\times481\times660/1750$ $4\times18.9\times26/68.9$	14 205.8	4.9 52.7	293.2 69 3154.8 742.4	95 209,475	184 405,720	2× 3810 2× 150	25.527 1005	Only Garratt express locomotive Europe. 1674 (66 ins.) gauge
	340	No. 4997-4999	2-6-6-2	1927	Beyer-Peacock	London, Midland and Scottish	$4\times470\times660/1600$ $4\times18.5\times26/63$	13.4 197	4.13 44.4	198.53 46.45 2136.2 499.8	124.65 274,853	157.99 348,368	2× 5029 2× 198	24.080 948	
	341	Class 20 A No. 721-760	2-8-2-2-8-4	1956	Beyer-Peacock	Rhodesian	$4\times508\times660/1295$ $4\times20\times26/51$	14.1 207.3	5.86 63	280.93 66.49 3022.8 715.4	138.2 304,731	226.6 499,653			1067 (42 ins.) gauge
		Class 59	4-8-2-2-8-4	1955	Beyer-Peacock	East African	$4\times521\times711/1372$ $4\times20.5\times28/54$	15.8 232.3	6.69 72	330.82 69.4 3559.6 746.7	161.6 356,328	255.1 562,496			Most powerful narrow-gauge engine. 1067 mm (42 ins.) gauge
			2-6-6-2	1928	Haine-Saint-Pierre	Ivory Coast	$4\times400\times560/1100$ $4\times15.75\times22/43.3$	12 176.4	2.75 29.6	177.2 1906.7	73.1 161,186	87.73 193,445	2× 2540 2× 100	13.970 550	Golwé type. 1 metre gauge
14.6	342		0-4-4-4-0		Lima	Greenbrier, Cheat and Elk	$3\times432\times457/1219$ $3\times17\times18/48$	14 200	4.51 48.5	174.83 39 1882 411	139.7 308,000	139.7 308,000		14.935 588	Shay type

Section	Illustration	Name of Locomotive	Wheel arrangement	Year	Builder	Railroad	Driving gear	Boiler Pressure atmospheres	Grate area	Heating surface firetubes and superheater	Weight		Wheelbase		Remarks
											Adhesion weight	Weight in Service	Coupled wheelbase	Total wheelbase	
	343		0-6-6-0	1916	Hartmann	Saxon State	$\frac{2\times440}{2\times680}\times630/1400$ $\frac{2\times17.3}{2\times26.8}\times24.8/55.1$	15 *220.5*	2.5 *26.9*	127.2 40.9 1368.7 440.1	92.2 *203,301*	92.2	$2\times$ 3550 $2\times$ 139.8	11.100 *437*	Klien-Lindner type
1	344	Series G12 (DR.BR 58)	2-10-0	1917	Henschel	Prussian State	$3\times570\times660/1400$ $3\times22.4\times26/55.1$	14 *205.8*	3.9 *42*	194.96 68.42 2097.8 736.2	82.5 *181,913*	96.7 *211,019*	6000 *236.2*	8500 *334.6*	Three-cylinder simple expansion
	347	Class P10 (DR.BR 39)	4-8-4	1922	Borsig	Prussian State	$3\times520\times660/1750$ $3\times20.5\times26/69$	14 *205.8*	4 *43*	220.7 82 2374.7 882.3	75.4 *166.257*	110.4 *243,342*	6000 *236.2*	11.600 *456.7*	A. Meister design, three-cylinder engine
	345	Group E	0-10-0	1922	Nohab and various other works	Soviet	$620\times700/1320$ $24.4\times27.6\times52$	12 *176.4*	4.46 *48*	188.8 47.7 2031.5 513.3	81.5 *179,707*	81.5	5780 *227.6*	5780 *227.6*	First locomotive series with interchangeable parts
	346	Series 02	4-6-2	1925	Henschel	German National (Reichsbahn)	$\frac{2\times460}{2\times720}\times660/2000$ $\frac{2\times18.1}{2\times28.3}\times26/78.7$	14 *205.8*	4.5 *48.4*	238 100 2560.9 1076	60.4 *133,182*	113 *249,165*	4600 *181.1*	12.000 *472.4*	First Standard locomotive
	351	Series 44	2-10-0	1925	Several works	German National (Reichsbahn)	$3\times550\times660/1400$ $3\times21.7\times26/55.1$	16 *235.2*	4.55 *49*	288 100 3098.9 1076	96.3 *212,342*	102.8 *226,674*	6800 *267.7*	9.650 *379.9*	
	348	Series 11	4-10-0	1939	Henschel	Bulgarian State	$3\times520\times700/1450$ $3\times20.5\times27.6/57$	16 *235.2*	4.87 *52.4*	224.1 80 2411.3 860.8	85 *187,425*	109.6 *241,668*	— —	10.900 *429.1*	
	349	Series 46	2-12-4	1943	Krupp and Schwartzkopff	Bulgarian State	$3\times550\times650/1340$ $3\times21.7\times25.6/52.7$	16 *235.2*	4.87 *52.4*	223.6 79.9 2405.9 859.7	108 *238,140*	155.8 *343,539*	6300 *248*	12.909 *508.2*	
	350	Class K5	4-6-2	1919	Baldwin and ALCO	Erie	$686\times711/2007$ $27\times27/79$	14.1 *200*	6.58 *70.8*	355.25 81.91 3824 882	89.36 *197,000*	138.83 *366,000*	4267 *168*	11.024 *434*	USRA Standard type 462-B
		USRA 282-A	2-8-2	1919	Several works	Several Railroads	$660\times672/1600$ $26\times26.5/63$	14.1 *207.3*	6.2 *66.7*	350.90 3775.70	99.79 *220,037*	132.45 *292,052*	5105 *201*	10.973 *432*	625 engines of the type built
		USRA 2102-B	2-10-2	1019	Several works	Several Railroads	$762\times813/1600$ $30\times32/63$	13.4 *197*	8.18 *88*	478.70 5150.80	132.9 *293,045*	172.37 *380,076*	6807 *268*	12.852 *506*	175 engines of the type built
.2	354	King's Class	4-6-0	1927	Swindon	Great Western	$4\times413\times711/1981$ $4\times16.3\times28/78$	17.6 *258.7*	3.19 *34.3*	204.47 29.08 220.1 312.9	68.58 *151,219*	90.42 *199,376*	4954 *195*	8967 *353*	Four-cylinder, Collet design
		B17 Class "Sandringhams"	4-6-0	1928	North British Locomotive Co.	LNER	$3\times445\times660/2032$ $3\times17.5\times26/80$	14 *205.8*	2.95 *27.4*	155.7 31.96 1675.3 343.9	55.22 *121,760*	78.49 *173,070*	4953 *195*	8458 *333*	Three-cylinder, Gresley design
	352	Green Arrow Class V2	2-6-2	1936	Doncaster	LNER	$3\times470\times660/1880$ $3\times18.5\times26/74$	15.5 *227.9*	3.83 *41.2*	225.91 63.14 2430.8 679.4	66.65 *146,963*	94.59 *208,571*	4725 *186*	10.263 *404*	Three-cylinder, Gresley design
	353	Royal Scot	4-6-0	1927	North British Locomotive Co.	LMS	$3\times457\times660/2057$ $3\times18\times26/81$	17.6 *258.7*	2.9 *31.2*	193.33 37.07 2080.2 398.9	63.5 *140,017*	86.26 *190,203*	4674 *184*	8382 *330*	Three-cylinder, Fowler design
	356	5P 5F Class	4-6-0	1934	Various	LMS	$470\times711/1829$ $18.5\times28/72$	15.8 *232.3*	2.58 *27.8*	150.13 21.14 1615.4 227.5	54.86 *120,966*	73.15 *161,296*	4572 *180*	8280 *326*	Two-cylinder, Stanier design
		Lord Nelson Class	4-6-0	1926	Eastleigh	Southern	$4\times419\times660/2007$ $4\times16.5\times26/79$	15.5 *227.9*	3.07 *33*	184.78 34.93 1988.2 375.8	62.94 *138,783*	84.33 *185,948*	4572 *180*	8993 *354*	Four-cylinder, Maunsell design
	357	School Class	4-4-0	1930	Eastleigh	Southern	$3\times419\times660/2007$ $3\times16.5\times26/79$	15.5 *227.9*	2.63 *28.3*	164.06 26.28 1765.3 282.8	42.67 *54,087*	68.17 *150,315*	3048 *120*	7772 *306*	Three-cylinder Maunsell design
.3	358	Group XX H V	2-8-2	1918	Hartmann	Saxon State	$\frac{2\times480}{2\times720}\times630/1905$ $\frac{2\times18.9}{2\times28.3}\times24.8/75$	15 *220.5*	4.5 *48.4*	227.05 74.0 2443 796.2	68.6 *151,263*	99.9 *220,280*	— —	11.960 *470.9*	Four-cylinder compound engine Meyer and Lindner design
		Group 746	2-8-2	1921	Breda	Italian State	$\frac{2\times490}{2\times720}\times680/1880$ $\frac{2\times19.3}{2\times28.3}\times26.8/74$	14 *205.8*	4.3 *46.3*	237.0 67.0 2550 720.9	66 *145,530*	93 *205,065*	5940 *233.9*	11.240 *442.5*	Four-cylinder compound with front Zara truck
	360	Series 4600	4-8-2	1925	Hanomag	Spanish Norte	$\frac{2\times460}{2\times700}\times680/1750$ $\frac{2\times18.1}{2\times27.6}\times26.8/68.9$	16 *235.2*	5.0 *53.8*	2240 99.85 24,102 1074.4	70 *154,350*	913.1 *249,386*	5550 *218.5*	12.675 *499*	Four-cylinder compound engine, Dr Glehn type, A. Wolff design 1674 mm (66 ins.) gauge

Section	Illustration	Name of Locomotive	Wheel arrangement	Year	Builder	Railroad	Driving gear	Boiler Pressure atmospheres	Grate area	Heating surface firetubes and superheater	Adhesion weight	Weight in Service	Coupled wheelbase	Total wheelbase	Remarks
	361	No. 41.001	4-8-2	1925	Epernay	French Est	$\frac{2\times450}{2\times660}\times720/1950$ $\frac{2\times17.7}{2\times26}\times28.3/76.8$	17 / 250	4.43 / 48	217.61 69.91 2341.5 752.2	74.6 / 164,493	117.2 / 258,426	6150 / 242.1	13170 / 518.5	Four-cylinder compound, De Glehn type
	363	Series 1700	4-8-2	1925	Maquinista	Madrid, Zaragoza and Alicante	$620\times710/1750$ $24.4\times28/68.9$	14 / 205.8	4.96 / 53.4	230.8 90.0 2483.4 968.4	64.3 / 141,781	103 / 227,115	5550 / 218.5	12450 / 490.1	Two-cylinder engine
	364	Series 214	2-8-4	1929	Floridsdorf	Austrian State	$650\times720/1900$ $25.6\times28.3/74.8$	15 / 220.5	4.70 / 50.6	283.3 77.8 3048.3 837.1	70.7 / 155,893	118 / 260,190	6210 / 244.5	12635 / 497.4	Two-cylinder engine. Giesl-Gieslingen and Lehner design
	365	Stalin Class	2-8-4	1933	Kolomna	Soviet	$670\times770/1850$ $26.4\times30.3/72.8$	15 / 220.5	7.04 / 75.8	295.16 148.4 3175.9 1596.8	80.7 / 177,944	133 / 293,265	5850 / 230.3	12605 / 496.3	Two-cylinder locomotive
15.4	366	Series 3.1201-1240	4-6-2	1922	Ateliers du Nord de la France	French Nord	$\frac{2\times440\times660}{2\times620\times690}/1900$ $\frac{2\times17.3\times26}{2\times24.4\times27.2}/74.8$	17 / 250	3.42 / 37.4	191.4 61.0 2059.5 656.4	56.3 / 124,142	99.2 / 218,736	4020 / 158.3	10420 / 410.2	Four-cylinder compound engine. De Glehn type
		No. 356. (Series 3701-3721)	4-6-2	1929	Rebuilt at Tours	French PO	$\frac{2\times420}{2\times640}\times650/1950$ $\frac{2\times16.5}{2\times25.2}\times25.6/76.8$	17 / 250	4.33 / 46.6	199.3 75.6 2144.5 813.5	57.3 / 126,347	101.8 / 224,469	4100 / 161.4	10700 / 421.3	Rebuilt by Chapelon
	368	Series 4701-4712	4-8-0	1932	Rebuilt at Tours	French PO	$\frac{2\times440}{2\times640}\times650/1850$ $\frac{2\times17.3}{2\times25.2}\times25.6/72.8$	20 / 294	3.76 / 40.5	212.77 68.08 2289.4 732.5	76.4 / 168,462	109.4 / 241,227	6000 / 236.2	10000 / 393.7	Rebuilt by Chapelon
	369	Series 151.A.1-10	2-10-2	1932	Le Creusot	French PLM	$\frac{2\times480\times650}{2\times745\times700}/1500$ $\frac{2\times18.9\times25.6}{2\times29.3\times27.6}/59$	20 / 294	5.0 / 53.6	244.77 91.64 2633.7 986	92.71 / 204,426	122.41 / 269,914	7200 / 283.5	12801 / 504	Four-cylinder compound
15.5	370	A-1	2-8-4	1924	Lima	Boston and Albany	$711\times762/1600$ $28\times30/63$	16.9 / 248.4	9.29 / 100	474.72 196.11 5108 2110.1	112.58 / 248,239	174.63 / 385,059	5059 / 199.2	12700 / 500	Woodward design
		Class 5001-5005	2-10-4	1938	Baldwin	Atchison, Topeka and Santa Fé	$762\times864/1880$ $30\times34/74$	21.8 / 320.5	11.29 / 121.5	551.55 240.5 5934.7 2587.8	172.36 / 380,054	244.03 / 538,086	7976 / 314	15291 / 602	
	371	Class 9000	4-12-2	1926	ALCO	Union Pacific	$\frac{2\times610\times813}{9\times635\times787}/1702$ $\frac{2\times24\times32}{1\times25\times31}/67$	15.5 / 227.9	10.006 / 108.2	540.0 236.9 5814.7 2549	160.57 / 354,057	224.53 / 495,089	9347 / 368	15921 / 627	Three-cylinder engine, with cylinders of different sizes
	372	Class 7000	4-8-2	1922	ALCO	Union Pacific	$737\times711/1854$ $29\times28/73$	14.1 / 200	7.8 / 83.9	461.8 173.65 4971 1881	104.42 / 230,746	156.49 / 345,060	6590 / 259.4	12575 / 495	
	373	Class F-3a Super-Hudson	4-6-4	1937	ALCO	New York Central	$571\times737/2007$ $22.5\times29/79$	19.3 / 283.7	7.62 / 82	389.97 162.95 1330.5 1753.3	48.08 / 116,016	163.3 / 360,076	4267 / 168	12294 / 484	Kiefer design
	374	No. 6405-6	4-8-4	1938	Lima	Grand Trunk Western	$610\times762/1956$ $24\times30/77$	19.3 / 283.7	6.85 / 73.7	357.85 133.14 3850.5 1432.6	107.5 / 237,038	173.59 / 382,766	6096 / 240	13449 / 529.5	
	378	No. 1200-1222	2-6-0+ 0-6-4	1943		Norfolk and Western	$4\times610\times762/1778$ $4\times24\times30/70$	21.1 / 310.2	11.34 / 122	617.79 251.11 6647.4 2702	196.11 / 432,423	261.86 / 577,401	2× 3759 / 2×148	18408 / 724.7	Simple expansion Mallet
	375	Class AC-11 No. 4177-4294	4-8-0+ 0-8-0	1940	Baldwin	Southern Pacific	$4\times610\times813/1613$ $4\times24\times32/63.5$	17.6 / 258.7	10.13 / 109	601.06 243.03 6467.4 2615	241.18 / 531,802	298.42 / 658,016	2× 5156 / 2×203	20498 / 807	"Cab Ahead" simple expansion Mallet
	376	Big Boy	4-8-0+ 0-8-4	1941	ALCO	Union Pacific	$4\times6.03\times813/1727$ $4\times23.7\times32/68$	21.1 / 310.2	13.94 / 150	534.64 189.8 5752.7 2042.2	247.21 / 545,098	350.17 / 772,125	2× 5563 / 2×219	22089 / 869.6	Heaviest and biggest steam locomotive in the world
16.1	379	Cornwall	4-2-4	1847			$445\times610/2591$ $17.5\times24/102$	— / —	— / —	97.17 1045.5	— / —	27.4 / 60,417	— / —	5029	Francis Trevithick design Rebuilt 1858
	380	L'Aigle	2-4-0	1855	Gouin	French Ouest	$420\times826/2850$ $16.5\times32.5/112.2$	— / —	— / —	— —	— / —	— / —	— / —	—	Blavier and Larpent design
	381	La Parisienne	0-6-0	1889	Boulet & Cie		$470\times700/2500$ $18.5\times27.6/98.4$	12 / 176.4	2.3 / 24.7	130.9 1408.5	42 / 92,610	42	5250 / 206.7	5250 / 206.7	Estrade design
16.2	383	Series 2751-2754 (220.011-014)	4-4-0	1896	Le Creusot	French State	$440\times620/2030$ $17.3\times24.4/80$	14 / 205.8	2 / 21.5	158.1 1701.2	30 / 44,100	51 / 112,455	2700 / 106.3	7250 / 285.4	Ricour design
	384		4-4-6	1900	Le Creusot	—	$510\times700/2500$ $20\times27.6/98.4$	15 / 220.5	4.68 / 50.4	297.7 3203.3	32 / 70,560	80.6 / 177,723	2800 / 110.2	12250 / 482.3	Thuile design
	385	Group S9	4-4-4	1904	Henschel	Prussian State	$3\times524\times630/2200$ $3\times20.6\times24.8/86.6$	14 / 205.8	4.39 / 47.2	260 2797.6	36.6 / 80,703	89.5 / 197,348	2560 / 100.8	11485 / 452.2	Wittfeld type. Kuhn design
	386	Group S2/6 No. 3201	4-4-4	1906	Maffei	Bavarian State	$\frac{2\times410}{2\times610}\times640/2200$ $\frac{2\times16.14}{2\times24}\times25.2/86.6$	14 / 205.8	4.7 / 50.6	214.5 37.5 230.8 403.5	32 / 70,560	83 / 183,015	2320 / 91.3	11700 / 460.6	Hammel design

Section	Illustration	Name of Locomotive	Wheel arrangement	Year	Builder	Railroad	Driving gear	Boiler Pressure atmospheres	Grate area	Heating surface firetubes and superheater	Adhesion weight	Weight in Service	Coupled wheelbase	Total wheelbase	Remarks
3		No. 03.154	4-6-2	1934	Borsig (AEG)	German National	570 × 660/2000 *22.4 × 26/78.7*	16 *235.2*	3.89 *41.9*	203.15 72.2 *2185.9* *776.9*	54.3 *119,732*	100.3 *221,162*	4500 *177.2*	12000 *472.4*	Trial engine, partly streamlined
	387	No. 05.001-002	4-6-4	1935	Borsig (AEG)	German National	3 × 450 × 660/2300 *3 × 17.7 × 26/90.6*	20 *294*	4.7 *50.6*	256.0 90 *2755* *968.4*	57 *125,685*	127.0 *280,035*	5100 *200.8*	13900 *547.2*	A. Wolff design
	392	Mallard (Class A-4)	4-6-2	1935		LNER	3 × 470 × 660/2032 *3 × 18.5 × 26/80*	17.6 *258.7*	3.83 *41.2*	239.34 69.57 *2575.3* *748.6*	67.1 *147,956*	104.6 *230,643*	4420 *174*	10897 *429*	Gresley design
	388	Coronation No. 6220	4-6-2	1937	Crewe	LMS	4 × 419 × 711/2058 *4 × 16.5 × 28/81*	17.6 *258.7*	4.65 *50*	260.81 79.5 *2892.4* *855.4*	68 *149,940*	109.8 *242,109*	4420 *174*	11278 *444*	Stanier design
	390	Merchant Navy Class	4-6-2	1941	Eastleigh	Southern	3 × 457 × 610/1880 *3 × 18 × 24/74*	19.7 *289.6*	4.5 *48.4*	227.7 76.36 *2450* *821.6*	64 *141,120*	9398 *207,226*	4572 *180*	11201 *441*	Bulleid design
		Hiawatha	4-4-4	1935	ALCO	Chicago, Milwaukee St. Paul and Pacific	483 × 711/2134 *19 × 28/84*	21.1 *310.2*	6.41 *69*	301.46 95.59 *3243.7* *1028.5*	64.41 *142,024*	129.73 *286,055*	2591 *102*	11455 *451*	Streamlined casing. Outside design: Otto Kuhler
	391	Class J.3 No. 5445-5454	4-6-4	1938	ALCO	New York Central	572 × 737/2007 *22.5 × 29/79*	19.3 *283.7*	7.57 *81.5*	388.97 162.11 *4185.3* *1744.3*	91.64 *202,066*	120.43 *265,548*	4267 *168*	12294 *484*	Outside design: Henry Dreyfuss
	393	Class T1	4-4-4-4	1942	Baldwin	Pennsylvania	4 × 502 × 660/2032 *4 × 19.8 × 26/80*	21.1 *310.2*	8.55 *92*	391.0 156.0 *4207.2* *1678.6*	121.9 *268,790*	226 *498,330*	7722 *304*	15824 *623*	Outside design: Raymond Loewy
1	396	No. 1-18	4-4-0	1864	Beyer-Peacock	Metropolitan (London)	432 × 610/1753 *17 × 24/69*	8.4 *123.5*	1.77 *19*	94.2 *1013.6*	31.5 *69,457*	42.72 *94,198*	2692 *106*	6325 *249*	Tank locomotive
	397		0-4-4	1883	Rogers	New York Elevated and others	279 × 406/1067 *11 × 16/42* 305 × 457/1067 *12 × 18/42*	— —	— —	— —	13 *28,665* 15.4 *33,597*	19.5 *42,998* 23.5 *51,818*	1524 *60* 1600 *63*	4877 *192* 5055 *199*	Tank locomotive. Forney type
		Terrier (Class A)	0-6-0	1872		London Brighton and South Coast	330 × 510/1219 *13 × 20/48*	9.8 *144*	0.93 *10*	47.47 *510.8*	27.94 *61,608*	27.94 	3658 *144*	3658 *144*	Tank locomotive. Stroudley design Inside motion
	398	Boers	0-6-0	1899		Paris Circle Line	430 × 600/1439 *16.9 × 23.6/56.7*	12 *176.4*	1.62 *17.4*	113.78 *1224.3*	44.6 *98,343*	44.6 	4450 *175.2*	4450 *175.2*	Tank locomotive. Type developed by French Ouest in 1885. Inside motion
		Group T5[1]	2-4-2	1895	Henschel	Prussian State (Berlin "S" Railroad)	430 × 600/1600 *16.9 × 23.6/63*	12 *176.4*	1.6 *17.2*	95 *1022.2*	31.4 *69,237*	53.13 *117,152*	2000 *78.7*	6800 *267.7*	Tank locomotive
	399	Group T12	2-6-0	1902	Union Foundry	Prussian State (Berlin "S" Railroad)	530 × 630/1500 *20.9 × 24.8/59*	12 *176.4*	1.73 *18.6*	107.81 33.4 *1160* *359.4*	50.8 *112,014*	66.32 *146,236*	38.50 *151.6*	6350 *250*	Tank locomotive. Dimensions of the third version, built in 1914 at the Borsig Works
2	402	Class M7	0-4-2	1897		LSWR	470 × 660/1702 *18.5 × 26/67*	12.3 *180.8*	1.89 *20.3*	110.7 *1191.1*	35.97 *79,314*	61.16 *134,858*	2286 *90*	7188 *283*	Tank locomotive
	403	Series 2.231-2.305	4-4-4	1901	La Chapelle	French Nord	430 × 600/1664 *17 × 23.6/65.5*	12 *176.4*	1.7 *18.3*	120 *1291.2*	32 *70,560*	63 *138,915*	1780 *70*	8750 *344.5*	Tank locomotive
	404	Series 620-641	4-6-4	1903	Maffei	Madrid-Zaragoza-Alicante	440 × 630/1544 *17.3 × 24.8/60.8*	12 *176.4*	2.85 *30.7*	126 *1355.8*	39 *85,995*	76 *167,580*	3300 *129.9*	10100 *397.6*	Tank locomotive. 1674 mm (66 ins.) gauge
	405	Series 5501-5545	4-6-4	1908		French PLM	$\frac{2 \times 370}{2 \times 580} \times 650/1650$ $\frac{2 \times 14.6}{2 \times 22.8} \times 25.6/65$	16 *235.2*	3.1 *33.4*	247.18 *2659.7*	48.96 *107,957*	103.98 *229,276*	4080 *160.6*	12310 *484.6*	Four-cylinder compound tank locomotive
	406	Group T18	4-6-4	1942	Vulkan, Stettin	Prussian State	560 × 630/1650 *22 × 24.8/65*	12 *176.4*	2.44 *26.3*	138.34 49.2 *1488.5* *529.4*	51.1 *112,676*	105 *231,525*	4100 *161.4*	11700 *460.6*	Tank locomotive
	407	Series 4.1201-1272	2-8-2	1932	Cail	French Nord	585 × 700/1550 *23 × 27.6/61*	18 *264.6*	3.09 *33.2*	181.5 64.2 *1952.9* *690.8*	85 *187,425*	122.5 *270,113*	5400 *212.6*	11400 *448.8*	De Caso design. Cylinder diameter later 640 mm
		Series 242 AT 1-120	4-8-4	1926		French PLM	$\frac{2 \times 420}{2 \times 630}/1650$ $\frac{2 \times 16.5}{2 \times 24}/64.7$	16 *235.2*	3.08 *33.1*	173 45.4 *1861.5* *489.6*	65 *143,325*	120 *264,600*	5910 *232.7*	14360 *565.4*	Four-cylinder compound with Serve firetubes
	409	Series 475-001	4-8-4	1935		Czech State	3 × 525 × 680/1574 *3 × 20.7 × 26.8/62*	16 *235.2*	4.8 *51.6*	226 64.4 *2431.8* *692.9*	57 *125,685*	118.6 *261,513*	5810 *228.7*	13870 *546*	
,1	410	Class 52	2-10-0	1942	Borsig (AEG)	German National	600 × 660/1400 *23.6 × 26/55.1*	16 *235.2*	3.9 *42*	177.6 63.7 *1911* *685.4*	75.1 *165,596*	84.1 *185,441*	6600 *259.8*	9200 *362.2*	
	411 (a)	Liberty	2-8-0	1944	ALCO and Baldwin	USA War Department	483 × 660/1448 *19 × 26/57*	15.8 *232.3*	3.81 *41*	164.71 44.59 *1772.3* *479.8*	63.91 *140,922*	73.66 *162,420*	4725 *186*	7087 *279*	

Section	Illustration	Name of Locomotive	Wheel arrangement	Year	Builder	Railroad	Driving gear	Boiler Pressure atmospheres	Grate area	Heating surface firetubes and superheater	Weight		Wheelbase		Remarks
											Adhesion weight	Weight in Service	Coupled wheelbase	Total wheelbase	
	411 (b)	Austerity	2-8-0	1934	North British Locomotive	War Department	$783 \times 711/1435$ *$19 \times 28/56.5$*	15.8 *232.3*	2.66 *28.6*	171.68 28.89 1847.3 310.9 *137,217 157,371 195*	62.23 *137,217*	71.37 *157,371*	4953 *195*	7569 *298*	Riddles design
	411 (c)	Austerity	2-10-0	1944	North British Locomotive	War Department Ministry of Supply	$483 \times 711/1435$ *$19 \times 28/56.5$*	15.8 *232.3*	3.72 *40*	181.25 39.3 1950.3 422.9	68.22 *150,425*	79.55 *175,408*	6400 *252*	9042 *356*	Riddles design
	411 (d)	Liberation	2-8-0	1946	Vulcan Foundry	UNRRA (Ministry of Supply)	$550 \times 710/1450$ *$21.7 \times 28/57$*	16 *235.2*	4.09 *44*	210.59 61.3 2266 659.6	74.75 *164,824*	85.67 *188,902*	4959 *195.2*	7671 *302*	
		MacArthur	2-8-2		Davenport	US Army	$406 \times 610/1219$ *$16 \times 24/48$*	12.94 *190.2*	2.56 *27.5*	127.4 34.75 1370.8 373.9	36.29 *80,019*	53.52 *118,012*	— *—*	— *—*	1 metre gauge
18.2	415		2-8-2	1945	Baldwin, ALCO and Lima	French SNCF	$597 \times 711/1650$ *$23.5 \times 28/64.9$*	15.5 *227.9*	5.16 *55.5*	250.74 65.4 2698 703.7	80 *176,400*	115.5 *254,678*	5181 *204*	10718 *422*	
	413, 421	Series 241-P	4-8-2	1948	Le Creusot	French SNCF	$\dfrac{2 \times 446 \times 650}{2 \times 674 \times 700}/2020$ *$\dfrac{2 \times 17.6 \times 25.6}{2 \times 26.5 \times 27.6}/79.5$*	20 *294*	5.05 *54.3*	244.57 109.38 2631.6 1177	81.6 *179,928*	131.4 *289,737*	6300 *248*	13460 *529.9*	Four-cylinder compound
	414	Series 242 A1	4-8-4	1946	Saint-Chamond	French SNCF	$\dfrac{600 \times 720}{2 \times 680 \times 760}/1950$ *$\dfrac{23.6 \times 28.3}{2 \times 26.8 \times 29.9}/76.8$*	20 *294*	5.0 *53.8*	525.7 120.22 2719 1293.6	84 *185,220*	148 *326,340*	6150 *242.1*	13500 *531.5*	Three-cylinder compound, rebuilt by Chapelon
		No. 160 A1	2-12-0	1940	Tours	French SNCF	$\dfrac{4 \times 520 \times 540}{2 \times 640 \times 650}/1400$ *$\dfrac{4 \times 20.5 \times 21.3}{2 \times 25.2 \times 25.6}/55.1$*	18 *264.6*	4.4 *47.3*	250.54 72.1 2695.8 77.8	120 *264,600*	137.5 *303,188*	8330 *328*	10780 *424.4*	Six-cylinder compound, rebuilt by Chapelon
	416	Series P-36	4-8-4	1950	Kolomna	Soviet	$575 \times 800/1850$ *$22.6 \times 31.5/72.8$*	15 *220.5*	6.75 *72.6*	243.2 131.7 2616.8 1417	74 *163,170*	134.9 *297,455*	5850 *230.3*	13450 *529.5*	
	418	Series 242.2001-2010	4-8-4	1956	Maquinista	Spanish RENFE	$640 \times 710/1900$ *$25.2 \times 28/74.8$*	16 *235.2*	5.3 *57*	293.73 104.57 3160.4 1125.2	78.6 *713,313*	145.5 *320,828*	6450 *253.9*	14480 *570*	Cunill and Augé design
	420	Britannia (Class 7-MT)	4-6-2	1951	Derby	British Railways	$508 \times 711/1880$ *$20 \times 28/74$*	17.6 *258.7*	3.9 *42*	229.83 66.7 2473 717.7	61.72 *136,093*	95.5 *210,578*	4267 *168*	10897 *429*	Riddles design
	422	Evening Star (Class 9-F)	2-10-0	1954	Crewe	British Railways	$508 \times 711/1524$ *$20 \times 28/60$*	17.6 *258.7*	3.74 *40.2*	187.19 49.7 2014.2 534.8	78.74 *173,622*	88.09 *194,238*	6604 *260*	9195 *362*	
	412, 417	Series 10	4-6-2	1956	Krupp	German Federal	$3 \times 480 \times 720/2000$ *$3 \times 18.9 \times 28.3/78.7$*	18 *264.6*	3.96 *42.6*	236.5 96 2544.7 1033	64.5 *142,223*	114.5 *252,473*	4600 *181*	12500 *492.1*	

INDEX OF LOCOMOTIVES

GENERAL INDEX

338

ACKNOWLEDGEMENTS

We are indebted to the following sources for photos and illustrative material:

Museums, Libraries

London: Museum of British Transport Clapham 89, 95, 101, 121, 355, 392; Science Museum 1, 2, 3, 4, 5, 6, 9, 18, 21, 30, 31, 35, 36, 38, 50, 52, 56, 60, 86, 87, 90, 118, 119, 124, 125, 151, 153, 201, 208, 279, 354, 353, 388, 394, 400; Victoria & Albert Museum 99; **Lucerne:** Verkehrshaus der Schweiz (Swiss Transport Museum) 139, 146, 185, 197, 250, 256, 284, 287, 311; **Madrid:** Museo del Ferrocarril 340, 402; **Munich:** Deutsches Museum 12, 103, 106, 130, 135, 141, 144, 147, 149, 212, 215, 247, 295, 401; **Nuremberg:** Verkehrsarchiv beim Verkehrsmuseum 107, 134, 157, 220, 222, 228, 230, 239, 242, 243, 252, 258, 273a, 275a, 276, 277, 278, 302, 345, 387, 399, 406; **Paris:** Bibliothèque Nationale Frontispiece 37, 152, 176; **Uzès** (Gard): Museon di Rodo 92, 93, 100, 108, 126, 129, 132, 188, 213, 246, 254, 328, 383, 421; **Vienna:** Österreichische Galerie 158; **York:** Railway Museum 19, 24, 154, 161, 282.

National Railroads

Bern: Swiss Federal Railroads (SBB) 241, 251, 273b, 275b, 298; **Madrid:** RENFE 324, 339; **London:** British Railways 422; **Paris:** SNCF 128; **Prague:** Czech State Railroads CSD 409.

Photographers, Private Collections, Archives and Journals

Aubert, Marcel 359; Fototeca Centrale FS, Roma 214; Dansk Jernbane-Klub 294; Foto Desrus 196; Dewhurst 320; Archiv Falaize 27, 45, 47, 61, 66, 69, 88, 94, 114, 131, 175, 210, 217, 227, 244, 245, 249, 290, 309, 368, 377, 379, 380, 386, 398, 407, 408; Eckert Kurt, Frankfurt/Main 329; Fenino, C.G. 281; Helmut Griebl Collection 310; Japan Times 186, 200; Kelland 120, 137, 232, 352, 356, 420; Lokomotivbild-Archiv Bellingrodt 109, 115, 117, 138, 162, 192, 224, 263, 286, 322, 327, 331, 343, 358, 410, 412; Miquel, Mario 405; H.M.P, Paris 240; Pressfoto, Prague 195; Ransome-Wallis P. 235, 296, 349; Schneeberger, Fritz 271, 413; Slezak, J.O., Vienna 299, 300, 416; Edit. Stédef/Broncard 419; Edit. Stédef/Cuenca 423; Strauss 365; Technisches Bildarchiv Konrad Pfeiffer, Vienna 183, 304, 332, 364; R. Todd-White & Son 28, 91, 122; Redactor Verlag, Frankfurt/Main 305, 347; La Vie du Rail 102, 110, 190, 204, 280, 325, 361, 362, 369, 384, 403.

Railroad Works

ALCO 289, 315, 317, 335, 372; Baldwin 306, 318, 334, 350; Fives Lille 159, 367; Hanomag 360; Henschel 229, 268, 270, 291, 326, 341, 344, 348; Lima 318, 342; Maffei 292, 346, 404; Maquinista 363; Timken 373, 374, 378, 391.

Illustrations of Paintings

Philippe Desgraves 163, 172, 218, 231, 248; Paul Devaux 223; C. Hamilton Ellis 206, 211, 274; A.J. Jöhnssen 293; A. Krause 297, 351; F. Witt 307.

All the other illustrations not mentioned above are from the author's personal collection.

The text and illustrations of this book were printed in July 1974 in the workshops of the Imprimeries Réunies, Lausanne — The binding was carried out by Buchbinderei Burckhardt, Zurich — Technical table adapted by David Jennings
Editorial: Giles Allen and Roswitha Beyer — Production: Franz Stadelmann — Layout: Hanspeter Schmidt, Studio S + T, Lausanne

Printed in Switzerland